THE POLITICS OF SEXUAL MORALITY
IN IRELAND

The Politics of Sexual Morality in Ireland

Chrystel Hug

Consultant Editor: Jo Campling

First published in Great Britain 1999 by
MACMILLAN PRESS LTD
Houndmills, Basingstoke, Hampshire RG21 6XS and London
Companies and representatives throughout the world

A catalogue record for this book is available from the British Library.

ISBN 0–333–66216–4 hardcover
ISBN 0–333–66217–2 paperback

First published in the United States of America 1999 by
ST. MARTIN'S PRESS, INC.,
Scholarly and Reference Division,
175 Fifth Avenue, New York, N.Y. 10010

ISBN 0–312–21685–8

Library of Congress Cataloging-in-Publication Data
Hug, Chrystel, 1957–
The politics of sexual morality in Ireland / Chrystel Hug.
p. cm.
Includes bibliographical references and index.
ISBN 0–312–21685–8
1. Sexual ethics—Ireland. 2. Ireland—Moral conditions.
3. Ireland—Social conditions—1973– I. Title.
HQ32.H79 1998
306'.09415—dc21
98–7078
CIP

This book is printed on paper suitable for recycling and made from fully managed and sustained forest sources.

10   9   8   7   6   5   4   3   2   1
08   07   06   05   04   03   02   01   00   99

Printed and bound in Great Britain by
Antony Rowe Ltd, Chippenham, Wiltshire

To Mary Robinson, *en toute connaissance de cause*

To X, *malgré elle*

Contents

Acknowledgements

This book started out as my doctoral dissertation in Irish Studies for the Universities of La Sorbonne Nouvelle and Caen. Tables, more details and anecdotes, and a more comprehensive bibliography have been left out from the original piece of research, and I hope this will not impair the present readers' understanding of the issues and grasp of the reasoning applied. The research involved could not have been conducted from anywhere but Ireland itself. Many individuals assisted me during the six years I lived in Cork. I wish to thank them all, and in particular:

Sandra Larmour McAvoy, my fellow researcher and friend, for support, expertise, perspective and intellectual stimulation.

The French Department, where I could confront my ideas to the real lives of my students, and in particular Professor Matthew McNamara, acting Head, for his trust, and Sylvie Campion for her support.

The staff of the Boole library of University College, Cork for their willing help during the long months of pure book-worming.

The Cork Women's Political Association for providing an insight, a platform and a vantage point.

Doing research was a great socialising factor. Many people in their various capacities responded most graciously to my numerous requests for information, statistics and documents. Many grateful thanks to my colleagues on campus for giving me their time and expertise, historians John A. Murphy and Dermot Keogh, political scientist Brian Girvin, medical ethics specialist Dolores Dooley, jurists Caroline Fennell and Peter Ward, and sociologist Paddy O'Carroll. For the same reasons, Senator David Norris, MEP Mary Banotti, Dr Gerry Waters, Senator and Dr Mary Henry, and former Minister for Health Eileen Desmond, also Ruth Riddick, Education Officer at the IFPA. In Edinburgh, I am indebted to historian Owen Dudley-Edwards for his support and advice.

My heartfelt thanks and daily loyalty go to *The Irish Times* and its incisive and thought-provoking columnists and specialist correspondents, among others Fintan O'Toole, Nuala O'Faolain, Denis Coghlan, Andy Pollak, and Jack Jones of the MRBI. Also to John Cooney, author and former columnist at *The Irish Press*.

Acknowledgements

A special word of thanks to Professor Paul Brennan for believing in a project only half-baked until precipitated by events, and for his clear guidance throughout, and to the rest of my dissertation committee, Professors Jean Brihault, Françoise Camus and Dermot Keogh for responding so positively. Also to Jo Campling, the consultant editor, for believing in the publishing project and steering it to completion.

I wish to thank most particularly my Irish women friends: Ann Duggan for her long-distance research assistance; Anne O'Leary, epitome of the 'new' Irish woman and role model, for providing a home when I had left mine for other shores and radiating so much positive energy; Caroline Jeffrey and Mary O'Sullivan for their logistical help; and so many others.

I wanted this book to be a tribute to Ireland and to Irish people, a concrete expression for my enriching and challenging time among them. The following is not about *l'Irlande profonde*, but it is just as real.

Last, my deepest gratitude to the two persons who opened up exciting vistas for me: Paul Brennan for helping me find my place in the world of Irish studies, and Pascal Ladreyt, for creating the very opportunity to live in Ireland and encouraging me to show in such a way my love for this country.

Introduction: Whose Morality? What Sexuality?

Politics, sex, morality. The association of these words is an old recipe for arousing interest. History, sociology and law, on the other hand, could be great enthusiasm deadeners, but in the context of Ireland (and throughout this book Ireland will refer to the Republic of Ireland), all these ingredients have fuelled endless debates and controversy, raging at regular intervals. The Irish don't just reconstruct the world around a glass of stout, as the image goes, but their propensity to question their own society can be fascinating to foreign eyes. Irish society has changed more over the last two decades than in the previous century, and the cathartic process reached all-pervasive proportions in the first half of the 1990s, notably at a time when the Catholic Church became embroiled in a number of controversial issues which markedly eroded its authority. These debates, which the French refer to as *débats de société*, as they are at the basis of our society, go beyond the question of private versus public morality, as regulated by the state for the common good of its citizens.

A close reading of public as well as religious discourse in Ireland in the twentieth century reveals a concern for the notion of social order, not surprisingly in a recently founded state, and one whose ideology was based on Catholic concepts at that. By contrast, a number of social phenomena will be blamed for fostering disorder, and their introduction into Irish society will be strongly resisted. In a country where Catholic morality, as we shall see, has been as central to the development of state law and state politics as it has been to the personal development of the Irish individual, any clash between its vision of order and the citizens' will be momentous indeed.

An apparent digression is timely in order to appraise the rhetoric of order and disorder in the sphere of morality. It is based on the concept of natural law, as expounded by Thomas Aquinas in the thirteenth century. This concept, however time-honoured, is still in force and relevant to some, and rests mainly on two precepts: first, that one must do good and avoid evil; second, that it is in nature that we can find the moral values that enable us to distinguish between good and evil. The

1

Catholic Church adopted this theory as its official doctrine in 1879, and to this day it still endorses natural law as the universal and obligatory moral law. But it insists on the fact that man, having been corrupted by original sin, needs the Church's dogma and a set of immutable principles to find the right way, guided by the Church and by the Roman pontiff in particular. Thus defined, natural law is but a different phrase for God's law. This was recently reiterated in the *Catechism of the Catholic Church,* published in English in 1994:

> The natural law, the Creator's very good work, provides the solid foundation on which man can build the structure of moral rules to guide his choices. It also provides the indispensable moral foundation for building the human community. Finally it provides the necessary basis for the civil law with which it is connected, whether by a reflection that draws conclusions from its principles, or by additions of a positive and juridical nature.[1]

Protestants (Anglicans and Nonconformists) subscribe to a different theory of natural law: for them, it is based on human reason, and they do not need the mediation of their churches, which do not give instructions but guidelines and do not play a mediating role when it comes to salvation. It is also important to state that Protestants believe in the supremacy of their free conscience, informed by their reason and not by a rigid dogma. What happens in a state such as Ireland, with its Catholic majority, is that Protestants, as much as atheists for that matter, are ruled by natural law as interpreted by the Catholic Church. The doctrine relating to the relations that must exist between Christians and the state is not fundamentally rejected by Protestants in that they recognise that divine authority is supreme, and that the will of the people is the intermediary between this authority and the three organs of state – legislative, executive and judiciary. In that sense Protestants do not reject the Preamble or even Article 6 of the Irish Constitution, which set out these principles.[2] Law and morality thus overlap, as the Church has inculcated obedience to the civil authorities, and the state has chosen to base its socio-moral laws on the idea of order and perfection. Where the Protestant concept of public morality diverges is when the state inserts in its Constitution and in its laws moral interdicts that leave no room for free will and conscience. When Ireland endeavoured to become openly pluralist, a number of questions were raised. Should the civil law be the vehicle by which democratic majorities, Catholics in this case, reaffirm the moral aspirations they share? Who would protect the rights of minorities?

When interpreting the Constitution, which is one of the functions of Irish judges, *whose* natural law were we talking about?

The Irish Free State leaned from the outset (1922) on the Catholic Church and on majoritarianism, i.e. the law of the highest number. The Irish felt they had the right to choose the kind of state which they wanted to live in – a state that would protect their beliefs and, by the same token, their identity. Since some 93 per cent were Catholic, they were going to give themselves Catholic-inspired laws. Let us take this opportunity to note that, although the Protestant churches were inspired by the same puritanism as the Catholic Church, the ideal of social purity being a Victorian prerogative as much as a Catholic one, there were nonetheless differences in degree and in the means employed. In Ireland, natural law and majoritarianism were used to justify the positive legislation relative to sexual morality, in particular that pertaining to contraception, abortion, homosexuality and divorce. Only these four socio-sexual issues will be examined here because, as well as being immoral in the eyes of the Catholic Church, the state intervened to regulate them, whereas sex outside of marriage, masturbation and artificial insemination, for example, are also so-called immoral practices but are not, and never were, illegal.

From the outset of this study, there was an impulse to trace the evolution of the laws relative to these socio-moral questions, but it was not altogether clear what their common denominator was. Why was Ireland rocked by these *débats de société*? Why did the Catholic Church heap so much opprobrium on these four aspects of conduct, and why did they incur state penalties? The reading of some religious texts offered the answer: they corrupt moral order – a moral order that rests on an ideology which condemns individualism on the one hand, and emphasises the primacy of the duties that the individual has *vis-à-vis* the community and God on the other. By extension, these practices corrupt society at large because they undermine the family, the institution on which moral order is built, the basic unit of society whose main function is to maintain order, economically as well as ideologically. It is clear that only one kind of family is being referred to: that based on a heterosexual, monogamous, procreative and indissoluble union. And, to bring us back to our point, anything that tends in another direction is a disorder. One Irish bishop expressed it explicitly: 'The question about legislation on such practices as divorce, sale of contraceptives, abortion and homosexual behaviour, which in varying degrees divide opinion in our society today, are questions about whether, or to what extent, freedom of conscience in this area can be reconciled with what public order requires, especially in so far as the latter entails care for the rights of others and for public morality.'[3] The new *Catechism of the Catholic Church*, in its third part, which deals with sexual and social morals, adopts an approach as unwaveringly damning as ever.

By bringing about moral and social disorder, these practices destroy the social fabric, and so they have been made illegal because they run counter to the common good. Thus these issues suggested themselves for scrutiny because of their recurrence in the Irish news, as well as in papal and episcopal declarations, and especially because they were immoral and illegal practices at the same time. The links that exist between them became clearer as the analysis progressed: the debate on divorce, when not raging, had never been far from the surface throughout the history of the state since its foundation in 1922. The debate on abortion commenced following the advent of the contraceptive culture, to use the Catholic Church's phrase. The homosexual militants have, for their part, been able to maximise their observation of and participation in the preceding socio-moral campaigns. Strategically, there have been some differences: in the case of divorce, a mix of referendums and legislative initiatives was necessary; the debate on abortion has been moved forward by contradictory referendums, weary legislators and determined women. The questions which were in the hands of the legislators, as opposed to the citizens, could be dealt with less fiercely – in fits and starts in the case of contraception, in one go for homosexuality, but they both required a nudge from the judiciary.

The aim of this book is to make sense of the profound changes affecting Irish society. A society still anxious to ensure the common good, to guarantee the natural rights of its citizens, but divided between the remnants of the normative morality imposed by the Catholic Church and what French philosopher Gilles Lipovetsky calls 'the triumph of subjective rights' when he claims that 'the moderate and liberal regulations are now socially legitimate, in a direct illustration of the triumph of subjective rights over unconditional obligations.'[4] This process is painful; it split the country, most notably in 1983. The process by which it is now accepted that the common good is not necessarily guaranteed by obedience to one's moral duties, as in the old order, but by the primacy of inalienable and fundamental moral rights, will be traced. The time of commandments is gone, self-denial is out of fashion, and, again to quote Lipovetsky, 'to the age-old supremacy of one's obligations towards God has been substituted the supremacy of the sovereign individual's prerogatives.'[5] In other words, the Irish are seeking a minimum consensus so that all, be they Catholic, Protestant, atheist, homosexual, divorced, or others can live in harmony.

The debate on the line between private and public morality took place against the backdrop of the Troubles in Northern Ireland. This adds another dimension to our argument: in the North, the Protestant majority governed and discriminated against the Catholics at all levels of social life, while in the South, the functioning of the state rested on Catholic ethics, with which minorities, be they Protestant or defined by something other than religion, did not identify. Pressing this point further, it could be contended that there has been in the island of Ireland, a fundamental confusion between majority rule and democracy, in an illustration of John Stuart Mill's phrase, 'the democratic oppression of majority rule'.

Politicians such as Mary Robinson, long before she was elected President, or Garret FitzGerald, Taoiseach (Prime Minister) in the 1980s, have often evoked the prospect of the reunification of the island to justify the passing of pluralist laws. It was during the Forum for a New Ireland, in 1984, that it was recognised for the first time by the nationalist constitutional parties that the Northern Irish Protestants' civil and religious liberties, as well as their sense of being British, should be protected in a new Ireland. But it was also in this very same forum that the Catholic Church challenged the argument that the laws of the state, based on its teaching, were sectarian, since the objective moral order had its source in human reason, and thus was accessible to all. Indeed, it had become clear to Irish citizens that they themselves could have access to the moral order, using their reason and their conscience: they now felt capable of being responsible moral agents. In this, they echoed Protestant rhetoric, according to which there are some cases when what is considered immoral is, in fact, the lesser of two evils.

Consequently, the advent of a new moral order will have come about despite the Catholic Church, thanks to the intervention of the powers mentioned in Article 6 of the Constitution. In this sense, this book is also an exploration of the dynamics established over the last 73 years between the Irish or European courts; the citizens, asked to voice their opinion in various referendums, or having recourse to so-called 'immoral practices' as responsible moral agents; the legislators, some timorous, some pioneers. This dynamic has brought about a shift from the objective moral order to a subjective one, which reigns beyond duty, and whose fundamental rule is not to harm others. It is impossible to refer to this post-moral order, to a pluralist Irish society and to subjective rights without referring to the election of Mary Robinson. Indeed, her election to the presidency, in November 1990, was one of the first signs that the decade was going to be marked by the emergence of a liberal political force. On that day, the Irish elected as Head of State a woman who, as a senator and constitutional lawyer, had actively fought for over 20 years in the direction of liberalism and pluralism, most notably in the areas of contraception, divorce, the rights of homosexuals and abortion. Watching and listening when the new president was elected in November 1990 was enough to sense that something momentous was happening: a distinct euphoria was palpable, and so was the sense of being at a crossroads. Who was Mary Robinson? At first, it seemed interesting to trace her career as a barrister, a senator and a feminist. At that stage, this foreign observer did not know that she had taken part in all the socio-moral battles, but her power as a symbol was already tangible. When we met, she graciously hinted that she would not be able to help directly. And it is only when the present research was being concluded that it appeared we had unwittingly achieved the initial aim – to retrace the literally subversive career of Mary Robinson and place it in context.

In February 1992, a year and a half after the presidential election, the X case hit the headlines. This was to be the real catalyst, both for the new moral order that will be examined here, and for this book itself. It quickly took on the proportions of an *affaire d'Etat* as the vast majority of Irish people were shocked, not to say shaken in their principles, faced with the callousness of the High Court judgment at the plight of a suicidal rape victim. The turnaround in public opinion was even more palpable then than it had been after the election of Mary Robinson, and became tangible from one day to the next. It seemed essential to go back in time and try to understand what the origins of this bizarre case were. The issues at stake were not only the right to an abortion, or the right to information about how to obtain an abortion; but also the place of Irish women in society; or what is really democracy; or the demarcation that exists or that one should establish between natural law, legislation enacted in the public interest and private morality in general. From the foundation of the state, these three areas were regulated jointly by the Catholic hierarchy and the legislators. Moral decisions taken by responsible individuals did not fit in the affirmation of the supremacy of the common good. The election of Mary Robinson and the repercussions of the X case brought into the spotlight the fact that Irish political culture was undergoing fundamental changes. At the same time, the legislation relative to contraception, homosexual practices and divorce were called into question. Headlines and feature articles, televised debates and conversations all dealt extensively with the ins and outs of one or other of these issues. The beginning of the 1990s will undoubtedly always be seen an intense period of socio-moral legislative activity and as signalling the end of a system of authoritarian and homogenising moral values. Indeed, there does not seem to be now, in the sphere of sexual morality, norms or sanctions.

It will be proposed that Mary Robinson's election is symptomatic of a society which will no longer be organised around order, duty and norms, but around minimal ethics based on the fundamental rights of individuals. It has now joined other Western societies in this new order. It will not be argued from the point of view of secularising theory because there is too much contrary evidence in Ireland, and it would also put us too firmly on sociological ground. Nonetheless, a cultural shift has occurred from a position of virtual 'moral monopoly' for the Catholic Church to a multiplicity of values and lifestyles.[6] Although the change in the Irish laws that concern us here has taken some 20 years more to come about than the change in corresponding legislation in other jurisdictions, it must be pointed out that Ireland became an independent state only recently, and went through an initial phase characterised by economic protectionism and cultural self-sufficiency, marked by the glorification of being different. Moreover, it is possible that this historical lag could turn to the advantage of Irish society, in that it can benefit from the experience of its neighbours, draw consequences and learn from their mistakes. Certainly, once triggered, change was finalised more quickly!

The methodologies used in this investigation were dictated by our position as a witness but also as a participant (as a delegate of the Cork Women's Political Association to the Council for the Status of Women, now called National Women's Council, a national umbrella organisation for some 152 affiliate groups), which gave rise to a personal conviction that Ireland was not so scrupulously Catholic, fundamentally conservative and basically different as the often self-imposed *cliché* went. It also gave rise to a great curiosity prompting us to make sense of the events taking place around us. There was a logic to these events, which needed to be made explicit.

It has been necessary to go back through the course of history, to use sociological tools (surveys, polls and any such empirical data) to observe Irish society, and to give special consideration to the law for it is, in Mary Robinson's words: 'a hidden infrastructure which conditions our society and pervades almost every aspect of our lives'.[7] As such it can be a powerful instrument of social change. Indeed, the Constitution, together with the judgments given in the socio-moral court cases and the laws themselves, reveal better than anything else what moral order, past as well as present, hinges on. An analysis of parliamentary debates completes the picture. Three categories of sources have been extensively used. First, the National Archives, as well as parliamentary debates and reports published throughout the period in question; books and articles written by journalists, historians, jurists, sociologists, doctors, theologians and philosophers; a great number of articles published in the Irish and British press, particularly *The Irish Times*, a newspaper of record, reliable for the facts presented and pluralist in its feature articles. Lastly, we benefited from interviews with protagonists, as well as with specialists, testing our impressions against their expertise. Thus, this book claims to be a sociological and legal history of the politics of sexual morality in Ireland (pending access to new archives), from the construction of the objective moral order after 1922, some of it having been kept over from the old regime, to the emergence of a new moral order, or a post-moral order, at the beginning of the 1990s.

Chapters 1 and 2 deal with divorce. As divorce is the occasion of the breaking up of the reproductive milieu, it is anathema to the Catholic Church, even more so than adultery. This issue will be dealt with first because it involves the state as a major player. As divorce is the issue where private life and public life overlap the most, this explains why it took so long for the right to a 'second chance' to take precedence over the upholding of the indissoluble family unit. General elements of Irish history and politics will also be introduced, such as the two Constitutions, of 1922 and 1937, which will allow us to follow closely the process of codification of Catholic moral ethics. This will provide an opportunity to introduce some key characters in the contemporary political, legal and social history of Ireland, in particular Mary Robinson.

Chapters 3 and 4 deal with family planning, or artificial contraception. Other historical indicators will be put in place, relative to the Catholic construction of sexuality in the early years of the Irish Free State. As far as the recognition of a right to marital privacy was concerned, legislators had a free hand, in the sense that they did not have to refer to the people in a referendum. Once the Supreme Court judges found in the Constitution itself the existence of such a right, the liberalisation of the Catholic-inspired laws took place slowly, progressively, over 20 years. It took four successive pieces of legislation to whittle away the impact of theology. In this domain, Catholic morality was particularly cut off from the reality of contraceptive practice, which accounts for its demise.

Chapters 5 and 6 deal with abortion, a taboo subject if ever there was one, until the beginning of the 1980s when it gave rise to an unprecedented moral war – the 1983 referendum – or how the supreme exercise of democracy turned out to be a double-edged sword, since it led to the insertion in the Constitution of a legal nonsense, as the X case would demonstrate nine years later. On this question the Irish state had simply adopted the British Victorian law, but a grouping of lay Catholic associations decided to 'copperfasten' a moral principle in a governmental text in order to protect society from any change in its mores.[8] Again, it was the Supreme Court judges who made abortion legal in certain circumstances, exhorting legislators to take over from them. In this area also, thousands of Irish women act every year as responsible moral agents, defying interdicts and disgrace: they travel to abortion clinics in England.

The last two chapters are devoted to the rights of homosexuals, the denial of which was also inherited from the British legal system, itself modelled on ecclesiastical law. Irish legislators intervened once, in 1993, most liberally. It can be noted that homosexual militants were particularly skilled at running the whole gamut of actions characteristic of an efficient pressure group, i.e. a court case, at Irish and European level, and the unflagging lobbying of politicians. They managed to get the most and the best of Irish tolerance, to give themselves a respectable and public face, thanks largely to the efforts of Senator David Norris, and to have a say in the final piece of legislation. Seasoned militants, they reaped the fruits of the preceding moral campaigns.

The contrast between the legal situation relative to socio-sexual questions in 1973 and that in 1993, both key years in this context, is striking. It is not a matter of knowing if these new measures are going to encourage promiscuity and deviance, for the reality has been indisputable for a long time. And this is a dimension that it will not be lost sight of. Every year more Irish women are going to England for abortions, officially 4 529 in 1995; there is a growing number of people, 87,800 according to the 1996 census, in broken marriages; there is no real reason why there would be proportionally fewer homosexuals in Ireland than elsewhere; and it is estimated that 15,000 Irish women were on the pill ten years before it was legalised (50,000 of them just before it was).

1 Divorce: From an Indissoluble Bond ...

Marriage is, in the Catholic tradition in particular, an indissoluble union between a woman and a man for the purpose of procreation, and as such, the legal impossibility of breaking this bond has its place in a study of the politics of sexual morality. Also, divorce dissolves a social contract and as such will have effects on housing, health, education and social benefits, and its effects are paid for largely by the state. It also challenges the traditional concept of the family as it opens the way to second (third, fourth, etc.) marriages and to re-ordered families, with their biological and/or social mothers and fathers, as well as the cohabiting of children with different parents. Divorce will be considered first in this study because, as it breaks up the marriage bond and opens the way to a second marriage, it is the socio-moral question that involves the state most. Public and private morality are thus equally at stake.

The ban on divorce by one of the first governments of the Irish Free State was an integral part of the construction of the moral order referred to earlier, as it sought to protect the family and society at large. It will provide an excellent opportunity to set the historical and political scene. The right to divorce is the socio-moral question that has in effect polarised opinion the longest. The recognition of a right to separate will be an important milestone in the edification of the new moral order, opening the way for the recognition of a right to remarry. On this question, as on the other three we will deal with, the Catholic Church stands apart from the other churches and it continues to affirm that the common good of Irish society is best guaranteed by something that sounds very much like its own theology, echoing the Gospels and their 'what God has joined together, let no man put asunder'. The *Catechism of the Catholic Church* reaffirmed recently that 'divorce is a grave offence against the natural law.... Divorce is immoral because it introduces disorder into the family and into society. This disorder brings harm to the deserted spouse, to children traumatised by the separation of their parents and often torn between them, and because of its contagious effect which makes it truly a plague on society.'

With the exception of the Brehon laws which permitted divorce under the old Gaelic system which collapsed in the sixteenth century, Irish courts never had the power to dissolve a marriage. Separating couples had to petition the courts for a separation of bed and board, and then the House of Lords at Westminster (from 1800, the date of the Union with Britain, to 1922), or the Irish Parliament for a dissolution proper. The English had done away with this system of private Acts of Parliament (in force since the Reformation) in 1857 by establishing divorce courts. This was in effect the first English divorce law, but it only applied to England and Wales, possibly as much from lack of interest as strong opposition on the part of Irish members at Westminster. Following the disestablishment of the (Anglican) Church of Ireland in 1869, the Matrimonial Causes and Marriage Law (Ireland) Amendment Act, 1870, was passed in Ireland: The jurisdiction of the ecclesiastical courts passed to that of new courts, but with no extension of their powers as in England in 1857, which implied that separating couples, once they had been granted a divorce *a mensa et thoro* (freeing them from living together), still had to petition Westminster with a private bill in order to be granted the right to remarry by a dissolution pure and simple of their marriage (together with the settlement of all ancillary orders with as many court actions). Both English and Irish parliamentary divorces could be granted on the same grounds, mainly adultery coupled with cruelty or desertion.[1] This should make clear that until the national referendum on the 1937 Constitution, it was possible to petition for a divorce in Ireland, and therefore the prohibition on divorce is not, as Mary Robinson put it, 'something that has been with us since the foundation of the State. It is not something that has been with us since the Irish people expressed a desire over the centuries to be a nation and so on. It is with us for less than 50 years. It is a recent provision, introduced in 1937.'[2]

GRAPPLING WITH THE ISSUE IN THE IRISH FREE STATE, LEADING TO THE BAN (1937)

As from 1922, once the Irish Free State was formed, it behoved the High Court in Dublin to grant decrees for divorce *a mensa et thoro*, and the Irish Seanad [Senate] to hear in committee and *in camera* the petitions for divorce *a vinculo matrimonii* (the full divorce which leaves the parties free to remarry). The new state inherited an almost complete set of state institutions, but it had to give itself a new Constitution, fleshing out the 1919 one. The committee in charge of the drafting of the 1922 Constitution was put under some pressure to include the principle of indissolubility of marriage, but its members had decided not to yield on this.[3] When Professor Alfred O'Rahilly, a latecomer on the committee, set to ensure that the interests of the Catholic Church would be taken into account, he realised that it had been agreed that no religious clauses would be inserted in the final draft of the Constitution.[4] Article 53 of his own draft stated unambiguously that marriage, 'as the basis of family life and national well-being', was under the 'special protection of the State'. As a consequence, the Irish state would recognise 'the inviolable sanctity of the marital bond'.[5] But he had against him that the pre-occupations of the constitutional committee and of the provisional government did not lay with religion, as the mood was conciliatory towards the Protestant minority. Also the agenda of the day was more political than moral, since it was necessary to draft a Constitution that would be acceptable to the British while appealing to the anti-Treaty-ists (including Eamon de Valera). Article 8 of the Constitution, on religion, was indeed unambiguous in prohibiting the passing of laws that would discriminate between religions. However this prohibition was subject to public order and morality, and historian David Fitz-patrick remarked that this qualification was meant to prevent some people from having recourse to illegal practices like 'mormonism and things of that sort', 'mormonism' being 'a contemporary code-word for remarriage following civil divorce'.[6] Having said that, the 1922 Con-stitution is certainly more secular than its 1937 counterpart, but its Preamble affirms nonetheless that 'all lawful authority comes from God to the people'. Undoubtedly, there was already a certain contra-diction inherent in the shaping of the new Irish state, in an attempt to reconcile secular and Catholic forces. It remains that if one hoped that partition would be but provisory, the Constitution had to be secular enough to accommodate Catholics and Protestants alike.

As three parliamentary private bills for divorce were awaiting con-sideration by the end of February 1924, it was necessary to devise a policy. Whereas the Attorney-General, Hugh Kennedy, was of the opinion that some provision should be made for divorce bills 'for those who approve of that sort of thing', the President of the Executive Council, William T. Cosgrave, asked a friend of his, the Archbishop of Dublin, for some advice. Dr Byrne was adamant that the Catholic Church could not condone divorce, even for non-Catholics, and added that anybody who wanted to settle in another country in order to divorce there could do so, as 'Ireland would not lose anything by this', a view that the Irish hierarchy spelt out at their plenary meeting a few months later. But for some long months no provision was made to deal with divorce private bills, and it was only in February 1925 that William T. Cosgrave proposed a motion in the Dáil that would prevent the introduction of such bills.[7] The only opposition, voiced by William Thrift and Ernest Alton, was based on freedom of conscience, which was thus denied to a large section of the community. Such an argument did not carry, and Cosgrave's motion was accepted without a vote. But, surprisingly, the Seanad refused to vote in favour of it. Even though there were more Protestants in the second chamber than in the Dáil, the vast majority of senators were Catholic and as opposed to divorce as their co-parliamentarians. But senators felt that such a motion was in breach of the Constitution and of the Standing Orders of the legislative assembly. Every citizen had the right to present a private bill, and therefore only a law, as opposed to a motion, could restrict an existing right. On 11 June, Senator Douglas tabled a motion in the Seanad, which stipulated that private bills for divorce should have their first reading in both the Seanad and the Dáil, which in effect meant they would never pass both stages, considering the strong Catholic majority in both chambers.[8] One cannot help noticing that the idea of enacting a law that would purely and simply prohibit divorce was not seriously considered by the Cosgrave government, because this would put the government in a situation 'which would bristle with constitutional complications' in Cosgrave's words, who also said he did not think legislation necessary, thus resisting pressures to go 'down the confessional road'.[9] Even with Senator Douglas' motion, divorce was not prohibited for ever, and it would be possible at any time to rescind it, should parliamentarians feel that people were ready to view divorce favourably. It is on the same day that the poet and Senator W.B. Yeats delivered his famous speech in which he protested against the catholicisation of Irish laws.[10] It does not seem that Yeats' views were shared by Protestants in general who did not want to initiate a campaign on this issue.[11] In any case, Cosgrave and the Dáil rejected the resolution adopted by the Seanad on 25 June: Why hear these bills at all, with all their unsavoury details, if there was no question of giving one's assent to the proposal? In other words, the resolution passed by the Dáil had been rendered inoperative by the Seanad, and that of the Seanad by the Dáil. In the meantime, the three private bills awaiting consideration had been withdrawn, 'and there the matter rested' as historians usually conclude, until 1937. We note once more that divorce could have been made illegal in 1922 and in 1925, as the bishops wished. The text of a piece of legislation, the Marriage Laws Amendment Act, 1927, together with a memorandum entitled 'Objections Answered' can be found in the National Archives. Despite the strong influence of the Catholic hierarchy on the new rulers, the new Irish state did not give its full weight to such an explicit enshrinement of the Catholic teaching in its laws. Just as when Cosgrave had proposed in March 1921 the setting up of a 'theological senate', which would decide if laws passed by the Dáil were 'contrary to faith and morals or not', the idea had not been taken up.[12]

So what was so different in the Ireland of 1937 to make divorce unconstitutional? For one thing, de Valera had been at the head of the Executive since 1932, and in April 1935, he set out to draft a new Constitution. He did not set up a Committee as was the case in 1922, and retained editorial control until completion. Even though de Valera and his followers were ardent nationalists, the reunification of the island was nonetheless a somewhat distant goal, and the spirit of compromise that had characterised the 1922 Constitution was no longer the priority. In effect de Valera wanted a state endowed with a nationalist, republican and Catholic Constitution to represent the will of the vast majority of Irish Catholics in the country. The Irish nature of the nation had to be ascertained even if it meant alienating Ulster Protestants. For example, de Valera said: 'I would not tomorrow for the sake of a united Ireland, give up the policy of trying to make this a really Irish Ireland – not by any means. If I were told tomorrow, "you can have a united Ireland if you give up your idea of restoring the national language to be the spoken language of the majority of the people", I would, for myself, say no.'[13] The same applied to the Catholic nature of the new state. Indeed 93.4 per cent of the population of Irish Free State were Catholic, and 6.6 per cent belonged to other religions. In 1911, on the territory covered later by the Irish Free State, there had been 10.4 per cent of non-Catholics. Catholics thus formed an overwhelming majority which was becoming more and more dominant. The new Constitution was meant to raise Catholic ideology to the status of government principle, and even though the nationalist doctrine was not explicitly sectarian, it proclaimed that Ireland was a Catholic state for a Catholic people. Indeed, in the words of Dermot Keogh, 'partition imposed its own ideological logic; ... What the establishment of the two states did achieve was the political institutionalisation of the religious divide.'[14] One notices in particular that de Valera's government dealt with questions where Cosgrave had temporised, and that it went further in the moralisation of legislation, in the construction of public morality: It passed laws forbidding the importation and sale of contraceptives (the Criminal Law Amendment Act, 1935) or regulating dance halls (the Public Dance Hall Act, 1935), both aimed at keeping in check public morality.[15] De Valera affirmed in a famous St Patrick's Day speech that 'since the coming of St Patrick, fifteen hundred years ago, Ireland has been a Christian and a Catholic nation. All the ruthless attempts to force her from this allegiance have not shaken her faith. She remains a Catholic nation.'[16] Article 2 of the new Constitution proclaimed that the state was the legitimate system of government for the whole of the island, which seemed to leave aside some one million inhabitants, approximately 25 per cent of the total population, who would never be able to adhere to some of the principles contained in the document. Without overestimating the influence and input of the Jesuits or of John Charles McQuaid, the future Archbishop of Dublin, it is clear that their submissions to de Valera were incorporated to some extent in the final draft. In particular, the great principles relative to the family and to property were directly inspired by recent papal encyclicals. Even the reformation of the Seanad was inspired by an encyclical, *Quadragesimo Anno*, dating from 1931, which sought to encourage industrial associations to offer vocational expertise to political leaders. Also, as far as outside influences are concerned, we note that Alfred O'Rahilly, whose project had been rejected in 1922, submitted it to de Valera, and there is some evidence it had some impact over the final draft.[17] For example, section VIII of 'draft C' which focused on marriage, the family and morality, had found no counterpart in the 1922 text, but Articles 41, 42 and 45 of *Bunreacht na hEireann* echo it quite strikingly. However, Dermot Keogh, who has traced in detail the tribulations of the drafting of the Constitution, warns that there were some fundamental differences between de Valera and McQuaid and that de Valera was in fact an *à la carte* Catholic, who had such 'an intimate knowledge of ecclesiastical politics' that it gave him the self-confidence to have 'a rather liberal view of discipline to ecclesiastical authority.'[18] And in the context of the time, the new Irish Constitution remained singularly attached to liberal democratic principles, and was also quite different from the Concordats signed between the Vatican and such states as Italy, Spain and Portugal. De Valera had rejected such a suggestion, made to him by some religious. There might have been a long-standing reciprocal and latent suspicion felt by both sides, dating back to the days when de Valera had stringently opposed the Treaty with Britain, itself supported by the Irish bishops. But de Valera felt that the position of the Catholic Church in the Irish people's hearts was a better guarantee for the Church than any concordat could ever be, an opinion close to heretical for many Catholics of the time.

As Dermot Keogh observed, both Cosgrave and de Valera were 'devout conservative Catholics', but they recognised that 'the laws and the Constitution of the country had to be inclusive' and they stood out 'against confessionalism'.[19] De Valera sought to find a balance between the rights of the church he considered to be the only true church and the civil liberties due to the others. Article 44, which gave a special position to the Catholic Church (repealed by referendum in 1972), while recognising the other churches, whether Christian or not, was written and rewritten, circulated and annotated, ending up a very diluted version of what some might have wished for. It seems that de Valera faced more opposition from those who desired a more confessional Constitution than from those who found it sectarian! O'Rahilly later wrote that Article 44 was but 'a piece of neutral scientific statistics expressed in fervent phraseology.'[20]

But, defending Article 44, de Valera himself said: 'There are 93 per cent of the people in this part of Ireland and 75 per cent of the people of Ireland as a whole who belong to the Catholic Church, who believe in its teachings, and whose philosophy of life is the philosophy that comes from its teachings.'[21] The Constitution would be the expression of a moral order centred on the superiority of divine law over positive law. Still, would a ban on divorce have found its place in the Constitution if the Catholic Church had not demanded it as a condition of its accepting the whole document? Indeed it would seem that, aware that the 'special position' granted was not much more than a formula, the Irish hierarchy had demanded the insertion of the ban on divorce to affirm the supremacy of its teaching. De Valera felt that all had to be subordinated to the central purpose of having the independence and sovereignty of Ireland recognised, and 'compromise with the Church was all important to nullify its opposition. If the Church came out against the Constitution the whole aim would be defeated and the referendum lost.'[22] As the principle of a ban on divorce appeared in all the submissions made to de Valera, it naturally found its place in the final document. Also worth emphasising is the fact that there was at the time a strong consensus between the churches on issues of morality: indeed, the approval of the final text of the Constitution by the Presbyterians, the Methodists, the Jewish congregations and the Church of Ireland 'further reflected the uniformity of views on moral issues between the Churches which existed in the country in 1937. Divorce, for example, was not the contentious issue it had become by the 1980s.'[23] In the Dáil, the debate on the insertion of the ban on divorce did not arouse much interest; it was even necessary to confirm several times that there was a quorum (20 deputies) during the committee sessions. Deputies Thrift and Alton did not voice their objections, as in 1925. Out of the 153 deputies, only three were women, known under the collective name of 'silent sisters', and they lived up to their soubriquet on that occasion.[24] Two lone deputies, Frank MacDermot and Robert Rowlette, expressed the opinion that the Constitution would widen the gap between North and South – all the more so as Northern Ireland was in the process of adopting its first divorce law. But de Valera's final argument was that 'with regard to the question of divorce in general, there is no doubt that sometimes there are unhappy marriages, but from the social point of view, without considering any other point of view, the obvious evil would be so great... that I do not think any person would have difficulty... in making a choice on this matter.'[25] Ignoring the purely social considerations, the argument was reminiscent of Pius XI in his 1930 encyclical *Casti Connubii*. In 1937, the rights of the individual were sacrificed for the common good. The family had to be protected by the state, even against the selfish whims of a few of its members. Article 41.3.1 and 2 would read: 'The State pledges itself to guard with special care the institution of Marriage, on which the Family is founded, and to protect it against attack. No law shall be enacted providing for the grant of a dissolution of marriage.'

DE FACTO SEPARATIONS AND SOME STATISTICAL INDICATORS OF MARITAL BREAKDOWN

A heavy silence now fell on the question of divorce. But the Troubles in Northern Ireland, which began in 1969, drew attention to the Irish denominational laws and relaunched the debate. Further, the reality of marital breakdown was acknowledged publicly in the early 1970s. A series of articles on the different aspects of marital breakdown and the various ways to face it was published in *The Irish Times* in October 1970, and the first poll on the desirability of divorce in Ireland dates from 1971: 73 per cent were against making divorce available, with only 22 per cent in favour. In 1974, 47 per cent thought divorce should never be legalised, but 48 per cent thought it should, in limited circumstances. By 1977, 26 per cent were still opposed, but 65 per cent then favoured the introduction of divorce.[26] It was as if economic changes had brought about a rise not only in living standards, but also in expectations. Welfare agencies and the newly set up, free legal advice centres recorded an explosion in the number of people coming to them with marital difficulties and seeking solutions. The debate on the pill that was raging somewhat dented the credibility of Catholic teaching and tradition of 'sacrificial tolerance'.

The fact is that a range of remedies in the event of marital discord was already at hand for couples, who wanted to put a more or less formal end to their marriage. Even if divorce was unconstitutional in Ireland, there were other ways to separate. As David Fitzpatrick pointed out:

> Persistent avoidance of divorce legislation could scarcely have been accomplished without widespread popular abhorrence of the dissolution of marriage. Yet, in its absence, other legal forms and social customs were developed to meet the fact or menace of marital breakdown.... If divorce was scarcely known in Ireland, separation in many guises was ubiquitous.[27]

Moral order was maintained on the surface, thereby concealing a multitude of more or less regular situations.

The history of marriage in Ireland is complex, but there are two points worthy of comment. First, Catholic marriages were not regulated by statute, and were treated differently in law historically from Protestant marriages.[28] Under the provisions of Matrimonial Causes and Marriage Law (Ireland) Act, 1870, civil law determined if a marriage was valid, whatever the religious rites observed, but the state imposed more rules on marriage other than Catholic before it validated it.[29] In fact, many Irish people until recently (1995) were not even aware of the civil formality – it is difficult to call it a ceremony – since it was not separate, in time or place, from the religious one. When they signed the register on their way out of church, very few people realised they had just signed a legal contract. Having said that, a Catholic marriage was valid even if the register was not signed, since its being celebrated by a priest in the presence of two witnesses sufficed.

Another very important factor is the fact that Ireland experienced a high rate of celibacy until well into the second half of the twentieth century. The fact that 30 per cent of Irish men and 25 per cent of Irish women born at the beginning of the twentieth century never married (in countries such as France and Britain, the rate and 'definitive celibacy' was 10 per cent for men and hardly more for women) is a striking illustration.[30] Even those who married did so at a more advanced age. Further, there were more men than women, and women emigrated in greater numbers (two phenomena specific to Ireland). It has been said that divorce was rejected in the 1920s in an effort to reinforce an institution that was not very popular. Conversely, the ban on divorce and contraception could not have encouraged people to marry! But, once married, the Irish were very fertile, a trend that was reversed with the subsequent rise in the marriage rate. David Fitzpatrick argues that traditionally marriage was a monetary transaction, and for this reason, the 'match' had to be irreversible, if not the wife's family should be given back their dowry. This is what he calls a structural obstacle to divorce which gave all its strength to the Christian arguments:

> Thus affirmation of the indissolubility of marriage became an essential ingredient of Irish ideology, capable of surviving the social conditions which had made such an affirmation expedient. As shown by the continuous reluctance of Protestant spokesmen to demand divorce facilities, resistance to divorce was not a specifically Roman Catholic enterprise.... Though the language of debate on divorce was often doctrinal, the impulse was social and cultural. The curtailment of divorce in Ireland cannot be attributed in origin to the Catholic hierarchy or doctrine.[31]

Nowadays, the number of people stating in the national census that they have no religion is increasing (from 39,572 in 1981 to 66,270 in 1991), as is that of people belonging to a minority religion other than Protestant (from 8,447 to 35,828). (Incidentally, people were not asked to state their religion in the 1996 population census!) On the other hand, the total number of marriages, at its peak in 1980 (21,792), has been declining (15,623 in 1995), as has been that of Catholic marriages (from a peak of 22,005 in 1974 to 15,255 in 1992, the latest figure available). The number of civil marriages (at the registry office) has been increasing, from 31 in 1961 to 388 in 1980 to 695 in 1992. This does not mean that the Irish are less religious, as economic factors might come into the picture, with civil marriages being substantially cheaper than church ones.

While there were two ways of getting married, there was none, until recently, to break the bond – even though there were two ways of having it annulled. Parallel to the High Court examining petitions for civil annulments, the Catholic Church has retained its own regional marriage tribunals which examine petitions. For the marriage to be annulled, by either party, an impediment must have existed at the time of the ceremony to make it invalid: that is, the marriage is deemed never to have existed. For the Catholic Church, the pre-existence of this impediment is paramount since a valid and consummated marriage is a sacrament and as such is indissoluble. The state applies the same condition since civil law in this area was based on ecclesiastical law prior to 1870. However, even though these two authorities apply the same principles to the petitions for annulment, they do not recognise each other's decisions: a marriage that the Catholic Church annuls is still valid in the eyes of the state, and vice versa. For the Catholic Church, any union contracted after one of its own annulments is a first marriage, but the person is a bigamist as far as civil law is concerned. And, as Senator Mary Robinson remarked:

> We have had over the years and continue to have, a significant number of so-called remarriages which, of course, are bigamous marriages. This is a blind spot of the Director of Public Prosecutions. There is a total failure to enforce the law, so that we have an undermining of the values of the law and we do not seem to want to know or want to care.[32]

An article (10 April 1994) published in *The Irish Independent* revealed that over the previous decade there had only been 'a handful of prosecutions and just two convictions for bigamy, though there are hundreds of such marriages in existence.' It is a strange fact that the state recognises the validity of a marriage celebrated in a Catholic Church with the priest officiating also as registrar so to speak, but does not recognise the annulment of this very same marriage by the Catholic Church: all the more so as the grounds on which a civil annulment is granted are modelled on those accepted by the Catholic Church. It has been suggested that the state does recognise ecclesiastical annulments and 'accommodate these bigamous marriages', as reported by former Taoiseach Garret FitzGerald.[33] Any such move would be discriminatory since the other churches do not annul their marriages.

Statistically speaking, there are far more petitions for ecclesiastical annulments (470 in 1994, and 300 granted) than for civil ones (72 in 1994 and 23 granted) – it would thus seem more important to be straight with God than with the civil authorities! But the two categories are increasing. Petitions for civil annulments are often a second-best resort when the request has failed in the ecclesiastical court; on the other hand, very few couples, having obtained an ecclesiastical annulment, proceed with a civil one. This would set them back further £4000, even though this used to be the only way to release them to remarry if they so wished. (By constrast, an ecclesiastical annulment costs around £450, less if they cannot afford the full amount.) When one examines statistics from the High Court or the National Marriage Appeal Tribunal, it is worth remembering that even though annulments are comparatively rare, what matters is the overall number of petitions, as it shows the true extent of marital difficulties.[34]

However relatively rare the number of civil annulments, there has been a substantial widening of the range of grounds cited and accepted in the last 20 years to cope with the increasing demand. As Mary Robinson pointed out at the time of the first divorce referendum:

> The number of petitions for nullity have increased a hundredfold in the last couple of years. There is a pressure on individual judges to grant decrees of nullity in circumstances where even five or ten years ago, the advice from a barrister would have been that there was no case for a nullity. The law is developing because of these pressures.[35]

This has led to a certain subjectivity on the part of the judges to such an extent that it can be difficult to ascertain if a marriage is valid or not before going to court. Some High Court decisions have in effect developed the civil law relative to nullity of marriage. For example, since *RSJ* v. *RSJ* in 1982, a degree of immaturity or incompatibility has become the most commonly invoked and accepted ground for annulment. This is flexible enough to leave a considerable degree of latitude to the judges. The irony is that, because of the ban on divorce, which is meant to protect marriage, the state is led to subterfuges that undermine marriage and discredit the law. The Catholic Church for its part reorganised its matrimonial tribunals in 1976 and revised its code in order to be able to receive more applications. By allowing the celebration of 'second marriages', which it calls simply marriages (the first never having existed), the Catholic Church implicitly accepts that some marriages do fail, and proceeds to do something about this social phenomenon. Its negligence is culpable as the new partners have no civil rights whatsoever as a couple (social security, pension, and the like). As for the wife of the first family, she is, in the words of Senator Catherine McGuinness (later a High Court judge), 'in return for the boon of getting out of an impossible relationship through nullity,... reduced to the position of an unmarried mother of illegitimate children.'[36] The situation was rectified for children when the state introduced the Status of Children Act, 1987, which abolished the status of illegitimacy. Indeed, until 1987, the children born of these second first marriages were illegitimate in the eyes of the state and were thus deprived of all rights. As for the children born of a marriage invalidated and rendered non-existent, they also became illegitimate and lost all rights!

Whatever the type chosen, a marriage annulment is a lengthy and costly procedure, which remains marginal and does not solve any of the problems created by a separation, including child custody, maintenance and the sharing of property. But in the minds of many Irish people, this procedure was the only one that gave a right to a second chance, the right to remarry; it was 'divorce Irish style'.

Some people wanting to formalise a second union but without going through an annulment can change their name by deed poll and appear married to their partner. Mary Robinson mentioned this practice in the Seanad: 'A significant number of women in a second relationship, change their name by deed poll, so that at least in a superficial sense they appear to be quasi-married. They gain some semblance of dignity and respectability in their relationship.'[37] It is impossible to quantify this practice since people changing their name do not have to give a reason for doing so. The High Court Central Office told us, on 7 September 1995, that 232 people changed their name in 1994, without specifying their ground for doing so.

Somebody who has obtained a divorce abroad can remarry in Ireland if the divorce is recognised in Ireland; if it is not, the person has married bigamously. Since October 1986 and the Domicile and Recognition of Foreign Divorces Act, the main condition for a foreign divorce to be valid in Ireland is that at least one of the parties was domiciled in the foreign country at the beginning of the procedure. But domicile is a very complex issue, different from that of residence, and so there are more foreign divorces that are not recognised in Ireland than is assumed. People may not realise their divorce is not recognised in law until it comes to inheritance. According to the 1991 census, 6,103 people had obtained a foreign divorce. This figure had risen to 9,800 in the 1996 census.

Another way of putting an end to marital life together is to prevent one's partner from entering the family home. Since the Family Law (Maintenance of Spouses and Children) Act was passed in 1976 and amended in 1981, a court can effectively issue a barring order to prohibit a violent husband, for example, from entering the home.

The court only has to be satisfied that this injunction will ensure the security and welfare of the spouse and children. It is also possible to obtain a protection order, which is an interim injunction prohibiting the violent spouse from threatening or frightening his family. The police can arrest without a warrant a person in breach of any of these orders. Since March 1995, this legislation has been extended to people other than legally married spouses, that is people in 'non-contractual' relationships. This brings attention to the fact that, until the introduction of divorce, cohabitation was not always chosen: some people did not (re)marry because of one of the partners' previous marriage, but they had no legal recourse if difficulties arose. In any case, applying for a barring order might sound like a drastic way of putting an end to marital life, but some 2,000 such orders are granted each year. The phenomenon seems to be on the increase: between 1976 and 1980, 2,000 women applied for such orders, and between 1980 and 1985, 15,000 did.[38] Further, nearly 3,000 protection orders are made each year. Minister Mervyn Taylor was heard to say: 'In 1994, there were 16,297 marriages. In the 12 months of the court year ending in 1994, there were 4,457 applications for barring orders.'[39] In other words, for every four marriages in 1994 there was one barring order sought!

Since the passing of the Domestic Violence Act, 1995, there has been an increase from an average of 74 barring and protection orders being sought each week in the legal year 1994–5 (or 3,878 in total) to an average of 122 a week in the first six operational weeks of the new Act (732 applications made). Having said that, barring orders, as a solution to marital problems – an original one in itself – are mainly sought by those in receipt of social welfare or on low income, since they are relatively cheap and quick to obtain.[40]

Mediation is another avenue, whose purpose is to help couples resolve their difficulties on the basis of a compromise accepted by both parties. A mediation service was set up by the state in September 1986, on an experimental basis. Situated in Dublin, its waiting lists were some three months long. There is now a second centre in Limerick, and they deal with approximately 300 couples annually. Counsellors help couples reach an agreement on their home, their children and their finances. This agreement has no legal force but can be endorsed by a solicitor, who will charge some £350 for a previously negotiated agreement; the mediation service is free. Worth noticing is the fact that the service prompts some 7 per cent to have another go at their marriage.[41]

The separation agreement is the most commonly used of all procedures and expedients, if one judges by the volume of family law cases undertaken by solicitors and legal aid centres. Unfortunately it is not statistically recorded and one can only approximate its scale. This agreement is signed by both parties in the presence of a solicitor following mediation sessions, or after each party has seen his or her legal advisers (which doubles the cost). It implies that they agree, or have reached an agreement concerning the splitting up of their possessions, the custody of their children, etc. It remains the simplest and cheapest way to separate. However, it is reversible at any time as the marriage remains valid. The only legal status of this contract (executory since 1848, but at the initiative of wives since 1882 only) is that if one party is in breach of his/her commitments, s/he can be sued by the other for breach of contract. Because the agreement can be drawn up and witnessed by solicitors, it can be relatively cheap and became the most popular way of formalising a separation.

The last alternative for couples in difficulties is judicial separation. As with divorce proper, the obstacles to a successful marriage appeared after the wedding. A decree of divorce *a vinculo matrimonii*, the form of divorce which did not exist in Ireland until the 1995 referendum, dissolves a valid marriage and results in both parties ceasing to be husband and wife and being free to remarry. On the other hand, a judicial separation, granted on similar grounds, loosens the marriage bond but does not sever it: it only lifts the obligation to live together and deals with related issues. Judicial separation, as currently featured in Irish legislation, was provided for in 1989, and we shall come back to it later. It replaced divorce *a mensa et thoro*, 'the Catholics' divorce', which orginated in Roman canon law and was available between 1870 (when the High Court inherited the jurisdiction of the ecclesiastical courts) and 1990. This decree did not allow for remarriage as it only lifted the obligation to live together, and the officiating judges could not solve related issues or make financial arrangements. It was exclusively fault-based and the only admissible grounds were cruelty, adultery and unnatural acts. Cruelty could be construed as the use of contraceptives or the practice of coitus interruptus against the other's wishes! It was a lengthy and costly procedure, and far from widely used: between 1946 and 1970, only 27 such decrees were granted, and between 1970 and 1981, an average of five separation judgments a year were granted by the High Court.[42] With the Courts Act 1981, the Circuit Courts have been allowed to hear such cases, which democratised the procedure a little, since they granted an average of 50 separations a year between 1982 and 1990.

The very fact that there are a number of ways of leaving one's estranged spouse proves that marital breakdown does affect Irish people, despite the pedestal on which the family has been placed in the Constitution. There seemed to be a growing number of people thus affected, but for a long time there was no statistical evidence to confirm this. In 1976, the National Economic and Social Council recommended the creation of a 'separated' category under the family status entry in the national census form, a suggestion that indicated an awareness of this social phenomenon.[43] However, it took three attempts before finding the right terminology, and this makes it diffi- cult to compare successive surveys. In 1979, there were 7,624 people in the 'other status' category (relating to persons who had obtained a divorce in another country); in 1981, 14,117 people ticked the 'other status' box if they were divorced purely and simply. In 1983, according to the results of the Labour Force Survey (a national survey conducted in the EC countries), 21,100 people said they were 'separated' (or deserted, legally separated, partners in an annulled marriage). Criteria and definitions changing at every survey, it is impossible to determine the number of broken marriages in Ireland. The Divorce Action Group (DAG), a group set up in 1980 to lobby for divorce in Ireland, estimated in 1983 that 70,000 people were in such a situation. This figure presumably included all those who would not recognise them- selves in any category other than 'married', such as all those women whose husbands had left to live and work in England and who would not think of themselves as 'other' or even as 'separated'.[44] More precise categories would eventually be used in the 1986 census, the results of which only became known after the referendum. It showed that 37,245 people were separated. In contrast, 1,304,095 declared themselves 'married'. Later surveys testified to the escalation of the phenomenon. The 1991 Labour Force Survey reported 46,700 sepa- rated people; the 1991 Census, 55,143, the 1995 Labour Force Survey, 85,600, and the 1996 census, 87,800. What all these figures confirm is that the ban on divorce did not protect the institution of marriage; and even if they are well below the divorce rates in other western societies, the upward trend is unquestionable.

Statistics concerning people benefiting from various state allowan- ces by virtue of their marital status or marital difficulties confirm the extent of the problem. Again, even though there are no objective statistics relative to the number of separated people and the way they separated, there is a certain number of indicators, such as the number of people receiving the Lone Parent Allowance, the Deserted Wife's Allowance or Benefit (one is means-tested, the other is not). These indicators are bound to be conservative because of the qualifying conditions. At the time of the introduction of the Social Welfare Bill, 1970, which introduced the Deserted Wife's Allowance, it was estimated that 1,000 women would meet the requirements. This was based on the Home Assistance figures. (Home Assistance was an allowance administered by the local authorities.) Six hundred husbands deserted their wives during 1969 and the first six months of 1970 (there had been up to 2,000 Irish husbands who disappeared in 1929–30); 220 were found, most in England where they had gone to find employment, often forming new families there, and three-quarters of them were persuaded to support their Irish families. Less fortunate wives could then apply for Home Assistance. Within six months of the 1970 law coming into force the figure of 1,000 was exceeded, and at the end of 1976, 4,783 women were receiving either the Allowance or the Benefit (introduced in 1973). Interestingly, this category and its associated benefits are unique to the Irish social welfare code, and as Nora Owen, then TD (Member of Parliament), would later say: 'This debate [on divorce] started in a uniquely Irish style in the early seventies with the introduction of the deserted wife's allowance. That was our first formal recognition that marriages break down in Ireland.'[45] The numbers continue to rise: recipients of the Deserted Wife's Benefit trebled between 1981 and 1991. Over the same period, the number of women receiving the Lone Parent's Allowance increased by over 400 per cent. Of course, the number of single parent families has increased dramatically over the last 20 years, a phenomenon attributable to the increase of births outside marriage (from 3.7 per cent of all births in 1975 to 8.5 per cent in 1985 to 22.2 per cent in 1996), but also to the dissolution of a growing number of marriages. The other reason accounting for the huge increase in the number of the beneficiaries of this benefit is the fact that, since 1990, it is paid to deserted women and men, as well as widows and widowers, single mothers, and separated people (of both sexes). It is estimated that this benefit alone costs the state some £93 million a year. The 15,757 women receiving the Deserted Wife's Benefit and Allowance cost the state £72 million in 1994. In all, some 22,000 people received a benefit of some kind in 1993 by virtue of their status as a deserted or separated partner.

The Social Welfare Act, 1970 marked a real turning-point in Irish matrimonial legislation. This was the first time that the state acknowledged the responsibility it has to support women whose marriage has broken down with the desertion of their husbands, who do not subsequently meet their obligations. Surely it is only fair that the state that insists on the indissolubility of marriage should shoulder responsibility for the victim of a broken but indissoluble contract. As jurist William Duncan observed: 'The new provisions do mark a change of policy in the State's attitude to marital breakdown – an admission of State responsibility in an area in which previously individual wives were largely left to fend for themselves.'[46]

Other measures have been taken that show the government's willingness to take into account, and even help, those who are affected by marital difficulties. A few examples follow: The Family Home Protection Act 1976, prohibits the sale or mortgage of the family home and its contents without the other spouse's prior written consent. If a man leaves to live in England to obtain a divorce there after one year (the minimum length of residence required), his wife can continue to live in the family home without worrying about being evicted because he has sold it without her knowledge. But this law does not give her any rights as to the proceeds of an eventual sale (except if the contract is in both their names). The Family Law (Maintenance of Spouses and Children) Act, 1976 holds that judges can issue maintenance orders and enforce them if a spouse fails to maintain his or her partner or dependent children. The Status of Children Act, passed in 1987, abolishes the status of illegitimacy and gives to children born outside of marriage the same rights, including inheritance rights, as children born in marriage. Children born of second unions, which could not be formalised until the introduction of divorce, benefit from this law in an effort by the state to acknowledge their rights. All in all, 'we now have a highly-developed system of family law containing an extensive range of sophisticated and up-to-date provisions to cope with the myriad of issues which can arise in the family law area'.[47]

To give credit where it is due, it is a fact that 'throughout the 70s Mary Robinson battled harder than any public figure in Ireland to remove the legal and social discriminations which attached to the status of illegitimate child.'[48] As early as 1974, she tabled a bill on the rights of illegitimate children, the Illegitimate Children (Maintenance and Succession) Bill. This was withdrawn in 1975 and replaced by another, which would require a referendum, the Sixth Amendment of the Constitution Bill 1978, when she realised that the government had not kept its promise to settle the question itself. From this bill, only the third measure, concerning the adoption of children, was retained, and approved in a national referendum in August 1979. But it is still Mary Robinson's action, as a lawyer this time at European level, in the *Johnston* v. *Ireland* and *Stoutt* v. *Ireland* cases, in 1986, which was instrumental in introducting legislation on the status of children. Not only did the 1987 law follow social thinking but it also followed the judgment of the European Court of Human Rights (ECHR) which had found Ireland to be in breach of Article 8 of the Convention and declared that the 'illegitimate child' 'should be placed legally and socially in a position akin to that of a legitimate child.'[49] In the context of the absence of divorce, this implied that children born of marriages subsequently annulled would not lose their rights. The Irish bishops distanced themselves from the legislation, saying they had not been consulted. They pointed out that

> legal reforms which take account of the rights of non-marital children should not undermine the principle that monogamous and indissoluble marriage is the legal basis of the family. It is not a question of giving equal status to marriage and co-habitation, but of giving equal rights to all children whatever the circumstances of their birth.

In 1980 the state put in place a system of free legal aid (administered by the Legal Aid Board) so that the most disadvantaged people could have access to the law. Between 85 and 90 per cent of the cases administered by the board are family law cases, of which 80 per cent are brought by women.[50] There are currently 30 legal aid centres in the country, which is inadequate to shorten the waiting lists which are often a few months long. It is again thanks to Mary Robinson's action, both as a senator and as a lawyer, that this system was put in place. In April 1978 and again in June 1979, she tabled a motion asking the government to set up a system of family courts and to introduce free legal aid in Ireland. Then, in 1979, she defended Ms Josie Airey at the ECHR, which again obliged Ireland to comply with its judgment. Ms Airey was in no position to meet the legal costs required to get a divorce *a mensa et thoro*, but the European Court ruled that every citizen has a right to a fair trial to establish his/her civil rights. As a result, 'the success of the Airey case in Strasbourg altered, in a fundamental way, the relationship between Ireland's civil law and the ordinary citizen of limited means.'[51] The Legal Aid Board dealt with 900 judicial separation cases in 1994 (at an average cost of £1500 each).[52] Last in this range of measures to cope with marital breakdown, the Courts Act passed in 1981, gave jurisdiction to District and Circuit Courts (more accessible regional courts) to hear family law cases (previously they had been heard in the High Court in Dublin). In the mid-1990s, 17 judges were appointed in the Supreme, High, Circuit and District Courts to cope with the backlog of cases, especially family law ones.

All this leads us to ask: if so many Irish couples experience marital difficulties, and if the government seems more and more willing to grant divorce – after all, what else does this wide range of laws and court rulings prove that ease the process of separation and come to the assistance of dependent partners – what was preventing the state from crossing the line and granting the right to remarry? Even though Article 41.3.1 of the Constitution pledges to protect marriage, it is more a profession of faith, a pious vow, than a promise of action. Moreover, most of the legislation mentioned above was introduced under the growing pressure of the separated couples themselves, not because of Article 41. As Mary Robinson said in the Seanad, 'we must be aware that the case can certainly be made that the absence of divorce legislation in Ireland is damaging marriage. It is damaging the very relationship which we seek to protect.'[53] As we have seen, there has been a steady decrease in the number of marriages celebrated each year in Ireland. If one takes the 1991 figure as an example, it represents 'a marriage rate of only 4.8 per 1,000 of population, which is the lowest on record since the early 1940s and also the lowest amongst the countries of the EC apart from France.'[54] This would be in keeping with the assumption that it is the concept of the indissoluble union that is being challenged, to be replaced by serial monogamy.[55]

THE CONSTITUTIONAL CRUSADE: THE FIRST DIVORCE REFERENDUM (1986)

As the ban on divorce was copperfastened in the Constitution, a national referendum was necessary to remove it. It is up to the government to call for a referendum, and it must be certain of victory before it launches on such a politically risky enterprise. As divorce is a minority issue, the majority had to be convinced that the ban was unfair to the minority. This minority was defined in the following way by Mary Robinson:

> In the context of marriage breakdown and divorce I do not mean a religious minority. There is no evidence at all, – indeed the evidence

is all to the contrary – that it is those of a religious minority who seek the right to remarry within our State, the Republic. The vast majority of those who seek the remedy of divorce are Catholics. Nonetheless they are a minority in that they are trapped in marriage breakdowns, and are unable to help themselves and they require that the majority who are not affected by this problem have regard for their human situation, their human rights in that situation and are prepared to take the necessary steps.[56]

At the beginning of the 1970s various voices made themselves heard in favour of the introduction of divorce in Ireland. Among them, the Committee on the Constitution, set up by Sean Lemass, successor to de Valera, published its report in 1967 in which it was suggested that those whose religion allowed it should have access to divorce. The proposition was criticised by both Catholic and Protestant religious. The report was quickly mothballed, deemed too radical by far: neither politicians nor the public were ready for such changes as those recommended – such as the end of the ban on divorce or a change in the articles on what constitutes the territory of Ireland. Only the deletion of the special position of the Catholic Church was endorsed by referendum in December 1972. It was the only question raised on which all political parties could agree; even Dr Conway declared he would not shed a tear over this loss of privilege (all theoretical). This deletion was a gesture of goodwill towards the Protestants of Northern Ireland, but what politicians did not seem to realise then was that basing their reforms on the possible welcome they would get from the Protestants of Northern Ireland would not suffice to appeal to them; nor to people in the Republic, as only 50.7 per cent of the electorate voted in that referendum. In fact, this poll proved that half the electorate were not concerned with Northern Ireland or by the call for 'a new Ireland' (in the words of the Taoiseach, Jack Lynch). The purely liberal approach, liberal in its own right, would take more time to have effect, but it would eventually bring about an evolution of conscience. Mary Robinson was one such proponent of liberalism and pluralism from the late 1960s. On the question of divorce, as on many others, Mary Robinson was one of the *avant-garde*: according to her definition of liberalism: 'Liberalism is the voice of dissent, especially when that entailed essential human rights.'[57] As already mentioned, she was, as a senator and as a lawyer, particularly active in family law and all the issues surrounding marital breakdown. She would take part in all the battles of the 'moral civil war' (in journalist Gene Kerrigan's words), not just that of divorce. This was after she was elected to the Seanad, first in 1969, followed by two re-elections, and also to Dublin City Council in 1979; she also stood twice for Labour in parliamentary elections, pushing forward on the second occasion the party's manifesto which advocated lifting the ban on divorce. But she was not endorsed by the electorate, as if the creation of a liberal pluralist society was not so much the doing of the people or of their Parliament, but the outcome of a combination of circumstances and of wills, to fight on behalf of the less privileged, and often despite them. She used the Seanad, even though she was aware that the important political and social debates of the time were taking place outside the Dáil, in Cabinet. Also, since a bill to amend the Constitution must be presented and voted in the Dáil before going to the Seanad, she was never able to present a private member's bill on the question of divorce. However, in April 1980, she drafted the Eighth Amendment of the Constitution Bill, which aimed at changing the wording of Article 41.3.2.[58] But the Labour Parliamentary Party decided instead to table a motion to set up a joint Oireachtas committee [of the two Houses], which would inform Parliament as to the appropriate way of amending the Constitution. The motion was tabled by Eileen Desmond on 29 October 1980 on the ground that 'Article 41.3 of the Constitution affects adversely the welfare of a growing minority of our citizens.'[59] She drew a very striking picture of reality as she saw it in her constituency, and in particular in her surgery. It was actually during their surgery hours that TDs saw for themselves the extent and effects of their constituents' marital difficulties. Parliamentary debates became progressively peppered with evidence which convinced some legislators of the need for change. But the government was not convinced 'that to legalise divorce would not bring much greater and more widespread suffering and social disadvantage,'[60] which sounded very much like de Valera in 1937 when he argued that a minority of people have to suffer to protect the common good. The government also reaffirmed that the family was under its unconditional protection. Interestingly, the very same morning, the Catholic hierarchy published a declaration condemning the coming into force of the new law on contraceptives. Obviously the Government could not be seen as saying anything that would go against the bishops: it was unthinkable to deviate from the right path a second time in such a short span of time. The die of the divorce debate was thus cast: the Labour motion was defeated by 62 votes to 15.

Fine Gael had been led since 1977 by Garret FitzGerald, an economist, a former Minister for Foreign Affairs and a 'Catholic intellectual'.[61] Born of a Presbyterian mother and a Catholic father, he was a partisan of liberalism and pluralism, as expounded in his writings.[62] The major themes of his 'revisionist nationalism', in the words of political scientist Basil Chubb, were that it was necessary to work towards the reunification of the island but only with the consent of a majority of the people of Northern Ireland; and, what is more relevant here, to set in motion changes in the Republic itself that would prove to the North its willingness to establish conditions that would make the prospect of a united Ireland at least conceivable in the eyes of some in the Protestant community. In other words, charity begins at home, and the Republic needed a civil rights movement too, like the one started in Northern Ireland. Articles 2, 3, 40, 41 and 44 of the Constitution should be modified, as well as the laws on censorship, contraception, abortion and the use of the Irish language. Such changes were 'the more immediate changes required within the Republic to create a favourable atmosphere for future discussions.'[63] Even if his ideas appealed to those 'who were able to free themselves from the shackles of the traditional nationalist myths', they did not engage people's interest nor the government's, and actually sounded like anathema in some quarters.[64] When, nearly ten years later, FitzGerald, now in power himself, launched his 'constitutional crusade', he met with the same lukewarm response, and indeed hostility. Fianna Fáil in particular made sure the crusade did not get off the ground, and Charles Haughey even said that he regarded this 'as a serious undermining of our national position – the equivalent of sabotage of our national policy of unity – to attack the Constitution in the way that Dr FitzGerald has done, to attack the *bona fides* of politicians of all parties in the South and to attempt to suggest that our State has a sectarian basis.'[65] As FitzGerald would observe, his crusade was still-born, but it was 'a time-bomb ticking away at the heart of the narrow and exclusive form of Catholic nationalism to which Fianna Fáil traditionally ties its fortunes.'[66] The day would come when his conception of nationalism and his sense of pluralism would be the order of the day.

The issue of divorce was an integral part of his crusade, and the programme of government of the new Fine Gael–Labour coalition (his second mandate) announced the setting up of a Joint Committee on Marital Breakdown which would analyse the issues relative to marital legislation. It did not meet until September 1983, because of the long drawn-out abortion referendum campaign, and the return to power, at the beginning of 1982, of Fianna Fáil, which was totally opposed to the introduction of divorce. Certain members of the Committee were legal minds as well as parliamentarians, such as Mary Robinson, Catherine McGuinness, Katherine Bulbulia and Alan Shatter. Fianna Fáil eventually agreed to take part and had seven members on the Committee. The Committee gathered figures first, then submissions (it received 700 written ones and 24 oral ones from various groups – around 90 per cent of them were in favour of the introduction of divorce), but the only consensus it managed to reach was on the desirability of holding a referendum, without voting on the desirability or necessity of a divorce law (only four of its members wished a stronger stance on divorce, including Mary Robinson). It can be noted that in a 176-page report, only 20 dealt with divorce itself (pp.71–91). Politicians were quite circumspect when it was published, and the press scathing. Witness this *Irish Times* editorial on 15 March:

> The Oireachtas Joint Committee on Marital Breakdown has failed to find an Irish, or any, solution to an Irish problem.... What is the point of such committees if they split on party lines, if they ignore expert opinion, if they cannot arrive at authoritative and preferably unanimous, recommendations [like suggesting which way the electorate should vote] to place before the Dáil and Senate?

On 3 April, the editorial of the same paper was as forceful: 'Who doubts that the constitutional ban will, in the fullness of time, join the "special position" in the dustbin? A shame that this report, which could have been a social and historical landmark, should go into the bin as well.' Because of the negative reaction it provoked, the report has been somewhat forgotten for the recommendations it made, but the following events would prove that the Committee members, in particular the parliamentarian lawyers, had cleared the way for a future law on divorce.

One might have thought that the publication of this report would have speeded up the process, but in fact the opposite happened. FitzGerald went on playing for time, insisting that it should be discussed in the Dáil first, then in the Seanad. The debate in the upper chamber only started at the end of June 1985 and was adjourned until September. Also, the government was deeply involved in the negotiations that would lead to the signing of the Anglo-Irish agreement at Hillsborough, and in local elections held in June which saw Fianna Fáil gain ground again. Fine Gael itself was very divided on the issue of divorce (even among the members of the Committee). Labour, which was in greater agreement on the issue, was beginning to understand that a divorce referendum was no longer a priority. The government was shrinking back from the idea of educating public opinion with a view to a referendum and leading the way. Politicians were hiding behind the idea that the Irish were not ready, and felt no need to prepare them.

There had been a few initiatives to introduce a divorce law following Mary Robinson's in April 1980, but they did not get very far. We shall list them to testify to the political energy surrounding the issue. On 3 June 1980, Dr Noël Browne (then a Labour TD) circulated his own Eighth Amendment of the Constitution Bill, which proposed lifting the constitutional ban, but did not suggest anything to replace it.[67] The Minister for Justice, Gerard Collins, denied most of the TD's arguments and the motion was opposed. In 1981, Mary Robinson tried to reactivate her bill, but Labour was still not in favour of such a procedure within the Fine Gael–Labour coalition of the time. In February 1983 and May 1984, Proinsias de Rossa, then a Workers' Party TD, was prevented from publishing his bill. He tried for a few months to attract the attention of the government on the issue with his own Eighth Amendment of the Constitution (Divorce) Bill, 1983 and Tenth Amendment of the Constitution (Divorce) Bill, 1984 which advocated a straightforward deletion of Article 41.3.2.[68] Quoting statistics and opinion polls, he concluded: 'As far as this subject is concerned, the general public is far ahead of many members of the Oireachtas.' In October 1985, Michael O'Leary, former Labour Party leader and now a Fine Gael backbencher, put forward his own two bills: the Tenth Amendment of the Constitution Bill, 1985, would delete clause 3.2 of Article 41, whereas the Marriage Bill, 1985, guaranteed that the people would take part in the drawing up of a law on divorce. Four TDs only supported him, when ten would have been required to see the bill reach second stage. While the debate on the marital breakdown report was taking place in the Seanad, and to oblige the Fine Gael half of the coalition to hold a referendum, Labour introduced in the Dáil its own Tenth Amendment of the Constitution (no. 2) Bill, 1985. Drafted by Mary Robinson, it was presented on 1 November 1985 by Labour TD Mervyn Taylor.[69] It was rejected at its second stage by 54 votes to 33, including most Fine Gael deputies. The latter were waiting for Fitz-Gerald to complete his consultations with the various churches on the changes to be made in marriage legislation, and for the government to present its own bill. The Fianna Fáil deputies abstained.

`Here one sees how such a wide-ranging issue, affecting the lives of thousands of citizens can be placed on the political agenda and no

longer be put in objective terms but in party terms. TD Proinsias de
Rossa was scathing:

> Recent opinion polls have shown that there is a growing demand for
> divorce to be provided under certain circumstances. To say that a
> referendum would not be successful at this time is a classic case of
> leading from behind. Is it simply that the Taoiseach has no confid-
> ence in his own ability or the ability of his party to convince the
> electorate that this major social reform is necessary? It seems more
> likely that he knows that he cannot rely on the support of his own
> party on this issue and therefore is not prepared to risk his political
> career, irrespective of the misery of those trapped in broken mar-
> riages.[70]

There had to be more to the Fine Gael deputies' refusal to support this
Labour bill than the consultations of their leader with the religious. As
Michael O'Leary observed, 'nobody expects the Taoiseach to reverse
the decision of the Council of Trent.... We are all aware that the
Church to which most of us belong has a settled view on the matter
of divorce.'[71] Whatever the case, it was the first time since 1937 that a
bill aimed at removing the constitutional ban reached its second stage,
and it might have gone further were it not for the Taoiseach's comment
that it was 'out of place and premature'.[72] At the time, opinion polls
showed that 77 per cent of people questioned were in favour of divorce
in certain circumstances (a record figure never matched since).

As far as the consultations with the churches are concerned, which
took place between 21 March and 7 April 1986, what did they reveal
of the religious' stance? The Presbyterian, Quaker, Jewish, Baptist,
Methodist and Church of Ireland leaders all told the Taoiseach
that the Republic needed some form of divorce. They had already
made submissions to the Committee. They underlined the sacred
character of marriage and the family, but acknowledged that it was
the duty of the state to dissolve those that did not work. Divorce could
thus be seen as a least evil, and as such as a civil right (by the Church
of Ireland notably). A blanket ban on divorce verged on grave
social injustice, and did nothing to promote marriage and family life,
according to the Presbyterian Church. Only the Catholic Church and
the Mormons were resolutely opposed to any law legalising divorce.
The former, for its part, had stated its point of view during the New
Ireland Forum (a peace conference seeking constitutional solutions to
the conflict in Northern Ireland, which met from May 1983 to
April 1984):

We have repeatedly declared that we in no way seek to have the moral teaching of the Catholic Church become the criterion of constitutional change or to have the principles of Catholic faith enshrined in civil law. What we have claimed, and what we must claim, is the right to fulfil our pastoral duty and our pastoral duty is to alert the consciences of Catholics to the moral consequences of any proposed piece of legislation and to the impact of that legislation on the moral quality of life in society while leaving to the legislators and to the electorate their freedom to act in accordance with their consciences.[73]

The Catholic bishops nonetheless went on the offensive in March 1985 with the publication of a pastoral letter, *Love is for Life*, read at mass on three consecutive Sundays. Much of what Cardinal O Fiaich and the bishops had to say to Garret FitzGerald and Alan Dukes, Minister for Justice, repeated this pastoral. But they offered no advice as to the desirability of holding a referendum; this was a purely governmental decision. The delegation agreed on certain points, such as the necessity to raise the legal age of marriage (from 16 to 18) and the creation of family tribunals. It was not felt that consulting the churches was a superfluous exercise, since so many marriages are celebrated according to religious rites, but it still sounded suspiciously like buying time, since none of the consultations gave rise to major revelations.

The referendum on divorce was eventually announced on 23 April 1986. The Tenth Amendment of the Constitution Bill, 1986 proposed that Article 41.3.2. would no longer ban divorce, but would allow the courts to grant the dissolution of a marriage that had failed for five years, if adequate provision was made for any dependent spouse and child. There was also a declaration of intent attached to the bill setting out proposed changes concerning the legal age of marriage, the family courts, the mediation service and separation procedures. The laws relative to these questions would be drafted and voted on *after* the deletion of the ban on divorce.

Was Ireland going to give itself, in one go, unlike its neighbours, a humane and compassionate divorce law based on consent? Indeed for a first law on divorce, it was relatively liberal since it introduced from the outset the concept of divorce as a possible amicable arrangement. This was due to what Evelyn Mahon calls the 'historical lag' – the fact that Ireland intended to benefit from years of experience in other jurisdictions.[74] Opinion polls on voting intentions had rarely been so favourable, and FitzGerald himself was feeling bullish. He had just signed the Hillsborough agreement with Margaret Thatcher on 15 November 1985, which aimed at establishing intergovernmental cooperation to defuse the conflict in Northern Ireland. It was a case of now or never for the Taoiseach and an important milestone in his constitutional crusade.

Despite the concept of divorce by consent, it remained a restrictive divorce law, since a five-year separation was required, in comparison to two years in Britain where there is mutual consent; also, the precise and limited grounds for divorce would be inserted in the Constitution. But it was necessary to be pragmatic, in order to have even the slightest chance of success in a national referendum, as it was obvious that nobody wanted to see the introduction of divorce on demand. It was decided that the campaign would be short, unlike the 1983 abortion referendum, to avoid a build-up of opposing forces, and the date was set for 26 June. There was not even a vote in the two chambers when the bill enabling the referendum passed all stages (Mary Robinson tried to table two amendments, one replacing the phrase 'the marriage has failed' by the more legal one, 'there has been a breakdown of the marriage'; and the other for the separation period to be two years rather than five).[75]

The final result is well known, and took many people by surprise. It provided fascinating material for political analysts, and made politicians weary: Why was the right to divorce not accepted by the Irish people in 1986? Why, despite the optimism, the growing visibility of the minority in difficulty, the stance of all churches but one in favour of minority civil rights, – why did this important milestone in FitzGerald's constitutional crusade fail? To explain this, it will be necessary to look at the fronts on which the campaign was fought, using arguments of a different order: that of the Catholic Church and lay groups which focused on a mix of theological and economical arguments; that of the government and the pro-divorce groups trying to find a solution to a growing social problem; and in the background, the larger question about the kind of society Irish people wished to live in – a Catholic state or a pluralist state, possibly willing to welcome the North? An analysis of the various opinion polls taken during the referendum campaign, will also enlighten us as to the outcome of the vote. What was the clinching argument? The prospect of moral and social disorder once divorce would be introduced in Irish society? The prospect of more financial hardship for all concerned?

The Catholic hierarchy announced from the outset that the clergy 'would use, but not abuse, the pulpit to present the Catholic Church's theological and sociological objections to divorce.'[76] Would they manage to do so without instructing people on how to vote? A new pastoral, an updated version of *Love is for Life*, entitled *Marriage, the Family and Divorce*, rehearsed their major themes, in an attempt to inform the faithfuls' conscience. The arguments employed and the language used left the bishops' intentions in no doubt, and there was an underlying suggestion that if the state did not leave the teaching of the Catholic Church enshrined in the Constitution, marriage itself would be undermined, and 'at one stroke, the legal concept of indissoluble marriage is abolished. From being defined in law as indissoluble, marriages, all marriages, become immediately defined as dissoluble.... The 'multiplier effect' of divorce as a factor making for instability in marriage is unavoidable and it is irreversible.'[77] This echoed what John Paul II said when he visited Ireland in 1979:

> Divorce, for whatever reason it is introduced, inevitably becomes easier and easier to obtain and it gradually comes to be accepted as a normal part of life. The very possibility of divorce in the sphere of civil law makes stable and permanent marriages more difficult for everyone. May Ireland always continue to give witness before the modern world to her traditional commitment, corresponding to the true dignity of man, to the sanctity and the indissolubility of the marriage bond.[78]

The Catholic stance contrasted with that of the Church of Ireland Archbishop of Dublin, Donald Caird, who said that 'the State has a perfect right to introduce divorce if it is necessary for civil order'. This leads to the suggestion that the Irish state was undergoing a fundamental metamorphosis in that it was adopting the Protestant approach as far as social issues were concerned – that is, a pragmatic approach, rooted in reality and based on individual conscience and responsibility.

What annoyed rational minds was the fact that looking at the situation in Britain or the United States (with some of the highest divorce rates) did not prove the religious' point, since these examples were not objectively transposable to the Irish situation, as they 'have long been secular and post-Christian countries and that the divorce trend is a consequence and a reflection of their culture rather than an intrinsic agent of social instability.'[79] What does one prove by comparing Ireland to countries with totally different cultures and ethics? It would be more convincing to look at divorce in Northern Ireland to get an idea of what it might be like in the Republic, since the North has similar ethics as far as marriage and the family are concerned. Curiously enough, such an approach carries little weight in the Republic and what happens up there in the socio-moral area is never of concern in the South. Certainly before the 1994 ceasefire, more Irish had been to England or had family there than in Northern Ireland. An opinion poll published in *The Irish Independent* on 2 February 1995 showed that 44 per cent of the Irish questioned had never been to Northern Ireland. The Irish media tried to clarify what the divorce situation in the North was. The Northern Irish Parliament, the Stormont, passed its first divorce law in 1939, thus adopting the English concept of fault, shortly after the South inserted the ban on divorce in its Constitution. The law was changed in England and Wales in 1969, with the Divorce Reform Act, which added, in parallel to the concept of fault, that of the irretrievable breakdown of the marriage (requiring two years' separation in uncontested cases, five otherwise). Pressure exercised in Northern Ireland by women's groups and the legal professions resulted in a new divorce law for Northern Ireland in 1978, which introduced the concept of irretrievable breakdown of the marriage, so that a divorce could be obtained on the basis of separation. Separation is now the most common ground on which a divorce is granted, whereas in England and Wales, 75 per cent of divorcing couples used the 'quickie divorce' procedure which enabled them to obtain a divorce in under six months, but required them to allege fault (this was done away with in 1996, and one year separation is now required). In 1995, 2,302 divorces were granted in Northern Ireland. With a population of 1.5 million, and an annual marriage rate of around 10,000, the divorce rate is 3.3 persons per 1,000 ever married, whereas it is 13.9 per 1,000 in England and Wales.[80] Interestingly, 5.6 per cent of husbands and 5.1 per cent of wives securing a divorce in 1995 were already of divorce status when entering the marriage. It is also important to remember that the Catholic Church in Northern Ireland does not grant any ecclesiastical annulment without a civil divorce being pronounced first. The constant progression of figures, even in Northern Ireland, was used by some Catholic religious and lay people to prove that once legalised divorce spread inexorably.[81]

The Catholic religious' argumentation was not always measured, and they could be formidable speakers. Some presented divorce as a Frankenstein monster and built up frightening scenarios. In a similar vein, Bishop McNamara compared divorce to the catastrophe at Chernobyl, 'a useful reminder of how negative radiation can filter across and permeate society. Divorce legislation has had a somewhat similar effect in the way it has permeated western societies and undermined the stability of marriage.'[82] Such dramatic statements had a greater impact on the average Irish person than any rational speech delivered by a minister or a senator, however well respected. Irish people were generally more exposed to anti-divorce arguments, coming more often than not from Catholics, either in the course of Sunday mass or during the communion and confirmation masses that were taking place throughout the country. These were occasions of captive listening, more so than when people read their papers or watched television. They forcefully confirmed the collective declarations of the Irish hierarchy, as that issued on 11 June, in effect a strong condemnation of the outcome of divorce on society and a plea to voters to decide 'whether other factors outweigh the damage which divorce would certainly cause to individuals, to families, to children and to the whole of society'. Catholics were reminded they could not vote as they liked, since it was a matter of 'serious conscientious decision'. In fact, 'in this case a person has to ask if the decision is in accordance with the law of God and based on what a person judges as best serving the common good and in the best interest of future generations.' This exemplifies the fact that, since Vatican II the Catholic Church acknowledges the importance of the individual conscience but stresses it has to be informed, and the Church itself is in the best position to inform it – which leaves little leeway to the individual if the true moral path is already marked out. This would seem to be in contradiction to the spirit of Vatican II, which was intended to give a greater say to lay Catholics and give a greater role to their private conscience. But back in Ireland from Rome in 1965, Archbishop McQuaid said to his flock: 'allow me to reassure you. No change will worry the tranquillity of your Christian lives.' And the letter of the reforms was adopted, if not always the spirit! Since then, John Paul II, elected Pope in 1978 and a great believer in theological conformity, has put emphasis on a more directive style, based on the magisterium, which is not at odds with the Irish hierarchy's stance on moral questions in particular. Indeed, the few priests who were tempted to speak out in favour of the constitutional amendment were allegedly prevented from doing so by the papal nuncio, Dr Alibrandi, who was not in favour of the ecumenism and pluralism in vogue after Vatican II.[83] More orthodox priests did not feel obliged, in their sermons, to focus more on conscience rather than on the evils of divorce, hence the greater impact of weekly sermons over political speeches or collective hierarchy statements.

Would the Irish have the independence of mind necessary to go against the Church and the law of God? It was going to be all the more difficult that they were also largely exposed to the lay anti-divorce militants. Catholic religious said they were not fighting a campaign but the weekly mass had the same role as a 'political' meeting, and lay Catholics took over the rest of the week. Indeed the anti-divorce groups were very well established, enjoying the benefit of the networks of the Church and of Fianna Fáil (both supposedly and officially neutral), and also of the large penetration in the country of Family Solidarity, a new group launched in 1984 to fight threats to marriage and the family. The group was organised by parish, whose infrastructure it used for its meetings. It was central to the Anti-Divorce Campaign (ADC), launched at the end of April 1986, to which it provided devoted crusaders, trained in persuasive canvassing methods. ADC sympathisers had generally the hang of things since most of them had already taken part in the abortion referendum campaign and had 'won'. Their spokesman, Joe McCarroll, was very skilled in the art of handling the media; their treasurer, and president of the campaign, Senator Des Hanafin, was an experienced and resourceful fundraiser; their legal adviser, Professor William Binchy, prominent in 1983 too, was well informed on divorce and its consequences in other jurisdictions, and, being telegenic and articulate, he was featured in a number of TV programmes, as sociologist Michele Dillon discovered during her research on the campaign.[84] Leaving theology to the professionals, without renouncing it, they focused on the financial aspects of divorce, that is on the now destitute first wife and children born of the first marriage, on dismembered farms later sold, and on the taxpayers called on to make their contribution – so much so that Professor of Law Kevin Boyle remarked that 'an outsider observer of the furore could be forgiven for thinking that the referendum was intended to remove the right to private property in the Constitution, rather than its clear purpose, which is to include a modest measure of civil freedom for citizens to rectify mistakes they have made in their personal relations.'[85] In general, the tactics used by ADC were defined thus by the 'other side', notably by TD Michael O'Leary: 'The opponents of divorce are introducing the politics of fear by misrepresentation into the public debate'.[86] The anti-divorce militants had long left the terrain of natural law and the ideal family to root their arguments in prosaic considerations.

The striking fact about this campaign rests in the extensive use made of sociological and economic arguments, of figures and statistics, what were also referred to as 'the facts'. But these socio-economic arguments sounded more like so many rationalisations of a fundamentally theological stance. They aimed at swaying the average Irish person, by reinforcing doctrinal and moral objections, and had a particular weight in Ireland, where property is a fundamental right in this traditionally rural country which took long enough to acquire it, and where the prospect of family farms being sold was inconceivable. The same goes for the family home whose purchase is the unparalleled priority of every Irish couple. It was also good tactics from the point of view of the large proportion of wives who did not have a career and income of their own. Fine Gael TD Alice Glenn employed this colourful phrase, 'any woman voting for divorce is like a turkey voting for Christmas.'[87] Such slogans expressed the fears of women, women as victims, who were holding on tight to marriage as if it was a bastion against a changing world in which they had as little power as ever. What ADC lost sight of was the fact that it is not divorce as such that impoverishes women, but the extremely vulnerable economic position they were in. Marriage gave them a title, social status, financial security. Why would they give it all up and for what? Irish society was not particularly friendly towards its unconforming citizens. Married women enjoyed numerous rights guaranteed by the Constitution, sometimes only on paper, but they would have significantly less as divorced women. ADC argued that it was precisely because Irish society discriminated against women that they needed to be protected from the effects of divorce, and it wanted to be seen as the champion of women's rights. The campaign against divorce was based on these premisses but it always presented women as victims rather than as free agents. There was never any question of changing the social and cultural circumstances that made women so vulnerable, as if they were 'naturally' dependent. But we are forced to accept that many Irish women recognised themselves in the picture drawn by ADC and this undoubtedly influenced the outcome. The question remained, would divorced women be worse off than all those women trapped in paper marriages or deserted women who received no maintenance from their estranged husbands, who might be head of a new household somewhere? The question was never asked in such a way, since ADC argued that the current welfare system coped well with marital breakdown. But as barrister Peter Ward proved in his later research, this system was not efficient. Whereas one of the anti-divorce arguments was that there were enough measures in place to cope with marital breakdown, Ward showed that this was not the case, contradicting one of the conclusions of the

Oireachtas Committee: it is not divorce that impoverishes women and children, but separation.[88]

On the politicians' front, several elements contributed to the defeat of the referendum. Fianna Fáil declared from the outset that they would not oppose the referendum as people had the right to decide the issue themselves, but that individual deputies and senators could campaign on whichever side they saw fit. John Cooney explained that this newly displayed neutrality was due to the fact that party strategists wanted to shake off the image that they were 'the bishops' party', in view of the fact that the pro-life amendment (see Chapter 5) was rejected in five Dublin area constituencies. Policy on marriage breakdown should be reviewed, and thus led Charles Haughey to allow deputies freedom of conscience in the campaign.[89] In fact, Fianna Fáil parliamentarians and activists for the most part campaigned on the side of ADC. For example, Michael Woods, in a 41-page speech to the Dáil, described the prospect of divorce in horror film terms, comparing divorce to a monster, an image taken up in no time at the pulpit: '[the first families] would become constitutional orphans.... Could it be that the Government have unwittingly created a constitutional Frankenstein which may sleep for a time but then rise and stalk the land?'[90] There were divisions on the government's side, the most notable coming from the Minister for Education, Patrick Cooney, who declared publicly on several occasions his opposition to the introduction of divorce in Ireland. He was not reprimanded by Fine Gael, which had decided that this was a matter of conscience and could be decided individually. There were also within the ranks of Fine Gael some fundamentalist Catholics, such as Oliver Flanagan, a long-serving TD and Knight of St Columbanus.

To offset disinformation, five days before the poll the government published an updated declaration of intent about the legislation it would introduce, once the amendment was accepted. In the light of the arguments used by the opponents of this amendment, it was decided to clarify the patrimonial effects of divorce and the rights of the first family. In retrospect, it is obvious that many of these details came too late and sounded too much like electoral promises. All along the government had been on the defensive, responding to ADC's objections instead of anticipating them. Initially it was mainly a matter of facing up to a growing social problem, and calling on the compassion of the Irish to facilitate the introduction of divorce. The government had neglected a very important aspect of any legislation on divorce, – the liquidation of the joint estate of the couple. It had not anticipated that the campaign would be fought on the socio-economic terrain, and it did not respond with enough facts to those deployed by ADC. It could have denounced the hypocrisy of ecclesiastical annulments often put forward as an adequate remedy to marital breakdown. It could have made more use of the available statistics, like the number of deserted women receiving social welfare, or the number of barring orders applied for each year. Unfortunately the state had never been concerned about these figures. It was only in April 1986 that people were asked for the first time in the population census if they were separated, but the results were not known during the referendum campaign. This allowed the opponents of divorce to idealise marriage, and the problem of marital breakdown remained quite abstract in the minds of the Irish people, as sociologist Paddy O'Carroll observed: 'Official lack of interest in marital problems, characterised, for example, by the total absence of any census statistics on the topic, ensured that reality did not impinge on popular consciousness to any great extent.'[91] It is also indisputable that, in comparison to the anti-divorce front which was united in its determination not to see the amendment through and speaking in one voice as it were, the campaign on the side of the proponents of divorce was less well orchestrated. Another handicap was the fact that the referendum campaign was led from Dublin, and provincial deputies, Fine Gael ones in particular, never really campaigned at the local level, as they would have done in a general election. Political scientist Brian Girvin noticed that

> by polling day, a significant minority of both Fine Gael and the Progressive Democrats were opposed to the introduction of divorce. Only the Labour Party and the Workers' Party, of the other political parties, were unequivocally in favour of divorce. Both canvassed actively alongside the Divorce Action Group, and identified closely with the issues.[92]

The pro-divorce group, DAG, did not have as great a foothold at local level as ADC, allied to Family Solidarity. Even though the group was set up in 1980, it was never, like the politicians, as present in the field as their opponents. Even if a substantial number were in favour of divorce at that stage, very few were inclined to canvass on the doorstep, and this in a country with 'almost a saturation rate of campaign penetration' at election time.[93]

Having said all this, the tactical errors made by the government could probably have been overcome if it had not had a major handicap, as far as its very argumentation was concerned. After all, it was the first time that the Irish had been asked to vote for a law that was fundamentally contrary to the Church a great majority of them belonged to. They had to be convinced that they could do so while remaining good Catholics. Actually the 'good Catholic' side of FitzGerald was often emphasised, as well as the fact he had first consulted all the churches. The Irish also had to be convinced that such a law was justified for the 'balance of the social good', but the social good had Catholic connotations that would be hard to remove. Defending divorce ran counter to such fundamental attitudes; hence the task was enormous. Also, in order to separate public from private morality, a challenge to the Church's socio-moral teaching, FitzGerald could not use the language of the Church. Therefore, as sociologist Michele Dillon has shown, he used a very intellectual language which did not engage the people.[94] The use of phrases like 'indissoluble monogamy' and the fact that the new law would not be of use to him, to his colleagues, to you and me, but to a 'hypothetical Irish person' did not augur well for the impact that the government campaign would to have. FitzGerald's arguments would remain much more abstract than those of William Binchy, which were strikingly true to life. It would have been far too prosaic on the government's part to praise the benefits of divorce in terms of financial benefits! So the reasoning used was more intellectual, it invoked minorities' rights, drawing parallels with Northern Ireland and, by extension, calling for a new Ireland, which would be full of compassion and generosity towards those, Catholics as well as Protestants, who wished to have a second chance. The government's slogan was 'Put Compassion in the Constitution!' but the Irish might not be ready to put individual freedom, with its hedonistic connotations first and to accept the new definition of the social good.

Those who campaigned in the field said later that it was obvious from the start that the amendment would be rejected. Some though were surprised at the narrower and narrower margin in the opinion polls. If the opinion polls prove one thing, it is that enough Irish people changed their minds in the course of the campaign to cause the result to tilt (25 per cent of the people changed their minds in three weeks). The first MRBI/*The Irish Times* opinion poll took place a few days after the referendum was announced and showed that 57 per cent of those questioned would vote to lift the constitutional ban, a greater majority than in all preceding polls. Indeed, until then, even when a comfortable majority of people said that divorce should be allowed in certain circumstances, a much narrower one said they were ready to vote for the repeal of Article 41.3.2. This discrepancy was accounted for by the fact that these Irish agreed with the general principle to allow for divorce in certain circumstances, but they shrank at the much larger and uncertain question of repealing the article at issue without knowing what would replace it. When one asked those who had replied in January 1985 that divorce should be allowed but, to another question, said they would vote against the repeal of Article 41.3.2, why, they replied that divorce should only be allowed in cases of irretrievable breakdown of the marriage, or in cases of violence and hardship.[95] Now that the people knew the government's intentions, which seemed sufficiently restrictive, there was a distinct majority who agreed that the Constitution should be changed. The next polls and the voting intentions of Fianna Fáil supporters show that the allegedly non-existent campaign of Fianna Fáil had borne fruit: 61 per cent of its supporters had said, on 25 June, the day before the actual vote, that they were going to vote against the amendment, compared to 46 per cent on 5 May. Generally speaking, all parties switched to the No vote, even the Progressive Democrats (PDs) whose leader, Des O'Malley, had insisted on the importance of separating the Catholic Church and the state, the *raison d'être* of his party. On 25 June, 40 per cent of voters were in favour of lifting the ban, and 49 per cent against: a sizeable majority in favour of the amendment had vanished within a few weeks. The categories which had shown a high proportion of 'for the amendment' on 5 May, like the Dubliners (67 per cent in favour), the middle classes and single people, were now divided 50–50, around 45 per cent. As for women, 31 per cent were in favour; 56 per cent against; and 12 per cent undecided. The campaign of ADC, centred on the interests of women, seemed to have had a considerable impact.

In the end, the turnout was 62.7 per cent, and the defeat was even more crushing than was feared, since 63.48 per cent of voters rejected the introduction of divorce in Ireland. Even in Dublin, the Yes vote only had a majority of 559 votes over the No vote (50.1 per cent to 49.9 per cent). The most resounding No came from Cork North West (78.5 per cent) and Roscommon (76.7 per cent). If the division in Dublin was roughly 50–50, in the rest of Ireland it was 69–31, which was a near repetition of the 1983 voting pattern (see Chapter 5).[96] This result seemed to prove that the Irish wanted to keep a Constitution stamped with Catholic values, that they did not want to question marriage as a lifelong commitment; and by extension, that they wanted to keep intact their identity. To be Irish is to be Catholic, is not to divorce – this is what makes us different. Did those who voted No do so because they were conservatives at heart, happy to live in a 'Catholic state', despite all – the broken couples, the re-ordered families and the people of Northern Ireland against whom this No vote was like a moral judgement? Senator Catherine McGuinness, a member of the Church of Ireland, felt that 'the amendment campaign has been a litmus test, like the Parnell controversy and the Mother and Child Scheme, about the type of society we want. We have shown we want a Catholic State and we should have the honesty to admit we aren't interested in a united Ireland.'[97] But the Irish had also opted for pragmatism: divorce is not a panacea, and maybe it was better to hold on to the status quo than change for something that did not always work well in other countries. Deliberations on the subject of divorce took place in Ireland at a time when the bad effects of various foreign divorce legislations had become tangible and well documented, particularly in the context of family instability and the problems children of divorcees seem to experience. It would not be easy for the Irish to accept that divorce could be for the social good. As for FitzGerald's crusade against the sectarian features of the Irish Constitution and legislation, it suffered a serious setback. Invoking the social good, minorities' rights and a pluralist Ireland had not had enough grip on a people who were not used to thinking in those terms. If it was a tactical error to focus on arguments that were not grounded in economics, at least next time one would be justified in starting from there.

The issue of divorce was not solved by the referendum. The social problem remained. It was not one of those one could hide or export; it would have to be tackled differently now. Those not too stunned by the defeat could see that divorce would end up being introduced in Ireland; it was only a matter of time. The editorial of *The Irish Times* announced on 28 June, the day the defeat was reported: 'There is a social momentum in the matter of divorce – beyond denomination and dogma – that cannot be halted. It will come in this State as it has come elsewhere; and it may not be so long in coming.' If among those who voted No, refusal to transgress canon law was paramount, fear was also a factor mitigating against change, fear of the unknown, of being dispossessed, of losing out – an answer had to be found to these fears.

A few months after the referendum, an MRBI/*The Irish Times* poll revealed that 70 per cent of those questioned would accept divorce in certain circumstances, and that a majority, smaller but nonetheless real (51 per cent), would vote in favour of lifting the constitutional ban.[98]

2 Divorce:... To the Right to a Second Chance

What took place in the area of family law following the defeat of the first divorce referendum appears to be evidence of a radically different strategy. The problem did not disappear as the 1986 census figures and later the 1991 ones, proved, bearing witness, as was pointed out earlier, to the growing anachronism that the ban on divorce was. They showed that the number of separated people was growing alarmingly, with a 48 per cent increase in five years. Irish people, the legislators included, began to accept that the absence of divorce did not protect the institution of marriage and that they resorted to all sorts of solutions to put an end to deadlocked marital situations, as detailed earlier. Seeing both the overt and the underlying opposition to divorce, in all political parties, how would it be possible to introduce major legislative changes in the wake of a resounding defeat? The introduction of divorce in Ireland was not on the agenda as a majority had rejected it in principle, and as it was out of the question to make civil annulment procedures more accessible for fear of hypocrisy, it remained to change the legislation on legal separation. This avenue which, by loosening the bond of marriage, has long been presented as the Catholics' divorce, because it is compatible with the dogma of the indissolubility of marriage, is a palliative that has developed wherever divorce is not available.

JUDICIAL SEPARATION: A LEGISLATION THAT DARE NOT SPEAK ITS NAME

It was Alan Shatter, a barrister specialising in family law, author of a lengthy volume on family law in Ireland, and a Fine Gael TD, who relaunched the debate. He had been a member of the Joint Committee on Marital Breakdown and in 1987 he tabled a private member's bill based on its recommendations. The Judicial Separation and Family Law Reform Bill, which would become the first private member's bill to become law in 30 years, and the second one in the history of the Oireachtas, had the initial support of all parties. Even Fianna Fáil, then in power, admitted in its recent *Programme for National Recovery*, that its policy on marital breakdown would be to deal with

49

the problems 'fairly and with as little acrimony as is possible'. The bill aimed at replacing the 1870 separation law, which rested on the Victorian concept of fault. Its intent was to make judicial separation a more identifiable remedy for people with marital problems, and it should put an end to the use of barring orders and suchlike in lieu of divorce proceedings.

The Law Reform Commission had examined the legislation regarding divorce *a mensa et thoro* and published a report in 1983 recommending change, particularly as far as the acceptable grounds were concerned.[1] The Joint Committee insisted in 1985 on the same requirement, and suggested replacing the current grounds by just one, irretrievable marital breakdown, in order to minimise conflict between the spouses. The Shatter Bill proposed that a judicial separation would be granted if there was irretrievable marital breakdown (which could be proved in six different ways) and mandatory mediation sessions had not led to reconciliation. Moreover the courts would be empowered to make maintenance orders, lump-sum payment orders, property transfer orders, orders extinguishing or changing inheritance rights, orders relating to the guardianship and custody of children, and orders relative to the sale of property. Concerning the ownership of family property, the court must take into account 'the contribution made by each of the spouses to the welfare of the family, including any contribution made by looking after the home or caring for the family.' Separation applications would now be heard in the Circuit Court only, and not in the High Court, certain days of the week being set aside for matrimonial cases; also, in order to make these hearings less distressing, neither the judges nor the barristers would wear wigs and gowns. It was an exhaustive bill, drafted by someone who faced these traumatic situations daily and who had drawn a lot from the Joint Committee.

At first, it seemed that it was widely supported, but it became obvious that the government was trying to empty it of its substance: it did not succeed in having its amendments adopted at committee stage, but it managed to stretch the length of the debates since that stage alone lasted seven months, and it tabled 36 amendments which covered more paper than the bill itself! One of its main difficulties with the bill was that it could not accept the phrase 'irretrievable marital breakdown' in the wording, and that it could be invoked to obtain a separation, since a separation is not a dissolution and it is always possible to get back together. The phrase belongs to the terminology of divorce legislation, and it is plausible that the Fianna

Fáil government wanted to avoid at all cost any resemblance to the English divorce legislation. There was a fear in certain quarters that divorce would be introduced by the back door, that 'the divorce lobby, despite rejection in the 1986 divorce referendum, aims to create a more compelling demand for divorce by increasing the number of separated people'.[2] Therefore the Minister for Justice tabled again, in front of the Dáil as a whole, that separation be granted for one of the five grounds proposed, but without breakdown of the marriage as a precondition. This time his amendment was passed by 72 votes to 70. Also, he tabled again his amendment intending to suppress from the bill that a couple could not apply for a separation if they were married for less than one year. It seems strange that a Minister from a party so anxious to protect marriage would support the idea that a couple could apply for a separation if they were married for a few months only. Again, the justification for such an amendment, and the determination to see it adopted, resided in the fact that this bar on appplications always appears in divorce laws, but not in separation proceedings. It was accepted by 77 votes to 72. The third major objection of the Minister concerned succession rights. Under the current separation law, the spouse against which the separation was pronounced lost his/her inheritance rights, whereas the applicant, for example, the battered, betrayed or deserted woman, kept hers. Gerry Collins suggested that since the courts had now all powers to protect the financial interests of the dependent spouse, all inheritance rights should be extinguished upon separation. This roused indignation: what battered, betrayed spouse, victim of inacceptable behaviour, would ask for a judicial separation if s/he knew that s/he would be automatically disinherited without being able to foresee what the judges would grant her/him? The other extraordinary aspect of this amendment was the inherent contradiction that if a judicial separation can at any time be revoked because the spouses decide to resume marital life, there should be no stipulation that they lose their inheritance rights. It is actually in a divorce situation that the divorced spouse has no right to inherit from a predeceased ex-spouse. Despite the strength of Alan Shatter's arguments, this amendment was accepted by 77 votes to 76. The bill was beginning to resemble precisely what a great number of women had feared losing in 1986 if they voted for divorce. But let us note that there was no statement from the hierarchy or from individual bishops, no demonstration organised by the Catholic lay groups, opposing Shatter's approach.

It seems that Fianna Fáil was alone in waging war on a bill that verged on – but only just – disobedience to canon law. At that stage, the amendments to the bill were such that Alan Shatter and Fine Gael even considered withdrawing it, as it was now a mere shadow of its former self. The solution out of the impasse was unconventional: the Minister for Justice and Shatter met outside the Committee and tried to find a compromise so that the bill retained its spirit and Fianna Fáil was satisfied that it was not a divorce law. The fact that they came back to the Committee with amendments in both their names was an almost unprecedented approach to legislation. The compromise was that the phrase 'irretrievable marital breakdown' was removed from the text, but a judicial separation could be granted if 'the marriage has broken down to the extent that the court is satisfied in all the circumstances that a normal marital relationship has not existed betweeen the spouses for a period of at least one year immediately preceding the date of the application.' This might not be the same as irretrievable marital breakdown, but it went a long way towards including a no fault element in a separation decree! This time, the bill was passed without any further obstacles, albeit by one vote only. One can understand that opposition deputies did not like to hear that the law was modelled on the English divorce law, for fear of unleashing the fundamentalist Catholic forces, but one has to admit that it did resemble the English divorce law, bar the right to remarry. Ireland gave itself a divorce law, but one that does not use the dreaded word, nor any usually associated with this kind of legislation, but the idea was definitely there: couples could separate after one year of experiencing difficulties in their marital life. Three fault grounds remained, and three no fault grounds were introduced. The courts would settle all financial and family arrangements as they saw fit. It is curious that no deputy queried the enormous prerogatives given to judges, but they were so busy making sure that no word would ring divorce alarm bells!

Obviously the new law was timely, since there were some 7,000 applications, and over 4,000 separations granted by the courts between its coming into force, on 16 October 1989, and 31 July 1995 (the end of the legal year). Even so, lawyers specialised in family law estimated that no more than a quarter to a third of couples in difficulty went to court to settle their disagreements. The substantial gap between the number of applications and of decrees granted is accounted for by the fact that some couples start proceedings and then settle amicably out of court (they presumably sign a deed of separation), but also by the fact that a large number of cases are still pending, sometimes for up to a year. Bearing in mind the gap between Shatter and the government at the time of the parliamentary debates, it is interesting to note that

the vast majority of separations are granted on the basis of an abnor-
mal marital relationship for one year, the marriage having effectively
broken down. Over a period of $2^1/_2$ years, 1,578 separations were
granted by the Circuit Courts because the marriage had broken
down; 305 on proof of the unreasonable behaviour of one of the
spouses; 92 for adultery; 54 for desertion; 89 after the couples had
lived apart for one year; and 66 after the couples had lived apart for
three years and only one spouse sought the decree.[3] A detail remains
to be mentioned: a judicial separation costs at least £4000 and this puts
it out of reach of many people, notably the not well-off but whose
income exceeds the legal aid threshold. Even so, the Legal Aid Board
data show that there has been a 400 per cent increase in legal aid
granted to people seeking a separation since the law came into force.
Another fact is that the courts cannot meet the demand. This begs the
question: How do you introduce divorce into a judicial system that is
already coming apart at the seams, with the judges sometimes hearing
up to 70 family law cases a day?

As family law cases are heard *in camera*, judgments are not published and nor are comprehensive statistics. The problem of marital
breakdown has become real because everybody now knows or knows
about somebody who is separated in one way or another. Indeed
couples who have been granted a separation decree are the tip of the
iceberg. According to a survey conducted by Gingerbread (a support
group for lone parents, be they single, separated, deserted, widowed or
other), 15 per cent only of the separated people surveyed opted for a
judicial separation; 20 per cent had a solicitor draw up a deed of
separation for them; 10 per cent had tried mediation, while 47 per
cent had no formal separation agreement or had negotiated it between
themselves.[4]

A tangible shift in public and political opinion concerning divorce
took place towards the end of 1990, following the election of Mary
Robinson as President of Ireland. Fine Gael fared quite badly in
this election, and its leader, Alan Dukes, resigned in favour of John
Bruton who, in his inaugural address as new party leader, announced
that his party would have 'the political courage to place difficult social
decisions before the Irish people. Fine Gael has the realism and the
compassion to raise the issue of divorce.'[5] The Labour Party leader,
Dick Spring, followed suit and also called for a new referendum.
He was echoed by the PDs, and the Workers' Party, while the Minister
for Justice of the Fianna Fáil–PDs government, Ray Burke, announced
that a White Paper on marital breakdown was in preparation. Its

publication was part of the second programme of government of this present coalition launched in October 1991 (a revision of the first one, which did not mention it at all). Had the time come when Fianna Fáil too was going to adopt the liberal agenda, which could now win votes, as it 'discovered the politically lucrative side of a liberal agenda. Fianna Fáil's role as protector of Catholic sexual morality would last only as long as it was seen to deliver votes and marginal seats. A reverse strategy in the 1990s was more likely to recapture the citadel of Dublin for the Party of Reality.'[6] In January 1992, Bertie Ahern, the Fianna Fáil Minister for Finance, spoke in public about his marital difficulties. In fact, his marital situation – separated from his wife and cohabiting with somebody else – was an open secret in political circles and in his constituency. Even though he was not the first politician to be living in a second union, it was still the first time that a Minister of his import-ance, number 3 in the government, admitted he was not part of a happily married couple. An article entitled 'Divorce in the Dáil' also revealed the marital arrangements of a number of TDs, MEPs and senators.[7] It has been suggested that Bertie Ahern chose that point in time to 'come out' about his private life because it could not later be used in the Fianna Fáil leadership contest to spoil his chances. Anticip-ating a little, let us note that this is precisely what happened in February 1992, when Albert Reynolds was elected by the Fianna Fáil party to replace Charles Haughey! Eventually, Bertie Ahern did become the leader of the party, in December 1994, with his partner at his side during the election. He also nearly became the first separ-ated and cohabiting Taoiseach – something that would finally happen in June 1997! Having said all that, Bertie Ahern's 'revelations' helped put divorce back on the political agenda.

THE RIGHT TO SEPARATE (1994)

The White Paper, *Marital Breakdown – Review and Proposed Changes*, was published in September 1992, after a gestation period of over 18 months and several delays, including that caused by the resignation of Charles Haughey, in February 1992. The new party leader and Taoi-seach, Albert Reynolds, declared when he took office that he hoped there would be a new referendum on divorce 'during the life of this government', and encouraged the new Minister for Justice, Padraig Flynn, to publish a White Paper addressing all the implications of marital failure as soon as possible. During the Fianna Fáil congress,

Flynn, despite his reputation as a staunch conservative holding fast to traditional values, made a speech that won him media praise for committing himself to legislate on reality rather than ideals. He admitted there was no running away from social problems, and added:

> I can quite easily foresee a situation in this country in the next ten years where social legislation will be passed which acknowledges patterns of living that many people would wish were not emerging. But the law has to deal with real life, real demographic and social factors, instead of ideals and aspirations, and, as Minister for Justice, that's what I'm going to be seeking to achieve, with every bit of energy and commitment I can bring to it.[8]

The publication of this report is an historic event since the largest party in Ireland, the most quintessentially Irish, the party one associates with the ideas of nation, Irish identity, traditional values, namely Fianna Fáil, was committing itself at last to a real debate based on social reality, and admitting implicitly that the introduction of divorce was inevitable. Flynn went as far as saying:

> I am stating here now, on behalf of the Government, that it is not a question of 'if', it is a question of 'when'. The 'when' will probably be some time towards the end of next year. I have no doubt that divorce legislation will be on the books in a certain short period of time.[9]

The White Paper proposed 'a full debate on the complex issues involved', and a referendum 'following the enactment of other legislative proposals in the area of family law'. One of the most difficult issues to be addressed was the provision of adequate maintenance, since very few maintenance orders currently made in the courts were being honoured; the threat to property rights was a related issue. The White Paper outlined the recent developments in family law and set out the legal alterations and legislative changes required if a divorce referendum was passed, but made no recommendation for or against constitutional change. It proposed the early enactment of a bill ensuring the statutory right of every spouse to an equal share in the family home (the Family Ownership Bill was in the process of being drafted). It favoured the replacement of the religious registration of marriages on behalf of the state by the introduction of a new civil registration ceremony, the introduction of special family courts, the ratification of a number of international conventions on the enforcement of the recovery of maintenance payments. It promised no fewer than five government bills. However, it did not seem to favour any one form of civil divorce, but listed five options, the last dealing with irretrievable breakdown of the marriage on a fault or no fault basis. It was the most detailed option and would add so many details to the Constitution that a referendum would be necessary each time it was felt necessary to respond to social change. This was more in keeping with the Minister's legendary conservatism and the fact that he was one of the staunchest opponents of divorce in 1986.

Could his new persona be trusted? Well, pragmatism, or even opportunism, in conjunction with the inexorable advance of a new socio-moral order, can get the better of the most traditionalist. Flynn went on to head employment and social affairs, including women's affairs at the European Commission, and has been praised for his work there by notable Irish feminists! The restrictions in the proposals do not necessarily challenge the Minister's good faith: the process of the demoralisation of legislation would not be achieved overnight, and this procrastination was inspired as much by aversion as by pure pragmatism. Also, it seemed that the divorce referendum would have a better chance of being passed if Fianna Fáil was in power in a coalition, leaving its political partner to do the dirty work of setting the process in motion, but ensuring victory with all its charisma, as it would give the whole project the legitimacy it required.

Interestingly enough, within the current Cabinet, the Taoiseach, Albert Reynolds, the Tanaiste, John Wilson, the Minister for Agriculture, John Walsh, the Minister for Marine, Michael 'Frankenstein' Woods, the Minister for Justice, Padraig Flynn and a Secretary of State, Mary O'Rourke, had let it be known in 1986 they were going to vote No in the referendum: so it would seem that the Fianna Fáil ministers had seriously questioned their convictions, and were advancing, little by little, in the direction of liberalism and pluralism. *The Sunday Tribune*, on 4 October 1992 commented:

> Fianna Fáil's progress on social issues tends to be crablike, a little bit sideways before the party feels it is safe to move forward. Yet, who would have thought just a few years back that Fianna Fáil would liberalise the laws on contraception, promise women access to information about abortion facilities, and commit itself to the repeal of the constitutional ban on divorce?

But Fianna Fáil was not going to lose sight of the fact that the liberal stand on socio-moral issues on the part of parlementarians such as

FitzGerald and Shatter had seen Fine Gael fall to 23 per cent in the opinion polls; they therefore intended to be more subtle about it. The debate on marital breakdown would be somewhat delayed as the 'little temporary arrangement', as Albert Reynolds called his coalition government, came to an end in November 1992 and threw the country into a premature and unwelcome general election. Its outcome was unexpected: Fianna Fáil had not had such a bad result since 1927 and lost nine seats (from 77 to 68); Fine Gael, since 1948, had its worst result and dropped from 55 seats to 45; the PDs gained four seats (from 6 to 10); while Labour had never scored so well, winning 33 seats, against 16 in the previous Dáil. Labour thus held the balance of power, and it took nearly two months to form a coalition, led by Fianna Fáil, with Albert Reynolds again as Taoiseach. There was another extraordinary outcome to this election, also due to what was called the 'Robinson factor', namely the fact that 20 women (including nine for the first time) were elected as deputies in this 27th Dáil (three more women would be elected in subsequent by-elections). This was the largest representation of women in the history of the state (there were also eight women senators). Two of them became ministers (Máire Geoghegan-Quinn for Justice, and Niamh Bhreathnach for Education) – the first time there would be two women in the Cabinet – and three other Secretaries of State. A new Ministry was created, that of Equality (of women, handicapped people, travellers, etc.) and Law Reform, placed in Mervyn Taylor's hands, one of the three Jewish TDs, a lawyer, well known for his liberal stand on sociomoral issues. The legislative programme of this new coalition included, apart from a number of pro-women measures, a commitment to reform family law, and in particular to hold a referendum on divorce where the only question left to be asked would be about the right to remarry.

In February 1993, the Second Commission for the Status of Women, chaired by High Court judge Mella Carroll, published its report, which the new government was committed to implement. It was a 535-page document, comprising 210 recommendations. These would radically change some areas of Irish society in order to guarantee the equality of women. The first report of the Commission dated back to 1972 and led to the formation of the Council for the Status of Women (CSW), in 1973. This was a government-funded body, acting as an umbrella group for the then 20 affiliated women's groups. It went on to represent 152 groups, or some 300,000 women. The CSW saw to the implementation of the reports' recommendations and lobbied the government in pursuit of this aim. It became the National Women's Council of Ireland (NWCI), during the summer of 1995. In the area of family law, the Second Commission favoured the holding of a divorce referendum and the measures recommended by the Law Reform Commission.[10] Therefore, with the new government in place, it appeared there would be a new political balance, with at least one of the two coalition parties committed to introducing a number of liberal laws relating to socio-moral issues; and with an unprecedented number of women members, all more or less prepared to legislate in favour of liberalism. As we mentioned above, the two driving forces necessary for the introduction of divorce were now united: Fianna Fáil for legitimacy and Labour for initiative and impetus.

In March 1993, as the debates on the White Paper began, the date of a second divorce referendum was announced. It would be spring 1994. Then, in June, the Matrimonial Home Bill was published. This guaranteed joint ownership of the family home, regardless of the financial contribution of either spouse. This would be a way of giving recognition to the unpaid work that married women do within the home, as proposed by the First Commission on the Status of Women. To the homemakers' great surprise, the judgment in the *B.L. v. M.L.* case had recently found that only a financial contribution could ensure the wife's share of the family home. Her work within the home could not be taken into account, despite Article 41 of the Constitution in which the state pledged to do its utmost to ensure that women would not be economically obliged to work outside the home.

The bill was approved by the Seanad on 3 November 1993 and was due to go to the President for her enacting signature. By that stage, the divorce referendum had been postponed to autumn 1994 because of the European elections. But the government's plans suffered a serious setback when the Supreme Court, on 24 January 1994, found the Matrimonial Home Bill unconstitutional. The bill had been referred to the court by President Robinson who, as a constitutional lawyer, wanted to prevent the bill, once enacted, from being contested by anti-divorce groups as being in contradiction of Article 43 on private property. (It should be noted that even some liberals, in favour of divorce, did not support the idea of mandatorily splitting up the property.) It would have been a major upset to have legal action taking place during the referendum campaign, which would have been marred by the pending judgment and a climate of uncertainty and anxiety, similar to that in 1986. The judges decided that automatic joint ownership of the matrimonial home constituted a failure by the state to protect the authority of the family and was against Article 41 of the Constitution. Just as they had based their decision in the McGee case (see Chapter 3) on the notion of autonomy within a marriage, they viewed the proposed provisions as a 'potentially indiscriminate alteration of what must be many joint decisions validly made within the authority of the family'.[11] This ruling was a severe blow to the government for whom the bill was to have been a central plank in the forthcoming divorce referendum. As tampering with the constitutional rights of the family was out of the question, the bill was dropped. However the fact that the court had not based its ruling on property rights saved the 1989 Act from being struck down too. As far as property was concerned, the 1989 Act allowed judges officiating in family law cases to take into account, if they so wished, the contribution other than financial that a spouse had made as a carer and a rearer of the family within the home. They had a huge discretion to decide who owed what to whom, who stayed in the family home, and who got what out of the sale of the house or the farm.

While it was decided to drop the Matrimonial Home Bill, a Cork man decided to test in court the constitutionality of the Judicial Separation Act. The plaintiff in this case, who was judicially separated from his wife after 13 years of marriage, was questioning all constitutional aspects of the 1989 Act, including its property provisions, and particularly the fact that it allowed for spouses to separate too easily. This legal challenge caused the government some concern as it intended to extend this Act to cover cases of nullity and divorce (when an amendment to the Constitution was carried). Indeed, while the case was pending, the government published the Family Law Bill, 1994, which would build on the powers of the 1989 Act. But the government's legislative strategy for the forthcoming divorce referendum now depended precisely on the constitutionality of that Act. The pending litigation had already forced the postponement of the referendum several times to the spring of 1995. A cloud of uncertainty now hung over the legislation throughout 1994, threatening the government's strategy and causing great distress to the some 6,000 people who thought they were legally separated and whose separation decree could be invalidated. This in turn created growing uncertainty in the referendum being carried at all, which spread to all political parties. It was feared that some deputies would dissociate themselves from the project if difficulty upon difficulty was heaped on the government. As for public opinion, support for the introduction of divorce remained solid, at 56–61 per cent, despite the difficulties the government was experiencing in implementing its legislative programme.

Judge Frank Murphy eventually gave his ruling in the *F.* v. *F.* on 28 July 1994, in which he upheld the constitutionality of the Judicial Separation Act. He said in his unpublished judgment:

> The factual relationship of marriage was buttressed through the centuries in form at least by its legal indissolubility and by social and economic factors. Judicial separation was regarded as a domestic and social disgrace and it is clear that in most cases the wife had no practical alternative to enduring a relationship which by any reasonable standards would be regarded as wholly unacceptable. The changed role and status of the married woman, however, has been clearly noted by the courts.... The granting of a decree of judicial separation ... is little more than an official recognition of an existing, and usually tragic, state of affairs and a not inappropriate attempt by the Oireachtas to reconcile the needs and rights of the parties to the marriage, the family, and the community of which the family is the fundamental unit group.[12]

The great merit of this judgment was that it recognised explicitly that there was such a thing as a right to separate, which had not been officially guaranteed yet. It confirmed that marriage does not necessarily last forever, and that this is in direct contradiction with natural law and socio-moral order as interpreted by the Catholic Church. It was 'an endorsement of the legislature's efforts to deal with the real and growing problem of marriage breakdown'.[13] The plaintiff appealed to the Supreme Court, which would find, on 14 July 1995, that the 1989 Act was constitutional. Judge Hamilton said unambiguously that 'in many cases the common good would require that spouses should be separated, notwithstanding the indissoluble bond of marriage between them.' By then, the divorce referendum had been postponed to the autumn of 1995.

THE SECOND DIVORCE REFERENDUM: THE RIGHT TO REMARRY (1995)

Minister Mervyn Taylor was now in a position to steer through the Oireachtas the Family Law Bill, the Civil Legal Aid Bill (putting the existing scheme on a statutory basis and extending it) and the Social Welfare Bill, which guaranteed no loss of rights under the social welfare system when a married, separated or deserted person became divorced. One of the main objections to divorce being that it impoverishes the spouses, particularly the non-earning one, the issue of social welfare had to be addressed. Indeed, what one often forgets in discussions on the division of assets and property, who keeps the house, maintenance and other sources of disagreement, is that for many couples who separate the issue is to decide how to share the debts or the unemployment benefit! This was not raised in the White Paper, which recognised that loss of entitlement to a prospective occupational pension may cause hardship for women after divorce, but 'the problem of devising a just method of dividing pension entitlements can only begin to be solved when it is placed in the context of the general debate on the definition of marital property, which debate has yet to commence in this country.'[14] It was feared that the anti-divorce groups would exploit women's anxiety about losing their rights to widows' pensions and inheritance rights.

The government guaranteed that no divorced person would lose out, but was this a realistic promise or a pragmatic argument? These issues are all the more important in Ireland where the proportion of married women in the labour force is less than in other Western societies. The *National Report on Ireland*, compiled for the 1995 UN Conference on Women held in Beijing, reported an upward movement in the number of married women working outside the home: some 47.3 per cent of married women aged 20–24, and 49 per cent aged 25–34 were in the labour force in 1992. In fact, 29.7 per cent of all married women were in the labour force in 1992, as opposed to less than 8 per cent in 1974. But the overall proportion of women in the labour force had risen very little, from 28 per cent in 1970 to 34.2 per cent in 1992.[15] Even equal pay, 20 years after the legislation introducing it, was often only an aspiration. According to the International Labour Organisation, Irish women's hourly wage in manufacturing was 68 per cent of Irish men's. The Irish state had thus to acknowledge, in financial terms, the role a woman had played in a marriage. It already did in the numerous cases where the working ex-spouse failed to pay maintenance after a separation. Since, as things stood, research proved that over three-quarters of women who secured maintenance orders would have been better off on social welfare payments, and that only 13 per cent of maintenance orders were fully paid up, the introduction of divorce would do little to alleviate these problems and would create more hardship if steps were not taken. The creation of the lone parent's allowance had been a great leap forward since priority was thus not given to marriage but to the fact one was a parent, whether single, separated or widowed, man, woman or homosexual. This focus on lone parents regardless of their circumstances remedied the high default rate on the part of fathers, but, as this only provided for people with a dependant child, the state would have to step back as it were and promise that any social entitlement that married people received (deserted wife's allowance or benefit, old age pension, widow's pension, etc.) would be left untouched after divorce. In short, divorce would not spell financial disaster for women. By the same token, the tax system would be examined so that people would not be worse off as a result of divorce. Even inheritance rights would not be totally extinguished! Such promises appeared to be the price of success in a divorce referendum; and, cynically speaking, it is simpler to amend a law than to amend the Constitution.

The situation in Ireland as regards the introduction of divorce was quite specific, since all ancillary questions had to be solved before the right to divorce could be granted. The Irish had been quite clear on that: they would not throw themselves blindly into a new era, when marriage ceases to be a sacrament and becomes a contract. The change in the national psyche would be momentous, when the ban on divorce as a mark of identity ceased. It was clear in 1994 that the state was prepared to make as many compromises as necessary to rid the Constitution of a sectarian clause (since Protestants were hostile to its retention), which had been overtaken by the reality of Irish society.

However, despite the efforts of the government to rid the referendum of all ancillary questions and thus facilitate the introduction of divorce, the Catholic hierarchy did not budge and refused to accept divorce as a fact. The attitude of the government and of all political parties had shifted over the years, public opinion too seemed to have accepted the proximity of change, but the collective voice of the Catholic Church and that of traditionalist Catholics still spoke the same language. Indeed while pieces of legislation went back and forth between Parliament and the courts, the Catholic Church was gearing itself up for its offensive against divorce. As early as March 1994, Archbishop Dermot Clifford, firmly on secular terrain, warned his flock that divorce would 'undermine stable family life', and would also increase social welfare costs. Instead of 'busily preparing the ground for divorce', the government would do better to put a check to the 'contraceptive mentality' which made couples selfish. That same Sunday, the Bishop of Galway's pastoral letter was read at all masses in the diocese. Dr James McLaughlin decried the growth of an 'anti-family culture': 'Sex outside marriage is condoned, abortion advocated under the "right to choose" and the social evil of divorce threatened on our society as if it were to be the solution to all marital ills....' In April, Bishop Brendan Comiskey complained to *The Irish Independent* that 'the media are ridiculing politicians, ridiculing religious leaders, ridiculing the Church, knocking role models....This State is in the business of legislating anti-family legislation.' And, speaking at a mass at the Knock shrine, the Archbishop of Dublin, Dr Desmond Connell, called on the faithful to 'look to our defences instead of contemplating surrender'; they had to fight to protect the family even if the state withdrew its support, it was a matter concerning 'our moral vision'.

On 18 May Cardinal Cahal Daly and three bishops were received by the Ministers for Law Reform and Justice, to voice their opposition to divorce. What was striking about this meeting was that neither the Taoiseach nor the Tanaiste were present, whereas the Catholic Church had sent its highest dignitaries, a discrepancy which would have been unthinkable in times past. This bore witness to the gap that now existed between the Catholic Church and the state, the latter speaking something of a lay language based more on civil rights than on moral order. Had it not spent the last 30 years putting in place, willy-nilly, all ancillary and palliative measures relative to the right to separate and then to the right to remarry? At the end of the UN International Year of the Family, was it not particularly ironic, and significant, that the programme of the new Irish government brought to power in December 1994 (with the same Dáil but with a Fine Gael–Labour–Democratic Left coalition in power, and a new Taoiseach, John Bruton) pledged to hold a referendum to lift the constitutional ban on divorce and to recommend a Yes vote?[16] The indissoluble Irish family was going to be subjected to its most concerted assault and might soon be no more.

What is striking in some of the bishops' declarations is the coalescence of the various socio-moral issues, all bringing disorder in their wake. As they pointed out, it all began with the advent of the 'contraceptive culture', dissociating marriage of its primary purpose: procreation. From then on, anything could be brought into play applying the same theories, notably those promoting the individual's well-being and self-fulfilment. If marriage was no longer indissoluble and procreative, so that the individual could develop according to his/her own values, the ultimate result was the multiplicity of the types of family, including temporary and sterile homosexual relationships![17] The offensive of the Catholic Church came when the political will had legalised the sale of

contraceptives in vending machines, decriminalised homosexual relationships, recognised the right to abortion in a foreign country or to
have one on Irish soil in certain circumstances – all of which occurred
within a couple of years and will be discussed in the following chapters.
This is why it was all the more urgent for certain people to orchestrate
the defeat of the second divorce referendum. It was actually considered possible at any stage of the campaign, because of the strong
mobilisation of the anti-divorce forces, their thorough penetration of
the Irish population and their strategies, refined by over a decade of
campaigning. Morover, the fact that the Catholic Church had been
embroiled in controversies of a moral nature, since 1992 particularly
(with the Bishop Eamonn Casey affair), did not necessarily imply that
bishops and priests could not exert immense influence over the voters.
In fact a backlash against traditional Catholic teachings could be overturned by fear of yet more social change.

Since the first referendum, 18 pieces of legislation had been enacted
dealing with problems related to marital breakdown. They also paved
the way for an unemotional campaign on the single issue of allowing
separated people the right to remarry. As for divorce itself, Mervyn
Taylor announced at a book launch on 2 May 1995 that the terms
under which people could be granted a divorce would be spelt out in
the Constitution, with the consent of the people. This minimalist
approach, adopted without an all-party consultative process, but with
the full backing of the Cabinet sub-committee on divorce, and the
Cabinet as a whole, might very well assuage doubters. Just as the
Minister for Health, Michael Noonan, had recently adopted a non-
confrontational approach with his Abortion Information Bill (see
Chapter 6), Taylor could not afford to ignore political realities and
decided to run the risk of alienating the pro-divorce lobby (who would
vote for divorce anyway) in order to ensure the victory of the referendum by securing the large middle ground of the voters. This group
represented 25–30 per cent of the electorate, who were open to the
idea of lifting the ban but had to be satisfied that the proposal was
workable and would not open the way to a 'quickie divorce' and a
'divorce culture'. This implied that any changes in the grounds for
divorce would be a matter for a referendum, preventing the Oireachtas
from implementing for a more liberal regime. The bottom line was that
most deputies, even those who had always held that the Constitution
was no place for such provisions, felt that the constitutional ban had to
be removed even if it meant restrictive provisions. Fine Gael raised
reservations, the PDs resented not having been consulted, but Bertie

Ahern, the Fianna Fáil leader, had, and such restrictiveness suited him and his party, and their backing was crucial. The lessons of the 1983 pro-life amendment seemed to be forgotten, namely that to put detailed measures on complex social issues in the Constitution presented the risks of being constantly reinterpreted in more or less satisfactory litigation and necessitating changes. The fact that it downgraded the role of elected Members of Parliament did not seem to cause great concern. *The Irish Times*'s editorial of 2 August reluctantly acknowledged: 'Pragmatism, rather than principle, appears to be the main force driving Government's policy on divorce. . . . One may not like the Government's minimalist approach, but there is little doubt that it has been politically adroit – so far.' It transpired a few days later that Taylor's Department had commissioned a confidential opinion poll carried out by MRBI which underpinned his decision. Overall, 57 per cent of those questioned were in favour of removing the divorce ban; given three broad options, 50 per cent favoured putting conditions into the Constitution, 20 per cent thought they should be left to the Oireachtas and 26 per cent wanted to keep the ban.[18] Soon after Taylor's unexpected announcement, two successive MRBI polls confirmed that his strategy was probably the right one: the first, published on 27 May, showed a 69 per cent support (the highest recorded in recent years, and a dramatic 10 per cent increase in three months) for the lifting of the ban, 52 per cent of those questioned wanting the conditions for remarrying to be written into the Constitution, and 52 per cent backing a three-year lapse between breakdown and remarriage. The second poll, published on 2 August, showed that 66 per cent supported the removal of the ban, 55 per cent felt the conditions saying when separated people can have the right to remarry should be inserted in the Constitution, and 43 per cent favouring a three-year interval between breakdown of marriage and remarriage (31 per cent five years; 14 per cent – four years).[19]

Meanwhile, the exact nature of the divorce jurisdiction to be proposed (in particular the length of the separation period required before a divorce could be permitted) was not announced before the summer so that the anti-divorce campaign would not have too early a start. The rest of the legislative programme was rushed through in the autumn also. In particular, the Family Law Act, 1995, was hailed as 'one of the most far-reaching pieces of reforming legislation in recent times. . . . [It] has, in effect, rewritten the law on a range of issues from pensions for separated couples to succession rights and the age of marriage. The entire package slipped through both houses in a matter of hours this week and, to Drapier's surprise, attracted little notice.'[20] It notably introduced as a legal requirement three months' notice of the marriage for it to be valid under civil law, and, in a marked change from the Judicial Separation Act, added a new asset, namely the spouse's pension, allowing for it to be apportioned or 'earmarking' it if necessary to provide adequately for the other spouse. With the Fifteenth Amendment of the Constitution (no 2) Bill, 1995, the amendment, if accepted, would not only remove the ban on divorce but enshrine in Article 41.3 the conditions required by the courts before they can grant a divorce (which, incidentally, is also what was proposed in 1986). The couple must have been living apart for a period of four years during the previous five (which case law already accepted to imply as much a withdrawal from a situation as from a place). Divorce would be based on the concept of 'irretrievable breakdown' without any need to prove guilt of whatever kind. There must be 'no reasonable prospect of a reconciliation'. Proper provisions for the spouse and children must be made by the court, which can make property adjustment orders; these cannot be adjusted after the remarriage of one of the spouses. Social welfare would be available to those in need, whether deserted, separated or divorced. The survivor's pension could be extended to people who had not remarried. Pressed, the government said the extra cost to allow for divorce (in addition to the £630 million a year widows, lone parents and deserted wives already cost the state), would be about £1 million over five years. The anti-divorce lobby estimated the cost of divorce at £350 million annually, resulting in a 10 per cent increase in income tax, and were adamant that it is wrong to undermine the marriages of 96 per cent of married people to show compassion to 4 per cent . Let us note that DAG put that rate at about 16 per cent (16,297 marriages celebrated in 1994, but 2,806 applications for judicial separations and 4,457 applications for barring orders lodged the same year), which is a more sizeable minority, but another disputed statistic.

For the anti-divorce lobby, the issue at stake was not just, as the government insisted, the right to remarry, but also the effect the availability of divorce would have on marriage in general. By 1995, 'a mood of somberness', as campaigner Joe McCarroll put it, was palpable internationally about divorce as social policy. Columnist Vincent Browne even admonished that the government

> must begin to acknowledge that divorce will destabilise marriages
> that otherwise might have remained intact and they have to

construct arguments that this disadvantage is outweighed by the advantages that the right to remarry will bring to those already in new relationships and to the children of these unions.[21]

In 1986, the argument that 'the balance of social advantage' lay with permitting remarriage in certain limited circumstances did not carry, but the Irish legislative and social context had effectively changed. Still, anti-divorce campaigners argued that making remarriage possible had the effect of radically changing the nature of marriage itself, so that

> the good being sought becomes unattainable because of the means by which it is to be brought about. . . . This has the paradoxical result that, instead of permitting those who are separated from their spouses and cohabiting with another person to achieve the dignified status of marriage, it transforms all existing marriages into a kind of cohabitation![22]

Moreover, which family would be protected by the Constitution, the first or the second one (or the third!)? William Binchy argued that

> it is beyond question that, with divorce, a second marriage during the lifetime of one's divorced spouse requires the Constitution to shift its support to the second family thus created. . . . A person who has been divorced can no longer claim protection from Article 41, since marriage, the basis of the article's protection, is extinguished by divorce.[23]

It seemed therefore logical that the entitlements associated with marriage, such as maintenance, inheritance and family property rights 'attach to the second rather than the first family'.[24] The claim that the first family would lose all legal rights was refuted, notably by the Attorney-General: 'Divorce dissolves the marriage bond between two people, but not the other familial relationships. The dissolution of a mariage by death or divorce does not dissolve the family.' It could still be argued that this did not solve the contradictions pertaining to the rights of first and subsequent families, on a purely practical, or financial, point of view. And what about the prospect of serial divorce?

Since the lead of the pro-divorce side had been whittled away in the course of the campaign in 1986, the present one would be shorter so that the lead would hold up. However, this strategy nearly backfired, and was only compounded by the fact the government had to withdraw its advertisements in the last week of the campaign. The prolonged delay before the wording was published on, 14 September, created logistical problems for both DAG and the anti-divorce campaigners. The government for its part meant to leave the campaign in the hands of an advertising agency which would put its case forcibly but rationally, since referendum campaigns are waged more in the media than on the doorstep as in a general election. But Patricia McKenna of the Green Party, despite her party's pro-divorce stance, launched a High Court challenge to the government's £500,000 information campaign on divorce. Wasn't the use of public funds to finance a one-sided campaign contrary to the Constitution? Even liberals felt uncomfortable at the fact that 'the Government may promise a neutral advertising campaign but it has been slow to explain how this will straddle the thinnest of lines which runs between general information and partisan political propaganda.'[25] Until the ruling, the government was unapologetic about providing information proving that divorce facilities were necessary in Ireland and distributed some 1.4 million copies of a booklet entitled *The Referendum on Divorce – Some Questions and Answers*, which was deemed to amount to 'contentious advocacy' for a Yes vote. The Supreme Court, by a 4–1 majority, ruled on 17 November, one week before the poll, that this strategy was 'an interference with the democratic process'.[26] There the question was settled that threatened to monopolise the whole divorce debate. Once again it was symptomatic that it was no argument that a government proposing a referendum should campaign for it, all the more so when it was government policy as expounded at the general election of 1992.

The government and pro-divorce lobby were accused of a lacklustre campaign, even though leading politicians and campaigners spoke compellingly on the reasons for lifting the divorce ban. The difficulty is inherent in the nature of the argument: divorce is not a good thing, or rather it is not a happy event in anybody's life, and as such is awkward to advocate (pro-choice campaigners have an even harder job with abortion). Rather, it is imposed on society to deal with social realities. Therefore 'the anti-divorce campaigners...had an easier but not an inherently stronger case to make.'[27] Still, Fine Gael put up a vigorous and aggressive campaign with frontliners Michael Noonan, Alan Dukes and Alan Shatter, whereas, in 1986, Garret FitzGerald personalised the issue while the party tore itself apart. Fianna Fáil did not campaign, as in 1986, and members were given a free choice. In 1986, Fianna Fáil had not been neutral, and the leadership did everything they could to scupper the government. In 1995, Bertie Ahern, the leader of the party, himself judicially separated, gave his unambiguous support to a Yes vote: the divorce referendum was about 'restoring marriage to a central place in Irish society', as well as dealing with the 'civil rights of minorities', quite a new argument from a Fianna Fáil leader.[28] An MRBI poll revealed, though, that only 52 per cent of the party's followers supported these liberal notions – a slim majority that eroded in the course of the campaign: in the next poll it had slipped to 48 per cent.[29] The message was clear at his first Congress as party leader: backbenchers and party members did not share the views of the leadership and the frontbench. But in general, none of the parties, whether Fianna Fáil, Fine Gael or even Labour, had remotely the same level of internal dissent as in 1986, and in any case party discipline was better enforced, particularly during the passage of the bill putting in place the referendum.

The thrust of the Right to Remarry Campaign was to appeal to the Irish's strong sense of compassion for the people trapped in dead marriages and to give them a second chance out of the 'legal limbo' they were now in. It coordinated the media campaign and provided speakers for their programmes and for public meetings; it organised briefing sessions for people from the affiliated groups and for parliamentarians. As it was important to be seen to support the family, not just 'undermine' it, the first Joint Oireachtas Committee on the Family and the Commission on the Family would be set up to recommend further support to families. The Minister for Health touched upon the issue of the reorganisation of Irish society according to a different order when he said:

> Irish society works through families, and marriage sets up families. We're at a situation now where there are many relationships operating totally outside the law. Any civil society when it comes to relationships between men and women and the raising of children must have their relationships ordered by law.[30]

Regularising these relationships in accordance with law was the best way of underpinning marriage, and a new social order.

On the anti-divorce front, three organisations ran independent campaigns: the Anti-Divorce Campaign (ADC) had more or less the same steering committee as in 1986, and a hardcore of activists who fought and won the 1983 anti-abortion and the 1986 anti-divorce campaigns. The No-Divorce Campaign (NDC) was led by Peter Scully, of Human Life International and Youth Defence, an altogether more radical and less legalistic grouping. Some 1,600 volunteer canvassers had been briefed by mid-October. They raised about £200,000 from supporters and claimed to be organised in each of the 41

constituencies. They used shock tactics and will be remembered for
their memorable slogans, particularly 'Hello divorce, bye bye daddy'.
Members such as former High Court judge and chairman of NDC,
Rory O'Hanlon, did use religious arguments. But the anti-divorce
campaign generally, was conducted on grounds on social policy, not
religion. This might have been more a matter of strategy than of
principle. It was remarked that 'paradoxically it is the opponents of
divorce who come nearest to this secular approach by restricting their
arguments to supposedly scientific evidence of the social consequences of remarriage, and deliberately avoiding the moral case.'[31]
Another notable exception to this strategy was the remarks made by
the leader and the vice-chairman of the third anti-divorce organisation, the Muintir na hÉireann political party, that the Law Reform
Minister Mervyn Taylor and pro-divorce TD Alan Shatter, being Jewish, 'may not have a full understanding of Christian marriage'. However, so 'disgraced' were the bishops in Ireland that the anti-divorce
groups operated almost independently of them, and their hardline
intervention was thought even by those who opposed change to have
been uniformly counter-productive. For example, Archbishop Dermot
Clifford held divorce responsible for all kinds of social, mental and
physical ills. Bishop Brendan Comiskey complained that divorce
opponents were alienated from the debate and warned that this
could lead to extreme right-wing violence like that of the Michigan
Militia in the USA: 'Make people voiceless and you make people
mad.' Dr Desmond Connell criticised the Taoiseach's views on the
separate roles of Church and state, and Dr Thomas Flynn declared
that divorced people would be excluded from the sacraments, including, apparently, the last rites. Mother Teresa of Calcutta called for a
No vote, and so did the Pope, which prompted some to say retrospectively that this caused a number of people to come out and vote
Yes who might not otherwise have bothered!

ADC chairman Des Hanafin repudiated allegations that the anti-
divorce forces had lied and used false evidence in their tactics (the tax
bill would be 10 per cent higher, fathers would desert their families,
women would be divorced against their will, first families would be
impoverished for the benefit of the second ones, etc), since 'those who
then [in 1986] called us "liars" and "scaremongers" spent the next ten
years trying to plug the legislative deficiencies we identified. And they
made a vey bad job of it.'[32] The last point is debatable. Nevertheless
the anti-divorce lobby identified the difficulties associated with
divorce, and even the Taoiseach in a radio interview five days before

the poll admitted, when asked if people would be poorer after divorce replied: 'Unfortunately that's true and there's no point in pretending otherwise.'

The erosion of support for divorce coincided with the statement of the Catholic bishops of 26 October, followed by a number of homilies on the sanctity of marriage in many dioceses (even though the parish priests were generally more muted than in 1986). The emphasis was entirely on the evils of divorce *per se*, but if the presentation was subtly different, the reasoning was similar to that they put forward in the 1920s when the young Irish State grappled with the issue. The Irish bishops concluded in their statement that the present proposal was 'false kindness, misguided compassion and bad law', which caused a miniature Church–state confrontation.[33] Indeed, the Taoiseach retorted that the divorce debate was about the duties of the state versus the teachings of the Church, and it was a matter of looking at a better ordered society. This could not be reconciled with Dr Desmond Connell's view that if one abandons principles in the search for pragmatic solutions to social problems, one introduces a fundamental disorder into society. The Minister for Health put the Church–state debate in perspective by observing that the referendum was 'simply proposing to separate the powers of Church and state when it comes to marriage. There is no question of undermining the role of either – it just involves a re-examination of how the two institutions interact and how that interaction can be improved for the common good.'[34]

The argument that laws must meet the needs of all members of society, not just Catholics, led to the argument that the Republic as well as Northern Ireland should cater for their minorities if Ireland as a whole was to be at peace. If the amendment failed, who would believe that the Republic could make compromises in order to reach agreement on 'a new political framework for the whole island', in the words of Austin Currie, Minister of State at the Department of Health. But even though the peace process in Northern Ireland was prominent in Irish politics at that time, 78 per cent of voters said they would not take into account the way Northern Irish people would view their society when voting on divorce.[35] Interestingly enough, the highest vote against divorce in Ireland in 1986 was in the border counties; this would be true again in 1995. From an outsider's vantage point, it was noteworthy that the divorce situation in Northern Ireland was analysed less than in 1986, and that the Protestant churches would be less vocal than in the previous referendum.

On the whole, it was a less 'hysterical' campaign than in 1986, mainly because the government adopted a low-key approach in the hope of getting the other side to be rational too, and of 'not disturbing a slumbering fundamentalist giant'.[36] But the government's strategy became more aggressive after poll results published on 8 November which showed an accelerated drop in support for divorce: the margin of support for divorce had shrunk from 31 points to 17 in four weeks, and in a fortnight support had slipped away at the rate of three percentage points a week.[37] If the amendment was defeated by the people, it would be bad news for the minority hoping for the chance to remarry, but it would be very bad too for the government and for the parliamentary process as a whole, since all Dáil parties had pledged support for the introduction of divorce. A 'full-blooded campaign' was necessary to win back those worried about the tax, property and inheritance implications of divorce, since the middle-class voters' support had dropped from 70 per cent to 57 per cent, and that of the working class from 62 per cent to 53 per cent.

What had been most influential of recent events? The launching of the opposed campaigns? The comments of President Robinson, who referred on an American TV channel to the 'extraordinary changes in marriage law and the judicial separation that exists', adding that 'a very thoughtful infrastructure has been developed since the last referendum. Issues had been discussed in a more open way to continue to open up as a modern society, while retaining Irish qualities recognised internationally'?[38] The Catholic bishops' statement? The literature distributed by the Ad Hoc Commission and the government? There seemed to be a slight increase in the number of those thinking divorce would destroy family life, from 22 per cent to 28 per cent, and would cost too much (7 per cent).[39] It seems the Yes campaign underestimated the level of thought voters would give to the issue, conscientiously weighing the pros and cons. The Cabinet sub-committee on divorce came up with an intense media campaign for the last 12 days of 'the campaign during which ministers from the coalition parties would unflaggingly appear to counter the estimated 4,000 anti-divorce canvassers nationwide, the thought-provoking leaflets and the countless interventions of well-briefed anti-divorce activists during radio chat-shows. Party posters finally went up in the last week of the campaign, and in the last four days the Taoiseach toured rural Ireland in an all-out effort. The final poll before the referendum showed that even though the swing towards a No vote was continuing (42 per cent), it had decelerated, which could be due to some extent to the greater involvement of the government parties in the campaign. Bearing in mind that in 1986 the original lead had been reduced by 15 per cent in the four months leading to the first referendum, the current trend towards a decline for support for divorce, however slight, was worrying. Also, despite the fact that the Oireachtas had passed a series of legal remedies to the problems caused by marital breakdown, and the fact that there had been a 48 per cent increase in the number of separated people between the two censuses, public opinion had not changed significantly, so there was undoubtedly no room for complacency on the part of the government and the pro-divorce lobby. It had to be accepted that the new body of family law legislation, the multiplication of cases of marital breakdown, the fact that the divorce terms would be written into the Constitution and that tens of thousands of new young people had now the right to vote, were not enough in themselves for people to grant the right to a second chance. What had also changed since 1986 was the body of evidence which had come out in various divorce jurisdictions about the effects of divorce, as to its cost and social consequences. Jack Jones, Chairman of MRBI, kept a close check on poll results and, as his polls had identified the swing against the Yes in 1986, he could tell on 21 November that the final result would be very close. But he added:

> Contrary to 1986, the current downturn has been much less dramatic and potent. During the past seven weeks, support for a Yes vote has dropped 15 points from 67 per cent to 52 per cent . During a similar period in May and June 1986, support for the amendment went from 61 per cent to 40 per cent, a drop of 21 points, and was of course defeated 37/63.[40]

Polling day for the 1995 referendum was exceptionally a Friday, so that students could be back in their home constituencies to vote. The normal voting hours of 9am–9pm were extended to 10pm, again to allow more people to vote. The weather was fine on the East coast, but very wet in the West which might account for some aspects of the final result. But the most striking fact about this result is that just 9,114 (0.56 per cent) out of 1.63 million voters decided the outcome: – an unprecedentedly small majority in a national referendum. A majority in favour of divorce of 130,000 in Dublin outweighed a 121,000 majority against outside the capital. Thus the referendum certainly revealed a country split down the middle. The Greater Dublin area, home to a third of the population, voted strongly in favour, narrowly cancelling out majorities against divorce in Southern and Western regions of

Munster and Connacht-Ulster. In Cork, Ireland's second biggest city, the result in favour was by a margin of just 11 votes! Most remarkably, there was a 15.01 per cent swing towards the Yes vote since the last divorce poll in 1986. A total of 16 of the 41 constituencies recorded a majority in favour of divorce, whereas in 1986 only six of the 41 Dáil constituencies returned a Yes vote and they were all in the Dublin area. This time, all 11 Dublin constituencies voted Yes.

However, considering that all six Dáil parties supported divorce, their advice was rejected by half the electorate, which 'revealed a huge gap between political leaders and party followers – particularly inside Fianna Fáil.'[41] The other worrying aspect of the result was that, as the anti-divorce campaigners claimed that the government had already spent up to £200,000 of public money before the Supreme Court ruling and this may have illegally influenced the result, they mounted a petition to the High Court maintaining that the result was invalid because the government had interfered with the conduct of the referendum to canvass a Yes vote. The Supreme Court (on appeal) would unanimously uphold the result on 12 June 1996. The Family Law (Divorce) Bill, 1996 was eventually passed on 20 November 1996, opening the way to the first modern Irish divorces.[42]

Despite the narrow majority (and this raises disturbing questions about referendums as democratic tools), the shift in thinking since 1986 was worthy of notice. It remained that the referendum was a 'defining moment' in Church-state relations, to borrow a much-used phrase at the time. The removal of a key feature of the 1937 Constitution, with the support of the Fianna Fáil leader to boot, marked a clear separation of Church and state. Indeed, as jurist Conor Gearty observed in 'When Church and State Divorce', 'despite such changes [in Irish society], the divorce referendum was still pivotal because it was the first opportunity for the people themselves to adjudicate in a clear contest between church and state. Earlier referendums in the eighties on abortion and divorce had been muddied by splits in the political ranks as to the right stance to adopt.' In view of all the above, he pointed out, 'the really interesting question is not why Ireland voted yes, but why it so nearly voted no. ... The paradoxical consequence of Friday's near electoral stalemate is the delivery of a clear, albeit negative, message as to how the Irish people do not want the future to develop.' A tentative answer to why Ireland so nearly voted No would have to do with fear, as in 1986, fear of social breakdown following a condoning as it were of marital breakdown, and fear of Ireland ceasing to be different. In that sense, it is not behind the times that one thinks, just because it feels that when 'the old order is falling apart', the family can be a safe refuge.[43] As we shall see, apart from the traditional families and the re-ordered families, there are many more types of families in Ireland, structured in non-traditional ways, and which are not the cornerstone of the old order.

The Yes vote won partly because the government and the pro-divorce side in general were pursuing a wider agenda than just divorce: they also appealed to a tolerant, pluralist and inclusive vision of Ireland, just as the No forces had been opposed to a wide range of socio-moral reforms over the last few decades; as a political comment-ator observed:

> The referendum result marks a coming of age for the liberal agenda, winning its first majority in a straight yes/no contest.... The liberal vote has gone from 33 per cent on abortion in 1983 to 37 per cent on divorce in 1986 and to almost 40 per cent in first prefer-ences for Robinson in the presidential election in 1990. It has now topped 50 per cent and can claim dominance for the first time.[44]

The following chapters will now deal with the other issues comprising the liberal agenda.

3 Contraception: From the Protection of Public Morality...

Contraception is, according to the Catholic Church, an immoral practice as it contravenes the natural purpose of the marital act, which is procreation. It is immoral to interfere with the natural cycle of human fertility because it is contrary to God's plan: a moral principle has thus been extracted from a biological law. Throughout the centuries the Catholic Church has said that contraception is an act against nature, going back to Augustine (†430) or Thomas Aquinas (†1274), to name but two of the most famous opponents of the practice.[1] The contemporary text, *Casti Connubii*, published in 1930, summarised unambiguously the secular position of the Catholic Church and was, according to John T. Noonan, 'as a distillation of past doctrinal statements,...a masterpiece'.[2] The first Pope to speak in 'positive' terms of contraception was Pius XII. He conceded in 1951 that the rhythm method for medical or social reasons was a valid option, thus dissociating for the first time the sexual act from procreation. This also implied that the Catholic Church accepted the importance of sexuality as a mode of expression. However, too large a dissociation (by artificial means) between sexuality and reproduction still begets moral disorder.

The Catholic theology and the official position of the Irish state were in accord until such time when contraception came to exemplify the conflict that exists between law and morals, public and private morality. Did contraception contribute to undermining the social fabric? Was birth control the state's prerogative or that of couples? This chapter will analyse how the teaching of the Catholic Church on contraception was institutionalised in Ireland, and how the state eventually detached itself completely from natural law – a very meaningful process since it was on the question of contraception that the state first confronted 'the law and morals dispute in its modern form'.[3]

THE CONSTRUCTION OF AN IRISH, CATHOLIC SEXUAL MORALITY

The ideology adopted by the new Irish state was both nationalist and Catholic: it glorified rural life and had a romantic vision of the family. The latter was going to be institutionalised through the common efforts of the state and the Catholic Church, as anything that threatened the family was seen to threaten the stability of society, and of the nation as a whole. As Michael Nolan wrote, 'in 1922, the Catholic Church became the most powerful ally of the new state, lending the weight of its immense authority to the cause of law and order and placing at the disposal of the new, mainly Catholic state its biggest ecclesiastical stake, namely its schools and system of clerical management.'[4] Once the 26 counties of Ireland gained independence, the role of the Church was compromised, which now had to join forces with the people against an enemy other than the British government: 'A nation that has defined itself in terms of an external enemy no sooner lost that enemy than she created a substitute within herself. In Ireland that internal enemy was immorality.'[5] Historian and political analyst Margaret O'Callaghan offered her interpretation of the virulent crusade of the Irish Catholic hierarchy to impose its 'almost hysterical puritanism in relation to questions of sexual morality.'[6] The bishops had been horrified by the violence unleashed during the Civil War, whose ferocity made them doubt the moral calibre of the Irish, because of 'their plasticity in the face of false teachings'. Hence their need for moral guidance. The Catholic Church's concern was clearly stated in a pastoral letter in October 1922:

> We deserve to impress upon the people the duty of supporting the national government, whatever it is, to set their faces resolutely against disorder, and to assist the government in every possible way to restore order and establish peace. Unless they learn to do so they can have no government, and if they have no government they have no nation.[7]

The Catholic Church was going to devote itself to purging society of the excesses of the war, by fighting an evil which had come from across the sea to corrupt the Irish, who were obviously weak and malleable. The evil traps were 'chiefly the dance hall, the bad book, the indecent paper, the motion picture, the immodest fashion of female dress – all of which tend to destroy the virtues characteristic of our race.'[8]

The preoccupation of the Catholic Church with sexual morality became more and more evident throughout the 1920s. And, as historian Sandra Larmour wonders, 'is there evidence of the intrusion of sexuality in the public sphere to such an extent that it was uncontrollable and had to be criminalised?'[9] In any case, from the early 1920s, the hierarchy, with the help of a number of Catholic lay groups, put pressure on the government to impose a Catholic construction of sexuality and to regulate it. The non-Catholics (some 7 per cent of the population) had to accept that 'this is a Catholic state and has a right to what is called "Catholic Morality."'[10] This principle was quite readily accepted by the population and the politicians. As John H. Whyte so justly remarked, ministers came from the same background as the bishops, they had the same values, they had been to the same schools and often were parents: there was no need to convince them.[11] The catholicisation of Irish laws was spontaneous, following the alternation of the two main parties.

Indeed, from its early days, the government of the Irish Free State showed a willingness to use the powers of the state to protect Catholic moral values. It is difficult not to notice, even at this early stage, the contradiction inherent is the clerical campaigns. The clergy were hostile to the intervention of the state in the area of morality and social support for families, considering these were the domain of the Church, but nonetheless they wanted the government to legislate in precisely these areas. Among a few examples of state intervention, the Censorship of Films Act, 1923 established a censor whose responsibility was to cut or ban any film that was, according to him, 'subversive of public morality'. The Intoxicating Liquor Act, 1924 reduced the opening hours of pubs, and was followed by the Intoxicating Liquor Act, 1927, which reduced the number of such places. In February 1925, William Cosgrave introduced a motion, detailed in Chapter I, which outlawed divorce.

To go back to what primarily concerns us here, birth control, like abortion and infanticide, was seen as 'the infliction of race suicide upon this nation'.[12] This was by no means an isolated phenomenon. Birth control propaganda and devices were banned in France by a 1920 law, and would remain illegal until the 1967 Neuwirth law (enforced as from 1972 only). Concerns with the declining birth rate and 'race health' were also prevalent in England during the 1930s.[13] Sociologist Tony Fahey confirms that this was not a new phenomenon: 'Sexual repression seemed to intensify in Irish Catholic culture as the 19th century progresses, though in this, as in other areas, Irish Catholicism was an extreme example of patterns common throughout the Victorian world rather than an utterly deviant case.'[14]

The *Report of the Committee on Evil Literature*, published in December 1926, on which the 1929 legislation would be based, found that birth control was widely practised in Ireland, as much in rural as in urban areas. It denounced the 'alarming' increase in sexual offences, in the number of illegitimate births and the great availability of contraceptives, and concluded that 'the propaganda has now assumed the character of a widespread dissemination of knowledge propagated to free vice of its most powerful restraints.'[15] About the bill that would come from the report's recommendations, the Minister for Justice was adamant that birth control propaganda would not even be discussed in Parliament (since its advocacy was in fact propaganda against the Irish race), and he declared: 'We have decided, call it dogmatically if you like, that this question shall not be freely and openly discussed.'[16] The Censorship of Publications Act, 1929 made illegal the publication of a great number of twentieth-century authors (whose work could incite sexual immorality and corrupt its readers), but also any publication promoting contraceptives. Notwithstanding the parallels drawn between Ireland and England, it is interesting to note that England passed the Infant Life (Preservation) Act that very same year, which allowed abortions performed to save the life of the mother.

With the 1929 law, Irish citizens could no longer read anything in relation to contraception, but nothing was yet in place banning the importation and the sale of contraceptives themselves. But towards the end of 1929, the hierarchy let the Minister for Justice, John Fitzgerald Kenney, know that they were none too happy about the state of the law regarding the sale of contraceptives. The Minister did not want to alienate Protestant support and would not commit his government to legislate more in Catholic moral terms. He only promised to keep checks on the delivery of contraceptive literature by post or hand.[17] William Cosgrave set up the Committee on the Criminal Law Amendment Acts (1880–85) and Juvenile Prostitution, which reported in 1931. That way clerical pressure was eased and the report would provide the basis for future legislation. The hierarchy was resisted this time, but when Fianna Fáil, a Catholic republican party, came to power in 1932, which 'promoted an idealised national identity', they favoured this 'patriarchal social/sexual code which they viewed as protecting women and criminalising 'deviant' behaviour'.[18] Eamon de Valera and Fianna Fáil showed themselves to be more receptive to the concerns of the Catholic hierarchy, all the more so as all the witnesses summoned by the Committee, which came to be known as the Carrigan Committee, unanimously testified to the 'degeneration in the standard of social conduct [that] has taken place in recent years'.[19] Despite the fact that Fianna Fáil was a political party whose ideology was based on strong republican ideals and that a number of its members had been excommunicated for their role in the Civil War (for being on the anti-Treaty side), it was a Fianna Fáil government that had the task of legislating on the Carrigan Committee's findings. The latter, which reported on the law on sexual offences and its application, gathered information and witnesses between 1930 and 1931, that is after the adoption of the legislation banning contraceptive propaganda. In relation to contraceptives themselves, it found that the evidence left no doubt that 'the practices so advocated have become extremely prevalent', and that

> so common in some places were such articles in use that there was no attempt to conceal the sale of them, and places were mentioned to which the supply of such articles come regularly by post to recognised vendors. At the same time, quantities of contraceptives advertisements are in circulation, and price lists are extensively distributed throughout the country by cross-Channel agencies in order to facilitate the direct purchase by private persons of the articles offered for sale.

It concluded: 'The Committee on Evil Literature made recommendations for the prohibition of printed matter, we recommend that the articles in question be banned by an enactment similar to the Dangerous Drugs Act, 1920.' Here, the Committee was referring to contraceptive drugs, such as quinine, which could be used for other purposes, and it is not quite clear what the committee was recommending – a total ban on contraceptive purposes, and registered use for others, or delivery on prescription whatever the use?[20] It is worth noting that the Carrigan Report was not published, not even for the benefit of deputies, nor were the minutes of the debates of the all-party committee in charge of drafting the new law. This committee had been put together by the new Minister for Justice, James Geoghegan, precisely to prevent debates in the Dáil as a whole in his concern to avoid airing such matters.

Despite the Minister's willingness to introduce legislation in accordance with Catholic teaching, a memorandum from the Department of Justice, dated 27 October 1932, questioned the impartiality of the Carrigan Committee. According to the official who wrote it, the

Committee had only heard one side of the story as it were, and 'so many of the witnesses represented societies the views of which were already known to the public, that a doubt arises as to whether any other case was put to the Committee and the object of this memo is to call attention to certain points which might be considered by the Government before a decision is taken as to the publication or adoption of the report.'[21] The official thought the report should be treated with caution and he advised against its publication as

> it contains numerous sweeping charges against the state of morality in the Saorstát [Free State], and even if these statements were true, there would be little point in giving them currency.... Unless these statements are exaggerated (as they may easily have been...), the obvious conclusion to be drawn is that the ordinary feelings of decency and the influence of religion have failed in this country and that the only remedy is by way of police action. It is clearly undesirable that such a view of conditions in the Saorstát should be given wide circulation.

Concerning contraceptives, he said: 'Again there is difficulty in ascertaining the relevance of this subject to the terms of reference'. But the civil servant's circumspection was not to be heeded, as the 1935 law would be even more severe than the report as far as contraceptives were concerned. Indeed, recommendation 16 of the report read 'that the sale of contraceptives should be prohibited except under exceptional circumstances'.[22] But no exception whatsoever would be mentioned in the legislation, whereas, concerning the other issues examined in the report, legislation would not go as far as its recommendations.

The complete ban on importing, selling and distributing contraceptives, echoing the teaching of the Catholic Church which prohibited their use, was ratified by the Criminal Law Amendment Act, 1935, whose full title was: 'An Act to make further and better provision for the protection of young girls and the suppression of brothels and prostitution, and for those and other purposes to amend the law relating to sexual offences.' This shows how the legislators saw a strong connection between fertility control and prostitution, as section 17 banned the importation and sale of contraceptives (the Carrigan Report itself dealt with birth control in the section on prostitution). Ironically, section 16(1) said that the fine for prostitution would not be more than £2, whereas section 17(2) set a £50 maximum fine for selling, offering, importing, etc. contraceptives in Ireland. Birth control and vice were indeed one and the same thing in the legislators' and the clergy's minds.

Public health might be threatened by such measures, and that of women was not considered at any stage, despite recommendation 16 of the Carrigan Report and a memorandum of the Department of Justice that acknowledged that fertility control might be a necessity for some women. This document, the heads of the original bill in fact, was dated 10 November 1933, and head 16, which dealt with this aspect of the problem, disappeared from the bill on which parliamentarians voted, for reasons still unclear.[23] In the context of the time, when poverty, maternal mortality, venereal diseases and tuberculosis were rife, such disregard for public health is somewhat shocking. A senator, Dr John Gogarty, and a deputy, Dr Robert Rowlette, protested that birth control was a medical necessity for some women, and that the law would cause an increase in the number of abortions and infanticides. Both accepted the moral arguments against birth control, but in response to their medical argument, which anticipated the McGee case (on which more later), the Minister for Justice retorted: 'There is no danger whatsoever of the thing that the deputy has in mind occurring.'[24] Out of the 18 amendments tabled, 16 were rejected without discussion, with hardly any opposition to section 17 of the bill, and certainly none to the Catholic principle underlying it. Indeed when contraception was about to be discussed, in 1929 and again in 1935, it was from a morality point of view only, taking on board the traditional concepts of family and women; it was not from a health (public or private) point of view, not did it acknowledge that such an option could be chosen in conscience. At the same time that the Church of England and the British Medical Council accepted, in 1930, that birth control was legitimate in cases where the woman's health would be endangered by a pregnancy, the Catholic Church reaffirmed its doctrine in *Casti Connubii*, and the Irish Free State inserted the latter into its legislation. The resolution adopted at the Lambeth Conference of Anglican bishops was immediately approved by the Church of Ireland (the Irish branch of the Anglican confession), and the Anglican bishops of Cork and Derry were on the Commission that drafted the resolution in favour of birth control.[25] In a sermon delivered in August 1930, the Anglican Bishop of Ossory declared: 'There are cases – hard cases – where the limitation of the family is not merely advisable but a moral duty.'[26]

Therefore the bishops belonging to the church whose theology was closest to that of the Roman Catholic Church no longer supported an absolute ban on contraception (and would recognise it as a right in 1958). However the legal ban on the sale of contraceptives did not give rise to much protest, even on the part of Protestants who could have invoked freedom of conscience. Such matters were not widely discussed. Protestants did not agree with the underlying totalitarianism of the Catholic Church, but they often agreed with its implicit puritanism. As we have seen, their position on birth control was more qualified, and they voiced their disapproval in the letters page of *The Irish Times*, which was a markedly Protestant paper at that time.[27] Generally speaking, the Anglicans did not think that the Irish particularly needed to be saved from immorality and debauchery. They were not worse than their neighbours, and their entry on the international scene brought about by independence was going to bring them as many good things as bad:

> We are firmly convinced, however, that the vast majority of the Irish people are just as moral and just as modest in their behaviour as the men and women of any other country in the world. Ireland is no longer a backwater. It is now in the full stream of the European Current and, much as we may regret it, we are bound to acquire some of the faults as well as some of the virtues which are the common heritage of the present generation. . . . We are not saints just as we are not scholars but taking the rough with the smooth, we are as good as our neighbours.[28]

Such a vision of society, rooted in reality, instead of being an ideal aspiration, was going to take several decades before it would inspire Irish legislators. In any case, it would seem that the new laws did not dissuade people set on reading a banned book or availing themselves of contraceptives. They could have them sent to their homes in a plain envelope.[29] As Sandra Larmour puts it: 'That the Catholic clergy continued to be concerned about the use of artificial birth control implies that some Catholics did import contraceptives.'[30] Publications, as unlikely as *The Nurses' Mirror and Midwives' Journal* and *Poultry World* featured advertisements that Catholic groups objected to because, though hardly decipherable, they seemed to promote prophylactic preparations aimed at curing all kinds of irregularities (read menstrual) quickly and definitively, in other words, interfering with a pregnancy! One may wonder, then, what the overall effect of such prohibitive legislation was. As Sandra Larmour suggests,

> from the point of view of the Catholic Church and Government the ban on contraceptives was a success in that it criminalised deviation

from a Catholic middle-class 'norm'. The impact on women's lives was immeasurable, particularly when it is remembered that by the law of the State they were denied access not only to fertility control, but to knowledge of all aspects of sexuality including information on sexually transmitted diseases.[31]

A ban on contraception also implied an increase in the number of backstreet abortions and infanticide, which was already described in the 1920s as a growth industry!

A WOMEN'S ISSUE

The famous 'Mother and Child Scheme' is a landmark in any study of the relationships between the Catholic Church and state in Ireland, in particular in a chapter about contraception. Until then, one could say that the Church and state had worked "hand in hand" and seen eye to eye in the socio-moral area. However the bill on public health, in a favourable historical context (the British Welfare State was extended to Northern Ireland in 1947), put forward by Dr Noël Browne, Minister for Health, and inherited from his predecessor, met with the total disapproval of the Irish hierarchy. It is interesting that 'a similar concern with the growth of State power on the part of the English Catholic Hierarchy had led initially to their opposition to the construction of the Welfare State in post-war Britain'.[32] The bill proposed providing free medical care for all mothers and their children to the age of 16. The Irish bishops found the introduction of a free health service for all regardless of resources unacceptable, and totalitarian in spirit. Moreover such interference of the state in a private domain, that of the family, traditionally the Church's, had to be opposed: it was not explicitly said in the bill that the state would take on the sexual education of women and young adolescents, but the bishops had read this between the lines, because it was precisely what they feared – that salaried doctors would provide gynaecological advice including advice on family planning to their patients:

> Education in regard to motherhood includes instruction in regard to sex relations, chastity and marriage. The State has no competence to give instruction in such matters. We regard with the greatest apprehension the proposal to give to local medical officers the right to tell Catholic girls and women how they should behave in regard

to this sphere of conduct at once so delicate and sacred. Gynaecological care may be, and in some other countries is, interpreted to
include provision for birth limitation and abortion. We have no
guarantee that State officials will respect Catholic principles in
regard to these matters.[33]

The obsession of the hierarchy in relation to contraception was also
tangible in their approaches to the Junior Minister for Health concerning the sale of tampons. Indeed, Ruth Barrington, in a fascinating
book on the politics of health in Ireland, recounts how the use of
sanitary tampons was strongly disapproved of by the bishops. Archbishop John Charles McQuaid contacted Dr Ward in 1944 to 'explain
their misgivings that the tampons could harmfully stimulate girls at an
impressionable age and lead to the use of contraceptives and whether
he would take action to prohibit their sale.' As she put it, Dr Ward
'acceded to the request'.[34] To come back to the 1950 episode, it
appeared that since Browne had opposing him the bishops, the doctors
(whose income largely came from mothers and their families) and the
rest of the government, he got no support when he refused to withdraw
the bill. Although he accepted that Catholic politicians should follow
Catholic moral principles, he advocated the independence of the state
in social matters, and as far as he was concerned this scheme was
purely a social matter. On 11 April 1951, forced by the leader of his
party, Sean MacBride, he resigned from government and from his
party (Clann na Poblachta). J.H. Whyte suggested he might have
wanted a showdown: 'he wished to bring about a collision between
the Irish State and a powerful vested interest. He might not win the
immediate battle, but even by fighting it he would crack the mould of
Irish society, and make easier that social change to which as a radical
he was committed.'[35] Until he disclosed the repeated interventions of
the bishops, Church–state relations were not discussed in Ireland. It
was the first and the last time that the Catholic hierarchy intervened
directly and publicly against a specific bill, and won.

At the same time that Britain legalised abortion and France contraception, Pope Paul VI published his encyclical, *Humanae Vitae*. His
predecessor, John XXIII, had set up a commission in 1963 to study
population and birth control. Eighty per cent of the commission members were in favour of some softening of the Catholic ban on artificial
contraception, but Paul VI refused to acknowledge their conclusions
and gave himself three years to publish his own. In July 1968, *Humanae
Vitae* confirmed the traditional teaching of the Catholic Church and

reaffirmed Pius XI's admonition that all sexual acts should be open to the transmission of life (albeit that recourse to infertile periods was 'lawful'). Paul VI condemned explicitly artificial contraception which 'intrinsically contradicts the moral order'. To approve artificial contraception would have led to the approval of other practices condemned by the Catholic Church, because 'the morality of sterilisation, abortion, even of adultery, pre-marital sex and homosexuality, are inevitably involved in the logic of argument about contraception'.[36] On 9 October 1968, the Irish hierarchy, after a two-day meeting at the Maynooth seminary, published a declaration reminding the faithful that 'sons of the Church may not undertake methods of regulating procreation which are found blameworthy by the teaching authority of the Church in its unfolding of the divine law.'[37] It is nonetheless interesting to note that Irish churchmen had prepared themselves for a change in the doctrine, as is shown in an article written by Kevin McNamara, then Professor of Theology at Maynooth, and later Archbishop of Dublin. His piece ended thus in his inimitable style: 'To conclude. It is not now clear that the ban on contraceptives cannot be revoked.'[38]

The encyclical provoked considerable reaction in the Irish media, expressed in particular in long feature articles and in letters to the editor, a page overflowing with the readers' mixed reactions. It would seem that everybody, churchmen, Catholic lay people and doctors had been waiting for several years for this papal declaration. The contraceptive pill had been introduced in Ireland in 1962, and because the sale of contraceptives was banned, it was only prescribed as a cycle regulator. The large number of Catholics who had started to practise birth control, sometimes with the moral support of their priest, would now have to readopt the traditional teaching, or ignore the papal declaration (which, even though it was not 'infallible' as Catholic jargon would put it, was nonetheless quite solemn). The number of Irish women taking the pill began to increase substantially towards the end of 1966 and sales increased by about 50 per cent in 1967 over 1966, according to a pharmaceutical source quoted in an *Irish Times* report, which estimated that some 15,000 women were on the pill, about 25 per cent using it for medical reasons and 75 per cent for 'social' reasons ('either that or there's a great increase in menstrual difficulties,' said a firm's spokesman).[39] A survey of Irish gynaecologists carried out in 1966 confirmed that three-quarters of them prescribed the pill for social reasons. A pharmacist in Dublin said his orders for the pill had tripled between 1965 and 1968. By the same token, there were only four different anovulents available on the Irish market in

1966; but there were at least ten different brands in 1968. Dr Karl Mullen, during an inter-hospital course for nurses, said in his talk on marital stress 'that in his experience, about 40 per cent of married couples in this country were practising methods of contraception other than rhythm'. In the December 1967 issue of the journal of the Irish Medical Association, Drs Declan Meagher and Dermot McDonald published a report on the marriage guidance clinic established in 1963 at the Holles Street National Maternity Hospital (advice being limited to the rhythm method since it was a Catholic hospital, with the Archbishop of Dublin as patron) where it said: 'the most significant finding... is the high incidence of coïtus interruptus. This finding highlights the urgent need for adequate marriage guidance services.... the use of the rhythm method imposes an intolerable strain on many marriages.' A footnote, added just before publication, announced that 'since the completion of this paper the policy of the clinic is to prescribe the Pill as a contraceptive for selected medical and social cases.' In the February 1968 issue of the same journal, the authors replied thus to the complaint of a colleague who had read their paper:

> The delay in the decisive papal pronouncement confirms that a state of doubt exists. We do not advocate the Pill. The issue for doctors is not the morality of taking the Pill, but rather the morality of refusing it for patients who feel entitled, in conscience, to take it. It is our duty to treat patients, it is the patients who make the moral decisions. In this situation we have concluded that to deny the Pill to couples who need it is at variance with the dictates of justice and charity. In common with all Catholic doctors, we eagerly await the time when our moral responsibility in this matter is clearly defined.

Their moral responsibility was indeed clarified in a most definite manner in *Humanae Vitae*. However, Dr Anthony Clare, in an article in *The Irish Times*, reported the results of a survey of final year medicine students at University College Dublin he had done with a colleague in 1966: 40 per cent of the Catholic students declared their willingness to prescribe the pill to their Catholic patients who asked for it; 88 per cent of all students, and 79 per cent of Catholic students wished to see the Catholic Church change its position on birth control, but only 60 per cent thought it would. These are quite impressive figures given the fact that UCD was the largest university for Catholic students where only Catholic concepts about marriage and the family were taught. In May 1968, Dr Michael Solomons wrote to the secretary

of the International Planned Parenthood Federation (IPPF): 'Recently
the large majority of the patients attending the family planning clinic at
the Coombe Hospital refused to hear any more about rhythm methods
and insisted on the pill or nothing. The clinic had to be closed.'[40] A
professor at the Maynooth seminary was heard saying during *Panorama*, a programme broadcast by the BBC in August 1968, that the
majority of the Irish accepted the papal decision and criticised those
doctors opposing it who 'would be first to resent us priests if we
interfered in purely medical matters, but they find it easy to interfere
with what is a purely theological matter and, in fact, is the teaching of
the law of God.' The birth rate between 1964 and 1968 corroborates
the relatively widespread availability of the contraceptive pill in Ireland: It had fallen from 64,072 to 61,004. Sociologist Robert Rose
noticed that, parallel to this decrease in the birth rate, the number of
marriages had increased, while the age of the husbands and wives
decreased, which should have implied a higher birth rate if things
were left alone.[41] Interestingly, the birth rate shot up after the publication of the encyclical: From 61,004 in 1968 to 68,784 in 1974 (an
increase of 12.75 per cent).

In the debate on artificial contraception, only the voices of married
women or mothers were sought. Whereas birth planning would be an
integral part of the demands made by Western women in the 1960s,
together with the right to freely dispose of their bodies, and was in
effect going to be at the centre of the movement for the liberation of
women, the situation was different in Ireland. The beginnings of the
Irish Women's Liberation Movement are not characterised by the
priority being given to access to contraception. In its manifesto, *Chains
or Changes? The Civil Wrongs of Irish Women*, published in 1971, the
lack of crèche facilities and the difficult access to contraception were
mentioned at the end of the 32–page booklet, and as feminist academic
Ailbhe Smyth later exclaimed:

> In retrospect, it seems ironic that a section dealing with such issues
> as the absence of childcare and contraception should have been
> entitled 'Incidental Facts'.... The focus on the nuclear family, on
> 'liberal' themes such as equal rights and educational opportunities,
> the low-key treatment of contraception and the absence of any
> reference to abortion, the lack of any analysis of sexuality or of
> sexual politics, these all seem surprising now in the 1990s.[42]

The movement for the liberation of Irish women aimed primarily at
fighting against the inequalities besetting them: it called for unmarried

mothers and separated women to receive state benefits; for women civil servants to be allowed to stay in post after marriage; for those women who were allowed to work to be assured of equal pay with men; for family law to guarantee them more rights, in particular in case of marital breakdown; for illegitimate children and their mothers not to be stigmatised; and finally, it called for a change in the laws on contraception. Only one fringe group called for the legalisation of abortion and contraception, the Women's Right to Choose Group, founded in 1978.[43] One of the specifics of the movement was the fact that even though it was not a mass movement attracting crowds, several founder-members worked in the media, including Mary Maher of *The Irish Times* and Mary Kenny of *The Irish Press*. Consequently they were in a position to attract wide attention on women's issues in very direct ways. Giving in to the growing pressure of feminist demands and that provoked by the prospect of joining the EC, the government set up the Commission on the Status of Women in 1970, even though there is little doubt that it viewed it with ambivalence and paternalism. The Commission published its first report in 1972, which read like a catalogue of all the injustices affecting women, including those listed above, accompanied by a series of propositions aimed at eradicating them. One of its recommendations stipulated that 'parents have the right to regulate the number and spacing of their family.... Information and expert advice on family planning should be available through medical and other appropriate channels to families throughout the country.'[44]

The most spectacular event staged by the movement remains the so-called 'contraceptive train', a day-return trip to Belfast on 22 May 1971, organised to bring back scores of condoms and spermicides in defiance of the law. Custom officers did not try to seize the illegal products, and the police did not try to arrest the women. It seemed to the movement that the government had decided not to enforce the law that day, but it also declared:

We further accuse the State of criminal irresponsibility in permitting 26,000 women in this country to use the only contraceptive pill legally available to them, imported as a cycle regulator, simply because it is a technical evasion of the law – despite the fact that such ovulents are, in many cases, medically unsuitable and damaging to women who might otherwise, in all conscience, choose other methods, at present illegal.... The Government by a political decision have decided not to enforce the Criminal Law (Amendment) Act. By default the Government upheld the constitutional rights of Irish men and women allowing for freedom of conscience and the right to control one's life.[45]

This does not mean that all doctors shared this point of view. In fact many of them were conservative when it came to such issues. They came from the same culture as politicians and churchmen. They had been educated in the Catholic system, up to and including tertiary education, which had taken place in Catholic hospitals. However, in 1970, Dr Solomons was invited to lecture at Trinity College Dublin on family planning in the context of the pharmacology and physiology courses for medicine students. He remarked that 'it was the first time that an Irish medical school had included the subject as a part of the curriculum.'[46] He was one of the founder members of the first family planning clinic in Ireland, whose beginnings he relates in *Pro-life? The Irish Question*. Despite the ban on contraception, the clinic opened in Dublin on 25 February 1969. It was called the Fertility Guidance Clinic, the name intentionally ambiguous to keep as low a profile as possible, and it aimed at providing efficient and informed contraception. It was opened with an initial grant of £1,000 from the IPPF and the advice of a lawyer who confirmed it was not illegal to open a family planning clinic, as long as the contraceptives were not sold, but provided free of charge. The doctors involved would introduce their patients to the various contraceptive methods available and advise them as to which would suit them best. The methods available at the time were the rhythm method, condoms, the cap and the pill. In fact only the pill was on sale in Ireland; the others had to be brought back from Northern Ireland or ordered from the IPPF, which sent them by post. Parents and friends of the associated members of the clinic brought back supplies of contraceptives in their luggage from any trip to the North or to England, at the risk of them being seized at customs. The coil was not on offer before September 1970 as it was a controversial contraceptive method (was it not more of an abortifacient?). But Dr David Nowlan, back from Jamaica where he fitted coils, had expressed surprise at the fact that Dr Solomons and his colleagues sent women to Belfast to get 'accidentally bombed or shot' instead of fitting them at the clinic. 'By the end of that year [1970] we had fitted almost 200 [IUDs].'[47]

The following statistics make interesting reading: 167 new clients came to the clinic in 1969 and 1,180 in 1970. Dr Solomons admits that most women were middle-class, but they opened a second centre in

1971 in a disadvantaged area, that year they saw 2,182 new clients. In 1972 they saw 4,202 or nearly half as many more every year. They gave 4,912 consultations in 1971, and 10,158 in 1972.[48] Despite an increase in the consulting staff, the waiting lists were not brought down. The 1972 company report said:

> The clinic staff have noted in the past year that the majority of patients are much better-informed about available family planning techniques and are becoming much more confident in discussing suitable methods. Credit for this is partly due to the wide dissemination of our booklet 'Family Planning – A guide for parents and prospective parents' which has sold 7,500 copies, and also to the publicity given to the question of family planning in all the news media.[49]

It was also in 1972 that the Rotunda Hospital opened a family planning clinic on its premises, thus becoming the first maternity hospital in Ireland to prescribe the pill. If the patient preferred a cap or a coil, she was referred to the Fertility Guidance Company, later called the Irish Family Planning Association (IFPA). However, as Dr Solomons noted, 'with a family planning service available in a state-supported hospital, the government's retention of legal status quo vis-à-vis contraception seemed hypocritical.'[50] A small group of people with a medical background had established the Irish Family Planning Rights Association (IFPRA) in October 1970, whose aim was to have the law changed so that the use of methods of artificial contraception became openly legal rather than being tacitly tolerated. After submitting various propositions to government ministers which had remained unanswered, they drafted a bill amending the 1935 law. This they confided to Senator Mary Robinson's care. At the same time, in December 1972, several members of the IFPRA set up a non-profit-making company, Family Planning Services Ltd (FPS), which would sell by mail order non-medical contraceptives (condoms and caps) which had to be imported. Dr Keith Wilson-Davis points out that within one year FPS received over 20,000 orders, 40 per cent coming from people referred by the two IFPA clinics.[51]

Thus the situation was that some 50 women could openly import quantities of contraceptives into the country without being troubled by the police; a family planning booklet could be published and run to three editions without being banned; medicine students began to be trained in contraceptive matters; and even a state-funded hospital dispensed artificial contraceptives. Still those Irish who practised contraception remained criminals under the 1929 (amended in 1946) and 1935 laws. In addition to this, they were living in a state of mortal sin. The debate on contraception focused on the question of knowing if it was an issue of private or public morality; if what one couple (married, of course) decided to do to space their children's births was for the state and the law to deal with, or if it was a matter of personal conscience. After all, the law was not against contraception *per se*, but against the promotion of contraception and the sale of contraceptives. Or, in other words, people could choose their favourite contraceptive method, find ways and means to get hold of the contraceptives themselves, but the state could not been seen to collaborate with something the Catholic Church abhors; it could not be seen legalising something contrary to the moral order. However we note that there was no question of banning the contraceptive pill as a menstrual cycle regulator.

The most famous pronouncement by a member of the hierarchy is that of John Charles McQuaid, Archbishop of Dublin, in a pastoral letter read at mass in March 1971:

> Any contraceptive act is always wrong in itself. To speak, then, of a right to contraception, on the part of an individual, be he Christian or non-Christian or atheist, or on the part of a minority or of a majority, is to speak of a right that cannot even exist.... Any change in legislation that would allow the sale of contraceptives would be an insult to the faith, gravely damaging to public and private morality, and would remain a curse upon our country.

This in effect presented the legislators as anti-Catholic, whereas the collective bishops' statement, presented by Cardinal Conway, had focused on the risk of changing the law. The curse referred to by Dr McQuaid applied to Catholics and non-Catholics alike, as, in the words of Dr Lucey, Bishop of Cork and Ross, some things are immoral *per se*, and 'the truth is that the Catholic Church is not the only Church to condemn the use of contraceptives and that contraception, like murder, lies, rape, adultery etc., is wrong even if the Church never said a word about it. Or the State either.'

The Irish hierarchy was confident the Irish would not question this and would convince their elected representatives to leave the law as it was: 'Civil laws on these matters should respect the wishes of the people who elected the legislators, and the bishops confidently hope that the legislators themselves will respect this important principle.' Moreover, as Cardinal Conway pointed out, 'the bishops' statement

is not concerned with private morality, but with the type of society
we want.' This point is highly contentious, but shows how the debate
on contraception clarified the role of the Catholic Church in the area
of public morality, which wanted to have a say in the choices facing
society as a whole, and not just a veto on one single question: the Priest
and sociologist Liam Ryan defined the role of the Church as being the
conscience of society.[52] The Church had to stress that the legalisation
of contraceptives would bring about moral as well as social disorder, by
promoting associated evils, since 'their very accessibility will occasion
an increase in promiscuity and a lowering of sex-moral standards.
Secondly the general acceptance of contraception may be the first
step on the road to abortion.'[53] The principle that the laws of the
state should reflect the moral aspirations of the majority of the people,
and a state whose population was 96 per cent Catholic had the right to
have Catholic laws, was rarely heard in the 1970s; still, it was expressed
individually by some bishops such as Dr Newman: 'My personal
position in the matter is that, in the first place, the Catholic people
of our State have a right – a political right – to the provision of the kind
of social framework that supports them in the living out of their
moral and religious principles.'[54] With regard to the question of knowing if Protestants had the same right, he would say: 'They have. But
if you have a situation where there is an incompatibility between the
rights, then, as there is no fundamental human right in question,
obviously the right of the majority has to be respected in a particular
way.'[55] Such words, in the context of the troubles in Northern Ireland,
triggered a public controversy, the only big clash in the 1970s between
the Catholic Church and the state, represented by Ministers Garret
FitzGerald and Conor Cruise O'Brien, who denounced the sectarianism of Dr Newman. It is interesting to note, in contrast, the resolution
taken at the Presbyterian Synod as it takes into account the contraceptive reality in Ireland and anticipates the stance taken later by
legislators:

> Family Planning is in itself a good thing. While persistent abstinence
> may be predictable for some married couples, it is fraught with
> danger for most. The use of contraception within marriage
> should not be regarded as in itself wrong. Nevertheless the decision
> to use them should not be taken lightly nor unadvisedly, nor
> should they be made the means of avoiding parenthood
> altogether for purely selfish ends. The Synod of Dublin calls upon
> the Government to amend the law with regard to the importation

and sale of contraceptives, and the law which forbids advocating their use.

As early as March 1971, a change of mood could be felt in political quarters, even within Fianna Fáil, the party in power, whereby laws should not make criminals of ordinary citizens just because their personal views differed from the majority of the people. Maybe the external political climate was conducive to this sort of change: 'A Government directly concerned with the problem of peace in the North, of negotiations with Great Britain, or entry to the EEC... will be more inclined to think in terms of the State not being the overlord of the individual conscience.'[56] It is a fact that the debate on contraception and the explosive situation in Northern Ireland were connected, chronologically and ideologically. As Dr David Nowlan put it, the Republic could not protest at the absence of civil rights in the North and at the same time prosecute those who fought for certain civil rights for a minority in the South – and actually it did not.[57]

The McQuaid pastoral did not come out of the blue: it was read on Sunday, 28 March 1971, just when the reading in the Seanad of an infamous bill was announced. All could be lost as the Taoiseach, Jack Lynch, had announced in February that he did not think that the state should legislate for public morality, and the Minister for Foreign Affairs, Patrick Hillery, had said at the beginning of March that 'the good government of Ireland requires us to legislate for the general good, not for our own private satisfaction. The legislature is certainly not bound to express inhibitions in matters in which adult people feel entitled to decide for themselves.' Indeed, 1971 will remain a crucial year in the fight for the right to contraception. As we saw, two family planning clinics were opened; the contraceptive train went to Belfast and back; and two opinion polls were published on the issue. In one, 73 per cent of the doctors questioned were in favour of the legalisation of contraception; in the other, 63 per cent of the Irish questioned thought that the sale of contraceptives should be forbidden by law.[58] Also in 1971, Senator Mary Robinson tried seven times to have her bills on contraception read in the Seanad. Also in 1971, custom officers seized a packet of spermicide jelly sent by post to a young mother in County Dublin.

Mary Robinson will remain in the Irish collective memory as the lawyer and senator who was one of the first parliamentarians to dare challenge the Catholic ethos by repeatedly tabling a bill to decriminalise those Irish who practised contraception. Between March and June 1971, over four months, the government refused six times to put her bill on the agenda. Mary Robinson, with the support of Trevor West and John Horgan, tabled a second bill, slightly different from the first, but nobody had seen either, since that was exactly the point of her unremitting efforts. A first reading of the bill would ensure its being printed and published. Senators and other politicians, as well as members of the public, could then judge on evidence what it was all about. In fact none of them waited to read the bill to comment, criticise, vilify, in effect 'we have the quite absurd situation where we now have a nation-wide debate on a non-existent Bill.'[59] Her bill, the Criminal Law Amendment Bill, 1971, was finally put on the agenda on 7 July. It allowed the limited sale of contraceptives in hospitals, chemist's shops and the like, as the Minister for Justice would deem fit. Also, publications about family planning would become available. A majority of senators opposed the first reading of the bill (by 25 votes to 14), something never seen before in the Seanad, as pointed out by Dr Wilson-Davis. Despite her disappointment and her frustration, Mary Robinson announced she was determined to table similar bills in the future, 'which will lead to the sort of society we would like to see here: A more pluralist and a more tolerant society'.[60] In February 1972, Noël Browne and John O'Connell, both Labour TDs and doctors, tried to have the same bill read in the Dáil, but its first reading was also opposed by a majority of government TDs, who created an uproar at the mere mention of the word contraception. Noël Browne pointed out again that the bill sought to have the rights of a minority recognised in a pluralist society,

> a right which should be accorded to the religious minority living in our society, as well as to the Catholics who felt they consciously had a right to use contraceptive methods if they wished to do so.... Dr. Hillery is touring the world, begging for help in America, Canada, France, the Common Market countries for minority rights in Northern Ireland. At least the North make no pretence of wanting a united Ireland. We do.[61]

The government announced it intended to present its own bill which would abide by the concept of private morality while regulating the sale of contraceptives. It was buying time as it knew the law had to be changed, but wanted to do it on its own terms. Such an important piece of legislation could not be left to the initiative of an individual senator or TD, however unpalatable the topic was.

THE McGEE CASE AND MARY ROBINSON'S PILL BILLS

A third force would intervene in the debate opposing the Catholic Church and the state on the issue of contraception, that is, between fierce opposition and *laissez-faire:* the judiciary. The five judges of the Supreme Court found that the ban on the importation of contraceptives was unconstitutional, and that a Mrs McGee had the right to limit the number of her children by artificial means. What is so extraordinary about this judgment is that the judges could find a Catholic-inspired law in contradiction with a Catholic-inspired Constitution. Did this point to a shift in meaning of what natural law is and what sustains moral order? In effect this court case changed the law on contraception overnight, and, as Gerard Hogan put it, 'the Supreme Court had sanctioned a radical change in the law which could not then have been brought through the ordinary legislative process.'[62] Mary McGee was 27 and lived in a caravan with her husband, a fisherman, and their four children (including twins). Her three pregnancies had been very close, and every one of them had been marred by medical problems. Her doctor strongly advised her not to have any more children as the next could be fatal. In J.H. Whyte's very words, 'Mrs Mary McGee was about as convincing a case as one could find of the need for artificial contraception.'[63] The rhythm method was obviously not working, the pill involved a high risk of thrombosis, sterilisation was apparently not considered, so she was fitted with a cap by Dr James Loughran, of the IFPA. Now she had to order the spermicide jelly by post from England, as it was not manufactured in Ireland. But the package was seized at customs, in accordance with the law that banned the importation of contraceptives. Dr Loughran and his lawyer encouraged Mrs McGee to go to court, as the seizure of the package put her life at risk if she was pregnant again – and this was in obvious contradiction with the Constitution which guarantees the rights of every citizen. While Article 15 of the Constitution forbids Parliament passing laws that are contrary to its spirit, Article 34 gives the High Court the power to interpret its articles, and the Supreme Court, the highest judiciary body in Ireland, power to overturn or confirm decisions taken by the High Court, its decisions being final and conclusive. These interpretative powers began to be used in the 1960s when, among other reasons, lawyers and judges tended to be trained more in the American than the English way, and they acknowledged the constitutional parallels existing between Ireland and the US. Encouraged by the Taoiseach, Sean Lemass, they became more and more inclined to interpret the Constitution, rather than take it at face value. In particular, in 1965, Judge Kenny in *Ryan* v. *The Attorney-General* based his judgment on the fact that the general guarantee in Article 40 over personal rights (the fundamental rights, including freedom of expression, religion, association, etc.) extends to rights not specified in the Constitution. The citizen has many personal rights which follow from the Christian and democratic nature of the state. This judgment created a famous precedent which would allow, from then on, the recognition of a number of implicit rights, that is to say, natural rights with which citizens are born and which even positive law cannot deny them.

The McGee case was heard at the High Court in July 1972.[64] Mrs McGee's lawyers (with Mary Robinson as junior counsel) contended that section 17.3 of the law was incompatible with the Constitution articles on the citizens' personal rights (40.3.1), and on the authority of the family (41.1.2). It seemed *a priori* difficult to prove that they could be incompatible, since both were based on Catholic social principles, and this is the argument that Judge O'Keeffe used to reject the case. According to him, the 1935 law did not explicitly forbid the use of contraceptives, so that the parallel drawn by the defence between this case and an American one was inadmissible. The latter, eight years before the McGee case, legalised *de facto* the use of contraceptives as it was proved that forbidding it was in breach of a right to marital privacy, a right implicitly recognised and protected by the American Constitution. In 1972, the American Supreme Court found that this right also applied to single people.[65] For the Irish judge, the personal rights of the citizen did not include a right to the protection of privacy, and the 1935 law was not inconsistent with the authority of the family. Mrs McGee appealed to the Supreme Court where the majority of the judges (four out of five) ruled in her favour, in December 1973, stating that the current ban was an unjustified invasion of the personal right that she had to the protection of the privacy of her marital relations. In Judge Budd's words: 'What more important personal right could there be in a citizen than the right to determine in marriage his [sic] attitude and resolve his mode of life concerning the procreation of children?' As for Judge Walsh, also in the majority, he relied on Article 41 to prove the unconstitutionality of the legislation. According to him, it protected husband and wife against any state intrusion in their private affairs, because the family is 'the necessary basis of social order and . . . [is] indispensable to the welfare of the nation and the State.' Another important element in the Walsh judgment is the fact that it echoed the Kenny judgment, referred to earlier, in that Judge Walsh said that the Preamble to the Constitution gave the judges liberty to interpret the rights of citizens by applying their own ideas of prudence, justice and charity: 'It is but natural that from time to time the prevailing ideas of these virtues may be conditioned by the passage of time; no interpretation of the Constitution is intended to be final for all time. It is given in the light of prevailing ideas and concepts.'

However liberal it may be, the verdict of the Supreme Court was based on well-known Catholic principles such as the primacy of natural rights and of the family. It is all the more extraordinary that they reached the conclusion we know from such premisses. But they did rely on natural law to justify that the family has rights over which the state has no hold. The state could have justified the ban on contraception by the fact that the practice is contrary to natural law – but only to that as espoused by the Catholic Church. The judges avoided having to choose between various interpretations of the natural law, while leaning on it to reach their decision. With this judgment, the importation of contraceptives for one's personal use was now allowed, but the ban on their importation for sale was maintained, with section 17.1 still in force, as was the ban on birth control propaganda. (IFPA and FPS were actually prosecuted in February 1974 and, interestingly, the case was dismissed.) The judges also pointed out that they offered no opinion in relation to the importation of contraceptives by unmarried couples. Such judgments can effectively and radically change the law but they are always limited to the case heard, known as a test case, without widening its scope. It is up to the legislators to take the matter further.

Mary Robinson was going to do just that. A month before the ruling, she had finally won the vote in the Seanad to have her bill read for the first time. It was a revised version of the 1971 bill. The main differences were its title, Family Planning Bill, 1973, and the fact that it would be the Minister for Health, and not for Justice, who would be responsible for the application of the terms of the future law. This time, then, the bill would be printed by Parliament, published and made available to the general public.[66] The move from a bill on the penal code to one on family planning testified to the determination to decriminalise contraception and place the issue in the realm of health – and feminine health at that. Mary Robinson's motivations and that of her colleagues, Horgan and West, had not changed. They wanted to have the issue debated in Parliament, since it was already being debated in all the other public fora in the country. It was a civil rights issue, detached from party politics as the three senators were in the 'independent' group. Family planning was also a civil right at international level, a fact acknowledged even by Ireland, which voted in Tehran in 1968 in favour of resolution 18 of the UN Convention of the Rights of Man.

As far as Irish political parties were concerned, they all seemed to be committed by then to some change, but the party in government, from 1965 to 1973, was Fianna Fáil and it did not seem in any rush to change the law, as it could foresee strong opposition from its backbenches. There was still a strong determination in all quarters, even in the Labour Party, to dissociate family planning from contraception. But between the first and the second reading of Mary Robinson's bill, that is between 14 November 1973 and 20 February 1974, the law had changed as a result of the McGee case. Without it, who can say that Mary Robinson's bill would not have met with the same resistance and the same fate as the first one? Paradoxically, the law on contraception had overnight become quite liberal, and as Mary Robinson herself said:

> As the law now stands, any person, married or unmarried, and with no age limit, can use contraceptives, manufacture contraceptives, distribute contraceptives and, since the recent judgment of the Supreme Court in the McGee case, import contraceptives. Also, the pill is regarded not as a contraceptive but as a cycle regulator and therefore does not come within the legislation prohibiting the sale of contraceptives. More than 38,000 Irish women, be they married or unmarried, use the pill under a prescription every month. However none of these people can inform herself fully on the subject.[67]

Indeed, the therapeutic indications were withdrawn from the contraceptive pills packs before being sold so as not to contravene the law banning birth control propaganda! If Parliament did not take over, others would try to test the constitutionality of the ban on the sale of contraceptives, as well as that of the ban on written information relative to them.   Mary Robinson, as a constitutional lawyer, found unacceptable that the law should be eroded on an *ad hoc* basis, by successive test cases, and felt that 'we must not abdicate to the Judiciary the function of gradually finding our laws unconstitutional and, therefore, in effect legislating.'[68] As in the case of divorce, the moral obligation to take into account the beliefs and behaviour of Protestants was also mentioned. On this issue too, the Protestant community, in the South as in the North, was expecting a 'gesture'. The clause relative to the special position of the Catholic Church had been removed from the Constitution in a referendum in 1972, because it was proof that the Irish Constitution discriminated in favour of the majority religion of the Republic. It was largely a goodwill gesture towards Northern Ireland, but Mary Robinson argued that it was not sufficient to remove such a clause from the Constitution if the laws exemplifying this special position were not removed as well. All the minority churches had made their position known by writing to all parliamentarians. This in itself was extraordinary. Family planning was a good thing in itself and should be left to the couples to decide in conscience, so that they would make their own decisions, armed with all the necessary information. The position of the majority church was well known, but Mary Robinson pointed out that: 'It is worth noting that family planning is now supported positively by all the Christian churches. This includes the Catholic church which is in favour of responsible parenthood, in favour of family planning. The difference between them relates only to choice of means.'[69]

Having said all this, it is necessary to keep things in perspective, and as Dr David Nowlan remarked, 'Senator Robinson herself has come to seem like some sort of revolutionary heroine, leading the battle for human rights through a reactionary Irish Parliament. But her bill, if passed, would give Ireland the most conservative and restrictive legislation on contraception in Europe, with the possible exception of Malta, and possibly, Portugal.'[70] Still, at the time, in the current social and moral climate her efforts were seen as subversive and her hate mail was substantial! On 26 November 1973 *The Irish Times* published a declaration by the Irish bishops, now quite worried that Mary Robinson's bill was finally going to be read. At first sight, they were strongly condemned any change in the law:

> The question at issue is not whether artificial contraception is morally right or wrong. The clear teaching of the Catholic Church is that it is morally wrong. No change in State Law can make the use of contraceptives morally right since what is wrong in itself remains wrong, regardless of what State Law says.

Using generalisations under the cover of statistics, the bishops proceeded by saying:

> Experience elsewhere indicates that where the sale of contraceptives is legalised, marital infidelity increases, the birth of children outside of wedlock (surprising as it may seem) increases, abortions increase, there is a marked increase in the incidence of venereal

disease and the use of contraceptives tends to spread rapidly among unmarried young people.

Up to that point there was nothing new about the stance of the Catholic Church on the issue. However this declaration marks a milestone in the history of Church–state relations because of the following passage:

> It does not follow, of course, that the State is bound to prohibit the importation and sale of contraceptives. There are many things which the Catholic Church holds to be morally wrong and no one has ever suggested, least of all the Church herself, that they should be prohibited by the State.

In fact, the Irish bishops had never before conceded that legislators were not obliged to forbid what was condemned in the name of Catholic moral principles. One look at the Mother and Child Scheme, for example, suffices to show that it was always the opposite! According to John A. Murphy, Pope Paul VI had even expressed to Garret FitzGerald, then Minister for Foreign Affairs, his hope 'that Ireland would continue to set a headline for Catholic countries' by not legalising contraception.[71] Was such a turnaround an abdication? Not quite, as the bishops qualified their magnanimous statement in the same breath: 'The real point facing the legislators is "What effect would the increased availability of contraceptives have on the quality of life in the Republic of Ireland?" This is a question of public, not private, morality. What the legislators have to decide is whether a change in the law would, on balance, do more harm than good, by damaging the character of the society for which they are responsible. There is a good deal of evidence that it would.' Of course, neither the legislators nor the people wanted a permissive and corrupt society; they all wanted to be good Catholics. The bishops knew this, and by pretending to leave them the freedom to choose, they hoped to bring them round to their point of view, that is, to maintain the ban on the sale and importation of contraceptives (to make their use as difficult as possible). They also knew that legislators were keen to reflect public opinion rather than try to make it change. Thus they did not have much to lose with such a declaration, but avoided the risk of being accused of interfering in public affairs. On the contrary, by posing as the conscience of society, the Catholic Church intended to continue playing an important role, by denouncing all the evils afflicting it.

On 27 March 1974, the day when senators were to vote on Mary Robinson's bill, they received the draft of the government bill on the same issue. Mary Robinson decided not to withdraw her own, and when it was rejected by 32 votes to 10, she said, 'I have always preferred quality to quantity and I am quite happy with that.'[72] The very title of the bill presented to the Dáil, the Control of Importation, Sale and Manufacture of Contraceptives Bill, 1974, said a lot about its intention. It was not a matter of legalising, but of controlling. This government bill was introduced by Patrick Cooney, Minister for Justice (from February 1973 a Fine Gael–Labour coalition was in power). Since the current situation was that anybody could import contraceptives into Ireland, for his/her personal use or give them away 'free', it was quite paradoxical that no restriction existed in relation to their importation, when their sale was forbidden. It had not been proved that the ban on their sale was unconstitutional, but the Minister for Justice felt the courts could very well decide that it was. Moreover, contraceptives were sold on the black market, there existed a mail order network and the companies even included samples with their order forms. It was thus necessary to regulate the importation of contraceptives while authorising their sale. The main points of the bill were that only chemists would be allowed to sell contraceptives, which authorised importers would provide. In remote places, a shopkeeper could get a licence if there was no chemist in the vicinity. It would be forbidden to display the contraceptives for sale or advertise them. Only married people could buy them, since the Minister did not think that 'there is a right, a natural right in favour of single people to have access to contraceptives. I do not accept that there is any such right because that implies a right to fornicate and in my opinion there is no such a natural right.'[73] Even though it would not be necessary to produce a marriage certificate, it was acknowledged in the Dáil that the ban on the sale of contraceptives to single people would not be absolutely respected. But it was felt that laws should be declarations of principle, for citizens who wanted such safeguards.

Such words nevertheless betrayed the notion that it is possible to impose a moral order, norms, lofty principles, by the simple fact of putting them on paper. On the contrary, what was not written did not exist. Was public opinion endowed with the same ideals? The first opinion poll on the issue was taken in 1971 and revealed that 63 per cent of the people questioned were against the legalisation of the sale of contraceptives, but four later studies produced different results. The first was done during the summer of 1973 by Dr Keith

Wilson-Davis. In a sample of 754 married women aged between 15
and 44, 59.6 per cent wanted to see the end of the ban, and 12.3 per
cent wanted it too, but in certain circumstances only (for example,
if people were married, if the woman had enough children); 24.5 per
cent were totally opposed to the legalisation of the sale of contraceptives. A second question was then asked, which was more precise:
if contraceptives were legalised, who should be allowed to buy them?
Seven per cent only thought they should be available to everybody;
26.8 per cent to married people; 6.2 per cent to everybody on
prescription, and 36.7 per cent thought they should be available
on two conditions: to married people and on prescription. Even
among married women aged under 25, the proportion of those
who thought that contraceptives should be available to single people
was only 21 per cent.[74] This reminds us of the questions asked in
relation to divorce: with a more concrete question, one gets a higher
proportion of restrictive views. Still, we are far from an unconditional
adherence to the teaching of the Catholic Church, and to *Humanae
Vitae* in particular. The second survey was done by Irish Marketing
Surveys (IMS) for the magazine *Hibernia*, in February 1974: it found
that 54 per cent of the people questioned were in favour of the sale
of contraceptives through chemists, and 43 per cent were opposed to
the legalisation of their sale. In the 16–24 years category or in the
highest socio-economic group, the percentage of those in favour of
the sale of contraceptives at the chemist's was as high as 70 per cent.
There was no reference to marital status in this survey.[75] Interestingly
enough, the same opinion poll institute did a similar survey for the
same magazine 18 months later, using the same population sample
and the same questions, but after the defeat of the Cooney bill (more
about this later), and it revealed that by then 47 per cent, instead of
54 per cent, were in favour of the sale of contraceptives at the chemist's (but the number of those opposed had also declined to 37 per
cent). Sixty-eight per cent of married women of childbearing age were
in favour, as in 1974. The undecided had jumped from 3 per cent to 16
per cent.[76] The fourth survey was done by Market Research Bureau of
Ireland (MRBI), in March 1974, on a representative sample of the
population, aged 18–60 without particular reference to marital status.
This showed 16 per cent wanted the sale of contraceptives to
be legalised for all, 42 per cent agreed, but for married people only;
and 33 per cent were opposed to any change in the law.[77] The
government probably relied on such results to affirm the validity of
its bill.[78]

However the results of these surveys do not match what was happening in the family planning clinics. A majority of people seemed to be saying that only married people should be able to use contraceptives, and very few voices granted this right to all, but what was the reality like? Was banning contraception sufficient for people not to use it? Did it suffice to exclude single people for them to refrain? The results of a survey done by Dr Eimer Philbin Bowman for a master's dissertation in psychology, showed that single people were not as chaste as one was led to believe. She had noticed that between 1961 and 1971, the marriage rate had risen from 5.5 to 7.4 per 1,000, but the birth rate had not increased in the same proportions: It had gone from 21.8 per cent in 1962 to 22.6 per thousand in 1972. On the other hand, illegitimate fertility had doubled, from 3.3 for 1,000 single women in 1961 to 6.8 in 1972. The number of abortions performed in Britain had jumped from 64 in 1968 to 1,421 in 1974. The 1974 annual report of the IFPA showed that in 1971, among the new clients of the Merrion Square clinic, 25 per cent were single, and at Mountjoy Square clinic, 10 per cent were. The first clinic was used mainly by middle-class women, whereas the second one catered for more deprived clients. But in 1974, these proportions were now respectively 32 per cent and 27 per cent. What is apparent then is that not only had the proportion of single women increased in three years, but also that the gap between the two clinics narrowed significantly. These figures contrasted with the opinion polls, and with what politicians said they knew about public opinion.

Intrigued by these results, Dr Philbin Bowman, decided to investigate the clientèle of the family planning clinics more closely and in particular those who were single and came to the Merrion Square clinic for the first time in 1974, more precisely between 1 January and 30 June.[79] Placing this survey in context, it should be remembered that it was conducted between the first and the second readings of the Cooney bill. Over the period chosen for the research, 47 per cent of the new patients were not married. The vast majority had marriage plans in the short term, but 19 per cent had none. A majority (63 per cent) were aged between 20 and 24 years. This is also the age bracket in Britain with the highest percentages of abortions and of illegitimate births, all aspects of a 'more widespread change in the sexual behaviour of young people'.[80] As for the contraceptive method used, 87 per cent were on the pill (67 per cent of all the clients, married and single, took it). The study focused on the 19 per cent who had no plans to get married, since they would be the most affected, or rather the most excluded, by future legislation. As the clinics were not allowed to advertise their services, and the media only reported discussions of the legalisation of contraceptives for married people, it was interesting to find out how these young women had heard about the clinic for the first time: 58 per cent had heard through a friend, 14 per cent through the media and 10 per cent through their sister, a parent or their partner. Let us mention that when the patients of the new Cork clinic were asked how they had heard about it, 40 per cent named the Bishop of Cork. He had enjoined the faithful from the pulpit not to go to the clinic that had just opened in Tucker Street and provided such and such services. A warning that surely backfired![81] Seventy-eight per cent of the sample had a steady and monogamous relationship. Of the 94 per cent who had already had sexual relations at the time of the study, that is to say at the time of their first visit to a family planning clinic, 42 per cent admitted they always used a contraceptive method, but it turned out that only 12 per cent used a reliable method (pill, condom or cap). Only one woman of the sample had come to the clinic on her doctor's advice, which betrays the pervading intolerance attached to the sexual activity of single people. Dr Philbin Bowman drew the following conclusions. Young Irish women seemed different from their British and American contemporaries in that fewer of them had sexual relations, and those who had started later. On the other hand,

> living in a more sexually conservative environment and having had to face greater pressures in coming to terms with their sexual behaviour, they have had to go further in rejecting the values of the society that would be necessary in a more permissive culture. It is arguable that one effect of this interaction may have been to select out the more independent-minded and there are some indications that the women in this sample may be the products of such a process.

The delay between the first time they had intercourse and their first visit to a family planning clinic (2 1/2 years on average) was worrying, and even if these young women were somewhat atypical in Irish society, they did provide evidence of a need for contraception. They also provided evidence of a change in attitudes, reflected in the steady increase in the illegitimate birth and abortion rates. Moreover, what was obvious was the fact that they wanted to live their sexuality in a responsible way, and still they remained on the margin of norms and of what was acceptable. Anticipating the events, the fact is that 47 per cent of the women who had gone to the Merrion Square clinic for the first time that year would had been liable to a fine of up to £100 if the Cooney Bill had been passed. Dr Philbin Bowman concluded:

> That they represent but one aspect of a more widespread change in the sexual behaviour of young people in general, is suggested by the other statistics referred to. It would seem advisable therefore, that before legislation is enacted, prescribing how the unmarried ought to behave, we should obtain some factual data on how they do behave.

How long would it be possible to prescribe norms and set them in concrete and in law? Having said that, a large majority of deputies, of all political persuasions, were convinced of the necessity to legislate to guarantee the right to marital privacy. Only two TDs, Oliver Flanagan and Michael Kitt, both of Fine Gael, invoked *Humanae Vitae* to express their opposition to the legalisation of contraception, and the government decided to allow a conscience vote to appease them. Fianna Fáil opposed the bill and imposed the whip, which saved its deputies from giving too much thought to the issue. The tone of the debates was somewhat unreal, often pure rhetoric.[82] Desmond O'Malley (Fianna Fáil) suggested allowing the importation of contraceptives by married couples for their personal use, in reasonable quantities. George Colley (Fianna Fáil) said it was not necessary to cover the country with contraceptives outlets since the Supreme Court had only stipulated that married couples should have 'reasonable access' to them. The Minister for Industry and Commerce, Justin Keating, admitted having flouted the law for years and so had some of his colleagues he would not name. For Michael Kitt, one of the two staunch opponents: 'I know perfectly well in my conscience that this is morally wrong. We all know that murder is morally wrong. How can you make that legally right?' And Oliver Flanagan, in an intervention that lasted three hours, made the point that

> this Bill is an attack on the family. It is an attack on society. ...Anything that is unnatural damages our society....I want to warn this House finally that if this Bill is passed it is the thin end of the wedge to complete moral disaster in so far as Irish society is concerned. ...As sure as this Bill goes on the Statute Books it will be the raising of the latch of the sluice gates of every kind of immorality with the ultimate result of abortion and everything that abortion stands for.

He thanked God for the fact that most chemists had said they would not touch or sell contraceptive appliances, and most conscientious doctors had declared they would not cooperate with the Minister for Justice. Only one woman TD spoke up during this debate. This was Eileen Desmond (Labour), and she was convinced that 'this Bill was brought in because it was clearly seen that the majority of the people want such a Bill. They want married people to have access to contraceptives.... Only in doing that [letting the Bill go to Committee] will we be sincere in discharging our duty to the people and, particularly, our duty to Irish women.'[83]

The debates ended theatrically on 16 July 1974. The result of the vote was never in much doubt, since the opposition was united and the government coalition divided, but the defeat was more crushing than what even the worst pessimists anticipated: 75 votes to 61. What was extraordinary was the fact that the Taoiseach, Liam Cosgrave (son of William Cosgrave) voted against his minister's bill, followed in the division lobby by six TDs, including the Minister for Education, Richard Burke. It had of course been noticed that the Taoiseach was a conservative Catholic and had not intervened in the debate. The day before, *The Irish Press* had published a photo of him kneeling in front of the newly appointed Bishop of Limerick, Dr Newman. No explanation was given for this vote, nor was any asked. People suddenly realised the difference there was between 'the Cooney bill' and 'a government bill', even though in February 1974 it had seemed to mean the same thing, when 'the government has decided, consequent on the recent Supreme Court decision in relation to the Criminal Law Amendment Act, 1935, to introduce a bill to provide for the necessary change in legislation arising out of that decision.' Following the defeat, Mary Robinson announced her intention to try once more to introduce a contraception bill, because, as she said later, 'I submit there is a responsibility on the Members of this House today to break out of that stalemate, to stop regarding the issue of family planning in Ireland as a political football.'[84]

Her bill was called simply Family Planning Bill, 1974, and it was a compromise between her relatively liberal bill of 1973 and the more conservative Cooney bill: anybody could import contraceptives for their personal use, but their sale would require a licence. The innovation was contained in section 8 of the bill which said that a contraceptive was considered as a medical appliance, which implied that adults who had a Medical Card, i.e. had a small enough income to have free medical services, could also obtain contraceptives free from their Health Board. About 30 per cent of the population benefited at the time from the General Medical Services, and as such the adult proportion could avail of free contraception.[85] On 17 December 1974, 23 Senators to 16 voted in favour of the second reading of the bill, but, almost a year later, this second reading still had not taken place. It eventually did, on 16 December 1976. The difference with 1974 was that there was no government bill on the horizon, and more senators spoke in favour of the bill than against. Still, when it came to the vote, 23 senators to 20 stopped it from reaching the committee stage. The gap was narrowing, inexorably, but not quite enough.

4 Contraception:...To a Responsible Sexuality for All

Fianna Fáil regained power in June 1977 with a majority of 20 seats. The Taoiseach, Jack Lynch, announced the intention of his government to introduce a law on family planning, and the task was given to Charles Haughey, Minister for Health, who took 18 months to finalise the draft bill. In the meantime, the militants against contraception had not remained inactive. As early as 1976, they brandished the motto 'contraception now, abortion next' and began to go round church halls and schools with foetuses in jars.[1] Irish newspapers now reported the official number of Irish women going to Britain for an abortion, and the IFPA had two calls a week from women wanting information about abortions abroad. The amalgamation was easy, but interestingly enough, it was also used by the pro-contraception militants who argued that a legal and informed contraception service would reduce the number of abortions.

A number of groups, including the Society to Outlaw Pornography, the Council of Social Concern, the Irish Family League, etc. sprang up, gravitating around the order of the Knights of St Columbanus and Opus Dei, in their efforts 'to counter unsubtle attacks on our religion, morality and culture, by certain women's organisations and by the lobbies for contraception, divorce and secular schools'. In effect, the opposition to the liberalisation of the laws relative to the family was masterminded by just a few persons who cropped up in various organisations, had access to influential circles in Irish society, and were very organised and very persuasive. The organisations overlapped, formed themselves into federations, and had separate actions with the same aim. The secret of their success, to quote the veteran campaigner John O'Reilly in 1968, was that 'an organisation or a group is never more powerful than when it influences events without itself being regarded as the initiator'. These people had effectively taken over from the Church. In November 1973, when the Irish bishops had decided to refrain and not try to influence legislators directly, by saying that what is forbidden by the Church does not have to be forbidden by the state, they had, in effect, shown the way forward for lay people. These would leap to the defence of the Church's teaching, and would say loudly and clearly what kind of society they wanted to live in. Faced with such an organised front, the militants for contraception did not really measure up. The Contraception Action Programme (CAP), the first campaign exclusively for contraception, was launched in 1976. They demanded free and legal contraception for all those who needed it, and distributed contraceptives in community halls. But the organisation disbanded in 1979 because their efforts resulted in 'nothing but a miserable bill' [the Haughey bill]. Legislation had to be introduced because of the 1973 Supreme Court judgment, 'the 1979 Bill would have been passed if CAP had never existed'.[2]

AN IRISH SOLUTION TO AN IRISH PROBLEM

In May 1978, Professor John Bonnar, with other members of the National Association of the Ovulation Method, met Haughey to describe to him the harmful effects of the pill and the IUD, and praise the Billings method. This was one of the first of over 18 organisations the minister met before his bill was drafted, including the eight Health Boards, the Catholic hierarchy, the Protestant churches, the Irish Medical Association (IMA), the Socio-Medical Research Council and the IFPA. But the joint parliamentary commission met only once and according to his political adversaries, Haughey did not formally meet the opposition party leaders. The Catholic bishops, who met him on 2 June 1978, used the same arguments as in their collective statement of April 1978, but they admitted that the current situation was highly unsatisfactory and that minimum legislation was necessary in the wake of the McGee judgment. Since unrestricted availability of contraceptives would have serious social consequences, the bishops advocated strict legal control and the assurance that contraceptives would not be available to young unmarried people. They remained convinced that changing the law would make people believe that morality had changed and they stated again that societies where contraceptives were widely used had seen a moral decline as regards sexuality. Their declarations prompted Mary Robinson to say: 'The bishops' recognition of the need for legislation is welcome, but the emphasis seems to be more on closing loopholes, following the McGee case, than on guaranteeing the human rights of Irish couples – whether

Catholic or non Catholic – to reasonable access to information and choice of methods of family planning.'[3]

The gist of the Haughey bill was that the eight Health Boards would provide a comprehensive information and advice service on family planning, even though they had never agreed to do this. Contraceptives would only be sold at chemists' and on prescription, even though the IMA had let the minister know that most doctors objected to prescribing non-medical contraceptives. A doctor would only prescribe contraceptives if he was convinced the patient required them for a *bona fide* reason of family planning or for medical reasons. The Minister for Health promised to set up a natural family planning service and to give grants to research projects in this area. Section 10 reaffirmed the ban on abortifacients, and section 11 provided for doctors and chemists to use a conscience clause if they objected to artificial contraception. Haughey had acknowledged from the outset that his aim was not to increase the availability of contraceptives, but to restrict it: 'It emerged clearly that the majority view of those consulted was that any legislation to be introduced should provide for a more restrictive situation in relation to the availability of contraceptives than that which exists by law at present.'[4] What greater restriction could one hope for than a law that limited the sale of all contraceptives, including condoms, to married people who had been given a prescription on the strength of their desire to plan their family? Whereas the Supreme Court said this decision should be left to the couple, in Haughey's bill, it was left to the doctor. Haughey's memorable retort to all objections was: 'This bill seeks to provide an Irish solution to an Irish problem. I have not regarded it as necessary that we should conform to the position obtaining in any other country.'[5]

The Dáil debates on the bill make more interesting reading than those on the Cooney bill. Even though the most vocal anti-contraception deputy was still Oliver Flanagan, a Knight of St Columbanus, arguments were more informed and less passionate and helped draw a picture of the contraceptive situation in Ireland as it was and as it would be once the law passed.[6] A number of deputies opposed the fact that the law would turn doctors into moral arbiters and Dr John O'Connell did not think they had the desire or the competence to do so and that 'what is suggested here is that doctors are now the rearguard of the morality back-up.'[7] It was also said that the bill did not meet the needs of the situation, but the political needs of the government, since it had been noticed that all opposition parties and a large part of public opinion were in favour of a change. But a Fianna Fáil minister needed a lot of finesse to come up with a bill that would take into account the McGee judgment, the birth control reality in Ireland, without provoking the wrath of its most powerful ally, the Catholic Church, and of its rural electors, usually unconditional backers of the Church. Fundamental objections to the bill were that it mirrored the Catholic position and did not take into account women's concerns, as Eileen Desmond pointed out:

> It could not be acceptable to anybody who has concern for human rights or for women as persons. ... I should like to know how many of those organisations represented young women, how many represented unprivileged women, women living in overcrowded homes, in bad homes or women suffering the tensions of having to share those housing conditions with in-laws. Judging by the Bill, I would not say they were represented.[8]

The bill would be of least benefit to those who needed it the most, as it was tainted with social discrimination. In 1978, some 48,000 women were on the pill, according to the IMA. Among them, 13,000 got it free as part of the GMS, as a cycle regulator, of course. Under the Haughey law, it would not be possible, since it stated that artificial contraceptives would not be covered by the GMS. To get around this, the doctor would still have to prescribe the pill as a cycle regulator! Contraceptives could be delivered free for medical reasons, as in the case of Mrs McGee, for example. The bottom line was that medical contraceptives could not be considered as ordinary medicines, and Haughey would have courted disaster in Catholic quarters if it had been stipulated that contraceptives could be prescribed free of charge. According to the bill, the Health Boards would not sell contraceptives, and neither would the family planning clinics. They could give advice, but a doctor would then have to issue a prescription marked '*bona fide* family planning', and the patient would then go to the chemist's. The question was whether the new system would cope with the 40,000–50,000 people who went each year to the family planning clinics, plus the 35,000 odd people who received contraceptives, including 12,000 condoms, through the post. Were there enough doctors trained in all birth control methods? There was a maximum of 120 general practitioners (including those trained in Britain) who had some training other than in natural birth control. The fact that the public benefit of the family planning clinics was not recognised was puzzling. Family planning clinics provided various tests and psychosexual counselling, and ran courses attended by doctors who then qualified for the diploma of the

Joint Commission of the Royal College of Obstetrics and of General Practitioners. About 100 out of the 1,200 general practitioners in the country were awarded this certificate from the only authority in family planning, the . . . IFPA.

It is a fact that between the McGee judgment and the passing of the law, public opinion was not very vociferous in demanding a change in the discredited legislation, but this false sense of contentment would only last as long as the family planning clinics remained open, as deputy John Horgan pointed out:

> The pressure for reform since the McGee case has lessened because of the success of the family planning clinics in providing a much wider range of contraceptive advice and materials to a much greater number of people than was possible before the judgement in the McGee case. Naturally, when the means and the advice are more widely available than before the pressure for change lessens, but I predict that if this Bill is passed. . . the pressure will again build up and the pressure for change in the law will then become a majority issue.[9]

The vote at the end of the second reading was not a resounding victory for Haughey, despite the 84 Fianna Fáil TDs, since 66 deputies voted in favour of the bill and 49 against. At the committee stage, a great number of amendments were tabled but very few were accepted. Such phrases as 'a family planning service', '*bona fide* family planning', 'abortifacients' were never clarified; the bill did not include definitions, and none were offered. John Horgan said: 'I believe that the phrase "*bona fide* family planning purposes" will go down in history as one of the most deliberately woolly and unenlightened phrases ever introduced into a Bill.'[10] This begs the question: Was the bill very hypocritical, or supremely pragmatic? One can venture that the phrase '*bona fide* family planning' was inserted to keep good Catholics and Fianna Fáil backbenchers happy, who wanted birth control practised in a family context. In fact, the phrase, without specifying if it had to be a legal marriage, belongs to the same category as 'natural family planning': they imply that the purpose of marriage is procreation, and even though the Catholic Church no longer expects continuous procreation, it still expects unselfishness on the part of the married couple spacing the births of their children. To call it 'natural' implies that anything else is unnatural, which in English also means against nature, perverse – a distinction that throws doubts on the ethical values of those using mechanical and chemical contraceptives!

Haughey knew that his bill would have a greater chance of passing if
it showed some goodwill towards the Catholic lobby, hence its sections
about natural family planning. The Health (Family Planning) Act,
1979, was passed on 26 June by 58 votes to 36. The bishops had
said in April and June 1978 that they wanted as restrictive a law as
possible, and that they did not foresee any clash between the Church
and the state as they trusted the goodwill and the good intentions of
the legislators. There was no clash, but then there was not much in this
law to displease them – save the very principle of artificial contraception.

The law, in force as from 1 November 1980, seems to have closed
more doors than it opened, on paper anyway. Chemists did not rally: a
survey taken three months after the law came into force, showed that
of 85 per cent of chemists operating in the five rural counties, only 11
per cent sold contraceptives.[11] The price of condoms shot up: a packet
cost £1.60 before the law, but more than doubled overnight to £3.45.
On top of that there was 35 per cent VAT and a percentage of the £100
import licence that had to be paid. Furthermore, according to Chris-
tine Donnaghy of the IFPA, prices were artificially low before their
legalisation, as English manufacturers were trying to develop the Irish
market![12] In any case, a survey published in 1982 showed that, at that
date, 80 per cent of the contraceptives bought in Ireland came from
unlicenced clinics, and that 15 per cent of all chemists had contraceptives in stock other than the pill.[13] Indeed the various family planning clinics went on to provide a comprehensive family planning
service, and not just to married couples. The IFPA now had six clinics
throughout Ireland, and only some of them asked for a licence from
the Department of Health: the Galway clinic saw 7,000 clients a year,
the Limerick one nearly as many. The Cork clinic was used by 12,000
clients. There were clinics in Bray and Navan. The two Dublin clinics,
in Synge Street and Cathal Brugha Street, had seen 50,000 clients the
previous year. They decided to go by the law, i.e. get a licence and to
employ a pharmacist on the premises (to deliver the contraceptives).
FPS did not obtain a licence, and the two Well Woman Centres did not
apply for one. They all sold condoms without prescription, and mail
order sales continued as before. As the economist Ursula Barry said:
'Once again the law was at odds with people's lifestyles and its partial
reform had not succeeded in strengthening its moral authority.'[14] The
inherent ambiguity in the terms of the law had taken over: family
planning had become normal practice in Ireland, after 45 years in
clandestine existence, whether 'family' referred to the constitutional

concept of the family (not defined there either, but interpreted as meaning 'in a marriage context') or to sociological reality.

A NEW ORDER: THREE CONDOM LAWS

The 1979 law will remain, despite its limitations, the first in the socio-moral area to be detached at its basis from the teaching of the Catholic Church, in a process whereby the state will increasingly refuse to criminalise practices merely because they contravene the moral beliefs of the former. The way was marked out, after a challenging judgment and the first contraception law, for more of the same. Citizens and professionals were still flouting the law, or at least getting round it, just as there was a general delusion that only married people anxious to plan their family availed themselves of the new services. Was this not doing a disservice to the state? Was it realistic to think that legislation could steal a march over Catholic morality and make good Catholics of its citizens? Was it not time to accept that it is possible to liberalise socio-moral laws without unleashing promiscuity and depravation?

The debate on the relations between the law, public morality and the private life of citizens was back on the agenda in 1985 when Barry Desmond suggested amending the 1979 legislation on family planning. He was Minister for Health in a Fine Gael–Labour coalition government formed after the legislative elections of 24 November 1982, whose Taoiseach was Garret FitzGerald. Their legislative programme announced straightaway that 'there will be a review of the operation of the present family planning legislation with a view to providing full family planning advice and facilities in all cases where needed.'[15] People knew perfectly well where Desmond stood: he was a member of the IFPA, and officially opened a new clinic for FPS in April 1984. He was even reported as saying that the current law was 'an ass'.[16] He proceeded to have the family planning situation in Ireland assessed and the findings were surprising: over 30 million condoms had been legally imported since November 1980, and they were sold in not more than a quarter of all chemists' and in the few family planning clinics (15–45 per cent of their patients came from another county).[17] These already sold condoms without a prescription, even in vending machines in some cases. One Well Woman Centre in Dublin, for example, had a vending machine installed outside the clinic, which pleased people who did not have to go inside and could buy condoms at any time of any day of the week. One clinic had legal proceedings brought against it, and Dr Andrew Rynne, then President of the IFPA, was fined £200 in 1982 for giving condoms to a patient at the weekend, when chemists' were closed. The fine was later lifted, but the judge said, 'anyone without condoms at the week-end will have to wait until Monday.'[18]

Doctors in general had asked for a change in the law so as not to be moral arbiters. A delegation from the IMA met the minister in July 1983, and during their AGM on 9 November 1983, a resolution was passed asking the government to change the 1979 law. There had been a significant increase in the number of illegitimate births, from 2.7 per cent of the total number of births in 1971, to 6.8 per cent in 1983. The number of marriages followed by a birth in the same civil year had doubled between 1962 and 1981, suggesting a corresponding increase in the number of premarital conceptions. Desmond felt he had a responsibility to bring down the number of unwanted pregnancies. A survey of 200 single mothers at the St James Hospital, Dublin, showed that only 18 per cent used contraception. In 1983, 3,677 Irishwomen went to Britain for an abortion, a figure on the increase. A confidential survey done in 1983 by the Medico-Social Research Board showed that the great majority of the single women coming for an abortion did not use any contraception. The 1983 report of this same Board showed that between 1971 and 1981, the number of illegitimate births increased by 112 per cent, whereas the total number of births increased by only 7 per cent. Moreover 33 per cent of illegitimate births in 1971 were to women aged under 20, whereas in 1981 this percentage reached 38 per cent (that same year, 79 per cent of illegitimate births were to women under the age of 25).[19] It was a fact that in 1985 Ireland, youngsters were sexually active at an earlier age, and the success of what deputy Alice Glenn called a 'sex hotline' vouched for that. This was a confidential phone line for teenagers to ask questions freely, put in place by the IFPA. Also, 20 per cent of the new clients of the two Dublin IFPA clinics each year were aged between 17 and 20. Over a third had been pregnant before coming to the IFPA.

A survey carried out in 1984 by IMS for the Health Education Bureau (which monitors the evolution of public knowledge and attitudes on health matters) showed that, out of a representative sample of 700 people aged between 18 and 50 years, 50 per cent were not satisfied with the existing legislation because of the restrictions relative to the availability of contraceptives; 64 per cent thought it should be possible to buy condoms without a prescription, and that doctors, family

planning clinics and Health Boards should sell them; 89 per cent
wanted the Health Boards to set up family planning clinics (but as
early as January 1985, the Midland Health Board had announced its
refusal to take part in such a scheme); 20 per cent thought there should
not be a minimum age to buy contraceptives; and 68 per cent thought
that single people should have access to contraceptives on the same
terms as married people.[20] The results of a poll published in *The Irish
Times* on 12 February seemed to corroborate these findings, particularly as far as the 18–24 year olds are concerned, 66 per cent of whom
demanded the unrestricted availability of contraceptives. The opponents of the bill would rely on the other findings of this poll to prove that
the Irish did not want any change in the law: whereas 41 per cent of the
people questioned were in favour of a law making contraceptives accessible to everybody, 24 per cent thought they should only be available to
married people, 17 per cent to married people on prescription and 15
per cent thought that nobody should have access to them. This means
that 56 per cent of those questioned were hostile to the new bill.
However the poll was taken *before* the publication of the bill, not after.

Among those hostile was certainly the President of a new group,
Family Solidarity, formed a few weeks after the 1983 abortion referendum in order to protect the family, the true measure of the grandeur
of a nation, against all attacks, and who said:

> Family planning for people who are not forming a family is merely a
> licence to fornicate and we think this is a threat to the family. The
> age limit is irrelevant. It doesn't matter. If you have unmarried
> people of 18 who are not prepared to make the commitment of
> marriage then we take the view that they have no right to sexual
> indulgence.[21]

More pragmatically, the Minister wanted to bring down the numbers
of illegitimate births, abortions and VD cases. The other aim was to
match the law relative to the sale of contraceptives with reality. It was
also a way of acknowledging that family planning was a women's issue
in a male-dominated Parliament and a male-dominated society. All
TDs received a letter from the Council for the Status of Women
(representing 35 women's groups) asking them to support the Desmond bill. There were 14 women TDs in this Dáil, and their support
was courted by their colleague Monica Barnes, of Fine Gael:

> This is a small Bill, but we have to make one of the most important
> decisions we have ever made.... If this small, much needed and not

very radical measure is not passed by this House, I and other politicians will have to wonder what we are doing with our time and with the money of the nation in being in a Chamber where we claim to be legislators but where the Hierarchy outside make decisions about legislation. That hierarchy does not include, and has no intention of ever including, the full participation or decision-making of women, yet in remarkably strong terms it makes grave moral decisions and gives directions on behalf of women.[22]

The Health (Family Planning) (Amendment) Bill, 1985 intended, in three short sections, to legalise the use of non-medical contraceptives (condoms, spermicide creams) which could be sold without a prescription to anyone over the age of 18, at chemists, family planning clinics, maternity hospitals and VD clinics. Incidentally, the age of civil majority was lowered only a few months earlier, in November 1984, by this same Parliament from 21 to 18. The legal age for marriage was 16, but would later be raised to 18 by the Family Law Act, 1995 (with the introduction of divorce). Even though this was mainly the regularisation of what was happening anyway, Desmond's law passed with a majority of just three deputies, and met the virulent opposition of Fianna Fáil and the Catholic Church. However Proinsias de Rossa (Workers' Party TD) pointed out that the new law fell short of the initial intentions of Desmond, as announced in January 1983, namely that he would like most sections of the 1979 law to be repealed, for example, that on natural family planning. De Rossa also pointed out that the definition of contraception still did not include sterilisation.[23]

The systematic opposition of Fianna Fáil, despite an earlier admittance that the law needed to be reviewed, was expressed barely one hour after the publication of the bill on 7 February 1985. Their main argument was that nobody in the country was asking for such a law, more worried as they were about the economic situation than the greater availability of contraceptives, which was seen as pure diversion. Besides, if 10 million condoms had been imported every year since November 1980, it proved that nobody was short of them and that they were 'in superabundance'.[24] To this cynicism it could be retorted that if people did not ask for a new law it was because they flouted the current one on a daily basis. Supply matched demand, in open defiance of the law.[25] In general Fianna Fáil TDs found unacceptable that contraceptives should become so easily available to teenagers, whom they never referred to as adults, even though they were now of age. They contested this was 'family planning' since such a law would break the family and usher in promiscuity. It was contrary to the spirit of the Constitution, which vowed to protect the family, and it was contrary to the traditional values of the Irish. In the words of Michael Noonan, 'as ever we in Fianna Fáil represent the values and traditions that make us Irish and we will continue to do so on your behalf.'[26] A final argument dealt with the reactions such a law would have on Northern Ireland. For some, liberal laws on contraception, divorce and abortion would not bring about the unification of Ireland. The Northern Irish were not interested in such a gesture. But the proponents of the legislation opposed the argument that contraceptives had been freely available in Northern Ireland for a number of years and covered by the British NHS since 1974; still, people there were no more depraved and did not give themselves over to debauchery and lust. Their abortion rate (performed in Britain too) and illegitimate births were actually lower than in the Republic (for illegitimate births, the rate was 6.45 per cent in Northern Ireland and 7.6 per cent in the Republic in 1985).

The Catholic Church did not react collectively as in 1973 or 1978, which prompted John H. Whyte to express some surprise. The explanation, lacking plausibility, was that the hierarchy had been caught unawares, the legislation being introduced in a hurry. Whatever the case, nine bishops managed nonetheless to express their opinion individually over ten days.[27] The individual reaction of some bishops was particularly virulent and turned a relatively 'minor issue' (in Desmond's words) into a Church–state clash: If one went by the declarations of the Archbishop of Dublin, Dr McNamara, and the Bishop of Limerick, Dr Newman, the question was not so much whether condoms should readily be available to the over 18s, but who governed the country and what sort of society the Irish wanted. They are worth singling out because they went against the previous declarations of the hierarchy, which seemed to accept a certain degree of separation between Church and state. Dr McNamara argued that one could not pretend that anything to do with sexual morality should be left to the individual conscience, as there was no such thing as '*à la carte* Catholicism.' Dr Newman reminded all politicians 'who profess to be Catholics that they have a duty to follow the guidance of their Church in areas where the interests of Church and State overlap.... Catholic politicians are strictly bound to take account of what the bishops teach where that touches on faith or morals.' Churchmen had not pronounced so clearly since the 1920s that legislators should apply the teaching of the majority church to the laws of the land. Indeed, according to Dr Murphy, Bishop of Cork and Ross, 'if individuals or minorities who represent dissenting values can succeed in having these values imposed on the majority, then a false concept of pluralism would turn democracy upside down.'[28] Lay organisations, encouraged by the declarations of some of the bishops, began to harass deputies by sending them threatening letters (e.g. threatening to kidnap their children if they voted in favour of the bill). They were condemned by Cardinal O Fiaich and Bishop Casey of Galway (a diocese where TDs were thus intimidated). The Church of Ireland bishops also entered the fray, saying they did not think that legislation alone could instil sexual morality, even though premarital and extramarital sexual relations were contrary to the teaching of Christ. They evoked the Anglican teaching that advocates responsible family planning and they added that since young people now had the right to vote at 18, they 'trust young people to show in their personal behaviour and sexual morality the same degree of responsibility'.[29]

The discussion over the Health (Family Planning)(Amendment) Bill, 1985 took five days of parliamentary time, and the issue polarised opinion for three weeks at the most, but it gave the state an opportunity to make a clear dividing line between its prerogatives and the Church's. The vote of the second reading, which was crucial as Desmond announced that the bill would not be amended, took place on 20 February 1985, the very day when, ironically, Margaret Thatcher, the British Prime Minister, proclaimed in Washington the determination of the Unionists in Northern Ireland not to be incorporated in what they saw as a theocratic state. Of course, the declarations of certain bishops and priests confirmed the impression the Unionists had that the Catholic Church was hostile to a pluralist society. The government imposed the whip, so that all members of the Fine Gael and Labour parliamentary groups had to vote in favour of the bill – a somewhat cavalier way to ensure victory, but a most pragmatic one. All Fianna Fáil deputies had to vote No, whatever their personal convictions. Dissident TDs on either side prepared themselves to be temporarily excluded from their parliamentary groups, and consequently to lose influence within them. Three Fine Gael and two Labour deputies voted against their respective parties. Dr John O'Connell who tried hard but unsuccessfully to liberalise the contraception laws, notably in 1972 with Dr Noël Browne, and who felt that the 1979 law did not go far enough, because he was recently accepted in the Fianna Fáil fold, found himself obliged to vote against Desmond's bill! Desmond O'Malley was excluded from Fianna Fáil after the vote for 'conduct unbecoming', as he was already excluded from the parliamentary group in May 1984 for expressing his disagreement with Haughey about Northern Ireland, and this extreme disciplinary measure was the only recourse left. He made an historic speech, a passionate plea for the separation of Church and state, for the supremacy of Parliament and for a radical republicanism.[30] It is still considered to be one of the most admirable contributions to the Dáil, preceding by a few weeks his founding a new party, the Progressive Democrats, based on such principles. However, about contraception, he said: 'at present the availability of contraceptives is probably far wider and less supervised than will be the case if the Bill is passed. For that reason I find it very difficult in conscience to put forward any opposition to the Bill.'[31] He seemed worried, like many others, about the subsequent legalisation of abortion and the advent of promiscuity.

Is it possible to see the outcome as a victory for the government and for the liberal forces of change when the vote in favour of Desmond's law was so narrow: 83 votes to 80? The Taoiseach declared that it was a victory for the state, and it is true that it was the first law (excluding the Intoxicating Liquor Act, 1960, which provided for the opening of pubs on Sundays at 12.30), to be adopted with the opposition of the bishops. In fact, Desmond's law was the first piece of legislation relative to an issue, traditionally of the Church's remit, which was adopted without first consulting it.[32] The important thing was that the law was adopted at all, and the use of contraception marginally liberalised. But the Church was going to win the next 'round' the following week with the Eileen Flynn case.

Eileen Flynn had been sacked from the school where she taught because she lived with a married but separated man and his two children, and she was expecting their own. This was totally unacceptable on the part of somebody who had the responsibility of educating children in solid Catholic values. Judge Costello confirmed the religious authorities' decision, which prompted *The Irish Times* to declare in its editorial of 11 March that Dr McNamara's policy was 'to preserve the Catholic culture and ethos in classrooms and bedrooms'.

Without straying too far from our subject, it is necessary to place the vote on the contraception law in context, as it took place against a background of more or less sordid cases, for it coincided not only with the Eileen Flynn case, but also with the Kerry babies case, an inquiry that lasted 17 weeks after two newborn babies were found dead within 100 km of each other. The vote also followed by a few months the death of Ann Lovett, a 15-year-old a schoolgirl, who died after giving birth to a stillborn baby. These were extreme cases, tragedies which periodically rock Ireland and shatter convictions the Irish hold dearly. Whatever the Catholic Church says, whatever God-fearing groups say, 'these things' happen, with or without permissive legislation, and victims feel driven to the brink because they have betrayed the prevailing ethics or feel unable to conform. The right to life of the unborn was written into the Constitution two years earlier, yet the death of viable babies did not evoke outbursts as passionate as that campaign had been.

Family planning legislation was not quite yet in keeping with public mores and thinking. On 26 February 1991, Judge Hanrahan at the Dublin Circuit Court ruled against the IFPA, this time accused of unlawfully selling condoms to a police inspector at the counter it ran in the Virgin Megastore in Dublin (a complaint lodged by an anonymous group). The Health Care Foundation, established by Virgin chief executive, Richard Branson, to fight the spread of AIDS, leased an area in the store to the IFPA. The fine imposed was paid by the rock band U2, as they felt 'the IFPA have much more important things to be doing than turning up in court'.[33] *The Irish Times* exhorted in its editorial of 27 February:

> It is difficult to avoid the suspicion that the real reason or the imposition of restrictions on the sale of condoms in Ireland is an attempt to impose some kind of authoritarian control on sexual activity.... It is now up to the Government to ensure that sense and good health prevail over sectarianism and bad law.

The government was also under pressure from the other parties to review the family planning legislation, in order to increase the number of outlets selling condoms in an all-out effort to stop the spread of AIDS, or as the Fine Gael spokesperson for Health, Richard Bruton, said, 'face up to the realities of life in Ireland in the 1990's'. And this is also what chemists did: whereas only 20–5 per cent of them sold condoms in 1985, the figure was 45 per cent in 1986, 70 per cent in 1987 and about 80 per cent in 1988. The prophylactic dimension of condoms certainly encouraged some to stock them, an importer thought: 'Irish chemists have been influenced by the AIDS scare. It has added the dimension of health protection to the condom and has encouraged those who might have otherwise have been more reluctant to stock them.'[34] Five companies distributed condoms to 900 chemists and to the 15 family planning clinics in the country. The Department of Health granted nine licences to import 18 million condoms in 1988; in 1989, the figure was 51 million owing to the increase in the demand caused by the AIDS campaign organised that year by the government. But the government was not unanimously in favour of change (there was now a Fianna Fáil–PD coalition government in power and the Taoiseach was Charles Haughey).

However, it seemed that once more a legal judgment showed the way, signalling that it was time to act. The Taoiseach committed himself quite explicitly two days after the judgment, during a radio interview: 'We will be coming to a decision very soon on dealing with legislation that has now become very unsatisfactory and outdated. ... We will certainly be amending the law to bring it more into line with the realities of today.' The Primate of the Catholic Church, Cardinal Cahal Daly, warned that a change in the law would have profound implications for the moral quality of life in Ireland, adding, 'it is not really a question of Church versus State. It's a question of legislators respecting the moral convictions to which people adhere and which are influenced by their membership of the Church.' He added that he did not agree with the common perception that the election of Mary Robinson to the presidency in November 1990 proved that the Irish wanted the legislation dealing with contraception, divorce and homosexuality to be liberalised. Whatever the case may be, Haughey seemed eager to modernise his party which should be more open to liberal opinion, seeing its losses in the last general election and the resounding defeat of its candidate in the presidential election. One knows of his previous stand on socio-moral issues, his 'Irish solutions', but he himself admitted that the situation had changed since the 1970s, the AIDS crisis not being one of the lesser symptoms. As *The Irish Times* remarked on 8 March, 'this has led to a change of attitude within FF, that most pragmatic of parties: It is now as concerned with keeping or gaining the support of more liberal urban voters as with maintaining that of its traditional rural backers, with their greater openness to the Church's teaching.' As on the issue of contraception, people on the whole tended to follow their own conscience to suit their own lifestyles, 'this Government can feel safe in pressing ahead with plans to make condoms more readily available to the public – irrespective of Dr Daly's view that such moves would have profound implications for the moral quality of life here.' Having said that, Haughey's proposal to lower the age at which contraceptives could be bought from 18 to 16 caused such disquiet within the parliamentary group that this became something to be considered only. Fianna Fáil had not changed that much! But Archbishop Desmond Connell expressed his surprise and his disappointment at the 'conversion' of the Taoiseach: he found 'extraordinary that no political party in the country is prepared to defend what so many people regard as fundamental values of family life.'[35]

Not everybody in Fianna Fáil had abandoned traditional values. The Minister for Health, Dr O'Hanlon, had said, after the initial IFPA ruling in 1990, that the current law on condoms matched demand and no change was necessary. In the Seanad, in March 1991, admitting the role that condoms play in the prevention of AIDS and other STDs, he concluded that 'the most effective way of avoiding transmission of these viruses is to stay with one faithful partner and remain faithful to that partner.' The Minister for Employment, Bertie Ahern, said in an interview that after a series of meetings with the Fianna Fáil delegates of his constituency, he doubted that it was a good idea, politically or morally, to allow youngsters of 16 to buy condoms. At this juncture, half a dozen bishops expressed very strong views on this relatively minor change to an existing law, proclaiming the moral law once more and alerting their flock. Such virulence can be accounted for by the arrival to the primatial archbishoprics of Dublin and Armagh of two ultra-conservatives, Dr O'Connell and Cardinal Daly whose uncompromising words gave the go-ahead to other conservative bishops such as Drs Newman and Comiskey. Not only worried about the consequences on young people of the wider availability of contraceptives, they were also worried by the fact that 'what the bishops saw as the liberal and secularist agenda ushered in by Mary Robinson's presidential victory, and beginning to be espoused by Fianna Fáil, was gathering momentum.'[36]

The other churches were more realistic and pragmatic: Methodist Rev. Graham Hamilton expressed his surprise that condoms should be held responsible for AIDS, and added that 'the only thing we can say to young people who do not necessarily accept the Christian position on marriage and who will be sexually active is that if they are going to be sexually active then they at least ought to...practise safe sex using a condom.'[37] Rev. David Bruce, of the Presbyterian Church, found

> puzzling the distinction drawn by some between 'artificial' and 'natural' methods of contraception, as if one were somehow more morally acceptable than the other....Regarding the provision of condoms in particular, their prophylactic use has tragically become much more pertinent in recent years....Let us pray, therefore, that what is eventually proposed and legislated for may not be an Irish

solution to an Irish solution, but a very realistic solution to a global problem.[38]

As the right to buy condoms at the age of 16 did not arouse much enthusiasm in the party rank and file (and the possibility of installing vending machines was not even discussed, excluded as it was as a matter of course), a compromise had to be found, within Fianna Fáil, and within the Fianna Fáil–PD coalition, since Haughey was adamant that the final decision would be taken by the whole government. Cynics, like Proinsias de Rossa, leader of the Workers' Party, noticed that 'Fianna Fáil's flirtation with liberal values has been one of the shortest political romances on record. It was not even a nine day wonder, lasting less than a week. At the first indication of rumblings from the backbenches and the rustling of episcopal robes, the Taoiseach is beating a hasty retreat back to the conservative Fianna Fáil position.'[39] On 14 March, the Fianna Fáil parliamentary group gave leave to the Minister for Health to produce a restrictive law, which would not allow the sale of condoms through vending machines, nor would it reduce the legal age at which they could be bought to 16. The IFPA was dismayed: a health issue had become a political battle.

As for public opinion, it seemed to have evolved faster than Fianna Fáil, judging by an opinion poll published in *The Irish Independent* on 14 March. Out of a sample of 1,057 people, 57 per cent were in favour of condoms being more widely available (38 per cent and against), and 53 per cent were in favour of 16-year-olds being allowed to buy them (41 per cent against). These results seemed to prove that being a practising Catholic did not necessarily imply a strict adherence to the line taken by the hierarchy on contraception in general, and on the availability of condoms in particular. A study, undertaken by the sociologist Fr Micheál Mac Gréil and published a few weeks earlier, revealed that 81.6 per cent of the Catholics questioned went to mass every week, but 52 per cent of the sample did not allow their religious beliefs to have 'a great deal of influence' on their political ideas. This figure of nearly 82 per cent marked a drop of 5 per cent since 1984 when the corresponding figure was 87 per cent, and 9 per cent since 1974 when it was 91 per cent.[40] Ireland's extraordinary level of mass-going would continue to dip, since an MRBI survey found in 1996 that only 66 per cent of those polled (of whom, 92 per cent were Catholic, a proportion close to the 1991 census) said they attended mass at least once a week, with the corollary consequence that only 21 per cent of

Catholics said they followed the teaching of their Church when making 'serious moral decisions'.[41]

O'Hanlon's bill was finally published in August 1991: the legal age to buy condoms would be lowered to 17, and the eight Health Boards would decide which outlets were locally allowed to sell them – a responsibility they immediately rejected. It had been made clear since 1979 that they wanted to have as little as possible to do with the marketing of contraceptives. In any case, what with the opposition encountered and a ministerial reshuffle in November 1991, the bill was shelved. The new Minister for Health, Mary O'Rourke (Fianna Fáil), seemed determined to attack the AIDS problem head-on, since it was inexorably invading Ireland, and was not confined to homosexuals and drug-users (the annual increase rate of AIDS among heterosexuals was 50 per cent higher than in Britain). But a second ministerial reshuffle occurred, and Dr John O'Connell replaced her.

From the outset, O'Connell declared that new legislation on condoms in the context of the fight against AIDS would be one of his priorities: since the introduction of serology tests in Ireland in 1985, 1,250 people had been found to be HIV-positive, 276 had AIDS, and 114 had already died. Also, the Health Boards would not be involved in the sale of condoms; he personally was in favour of sales through vending machines. Moreover he intended to encourage hospitals to perform female sterilisations and expressed the hope of seeing fewer representatives of the Catholic Church on the management boards of hospitals which received 98 per cent of their funding from the state. After a long gestation period, the new Health (Family Planning) Amendment Bill, 1992, was published on 1 July. Whereas under the 1991 bill condoms and spermicides would have been widely available without prescription, the 1992 bill would concern itself with condoms only. Spermicides, which are contraceptives, not prophylactics, would from now on be considered as 'medical preparations'. Since the expression would now include 'any drug or preparation intended to prevent pregnancy', the pill too would be considered as a medical preparation, and would thus be excluded from the legislation on contraceptives! Medical preparations, unlike contraceptives, were part of the GMS and were supplied free to those with a Medical Card. The irony that the pill was no longer considered as a contraceptive went unnoticed! the reason being that the pill was already supplied free to disadvantaged people since it was implicitly understood by all concerned (the patient, the doctor and the GMS) that it was prescribed as a cycle regulator! In fact, somebody at the GMS (Payments) Board drew our attention to the fact that doctors did not have to specify the reason for their prescriptions, and Dr Waters pointed out to us that most doctors did not know that the pill could only be prescribed as a cycle regulator![42]

The new law would not change anything in daily practice, but it is still important to point out this official regularisation. Anybody over the age of 17 could now buy any contraceptive, but anybody younger would have to be married or obtain a prescription to do so. The Health Boards would not have to decide which outlet was allowed to sell condoms, as any outlet not expressly excluded in the law could sell them. The excluded places were schools, sport centres, youth centres, stalls and vending machines. Reading the parliamentary debates on this bill reveals a major difference with the reading of the discussions pertaining to the 1979 and 1985 bills: it takes considerably less time! For example, the second reading took place on 8 July, every deputy being limited to 15 minutes, some even had to share their speaking time with another TD (the only woman who spoke, Nuala Fennell, had just five minutes). The final readings took place the following day, at the end of which the law was passed in the Dáil by 67 votes to 56. The Minister was accused of rushing things through so that opposition could not be organised, but, having said that, there was a general consensus within the Dáil. In fact, the main objections to O'Connell's bill were about the ban on vending machines, and the legal age of 17. But would a majority of TDs have followed him if he had gone further in the liberalisation of the 1979 and 1985 laws? Generally speaking, this bill was more progressive than O'Hanlon's, but the fact that the legal age for buying condoms was now the same as the heterosexual age of consent (there was no homosexual age of consent, since it was still a criminal activity in 1992) did not take into account the fact that within ten years, between 1981 and 1990, 5,518 babies were born to single mothers aged 17 and under. The fact that vending machines were banned was, according to some TDs, unjustifiable if most outlets were now allowed to stock and sell them. Pubs and discos already applied a minimum age, 18 or even 21, so why not install vending machines in their toilets? (A number of them already had, as part of of a 'Condom Sense' campaign.) The Minister admitted being in favour of such a measure, but felt obliged to 'strike a balance' to respect public opinion which did not seem ready to accept the introduction of such devices in public places. He hoped that 'if circumstances and attitudes change,... we will be bringing in a Bill to meet the changed needs.'[43] In the Seanad, he went as far as saying that 'in a year or two circumstances may change and we may have to introduce another Bill.'[44] The question then was: were people prepared to order a packet a condoms with their pint of beer? Dr O'Connell thought that

> maybe it is a good idea that we ask people to go up and ask for them; there is nothing disgraceful, nothing wrong, nothing sinful, nothing morally wrong in sexually active people asking for condoms.... Maybe the best thing we have ever done is to ask people to do this, to go and ask for condoms. We have come a long way from the time of the debate on the 1985 Bill. We would be appalled today if the 1979 Bill were brought in but it met the needs of the time. The 1985 [Bill] followed.[45]

It is interesting to note that none of the TDs who spoke in the debate were in favour of the ban on vending machines nor of a minimum legal age. Richard Bruton wondered: 'Who are the people who are telling the Minister not to make changes? There are none in the House this evening that I can detect. Where are they? The Minister is out of touch with what is happening in the country and around him in the House.'[46]

An important amendment had been introduced by the Minister himself on 9 July: he would have to see to the setting up of a comprehensive service of family planning, giving due recognition to the pioneering work of the family planning clinics. He also accepted an amendment whereby state grants would not be destined solely to research in natural family planning, something de Rossa called 'a quiet revolution in terms of attitudes to contraception.... This is a watershed in our dealings with this extremely controversial issue.'[47] But the Minister rejected the amendments concerning the legal age and the legalisation of vending machines. Brendan Howlin, Labour, tabled 21 of these, which augured well since he would be the next Minister for Health. An independent Senator, Brendan Ryan, expressed incomprehension: 'I cannot understand how it is morally superior not to have vending machines but hopefully to have condoms freely available on the shelves of every supermarket in the State.'[48] In fact, very few supermarket chains agreed to sell condoms, probably due to concerns about the legal age, which would not be easily enforceable, and which might lead to them being prosecuted.

Reading the Seanad debates on the issue is interesting (all bills are discussed and voted upon in the Seanad before being signed by the President; some bills originate there) not just because the arguments opposing the bill were similar to those in the Dáil, but also because the debate was dominated by David Norris, a well-known homosexual. As Brendan Howlin had already noted, the definition of contraceptives included condoms (but excluded the pill), which seemed to contradict the legislators' main objective which was to fight a deadly disease! David Norris noted that homosexuals do not use condoms to prevent a pregnancy, but to prevent the spread of an infection. Indeed, some condoms are designed solely with this in mind (For example the brand 'Mates'). The question remained whether such brands were covered by the law. But what nobody could get a government minister to say or to insert in a law was the fact that condoms were used by homosexuals to protect themselves against AIDS, because homosexuality was a criminal activity in Ireland. This explains that the very title of the bill is marked with this refusal to call things by their proper name: it was not about planning a family, any more that it had been in 1979, but about not having one for some, and protecting themselves from disease for others. The Catholic hierarchy issued a statement only when the law was passed. This said that 'sexual intercourse outside marriage is an abuse of sex and is in itself sinful', and that 'no campaign to limit the spread of AIDS can succeed unless it is based on sound moral principles.' They concluded, in more qualified terms than in 1985, that: 'there are many things which are sinful and which the law cannot reasonably be expected to prohibit. Neither can the law make what is morally wrong become right.'

A few months later, on 20 November 1992, Senator David Norris officially opened the first condom shop in Dublin, Condom Power, which stocked 500 different sorts of condoms. That same month, the government fell and a general election took place on 25 November 1992, the same day as the three referendums on abortion. As seen previously, Labour emerged victorious, which is an important development in our context as the party was firmly on the 'liberal' wing when it came to socio-sexual questions. Even though the election resulted in a coalition government between Fianna Fáil and Labour, radical changes in this area could be expected. The new Minister for Health was Brendan Howlin. One notes with the benefit of hindsight that such TDs as Barry Desmond, John O'Connell and Brendan Howlin, who had been vocal in Parliament on the issue of contraception since the early 1970s, eventually got the opportunity to act in their capacity as Minister for Health. Howlin got the most elbow room, but the 'spadework' spanned some 20 years. He launched a national campaign against AIDS on 24 May 1993, and one of the first initiatives was to liberalise the 1992 law. Thus fell the last barriers bringing the law into line with the sexual reality in Ireland, and with other EC countries which all allowed the sale of condoms through vending machines. This followed the publication in February of the results of a Durex survey, which revealed that the condom was the most popular contraceptive method in Ireland (28 per cent of those surveyed with 24 per cent using the pill). Sixty-one per cent of the sample thought condoms should be sold through vending machines. According to the London Rubber Company, makers of Durex, 5.8 million condoms were sold in Ireland in 1992, and while this kind of figure is not unusual in other Western countries, in Ireland, it takes one by surprise![49]

The second initiative was a media campaign aimed at encouraging people to use condoms. A series of seven spot advertisements were broadcast, whose message was: 'Protect yourself, use a condom'. Objectively, one has to say that these ads did not express *joie de vivre*, let alone debauchery. They aimed more at shocking than pleasing: for example, one of the personalities featured concluded with the admonishment: 'Never sleep with a man who's prepared to kill you'. The latest official figures on AIDS were now: 341 cases of full-blown AIDS, 1,368 HIV-positive and 150 dead. Within one year, seropositivity had increased by 9 per cent among drug-users, 17 per cent among homosexuals and 20 per cent among heterosexuals.

As for the new law, the Health (Family Planning) (Amendment) Bill, 1993, it was, in Howlin's own words, 'an historic bill and closes a chapter which it has taken a long time to close.'[50] The definition of contraceptives would now exclude condoms, which could be bought with no minimum legal age. Condom vending machines could be installed in all public places, with the Minister for Health retaining the right to ban them in places he deemed 'inappropriate', including secondary schools (even though a recent study on 2,000 pupils in their final year at secondary school, in the Munster region showed that one pupil in four already had sexual relations). Restrictions concerning import and manufacturing licences would be withdrawn, and advertising would be allowed (in shop windows, for example). Rarely had any bill of such nature provoked so few adverse reactions! On 2 June, the spokesperson of the Catholic hierarchy repeated verbatim the same declaration as a year earlier. Again a few readers expressed indignation in the letters page of their daily papers. But the law was adopted without a vote, on 3 June 1993, after a $4^1/_2$ hour debate. The spokespersons for Health of the other three major parties gave their support to the Minister. Only three TDs voiced opposition. With a 37-seat majority, the government was insulated from pressure groups. It could be argued that the smooth adoption of this law was not entirely due to the so-called sea-change in Irish society, but that the AIDS threat and its spread accelerated the process. After all, condoms are not considered contraceptives, but as essential devices to protect public health, and as such are available everywhere to everybody. This was noted by a number of deputies, including Alan Dukes, of Fine Gael: 'another illustration of the contortions of thought that have been brought to this issue year after year.'[51] As Charles Flanagan, Fine Gael spokesperson for Health, noted, a comprehensive family planning service was still lacking, its provision less than uniform in maternity hospitals, and sterilisation services varied greatly throughout the state.[52] It could well be that AIDS, like the McGee case, or the IFPA case to a lesser extent, forced the hand of legislators, so to speak, and allowed for the recognition, in fits and starts it has to be said, of the right that Irish citizens have to disengage their sexuality from a particularly constraining moral interdict. There were still a few moralising aspects to this legislation, including the fact that contraceptives were not free to the disadvantaged as contraceptives, and that sterilisation was not considered as contraception but as a therapeutic operation. The question of sterilisation is another good case in point and is worth examining.

A LEGAL BUT DISORDERLY FORM OF CONTRACEPTION: STERILISATION

What then was the situation regarding sterilisation, an operation mentioned throughout the years during the debates on contraception, but never acknowledged as such? The most striking thing about sterilisation is that the state never tried to regulate its practice nor ban it. Nothing in its laws precludes sterilisation, as it relied on doctors and the Catholic Church for that. But, as Dr David Nowlan once, remarked it could be because legislators did not think of it in 1935![53] When the question was discussed by the Council of Europe, with the adoption of resolution 75–29, the Irish representative abstained. This resolution recommended that sterilisation for the purpose of family planning be made available by health services in member states. In keeping with the legislators' disinterest, Brendan Corish, Tanaiste and Minister for Health in 1975 when the resolution was adopted, said that 'he didn't remember anything about it'.[54]

If the state had not really given the question a thought, the Catholic Church had, and was quite clear about it: this surgical operation aimed at preventing procreation is forbidden as it contravenes the moral order. A Vatican decree in 1940 stated that: 'Any direct sterilisation, whether of man or woman, whether perpetual or temporary, is forbidden by the law of nature.'[55] Paul VI, in *Humanae Vitae*, in 1968, remarked it was an intrinsic disorder. In fact, the Catholic Church opposes sterilisation even more virulently than it does contraception, because it is effectively irreversible.[56] In Ireland, the practice was condemned several times, notably in the publication of the ethics code of Archbishop Ryan, and the episcopal pastoral, *Love is for Life*. Emily O'Reilly relates how Professor Bonnar called, at an Irish Nurses Organisation Conference in March 1977, for the establishment of ethics committees in all Irish hospitals 'to design and monitor hospital policies in contraception, sterilisation and other questions of ethical or moral concern', ensuring that the Catholic ethics would prevail in hospitals, particularly in gynaecology, obstetrics and birth control.[57] The social climate was such that it was foreseen that women would soon be clamouring for contraception, sterilisation and other morally objectionable facilities. In December 1978, the Archbishop of Dublin, Dr Ryan, published the ethical code whereby Catholic-run hospitals should put together these committees.[58] This set of guidelines greatly influenced the way these hospitals were run and the way staff worked, even though it largely legitimised what was already in place. Therapeutic sterilisations appeared to be allowed, but in reality,

> in some cases, it is difficult to get the cooperation of nurses and other hospital staff, but mainly the absence of this essential service is a result of hospital ethical committee rulings. All these committees, right throughout the country, have placed an embargo on tubal ligation, reflecting the Archbishop's wishes.[59]

A consultant had to get the approval of the ethics committee to carry out a sterilisation, and this is still the case in private Catholic hospitals. The committees would typically include members of the Catholic clergy, local councillors and medical staff. The latter received even more explicit instructions from the Catholic bishops through *Love is for Life*, published in 1985, and the following is worth quoting for its level of argumentation:

> When surgical sterilisation was practised in Nazi Germany some 50 years ago, it aroused general disgust and revulsion. It is surely a sign of moral decline that now the same operation is widely regarded as morally acceptable and even socially 'progressive'. It was of course

predictable that the propaganda for contraceptives, and especially for the contraceptive pill, should lead to acceptance of sterilisation.... This teaching [of the Catholic Church] declares that any form of sterilisation, whose direct and immediate and intended effect is to render the sexual faculty incapable of procreation, is direct sterilisation, and as such is absolutely forbidden according to the doctrine of the Church. Catholic hospitals may not provide facilities for such operations. Catholic medical personnel may not co-operate with them.[60]

Such peremptory statements account for the insistence of the Board of the Adelaide Hospital to see its ethos preserved when it was relocated in the new regional hospital planned in Tallaght at the beginning of the 1990s. As the only Protestant teaching hospital in the state, it was worried that 'its particular denominational ethos' would not be represented in the new Board (because of a merger with another two hospitals). What then is the 'Protestant ethos' in the medical world? In such a hospital, 'the privacy of the relationship between patient and doctor' was respected, and procedures such as sterilisation and genetic counselling involving methods of contraception were available in the best interests of the patient. The Protestant churches do not draw a distinction between what is medically necessary and what is a conscientious decision, nor between what is irreversible contraception and continuous contraception:

Decisions on family planning are the responsibility of each married couple, in ways that are mutually acceptable to husband and wife in Christian conscience. Vasectomy differs from other forms of family planning in that like tubal ligation it must be regarded as irreversible so the consequences should be carefully considered. A responsible decision to use permanent methods of contraception (e.g. vasectomy) differs little in principle from a decision not to have further children and to use other forms of contraception continuously.[61]

Having said that, a number of people are sterilised in Ireland (others go to Britain). As far as male sterilisation, or vasectomy, is concerned, things are straightforward. The state allows family planning clinics to perform them and it is a simple operation, lasting some 15 minutes. The first vasectomy was performed in Ireland in February 1974 by Dr Andrew Rynne, in the IFPA Mountjoy clinic, and he went on performing them in Clane and Dublin.[62] Only 12 per cent of vasectomies are performed in hospital under general anaesthetic, the others are done in family planning clinics or at the doctor's surgery. The operation costs around £130, and most (79 per cent) do not get any financial support from the Health Boards. According to the IFPA figures, 1 per cent of contraceptive users choose sterilisation, the vast majority of them being men. There were 3,130 vasectomies in 1992, a 66 per cent increase in six years from the 1986 estimate (1,980 vasectomies): Presenting the results of his study, for which he contacted all the hospitals and family planning clinics in Ireland, Dr John O'Keeffe comments:

> Vasectomy is a very reliable, cost-effective and usually safe method of family planning. It is of course a major decision to make but one which is increasingly requested in Ireland today.... With this survey we have a clearer picture of the place of vasectomy within the contraceptive services on offer in Ireland today.... [63]

Research conducted by Dr Deborah Orr in the late 1980s showed that couples seeking vasectomy were middle-class, married for an average of 11.3 years with 3.4 children, and aged between 30 and 39.[64]

More men are sterilised in Ireland than women, the ratio being 3:2. Djinn Gallagher reports that 'according to the latest figures available, Ireland is the only country in the world which performs more vasectomies than tubal ligations.'[65] Despite the absence of legal restrictions, female sterilisation has always been more difficult to obtain, owing to the fact it is a more complex operation than a vasectomy, requiring a general anaesthetic and a three-day stay in hospital (for a laparotomy). But, as Dr Rynne declared in 1982, 'most hospitals will not perform tubal ligations for contraceptive purposes, and many will object to them even for therapeutic reasons, even though, in many cases, the patient's health may be threatened by a further pregnancy.' The first Irish doctor to perform female sterilisations was Dr George Henry, then president of the medical committee of the IFPA, in the Adelaide hospital where he was a consultant gynaecologist. It is reported that he performed 100 sterilisations in 15 months.[66] Another doctor, Dr Edgar Ritchie, started providing the service in 1972 in Cork, at the Victoria Hospital, another establishment which had no objections. In fact, much depended on the hospitals where the consultants practised. When Dr Henry became Master of the Rotunda in Dublin, he only supervised 31 in one year, because of the opposition of the nursing staff. Dr Solomons admitted that he was in no position to perform many tubal ligations because of the nurses' ethical objections:

Whether or not a doctor was able to perform this operation was a lottery, depending on the hospital in which one worked. The matron and the theatre sisters in Baggot Street Hospital came up with a solution. 'Ask the parish priest', they said. 'if he approves we'll have no objection and we'll get two nurses who are willing to assist you.' It was a different story at Mercer's Hospital, where the otherwise cooperative theatre sister stated, 'you are not going to do that in my theatre.'[67]

In 1985, a motion to make sterilisation 'readily available' to Irish women was defeated at the AGM of the Irish Nurses Organisation by 65 votes to 30, with eight abstentions. The motion had been tabled by a nurse who believed there was a demand for the service in Ireland, since in 1984, about 1,200 sterilisations were performed, including 50 per cent at the Whitethorn clinic. This clinic deserves more than a passing mention because of the pioneering work done by its director, Dr Gerry Waters, and of his flamboyant personality, particularly in his altercations with the pro-life movement. The Whitethorn clinic was the first private clinic of its kind, that is, one that specialised in sterilisations. This somewhat luxurious establishment was opened in September 1984 in Celbridge, near Dublin, and offered tubal ligations, performed twice a week by a renowned Harley Street gynaecologist who commuted between London and Celbridge. On the first day, the women occupying the 12 beds said they were delighted they did not have to go to England or wait 12 months for a bed at the Victoria Hospital.[68] The Whitethorn clinic already had a 200-name waiting-list. The operation then cost £250, and Dr Waters had set up an ethics committee comprising an anaesthetist, the English gynaecologist, a nurse and himself, in order to be seen to follow the rules. The patients had to be over 30 and bring with them the written consent of their husbands (the same was true of vasectomy candidates), a prerequisite later dropped. Out of the first 12 patients, two required the operation for medical reasons, the others because they did not want any more children. Dr Waters felt that his initiative would contribute to the reduction in abortions performed in Britain by eliminating the risk of undesired pregnancies since '18 per cent of the women who go to England for abortions are married women who would be sterilised if they could.'[69] Eighteen months later, 800 women had been sterilised in his clinic, an average of 45 a month. Some statistics were then published: 87.8 per cent of these women were Catholic, 8.6 per cent belonged to one of the Protestant churches, the others had no religion or were not Christian;

95 per cent were married, four were single, two divorced and 24 separated.[70] To those who expressed surprise at the lack of opposition to the opening of such a clinic, he would reply that he had not announced its *raison d'être* until late during construction! His colleague, Dr Rynne, got into more trouble with an opponent of sterilisation, which caused delays in the opening of his own clinic, which was going to perform tubal ligations among other services. But the clinic, also near Dublin, in Clane, eventually opened in October 1985, and it is actually there that *in vitro* fertilisation techniques were developed for the first time in Ireland in 1987.

Another pioneer was Dr Michael Mylotte who performed some 100 sterilisations a year in the Galway Regional Hospital. This prompted the Archbishop of Galway, Dr Eamonn Casey, to send a letter in August 1985 to the doctors in the area, reminding them that sterilisation was 'repugnant to Christian teaching'. When Dr Mylotte remarked that, as a gynaecologist providing a service for people with medical and social problems and a Catholic, he did not agree with the Church's stand, 'almost at once, and as if by coincidence, there were calls for an ethical committee to be set up at the hospital.'[71] Shortly afterwards, the same bishop oversaw the sale of a private hospital to a group of doctors on the written condition that they would not perform sterilisations there. Public opinion, still reeling in the aftermath of the abortion referendum, did not grasp the implications of these ethics committees, and sterilisation remained a non-issue.

To overcome the barrage set up by the ethics committees, consultants sometimes had recourse to drastic solutions to their patients' problems: they performed hysterectomies, i.e. the removal of the uterus, on women who would only have required tubal ligation. This is a major operation, but easier to justify, by saying there was a prolapse of the womb for example. Such a trend is difficult to quantify, or even substantiate. One can only go by the declarations of a number of doctors over the years. It was corroborated during a conversation the author had with a radiologist, recently arrived from England, to work in a Catholic hospital in Cork. She was struck by the high proportion of women she X-rayed whose uterus had been removed. She understood the 'therapeutic indication' given to hysterectomy in Ireland by talking with these women. In 1988, 3,069 women had their wombs removed in general hospitals (excluding maternity hospitals), 1,934 in 1990.[72]

Another striking feature relative to sterilisation is the fact that most tubal ligations were performed in hospitals and clinics around the country, and not in Dublin, a fact recorded by the Second Commission on the Status of Women: 'The availability of sterilisation is piecemeal, and mainly outside the Dublin area.'[73] In 1991, for example, approximately 1,745 sterilisations were performed in state-funded hospitals (including 438 at the Victoria Hospital, Cork, 400 at University Hospital, Galway, 350 at the Adelaide in Dublin, 334 at the Rotunda), and 370 in the Whitethorn and Clane clinics.[74] Private clinics developed this service as it was so difficult to obtain it in public hospitals. Since the beginning of the 1990s, a liberalisation in the Dublin hospitals has begun to redress the balance, a fact observed by Maria O'Sullivan in the course of her research on sterilisation: 'The development of private clinics arose in the absence of a public service. This led to a situation whereby sterilisation was more freely available in the provinces than in Dublin. It was these developments in the provinces, one of my interviewees explained, which forced the liberalisation of the service in Dublin.'[75] Consultants came to resent the interference of the ethics committees in their privileged relationship with their patients. Dolores Dooley, a lecturer in medical ethics at University College Cork, notes that consultants could not agree to the fact that their decisions, taken in conjunction with their patients, had to be submitted to a committee whose medical competence they did not necessarily recognise. 'They had a gradual perception of their autonomy. The committees were seen as interfering with the integrity of the relationship between the woman and her doctor.'[76]

Over time the main hospitals have issued new guidelines, doing away with ethics committees in many cases. For example, a recent report of the Eastern Health Board (which covers the Dublin area) mentions that out of nine hospitals surveyed, only one, the Meath Hospital, still requires the approval of an ethics committee before a sterilisation can be performed. Having said that, individual cases are 'reviewed by the Master' in the Coombe and Holles Street Hospitals.[77] In 1991, only 58 sterilisations were performed in the Coombe, as opposed to 225 in 1992, once the new guidelines were in force, a four-fold increase. In the Holles Street National Maternity Hospital, it was decided, also in 1992, that women could be sterilised without reference to an ethics committee. The new guidelines stated that 'the hospital considers that tubal ligation may be appropriate for some women'. Only ten sterilisations were performed in 1991 in that hospital, as opposed to some 400 in the Adelaide, a Protestant establishment. What is not clear is whether the final decision is left to the woman, or if the consultant or even the Master of the hospital has not taken over the prerogative of the

ethics committee. If some criteria are to be applied, 'these criteria have
the denigrating consequence of defining sterilisation as necessary for
curing or alleviating a pathology. Sterilisation is not seen a as an
opportunity to allow women to exercise choice.'[78] The insistence that
the husband or partner must consent, that the woman should be over
35 and have children betrays pro-natalist tendencies rather than an
acknowledgement of the right to self-determination. The woman's
decision is thus no more than a request.

At present, it can be said that if nearly 30 public hospitals perform
sterilisations, according to the Department of Health, eight of them
apply a lot of restrictions. The document *Family Planning Policy –
Guidelines for Health Boards*, issued by the Department of Health,
lists the hospitals offering tubal ligation, which is something the
Department of Health refused to do in the 1980s, for fear that 'ethical
committees would spring up all over the place. Or, as one consultant
put it, "he's [the Minister for Health, then Barry Desmond] afraid of
the bishops coming down and queering the pitch." '[79] A sure sign of
the times, Dr Waters closed his clinic in December 1995, after 11 years,
because the need for such a specialised clinic had disappeared with the
hospitals offering the service.

As far as sterilisation is concerned, as a permanent and irreversible
form of contraception, the ban did not come from the law or the
meddling of the state in the area of medical practice, but from the
Catholic Church, from which medical staff took over. It did not necessarily mean it would be any easier to see the end of it, but at least it left
room for individual initiatives. As for the people, they seem to endorse
sterilisation. A survey, *Women and Health Care in Ireland*, commissioned by the National Maternity Hospital, Dublin, was published in
1996 by the Economic and Social Research Institute. It showed that 87
per cent of urban women and 74 per cent in rural areas support the
availability of male and female sterilisation. There still remained the
obvious social discrimination since only women who could afford
the £500 a sterilisation cost could avail themselves of it.

In the area of contraception, in its temporary or permanent forms,
the last legal and moral obstacles disappeared with the 1993 law, but it
was necessary to eradicate the last socio-economical obstacles by
giving wider access to contraception to the less well-off, in terms of
information or cost. Since the pill could be prescribed free of charge, it
was a matter of extending this to other contraceptives, so that patients
would be given a wider choice, which might be medically desirable.
The Department of Health estimated that 280,000 women aged

between 16 and 55 were covered by the GMS.[80] It was hardly surprising that the new government in late 1994, in which Labour and Democratic Left had seats, would include family planning in its programme. The Minister for Health, Michael Noonan, announced in March 1995 that sterilisation, male and female, and other methods of contraception (IUDs, diaphragms, spermicides, etc., excluding condoms) would be freely available to Medical Card holders before the end of the year. The IFPA welcomed this decision as 'the most significant development in publicly-funded family planning services since the decriminalisation of artificial family planning methods in the 1970s'.[81] The Catholic Church took this opportunity to repeat that sterilisation as a contraceptive method remained 'morally unacceptable'. The government also demanded that the Health Boards put in place a comprehensive family planning service in their regions. Some Boards proceeded to draw reports on the local contraceptive situation to assess the level of service required and the ways to deliver it. For example, the North Eastern Health Board found the following in a survey of more than 1,000 women aged between 16 and 45 in the region: 64 per cent said they used some form of contraception; their favourite methods were the pill (for 45 per cent) and condoms (44 per cent); 60 per cent went to their GP for family planning services; but nearly 50 per cent said 'the availability of family planning services was poor or very poor in their area', and 25 per cent said 'they did not have access locally to the family planning services they required.' Nearly 40 per cent felt 'the most significant improvement that could be made to family planning services was to provide them locally'. The Board surveyed its doctors too, and 89 per cent of them answered, of whom only 36 per cent (i.e. 42 doctors) had a Family Planning Certificate, a formal qualification in family planning; 96 per cent prescribed the pill, 83 per cent gave information on natural family planning and 86 per cent provided post-coital contraception. Only 34 per cent fitted diaphragms, 14 per cent IUDs and 2.5 per cent performed male sterilisations. The findings of this survey show the way forward unambiguously. Incidentally, we are struck by the high percentage of doctors providing post-coital contraception, which is a form of abortion (before implantation). In 1991, about 26 per cent of first-time visitors to IFPA clinics came for the so-called morning-after pill; 34.2 per cent did in 1992, and more than 35 per cent in 1993.[82] In fact, the morning-after pill is not available in Ireland, therefore it is a non-issue, and as such it cannot be banned. The patient is given four tablets of high-dose contraceptive pills and not a proper morning-after pill as one would anywhere else.

This reminds us of the old days when therapeutic indications were removed from the packs of pills lest they be assimilated to birth control propaganda![83]

Four successive contraception laws have eroded the grip that Catholic teaching has had on individual consciences as far as contraception is concerned. Four laws were needed, as well as umpteen bills, tabled, rejected or shelved, a few directives and some 20 years of dogged determination on the part of a number of politicians, doctors and responsible citizens. Contraception thus became a *fait de société*, but also a right, whatever one's social class or marital status.[84] The fact that politicians proceeded, literally by trial and error, bears witness to the difficult but inexorable process of legal de-moralisation. In the case of contraception, as with divorce and homosexuality, it took a few individual initiatives at parliamentary level which failed lamentably at the time, but cleared the ground and heightened public awareness of the issue.

It is interesting that, whereas in some Western countries, slogans such as 'a child when I want, if I want' cover the right to have an abortion as well as that of taking the pill, these two issues have been quite distinct in Irish women's minds, whether militant or not. The two practices partake of the same disorder in the eyes of the Catholic Church, but contraception is accepted by the overwhelming majority of Irish citizens and politicians as the expression of a responsible sexuality, whereas abortion has become accepted only very recently, as something that happens at all in this part of the world.

In the case of abortion, moral objections are stronger, seeing that another life is at stake, and legal obstacles are greater since it is illegal as well as unconstitutional. To what extent has abortion a place in the gradual imposition of a new moral order based on individual moral choices? The following chapter will attempt to retrace a long-drawn-out and painful coming to grips with the issue.

5 Abortion: From the Right to Life...

As one cannot speak of a right to abortion without entering the fray, let us talk about the right of women to take a moral and responsible decision when they feel they cannot, in conscience, bring their pregnancy to full term. This is a decision that the Catholic Church does not recognise since it views abortion as an 'abominable crime' which no circumstance, however exceptional, can make into a moral act. It only reconciles the right to life of the mother with that of the foetus by the double effect principle: if by trying to save the life of the mother from immediate danger, one ends inadvertently that of the foetus (as in cases of an extra-uterine pregnancy or a cancer of the uterus). Is there no other way to reconcile the rights of the woman with that of the foetus when they are in conflict? Is it not possible to come closer to the Protestant concept of the problem? Any woman involved in this moral dilemma deserves all the compassion from her fellow citizens, who should recognise she is well able to take a moral decision. Should not the state adopt this kind of approach which admits 'there are cases when...'?[1] These questions are particularly acute in Ireland, where it has become impossible, since 1992, to reconcile the doctrinaire position of the Catholic Church with the fact that a growing number of Irish women effectively take the decision to have an abortion. As it took the Irish state 22 years (from 1973 to 1995) to liberalise access to contraception, one wonders if it will ever recognise the decision taken by its female citizens to terminate a pregnancy. The question has only been asked officially since 1992. Ten years earlier the subject was taboo, and before that very few people defended the right to choose, or even the right to an abortion in grave circumstances (Senator Noël Browne was an exception, as early as 1974).[2] As surprising as it may seem, even feminist groups drew a distinction between contraception and abortion, not only in order to obtain the right to prevent conception, but also because such an association would have alienated a majority of citizens and militants too. To these people, abortion was quite distinct from contraception, in that it involves another human being, one of the key arguments put forward by the Catholic Church. But the two practices cannot be fundamentally different, since, according to churchmen, one opens the way to the other.

Paradoxically, abortion only became an issue, dominating political debates and polarising opinions, when an amendment to the Irish Constitution was proposed to include a guarantee of the rights of the foetus, and not to legalise an existing situation. Seeing the quasi-general disinterest in the issue, the relentless determination of the groups opposing a possible legalisation of abortion is all the more surprising, and the divergence of opinions, in 1983 for example, did not so much oppose the opponents of abortion to the proponents of legal abortion, as the opponents of the inclusion of an essentially Catholic principle into the national Constitution. For most Irish people, abortion was murder, and the right to 'choose' was rarely invoked. It would take the X case, in 1992, to bring them to qualify this condemnation. The X case seemed inevitable, once the logic of the law was pushed to its limit, and it called into question the socio-moral control mechanisms so imbued with Catholic ethics.

It is not just that abortion has become a topical issue since 1983, it is also an issue that exemplifies all the complexities inherent to questions of public law and morality. The insertion of the above-mentioned amendment is a clear example of the links established between the two. It is also a question that cannot be analysed solely in the context of the Irish state since abortion in Ireland is a European question, not because of European interference, but because Irish laws oblige Irish women to get abortions in Europe.

Why was it deemed necessary to reinforce the illegality of abortion, which was uncontested, by inserting it into the Constitution? How could a supremely democratic decision (a referendum) take a desperate 14-year-old to court? What are the implications at European level of a legislation based on Catholic ethics? And finally, how did the Irish swing within nearly ten years from a plebiscite for the right to life (of the foetus) for a plebiscite for the right to live (of the mother)? The present development should help us understand how a paradoxical situation has been reached. At present, abortion is legal in Ireland in certain circumstances, but the state only formally recognises the right to obtain information about abortions in another jurisdiction and the right to go there for that purpose. Further, only a professionally suicidal doctor would attempt to perform an abortion in Ireland since the procedure is still banned by the Medical Council, whereas a large and growing number of Irish women defy the law and have an abortion abroad. We should remember that Ireland has, despite censorship and prosecutions, a relatively high rate of abortions (8.89 per cent of live births in 1993, according to official figures, i.e. 4,399 abortions for 49,456 live births): There is therefore a reality out there, beyond moral, social, legal and medical arguments.

ABORTION IS ILLEGAL

Abortion has been illegal in Ireland since the enactment of the Offences against the Person Act in 1861, a law adopted by the British Parliament when it still ruled over the whole island of Ireland. As Pauline Jackson observed, the 1861 Act

> was only one of a number of laws passed in Western countries in the late nineteenth century restricting abortion and sexual behaviour. The Act deals with sexual relations between males and females, males and males, minors and adults, seducers and heiresses and animals and humans. In the reproductive sphere it criminalises abortion, attempts to procure or assist at an abortion, and regulates concealments of births.[3]

Sections 58 and 59 in particular deal with 'miscarriage', and refer to people who procure illicit miscarriages, without offering any definition of 'illicit', but inferring there might be licit abortions, probably in cases of severe risk to the life of the mother. Without being repealed, it was completed in 1929 in Britain by the Infant Life Preservation Act, which was intended to combat the high rate of infanticide; it also contains a clause that strongly qualifies the 1861 law by saying that the person will not be found guilty if it can be shown that s/he performed an abortion to save the life of the mother. In 1939, the *Rex* v. *Bourne* case created a precedent that brought about the liberalisation of the law, then the legalisation of abortion in Britain. The 1861 and 1929 laws were interpreted quite unexpectedly by Judge MacNaghten who insisted that if it was not possible to prove that Dr Bourne had not acted in good faith to save the life of the mother (a girl of 14 who had been gang raped) to prevent her becoming a 'mental wreck', he should be acquitted – and he was. Eventually, the British Abortion Act of 1967 set out the circumstances in which a termination can be legal, that is when two doctors agree that the continuation of the pregnancy would put the life of the mother at risk, or her physical or mental health, or that the child would be grossly handicapped. Northern Ireland was excluded from its terms because of the opposition of its elected representatives and various church leaders. Abortion is still illegal there under the 1861 and 1929 laws (the latter was extended to the Province

in 1945 under the title of Criminal Justice (Northern Ireland) Act).
But as the interpretation of the law in the Bourne judgment did not
apply to the Province, doctors feel they have no option but to refuse to
perform abortions on their patients, not knowing how the word 'unlawfully' will be interpreted in court. Still, some abortions are performed
in Northern Ireland, without any real legal foundation, depending on
the doctor's decision. It is estimated that up to 500 therapeutic abortions are carried out each year in Northern Ireland, whereas approximately 1,800 women go to England (precisely 1,816 in 1989, 1,855 in
1990, 1,775 in 1991 according to OPCS figures). The report of the
Northern Irish Association for Abortion Law Reform mentions that
'there have been five known deaths in Northern Ireland since 1967 as a
result of illegal abortions, and probably more which have been officially registered in some other form.'[4] An opinion poll, taken yearly
indicates that people do wish for an extension of the 1967 law: in 1994,
79 per cent wished for abortion to be made legal if the doctor thinks it
is necessary for the physical or mental health of the mother, 78 per
cent in cases of rape or incest, 59 per cent if the baby will have serious
abnormalities, and 30 per cent 'on demand'.[5]

   When the Republic of Ireland journal the European Community in
1973, it was particularly worried about the possibility that legalisation
of abortion might be imposed, as Ireland was the only country in the
EC where all abortions were illegal. The 1979 family planning law
reasserted that sections 58 and 59 of the 1861 British law do constitute
the Irish law on abortion. But a recommendation from the European
Parliament in June 1981, even though it did not have the impact of a
directive, revived the anxieties of Irish MEPs and the opponents of
abortion. It recommended that decisions be taken at national level
'such as to obviate the need for journeys of this type [women seeking
help abroad] which make any form of social aid impossible and lead to
unacceptable commercialisation, and to ensure that every woman who
finds herself in difficulty can obtain the necessary assistance in her own
country.'[6] Ailbhe Smyth observed that 'this recommendation was
rejected by Irish members of the parliament, who rejected the entire
report on the basis of its inclusion.'[7] Their attitude echoed Irish
episcopal pronouncements as in *Human Life is Sacred* (1975) and
Love is for Life (1985). In one of his most recent encyclicals, *Evange-
lium Vitae*, Pope John Paul II had condemned abortion very strongly:

> The moral gravity of procured abortion is apparent in all its truth if
> we recognise that we are dealing with murder. The one eliminated is

a human being at the very beginning of life.... No circumstance, no purpose, no law whatsoever can ever make licit an act which is intrinsically illicit, since it is contrary to the law of God written in every human heart, knowable by reason itself and proclaimed by the Church.

In contrast, the position of the reformed Church is somewhat qualified as the key-declaration of the Anglican bishops in England on the issue proves:

In certain circumstances abortion can be justified. This would be when,... it could be reasonably established that there was a threat to the mother's life or well-being, and hence inescapably to her health, if she were obliged to carry the child to term and give it birth....[8]

The reformed church was actually strongly opposed to abortion in the sixteenth century, but countries with Protestant majorities such as Britain and the United States were the first to liberalise the early laws banning abortion, which denotes a tangible evolution in Protestant ethics. Generally speaking, Protestants reach moral judgements in a different way from Catholics: they tend to view ethical problems *in situ*. As far as abortion is concerned, they give more weight to individual circumstances: is the pregnancy the result of rape? will the baby be grossly deformed?

ABORTION IS UNCONSTITUTIONAL

The Catholic condemnation was in place, but how could the Irish courts be prevented from ever finding a right to abortion? How could legislators be prevented from introducing legislation allowing abortion? How could Ireland be protected from European interference since European law has prevailed over Irish law since 1973? It appeared to a number of people that the insertion of a moral principle in the Constitution was the solution.

It has been shown previously to what extent the Irish Constitution has a symbolic but also effective importance, at all levels of social life; thus one understands better why it was deemed necessary to copperfasten a declaration of principle in a document, which is used elsewhere to determine the structure of government. For some, the Constitution already acknowledged the right to life of the unborn child: It seemed guaranteed by Article 40.3.2, as interpreted by Judge Walsh in two cases as including that of the foetus.[9] For others, such a right was not guaranteed. A moral theologian, Fr Maurice Dooley, in an article published in 1974, and the Irish Family League (formed in 1973), touched early on the idea of a constitutional amendment.[10] Lawyer William Binchy attracted the attention of the anti-abortion lobby with an article in which he demonstrated that the concept of marital privacy, established with the McGee case, could easily be extended to include the right to abortion.[11] Finally, an article published in February 1980 on the activities of the Women's Right to Choose Group (WRCG), under the title 'Feminists plan abortion campaign', confirmed to Catholic activists that the time had come to act.[12]

It had become plausible that socio-moral attitudes could change in Ireland quickly and fundamentally so that abortion would appear as an option, let alone a right. It was precisely to avoid the right to abortion ever being recognised that the Pro-Life Amendment Campaign was launched in April 1981. The objective of this umbrella organisation, of some 14 associations, was to have included in the Constitution an amendment guaranteeing the right to life of the unborn child, from the moment of insemination. Since abortion was already illegal, PLAC wanted to make sure it could never be legalised, whether by Parliament (as in Britain in 1967) or by the courts (as in the US in 1973 following the *Roe* v. *Wade* case), or by a European directive. *Roe* v. *Wade* was a famous court case in which the American Supreme Court decided that the right to marital privacy made abortion legal. It was the extension of a 1965 decision establishing a right to contraception, ensuing from the right to marital privacy. PLAC felt that the unborn child's life was in danger because the Irish Constitution offered it no explicit protection (nor implicit, according to them). The danger was all the more imminent in so far as the Supreme Court had, in 1973, found there was a right to marital privacy. It might, one day, recognise a right to abortion on demand. The 1979 Health (Family Planning) Act, because it proved in itself that Irish society was moving in a direction that some did not like, acted as a catalyst to the launching of a campaign aimed at protecting the rights of the unborn child. While the family planning law was being discussed, the Dublin Well Woman Centre opened, and offered to help women with crisis pregnancies by referring them to English clinics if they opted for an abortion. A similar advice centre, the Irish Pregnancy Counselling Centre, was opened in 1980 by the most radical feminist group at the time, the WRCG, the only one to advocate the absolute right of women to choose if they wanted to carry a pregnancy to full term.[13] Such centres were the first to discuss abortion as an option, a service which was not yet illegal. These developments, which signalled that the liberalisation of socio-moral codes was reaching Ireland, threatened traditional values and Catholic morality. PLAC was formed to prevent the 'abortionists' from moving any further, and attack was deemed to be the best form of defence. Abortion was viewed by these militants as 'the last line of defence against the encroaching moral decadence of Europe.'[14]

As the abortion referendum campaign has been so well documented by Tom Hesketh in the published form of his doctoral thesis, *The Second Partitioning of Ireland? – The Abortion Referendum of 1983*, we will not delve too deeply into it here.[15] The campaign early on took a medico-legal turn, thanks to the professional occupation of its members, and the strategy chosen by its chairwoman, Dr Julia Vaughan. Another aspect of the strategy was the necessity of ensuring the support of politicians. In April 1981 the Taoiseach, Charles Haughey, and the leader of the main opposition party, Garret FitzGerald, were approached by PLAC, and vouched to amend the Constitution for the sake of the unborn. One essential factor accounts for the influence that PLAC exerted on politicians – the fact that the pre-referendum campaign coincided with a period of great political instability. The necessity of such an amendment might not have imposed itself so easily in different circumstances, but there were four general elections between 1979 and 1982, including three between 1981 and 1982 alone. There was a regular alternation between Haughey and Fianna Fáil, and FitzGerald and Fine Gael. Every election campaign provided an opportunity to court support. In February 1982 Haughey was returned to power, and he announced that the new government was going to come up with a suitable wording, and a national vote would be called. This period is notable for 'the largely unquestioning acceptance by the politicians of the right of PLAC to make demands on the issue, and of their consequent duty to act when PLAC demanded they should.'[16] The announcement that the government was planning to put in place a referendum in the same year galvanised groups and individuals opposed to any amendment. Senator Mary Robinson, for one, argued that abortion was a problem that would not be solved by an adjunct to the Constitution:

Abortion is a problem. The pro-life amendment is not a solution. It would not even be helpful in solving the problem. In fact it would be counterproductive, and costly, not only in terms of the expense of

financing a referendum.... [A more adequate response to the problem of abortion included] the introduction of proper sex education
into the schools, and a just, fair and practical contraceptives
Bill.... Not all abortions are a result of unwanted pregnancies.
Many women who have abortions would clearly like to keep their
child but are the victims of circumstance. Circumstance can mean
our still cruel attitude to unmarried mothers, or, let's face it, simple
economic pressures. Couched in brutal terms, if the State wishes
to adopt a pro-life attitude, it must ensure that parents, either single
or married, are not penalised economically for having children.
The State could go a long way towards providing housing for single
parent families ... and child-minding facilities for working single
mothers. In this country, the State crèche is still a thing of
the future.[17]

Mary Robinson took an original line in that she identified the causes
behind abortions rather than condemning or justifying them without
qualification. The amendment for her was a profoundly inadequate
answer to the lack of sexual education or to financial hardship. At the
same time, the Protestant churches began to denounce the sectarian
character of the amendment. Despite the fact that they were not in
favour of abortion in the absolute, that they even worked hand in glove
with the Catholic Church in the anti-abortion group LIFE, and that all
Christian churches opposed the extension of the 1967 English abortion
law to Northern Ireland, they accepted that in certain serious cases
abortion could be the lesser evil. Their point of view was that it was
dangerous to legislate without taking into account hard cases like rape
and incest, and that this amendment reinforced the sectarianism pervading Irish society by alienating the Republic's Protestants as well as
those in the North.[18]

The Anti-Amendment Campaign (AAC) was officially launched in
June 1982. The initiative to develop a counter-strategy belongs to the
WRCG. Despite this, it was eventually decided to oppose PLAC from
a less radical platform than the right to choose. As Vicky Randall put
it, 'The fact is that Ireland's feminists were not campaigning to liberalise abortion; they were resisting moves to reinforce the abortion ban.'[19]
Since a growing number of Protestant churchmen and Catholic liberals
were making themselves heard, it was more realistic to build a campaign on a more 'respectable' basis: it would have been counterproductive to choose this point in time to try to convince public opinion
that abortion should be legalised. The basis of such a campaign would

have been far too narrow and would have been grist to PLAC's mill.[20] A number of members insisted that it should be made clear they were against abortion. The most radical members of the campaign were progressively less heard, and as from June 1982, the few declarations on abortion were qualified, and focused on extreme cases. The liberal wing of the campaign had succeeded in imposing the religious (anti-sectarian), medical and legal arguments, so as to be on the same terrain as PLAC and reach the greatest number. Leading lawyers rallied AAC, indeed some were instrumental in the setting-up of the campaign. In late July 1982, the intervention of Michael O'Leary, lawyer and leader of the Labour Party, marked the end of the political consensus that had seemed so far to be on PLAC's side. From then on, other Labour members would publicly oppose the amendment, thus putting pressure on their coalition partners, but also dividing the party as no other party was divided during this campaign, even Fine Gael. All sorts of groups formed and affiliated to AAC, and the large support shown by the legal professions culminated in the setting up of the Lawyers against the Amendment Group. It is to be noted that more lawyers supported AAC than PLAC, and conversely for doctors.

AAC led the debate for several months thanks to a systematic critique of the amendment, totally detached from the issue of abortion itself. An opinion poll, published in September, seemed to indicate this was good strategy since to the question: Should there be a referendum to amend the Constitution so that no future law could legalise abortion? 43 per cent of the sample were in favour but 41 per cent were against. If the sentence to be inserted was 'No Irish Government can adopt laws allowing abortion', 47 per cent would vote in favour, 36 per cent against and 17 per cent did not know or had no opinion. But when the question was asked if they had heard of the very possibility of such a referendum, 50 per cent said they had, and 48 per cent said they had not![21] which corroborated Mary Robinson's remark:

I said to them [some social workers], because I was very interested, 'what is the view or discussion in your area?' and they said: 'what discussion? What amendment? It never comes up. The women I deal with, ordinary working-class women, never mention it. They do not even know that there is a proposal to amend the Constitution.' I am sure that is true. We have this unreal debate taking up vital parliamentary time, dividing us politically, and as a country dividing churchmen against churchmen and individual against individual, even dividing families. Yet, the people in the front line, coping with economic and social difficulties, with real needs that we should be diverting resources towards, are completely unaware, and there is no reason why they should ever become aware because it is totally irrelevant to them....[22]

The poll reveals not only widespread apathy and confusion, but also that the number of people opposed to such a referendum was high in a country where it is said that opposition to abortion is quasi-absolute. That poll showed that either the WRCG could have focused its campaign on the right to choose, or that AAC had managed to convince people of the danger of such an amendment who would have been opposed to abortion. An international study on attitudes and values confirmed the abhorrence the Irish felt towards abortion: in the case of a child who would be born handicapped, 68 per cent were opposed to abortion (compared to 33 per cent of the sample in Northern Ireland and 17 per cent in Britain); abortion for purely social reasons was rejected by 86 per cent of the Irish (83 per cent in Northern Ireland and 64 per cent in Britain); and concerning therapeutic abortion, when the health of the mother is in danger, only 49 per cent of the Irish were opposed (20 per cent in Northern Ireland and 7 per cent in Britain).[23] These results can be compared to a similar study done in 1973. Then 74.3 per cent of the Irish Catholics sample thought that abortion was always evil; 5 per cent could envisage it as a solution in cases of rape or illegitimacy; and only 1.3 per cent thought that it was 'in general a good solution'.[24] A slight evolution could be discerned, in the case of extreme circumstances. Moreover the question 'Would you be in favour of an abortion if your own daughter was raped?' was not asked. Strengthened by these results, AAC focused on the slogan that voting Yes in the referendum would endanger women's lives.

On 2 November 1982 the Fianna Fáil government published its wording of the amendment: 'The State acknowledges the right to life of the unborn and, with due regard to the equal right to life of the mother, guarantees in its laws to respect and, as far as practicable, by its laws to defend and vindicate that right.' The wording itself sounded like a compromise, all the more so as it got the initial cautious approbation of Protestant churchmen, as well as the equally cautious approval of PLAC and the Catholic hierarchy. The latter said that 'the text of the proposed amendment does seem to contribute positively to safeguarding the right to life of the unborn and as such it is welcome.'[25] The minority churches had not changed their minds on the desirability of a referendum on the issue, but since the wording did not explicitly exclude exceptional cases in which an abortion was acceptable to them, and since if wording there would be, this one was probably the best they could hope for, they adopted a pragmatic stance. In fact, as Tom Hesketh pointed out, the minority churches and PLAC approved the wording for opposed reasons: the former because it did not outlaw abortion in some cases, the latter because it finally accepted that with this wording the law could not be liberalised. PLAC was initially worried, as John O'Reilly later said: 'the word 'unborn' seem[ed] to pose problems. [Did] it mean protection from 'fertilisation' or from such undefined point as 'viability'? [Was] it really a protection to the unborn child or was it the gateway to abortion?' In the light of the 1992 events, this appears premonitory. Mary Robinson herself said that this wording 'would throw the entire matter into the lap of the courts'.[26] AAC attacked the wording from all angles, as its members opposed the very idea of a referendum, but again, to be strategically coherent, they adopted a single stance whereby such an amendment would have serious consequences on medical and legal practices currently in force in Ireland: 'The strategy emerged at a news conference held in Dublin on November 9, chaired by Senator Robinson. It was announced that a "medico-legal body within the AAC" had concluded that the amendment threatened the IUD, the progesterone-only pill and the low-dose pill....'[27]

FitzGerald gave his immediate and wholehearted support to the Fianna Fáil wording and assured PLAC it would be part of the programme of the government of Fine Gael after the coming election. Bearing in mind he had just launched his constitutional crusade aimed at bringing Northern Ireland and the Republic closer, it is not clear why he would show so much eagerness to include in the Constitution a clause that was widely deemed to be sectarian. Moreover, throughout 1982, he repeated that the insertion of a pro-life amendment would only be part of a general review of the Constitution.[28] His immediate enthusiasm can be accounted for by the fact that at first sight the wording was not sectarian, and it guaranteed equal rights to mother and foetus. He was especially anxious to defuse the electoral value of the amendment by subscribing to the Fianna Fáil wording.[29] It was the third general election within 18 months, and, as FitzGerald himself said, 'to allow a serious election, crucial to the future of the country to be turned into a circus over this issue would have been totally irresponsible.'[30] A Fine Gael–Labour coalition was returned to power after the election on 24 November 1982, and this time they vouched to have the amendment adopted in the Dáil. The amendment was thus accepted without its legal and medical implications been examined. The Attorney-General, Peter Sutherland, only commented on them in mid-January 1983 and found them to be dangerous. His objections had to do with the ambiguity of certain terms including 'right', 'equal', 'life', 'unborn child', 'with due regard' and 'as far as practicable', which, considering the length of the amendment, constitutes a substantial amount of ambiguity, which could lead to conflicting judicial interpretations!

His objections reopened the debate, at a time when FitzGerald was being attacked from within his own ranks for sacrificing his liberalising 'constitutional crusade'. In parallel, the minority churches came back on their lukewarm approbation, spurred on by AAC and its traditionally conservative members, the lawyers and doctors. This reversal brought into sharp contrast the inherent contradiction in FitzGerald's position: How could he consider changing the Constitution to bring about reconciliation with the Northern Irish Protestants while promoting an amendment to which all Protestant churches were opposed? As he could not accept his crusade being discredited, nor could he accept the amendment changing existing medical practice, it was decided to change the wording.[31] Unfortunately it is precisely in March 1983 that the hierarchy began to give its open and warm support to PLAC, which augured badly for the possibility of finding a wording that would satisfy the Catholic Church as well as the Protestant churches.

On 24 March 1983, the Fine Gael wording for the amendment was published. This read: 'Nothing in this Constitution shall be invoked to invalidate any provision of a law on the ground that it prohibits abortion.' This forbade the Supreme Court from finding an implicit right to abortion, but it left open the possibility that, one day, the Irish Parliament, without referring to the people, could pass a law introducing abortion. The Protestant churches liked this wording better, but PLAC, Haughey and most of Fianna Fáil, Fine Gael and even Labour found it unacceptable. The editor of *The Irish Times*, on 25 March, could not help but express his surprise: 'It is very difficult to understand how TDs of various parties can have so little faith in the Oireachtas as to assert that abortion cannot be left, as a subject, to the elected representatives of the people.' It is as if the Irish have not rid themselves of a lively suspicion of British legislature, and have transferred it to their own laws and legislators. They seem to think that referendums are a better way of judging the will of the people, which is strange in a country so marked by the concepts of minority and majority. They should be in the best position possible to know that the will of the majority can be tyrannical. Within Parliament itself, the Fine Gael amendment was defeated, which implied that deputies accepted that they and their successors could never change the law on abortion. On 27 April the Fianna Fáil wording was adopted by 87 votes to 13, after a two-month long preaching campaign on the part of Catholic churchmen. On 29 March, the hierarchy had issued its collective declaration which was more down to earth than spiritual, and concluded: 'the Constitution is our greatest legal protection against violation of the right to life. Surely the most defenceless and voiceless in our midst are entitled to the fullest constitutional protection...'.

In the Seanad, the wording was adopted by 18 votes to 15, and the debates preceding this vote will go down in history for 2 1/2 hour-long attack on the amendment delivered by Mary Robinson. She examined in detail all the ambiguities of the wording, and all the possible medical and legal consequences of such an amendment. She particularly condemned the intervention of the Catholic hierarchy:

> In other words, they [the Catholic bishops] have entered into the political arena on this. It is something I am sure historians, commentators and social scientists will comment on. It has already been referred to as the mother and child scheme, mark II. In my view, it is. We are witnessing the forces of the Catholic Church moving in on a political debate, taking sides on it and using the resources of the Catholic Church to advance those sides.[32]

She underlined the fact that all the minority churches had pronounced themselves against the amendment, because

> the problem with this constitutional amendment is that it is a Catholic way of doing things. One is morally right and, therefore, one puts it into the Constitution, assert it and that is the end of it. The Protestant ethos, and the ethos of the Chief Rabbi on behalf of the Jewish community, and the ethos of other groupings in the State, would be one of freedom of conscience of the individual, that it is a moral issue which one does not put in any form into a Constitution for cultural or religious reasons. It is not so much the precise wording that is causing the fear. It is that it indicates a closed, pre-emptive society which is going to fasten down a debate, prevent freedom of conscience, make certain citizens feel less citizens of this State because they simply do not subscribe either

to the approach or to the wording of reducing this to a constitutional amendment.[33]

She also echoed the Protestant churches by stressing that such an amendment would do nothing to solve the social problems at the root of the relatively high abortion rate in Ireland: 'We do not appear, even in the course of a debate on this constitutional amendment, to want to address ourselves to the real issue of why it is that despite the substantial and certainly religious environment in this country and the concern for family life that is clearly evident here we have an unprecedented and, as far as the foreign jurisdiction is concerned, an artificially high abortion rate.'[34] Despite her intervention, the bill passed all its stages. However, a date for the referendum was not set, as two legal actions were started under various pretexts to prevent this. As the results of an opinion poll had just been published and they showed an increase in the number of people opposed to the referendum, the government was not unhappy to postpone the vote. In fact, an increasing number of people were against the idea of a referendum, but if it took place at all, a majority of them would vote in favour of the amendment![35]

The referendum campaign was the longest, the most virulent and the most polarised there ever was. On the one side, PLAC, the pressure group made up of associations all unconditionally opposed to abortion; on the other, AAC, a grouping of people and groups opposed to the idea of a sectarian clause being inserted into the Constitution, generally thought of as being 'for abortion', which was in most cases an incorrect shorthand phrase. This does not bear witness to the atmosphere of conflict pervading doctors' surgeries, such respectable associations as the Medical Council, courtrooms, congregations, workplaces and so forth where sympathisers and adversaries of the amendment worked side by side. The debate focused on two themes: the medico-legal quarrel, which did not get anywhere, as the two lobbies, PLAC and AAC, each had such strong medical and legal support with their own interpretations of the amendment. The only result as it were was that the vision of babies being killed in the womb was stronger in the minds of the Irish than the potential danger in which the amendment would put women (perhaps they trusted their doctors more than their legislators?). The central plank of the AAC campaign, that the amendment would put women's lives at risk (their health was hardly mentioned; and their rights were not mentioned at all), did not carry enough weight.

The second theme was much wider and concerned the nature of Irish society. This debate was quite politicised since, generally speaking, the left supported AAC and the right PLAC. The cleavage lay along other lines than 'for or against abortion', and as such it was more a question of politics than morality. Abortion itself, as we said, was rarely discussed, since AAC's most radical members strategically accepted not to focus the debate on the right to choose. As for PLAC, the issue was much wider than abortion since it was about the social and moral future of Ireland: the old values were in danger, and were already somewhat eroded by 1983. When the hierarchy took sides with PLAC, individually first, then collectively, the intention was clear. Abortion was not just a pretext but it was certainly the best chosen moral question since it met with quasi-general condemnation; also, choosing it was an attempt at putting a check on the process of secularisation of moral values, a process already well under way. Brian Girvin echoes this: 'The campaign was a riposte to the secularizing tendencies which had appeared so strong throughout the 1970s. In addition, abortion appeared to be the issue around which the maximum support for traditional values could be generated.'[36] Dick Spring was the party leader to raise such political questions:

> Is it possible that the campaign reflects a reaction to a different reality – that there had been some, limited, progress towards improving the status of women in Ireland, that family planning, once fiercely resisted, is now widely practised, that legislators, or some of them, are increasingly conscious of the need to change attitudes towards a wide range of social issues, such as illegitimacy, the treatment of children under our laws, and the growing problem of marital breakdown? In other words, is it possible that this campaign represents no more than a backlash against the slow liberalising of our society...?[37]

It obviously all depends on what one means by 'liberalising', or by progress, as the priests of a Cork parish said more or less the same thing but in a radically different way:

> Unless we say a resounding 'yes' to that, the people who would like to have the Godless society will be encouraged to come back to us with some other proposals after a year or two.... So that you won't be conned by their language, may we alert you to the fact that you are only being shown a tiny tip of the iceberg; the really nasty stuff is still submerged.... You can stop the rot now.[38]

What had happened to earlier declarations that what the Church taught did not have to be transcribed in law, or the fact that the state's role was not there to make better Catholics of its citizens? Facing the spectre of pluralism, the Catholic Church took refuge behind its authority and waved the prospect of 'horrors' yet to befall – legalised divorce, decriminalised homosexuality, a contraceptive culture.

After two and a half years of fierce campaigning, from January 1981 to September 1983, the eighth amendment to the Irish Constitution was accepted in a national referendum by a majority of two to one (66.9 per cent in favour, 33.1 per cent against). Victory was unambiguous, even though the turnout was only 54.6 per cent. Did the abstainers represent a silent No, as Dick Spring suggested? Was this a protest vote from people opposed to the very idea of a referendum, whose size, according to Brian Girvin, should worry the Catholic Church, considering its intensive exhortations to vote Yes?[39] It is in this sense that PLAC's success is the most mitigated. When one examines the result of the referendum in comparison to the whole electorate, it appears that the amendment was supported by only 35.79 per cent of the electorate.[40] On the contrary, were the abstainers in favour of the amendment, but not sufficiently motivated to go out and vote, as Brendan Walsh suggests? This thesis is plausible since the turnout was low in the South and West of Ireland, rural and traditionally conservative areas, from where one expected a resounding Yes.[41] But, again, if one takes into account the massive efforts deployed to bring people to the polls and the unremitting door-to-door canvassing of PLAC, we would suggest that, without going as far as pointing to a protest vote, there was a substantial number of people for whom the amendment was a question of no importance; a number of people impervious to the message of the media, to the priests' sermons, for whom abortion remained an abstract question.

This victory for PLAC and the Catholic Church proves paradoxically that there is such a thing as a liberal force in Ireland, to which this campaign gave an opportunity to express and organise itself. Even if AAC was going to be disbanded after the referendum, the campaign had forged links. These might not be strong enough yet to counter the traditionalist forces, which was better organised and financed, but this liberal force had become visible, and credible, and this was the real revelation as far as politicians were concerned, since it would be a force to be reckoned with. Indeed, even if the finance sub-committee of PLAC was not disbanded like the rest of the organisation, and would give rise to the future campaign against divorce or to the group Family Solidarity (whose aim was to protect and promote the family), at the same time, Parliament was going to widen the legality of contraception, as we saw in Chapter 4. No doubt the traditionalist forces had the situation well in hand in the 1980s, in the sense that they could successfully mobilise the support of voters; but the liberal forces were going to infiltrate Parliament and leave their mark on legislation.

But were the instigators of PLAC going to call it a day? Was the insertion of this amendment pure rhetoric? The most obvious target, already identified, apart from doctors and women going for an abortion in Britain, was the centres providing the latter with information. Would the militants manage to limit a right, recognised by Irish and European law, to information?

The 8th amendment became Article 40.3.3 of the Constitution, and until February 1992, was never put to the test in court. It had not prevented one woman from leaving Ireland to obtain an abortion, so presumably it had not prevented one single abortion. SPUC and other anti-abortion groups always said they wanted the right to life of the unborn child to be protected within Ireland, but it was not their intention to harass individual women. What is original about the Irish situation is that there are anti-abortion groups whereas abortion is not legal, and any demand for the 'right to choose' was always minimal and marginal. The Society for the Protection of Unborn Children Ireland was launched in 1980 and would become one of the most active groups within PLAC. Its aims were clear: 'The prevention of the decriminalisation of abortion... and the doing of all other things as are incidental or conducive to the attainment of the above object.' In 1983, at the height of the abortion referendum campaign, the group had some 4,000 members, in over 40 regional branches. After the victory, they focused on indirect action: 'In order to defend the right to life of the unborn, we must close the abortion referral agencies which are operating in Dublin quite openly and underneath the eyes of the law. These clinics must be closed and if the 1861 Act cannot close them, we must have another Act that will.'[42] These 'abortion referral agencies' offered a non-directive counselling service to women faced with a crisis pregnancy, examining with them all possible options, and giving addresses in Britain if the women chose a termination.

Even before the constitutional ban on abortion, the Irish Pregnancy Counselling Centre was targeted for closure. And in October 1986, SPUC obtained an injunction against two such centres: Open Door Counselling and the Well Woman Centre. The former opened in 1978 and the latter, which provided various services relative to women's mental and physical well-being, in 1983. The centres were accused of facilitating the murder of babies, in breach of Article 40.3.3, by providing information and arranging appointments at British abortion clinics. In December 1986, the Hamilton judgment (in the High Court) ruled that it was now illegal in Ireland to provide information that would facilitate abortions in Britain. The centres stopped providing the litigious information, but a telephone network was established, and information took precedence over counselling. The centres (WWC being defended by Mary Robinson) appealed to the Supreme Court, which rejected their appeal on 16 March 1988 on the grounds that 'there could not be an implied and unenumerated constitutional right to information about the availability of a service of abortion outside the State which, if availed of, would have the direct consequence of destroying the expressly guaranteed constitutional right to life of the unborn.'[43]

A few months later, in September 1988, SPUC, on the strength of the Hamilton judgment, obtained an injunction against three students' unions for publishing addresses and phone numbers of British abortion clinics in their student handbooks. These organisations had been at the forefront of the struggle for reproductive rights, since, for example, TCD students had started to 'give away' non-medical contraceptives in April 1974, and the UCD students' union had followed suit in November 1975. The students case went from High Court to the European Court of Justice, Supreme Court and back again, and it deprived not only students of information, but all Irish women, as in the following months, women's magazines such as *Cosmopolitan* and *Company* started publishing a special edition for Ireland, without their page of addresses of abortion clinics. Supplements on abortion were later self-censored; an edition of the *Guardian*, a British newspaper, was sent back; books on feminine health removed from the library' shelves. The 'SPUC cases', as they became known, were taken to Europe (and defended by Mary Robinson, until her election to the presidency), that is, one to the court of the European Community (now European Union) and the other to the court of the Council of Europe.

Though largely theoretical, these judgments demonstrate the irreconcilable and inherent contradictions between the Irish and the European reasoning. ODC and WWC took their case to the European Court of Human Rights (ECHR) which sits in Strasbourg and hears cases brought by people who think their rights as defined by the

Convention of the Rights of Man (signed by the 26 members of the Council of Europe) have been breached in their own country. The final judgment of this court was given in October 1992, in the midst of yet another abortion referendum campaign. The ECHR found Ireland to be in breach of the Convention: the health of Irish women was being put at risk by the ban on information as it was the cause of later abortions and deprived women of post-abortion check-up. The services provided by the centres being non-directive, they could lead to the women choosing a solution other than abortion. Consequently the link between abortion information and the destruction of life was not as real as the Irish government contended. Moreover, finding the phone number of a British clinic in a phonebook or through the grapevine was no guarantee that the operation would take place under the best conditions and time limits possible. The ban on information did not prevent a growing number of Irish women from having an abortion abroad: its aim might have been 'legitimate', but its effects were 'disproportionate'. Implicitly, this meant that the moral aspirations of a society cannot be placed above practical considerations. Interestingly, the appeal was heard in the wake of the X ruling, to which we will return in Chapter 6. Counsel for the State had then to concede that since there was now a category of women in Ireland who could legally get an abortion, they should be able to get the necessary information on this service. The ban on information, inherent as it was to Article 40.3.3, was suddenly no longer absolute.

The students taken to court by SPUC made a reference to the European Court of Justice (ECJ) which sits in Luxembourg and guards the Treaty of Rome, the Constitution of the EC/EU as it were.[44] The court established that abortion is a medical service. However, it conceded that a member-state can curtail certain community rights, such as that of availing of a service, on the grounds of public morality, if these measures are not disproportionate. Such a ban was not disproportionate to the aim sought, 'since that aim is intended to effectuate a value- judgement, enshrined in its Constitution, attaching high priority to the protection of unborn life.' For the Advocate-General, measures 'which would be disproportionate – in as much as they would excessively impede the freedom to supply services – would include for example a ban on pregnant women going abroad or a rule under which they would be subjected to unsolicited examinations upon their return from abroad.' With hindsight, one is struck by the irony that what was deemed 'impracticable' by PLAC in 1982 and 'disproportionate' in 1991 did take place in February 1992, as we shall see.

Still, as banning the student associations from providing addresses could not be regarded as a restriction of the right to avail oneself of a legal medical service because there was no commercial link between the two, some women's health centres then signed contracts with abortion clinics in Britain. For £1 a year, the IFPA began to provide a non-directive counselling service to women in crisis pregnancy and the addresses of the British Pregnancy Advisory Service clinics if the women opted for an abortion, as well as a post-operation counselling service on their return.

The students' case went back to the High Court in July 1992 where Judge Morris granted SPUC a permanent injunction restraining the student leaders from distributing information on abortion abroad and awarded the costs against them. (The students' appeal to the Supreme Court would be allowed in March 1997 and the restraining order lifted, as the judges all accepted that the law had since changed significantly in the matter of abortion information.)

The SPUC cases proved that an ordinary citizen can enforce the law as in Article 40.3.3 and deprive women in distress of the necessary information relative to their decision to terminate their pregnancy. As long as the right to 'travel', as it became euphemistically known, and the right to information were not explicitly recognised by Irish law, Irish women would not be in a position to take moral and responsible decisions in an honest manner. Censorship has often been used in Ireland to stifle ideas, as if stopping the circulation of ideas stopped people from behaving immorally and put checks on their freewill. But as far as abortion is concerned, it was something of a failure: the only effect of this censorship of information has not been a reduction in the number of women getting an abortion in Britain, but an increase in their isolation and their anguish.

ABORTION: AN ENGLISH SOLUTION TO AN IRISH PROBLEM

Despite the inflexibility of the law and the vigilance of SPUC, it is an indisputable fact that Irish women have recourse to abortion, in quite large numbers. As far as the majority of Irish people are concerned, it is as if this reality has only existed since the beginning of the 1980s, even though it is not a particularly recent phenomenon, as some research attests.[45] According to Pauline Jackson, the Bourne judgment opened the way to Britain for Irish women. As there was no prosecutions for illegal abortions in Ireland in the years that followed the judgment (1938 to 1942), 'from this we may surmise that the so-called abortion trail to England started not in 1967 but some thirty years earlier, about 1937.'[46] We will only venture that it might be a bit rash to think that the Bourne case made abortion that much more accessible (a number of British doctors were still prosecuted). Nonetheless, even at that time, despite censorship and the lack of cooperation of most Irish doctors, imbued with Catholic values, women had already found ways to solve their difficulties. But because of the travel restrictions imposed on civilians during the Second World War, Irish women could not go to Britain, and the rate of prosecutions for illegal abortions drastically increased: 25 cases between 1942 and 1946.[47] The rate of illegitimate births increased in parallel: 3.93 per cent of all live births in 1945, the highest rate between 1864 and 1977. After the war, the number of prosecutions decreased: 12 cases between 1947 and 1956.[48] The number of prosecutions leaves to the imagination the actual number of abortions performed, since one only heard of those that went wrong, when the women ended up in hospital or died. Since 1967, the date of the legalisation of abortion in Britain, there has been a steady increase in the number of Irish women going there for a termination of pregnancy, and a simultaneous decrease in the number of prosecutions for backstreet abortions.[49] The double ban (illegality and unconstitutionality) on the procedure, dating back to 1983, has not managed to stem this increase: from 64 Irish women in 1968 to 4,529 in 1995 (4,894 in 1996). It is estimated (by the nursing staff concerned) that if 4,529 Irish women gave the clinic their name and address, about as many were too terrified to do so and gave the address of a hotel or of those, friends or relatives, who put them up during their stay in England and Wales (abortious performed in Scotland are not included). The official figures seem to be well short of reality.

Various studies have shown that it is mainly Irish women aged between 20 and 29, living in cities, who take advantage of the English law.[50] Dr Dermot Walsh reported in 1975 that 88 per cent of the Irish women getting an abortion in Britain in 1971–2 had invoked the ground of 'mental or psychiatric troubles' in order to obtain the go-ahead that two doctors have to give before the operation can take place.[51] Dissimulation is thus an added burden for Irish women who already have to cope with the stress of an unwanted pregnancy, of doing something criminal and immoral. They have to pretend they are mentally unstable to boot. The positive thing about having an abortion in Britain is that it is a legal operation performed in the best medical conditions possible. But it remains an expensive procedure, if one adds to the £250 for the operation itself, the same again for the fare and other expenses, a prohibitive sum of money, especially if it has to be raised unknown to one's nearest and dearest.

What about backstreet abortion, then? Surely it remains a possibility in a country long in the throes of economic problems. A commentator on religious affairs, Seán Mac Réamoinn, asks:

> And what of those who quite simply cannot afford to travel? Are we sure that the 'back-street' operator is no longer with us? Indeed, one of the nastiest aspects of the situation here is the way it imposes on the poor and helpless a morality which those who can afford it may evade. Over these last weeks I have been haunted by the thought of Ann Lovett and her baby in a Longford field...[52]

Ann Lovett's story exemplifies the intolerable suffering and secrecy surrounding the issue. There are no statistics on backstreet abortions, and no resounding cases since the 1950s, no substantial rumours in the media or in conversations. The only exception being the investigation that a Dublin clinic was subjected to in February 1997.[53] However, seeing that Ireland is such a rural country, that access to information was banned, that contraceptive methods are not readily available everywhere or have been so for a short time only, it is not entirely impossible that some have recourse to self-induced abortion or ask somebody to help. Having said that, there is no ground to suspect the existence of a background network of abortionists. It is no secret, though, that abortions can be classified in hospitals under another name. For example, when applying the double effect principle, one removes the tubes to put an end to an extra-uterine pregnancy, or one performs a 'D and C' (dilatation and curettage), a ten-minute operation which can be legally performed to solve the problem of painful or heavy periods. Robert Rose reports in his doctoral thesis on fertility control in Ireland:

> The chemist stated that I should consult more people in his line of work since they were now and again asked for something 'to bring on a late period' and that consequently they 'had their finger on the problem.' Dr Y, on the other hand, admitted that between 1964 and 1968 he had performed around 60 abortions himself....Dr Z informed me that during 1973 and 1974, in Dublin's major hospitals there were probably five to ten dilatation and curettage patients per day. Of these, what number can we assume were there to wilfully

terminate an unwanted pregnancy?...In any event, Dr Z suggested that it is rumored among his colleagues that fetal material is sporadically found as the result of dilation and curettage therapy initially prescribed to control heavy menstrual discharges.[54]

We would be tempted to add to this that practices whose legality can largely be questioned are undoubtedly avoided seeing the litigious climate that currently reigns in Ireland. It is more likely that nowadays compassionate doctors give all the relevant information relative to a legal abortion in Britain. Dr Paddy Leahy goes even further. Now in his mid-seventies, he revealed in 1992 that in the previous two and a half years he had accompanied five teenagers to England for an abortion – three in 1992, including two who were under 15 and the third who was just a little over 13.[55]

Generally speaking, one can say that the geographical and linguistic proximity of Britain, the fact that the Irish are not insular and have a long tradition of going as far as necessary to find solutions to their difficulties, as well as the existence of networks established as a result of the emigration of family or friends to British cities, have brought about the disappearance of backstreet abortions as they were practised in bygone days. It remains true that for those who do not have the means or the courage (to leave, to lie, to defy interdicts), infanticide is still a last-minute solution. News of a baby found dead on a beach, on the steps of a church, in bushes, with the police concerned about the mother's health, who can come forward in all confidentiality are commonplace.[56]

The ban on abortion information certainly caused a lot of panic and anxiety to more than a few Irish women facing an unwanted pregnancy. Before the Hamilton judgment, they could discuss their options at ODC or at a WWC clinic. In those days (from the mid-1970s when such services began to appear to 1987), an Irish woman going to Britain for an abortion could give it mature reflection and make an informed choice. Staff in the British clinics have noticed that, since 1987, Irish women often arrive in a state of panic and, as they cannot return after due reflection, they have an abortion there and then. The Ulster Pregnancy Advisory Association has also noticed that the number of women from the Republic going to Belfast for some information or even phoning to get some advice significantly increased within eight months following the Hamilton judgment.[57] Another consequence of the information ban is the increase in the number of late abortions: according to the British Pregnancy Advisory Service, the number of late abortions (after 12 weeks) went from 7 per cent of the total number of abortions in 1986 (the year preceding the Hamilton judgment) to 14 per cent in 1988 (the year following). The same applies to abortions performed after 16 weeks. According to the Irish Women's Abortion Support Group (IWASG) in London, only 3 per cent of Irish women who used their support service in 1986 had abortions after 16 weeks' gestation. By the first half of 1987 this figure had doubled to 6 per cent. Recent figures suggest that 85 per cent of the Irish women who go to Britain for an abortion are less than 12 weeks pregnant. Among these 85 per cent, 35 per cent are less than nine weeks pregnant, and 50 per cent are between nine and 12 weeks pregnant.[58] It remains that all these Irish women were penalised by the information ban, those who go to Britain as soon as they find out they are pregnant and do not always take time to consider all their options, and what they really want; those who wait too long, because they do not know how to go about it or where to go, or might even have tried to induce a miscarriage themselves (another current practice according to BPAS). Still, the increase in the official figures proves that they were not dissuaded from going ahead with what seemed to them to be the only solution. It can be noted that while the X case was raging, that is during the first quarter of 1992, 1,162 Irish women nonetheless went to Britain, the highest figure ever recorded for one term, showing a 10 per cent increase over the 1991 figure! Statistics have come to replace the testimony of actual women, silenced by the information ban. Only two television programmes have documented the state of mind of such women: *The Silent Export* and *50,000 Secret Journey*, which were broadcast in 1994.[59]

Let us try to imagine what such a woman goes through. The money for the termination and the trip itself has first to be found, or perhaps a part of it only as the British clinics have been known to say 'come over anyway'.[60] Then some reason for a short trip to Britain has to be dreamed up. After travelling all night, she must wait for the clinic to open, but cannot have breakfast. Just one hour before the operation doctors and counsellors will mention for the first time the other options open to her. A bus will take her and a group of women to where the operation will be performed. The next morning she is discharged and has to wait until the evening for the train that goes to the ferry. Another night of travelling and she is back in Ireland at dawn.[61]

Across the Irish Sea, BPAS, a non-profit-making charity, welcomes the largest number of Irish women who do not qualify for an abortion under the National Health Service (as one has to be resident in Britain for at least six weeks). It sees about 1,000 Irish women every year. The Women Health Clinics Marie Stopes (there are three in London) welcome about 2,000 Irish women a year. The IWASG, set up in London in 1981 by some first- and second-generation Irish women, organises transport, accommodation and appointments at the clinic once the Irish women in need have found out how to contact them.[62] There is a similar group in Liverpool, Escort, which can even organise for somebody to collect the women on their arrival at the ferry or at the airport and take care of them for the duration of their short and stressful stay. Parallel to this support network in Britain, an underground network was established in Ireland, with an illegal helpline whose number could be found amidst graffiti in public toilets, on the grapevine or from an understanding doctor. Paradoxically, the English phonebooks can be found in city libraries or bought from Telecom Eireann, the Irish phone company. And for a couple of pounds anyone can buy the *Dáil Debates* of 21 May 1992 (or read them in the library) during which a deputy used his parliamentary privilege to read out the number of the seven Marie Stopes clinics uncensored. All the Irish papers published *in extenso* his intervention the next day! Lastly, the student unions kept defying the law by printing abortion information in their yearly handbooks.

All this goes to show that a substantial number of teenagers and women have to make this journey, during which they were all liable to be stopped and arrested, or at least that was the case until March 1992. Nonetheless, whatever their social class, whatever the difficulties encountered, despite their guilt at wanting an abortion, the number of Irish women going to Britain for an abortion has not decreased, not since the 8th amendment nor since the Hamilton judgment. Ireland has never got rid of the problem, it has only exported it, taking advantage of its neighbour's liberal legislation. Was it going to face up to the problem once the X case burst like a bombshell?

6 Abortion:...To the Right to Live

The abortion debate had seemed closed since 1983. The official figures relative to Irish terminations in Britain were published in the newspapers, without comment. The only pending question was that of information, since both the women's centres and the student unions were awaiting a verdict at Irish or European level. The right to choose was not on the agenda, only the right to information mobilised the campaigners. But in February 1992, a case hit the headlines which turned out to be much more than a *fait-divers*, since it called in question the national legislation and Constitution, became entangled with the European Maastricht Treaty and shook public opinion notably and irreversibly.

THE X CASE

On 12 February it was learnt that the Attorney-General, Harry Whelehan, the principal law officer, had been granted an interim injunction against a 14–year-old rape victim and her parents to make them return from Britain where they had gone to seek an abortion. The girl had been the victim of sexual abuse by a family friend over several months. When she became pregnant, the parents decided, against their moral convictions, to take her to Britain for an abortion. But because they contacted the Irish police to check the admissibility in court of a DNA test to prove paternity, the Attorney-General was notified and used his powers as the protector of the Constitution and of public interest to have the life of the foetus protected. In the light of the recent SPUC cases, this new vindication of the right to life of the unborn was fully in keeping with the logic of the law. Even though PLAC rejected all suggestions of extreme scenarios as 'hysterical', the lawyer William Binchy had written about the suitability of injunctions to prevent abortions from taking place.[1] In the High Court, Judge Costello granted a permanent injunction preventing Ms X from leaving the country for the duration of her pregnancy. The rationale behind this seemed rather callous. There is a hierarchy of rights, and if the constitutional right to freedom of movement is going to be used to flout another constitutional right, the court can intervene to restrain the former.[2] As for the fact that the girl was suicidal, the judge deemed the risk that she put an end to her life to be 'much less' and 'of a different order of magnitude' from the certainty that the unborn's life would be terminated if it was not protected by means of an injunction. Even though the Treaty of Rome guaranteed freedom to avail oneself of a service such as abortion, and to go from one country to another for that purpose, it was recalled that Ireland can derogate this 'on grounds of public policy, public security or public health'. Article 40.3.3 and its legal consequences amounted precisely to a derogation on the grounds of public policy, which arose from deeply held moral convictions. Consequently Judge Costello did not think that 'a measure which empowers a court to stop a woman going abroad (which taken in conjunction with constitutional principles is one of the effects of the 8th amendment) to terminate the life of the unborn is disproportionate to the aim which the 8th amendment seeks to achieve.' This verdict was received with shock in all quarters, and was symbolised by a cartoon published in *The Irish Times*, representing a pregnant youngster holding a teddy bear by the hand and standing in the middle of a camp the shape of the Republic of Ireland surrounded by barbed wire. The caption read: '17th February 1992. . . The introduction of internment in Ireland... for 14-year old girls. . .'[3] The country was appalled, marches were organised, debates upon debates dominated public fora and homes. Even President Mary Robinson summarised, with sobriety, what she witnessed:

> I cannot but say that this has been a very difficult week for women and girls in Ireland. You know as well as I do that as President I have no role to play or function to play in relation to this specific issue. But because I am very much in touch I think I am in a very good position to know. . . of the anxiety, of the sense of frustration, of the sense of helplessness and also, I think, arising out of this increasing self-development of women and confidence that has been talked about, a sense that we must move on to a more compassionate society – that we must in fact pull together and make progress in this very difficult area.... I have this very real sense, . . . that at the moment we are experiencing as a people a very deep crisis in ourselves. I hope we have the courage, which we have not always had, to face up to and look squarely and to say this is a problem we have got to resolve.[4]

Family Solidarity was indignant that the President had not referred to the rights of the unborn child. But the anti-abortion groups were generally dismayed by the X case, because it instantly and substantially eroded the anti-abortion consensus reigning in the country. And this is a fact. The President's speech had no precedent, and one witnessed other extraordinary things in the country in the following days and weeks. The singer Sinead O'Connor revealed she had had two abortions and forced her way to talk to the Taoiseach as she was exhorting the teenagers of Ireland to take to the streets – which is what whole uniformed classes of them did, throughout Ireland. It was a debate they had not taken part in in 1983, but neither had their big sisters. An opinion poll taken a few days after the verdict revealed that 64 per cent of the sample did not agree with the High Court's decision (25 per cent did), and that 66 per cent wanted the 8th amendment to be reviewed to allow for abortion in certain limited and defined circumstances (28 per cent were opposed).[5]

Such a change of heart since the 1983 referendum begs the following question: Did the Irish know precisely what they were voting for at that time? Were they aware that by voting yes to the pro-life amendment, they would prevent a teenage rape victim from having an abortion, or did they think that the clause 'with due regard to the equal right to life of the mother' would cover the extreme cases (this was never officially clarified)? Or, had attitudes changed so drastically in nine years?

A recent study on European values shows that the Irish were more tolerant towards abortion in 1990 than in 1981 (the date of the previous study). To the question, would you approve of abortion where the mother's health is at risk by the pregnancy, 45 per cent said yes in 1981, 65 per cent in 1990. And where it is likely that the child would be born handicapped, 25 per cent said yes in 1981, 32 per cent in 1990.[6] The question asked did contain the word 'health' which, according to the definition of the World Health Organisation, includes physical, psychological and social well-being. Can one admit that rape shatters this well-being and puts the mental health of the woman sufficiently in danger to justify an abortion?

The government, in its embarrassment, offered to pay all the X family's costs if they appealed to the Supreme Court. This generous offer implied that the government hoped that the injunction would be lifted and the girl would have her abortion, whereas the state's lawyers would do their utmost to make sure the injunction was upheld. Nonetheless the offer marks a cathartic turnaround in the attitude of Irish legislators: moral principles, because of their remoteness and inflexibility, do not stand up to the reality of things and, once inserted in a document, create aberrant situations like the X case, which have to be corrected out of compassion. Uncharacteristically, the five Supreme Court judges handed down their verdict within a few days, and quashed that of the High Court: the girl could go abroad for an abortion.

The text of the judgments, one from each judge, was made public the following week and explained the reasoning behind the extraordinary fact that, with a majority of 4 to 1, abortion was now legal in Ireland under certain circumstances. The verdict was historic in the sense that it offered an interpretation of the 8th amendment, which was unexpected and totally contrary to what the pro-life campaigners had set out to achieve. But, as the President of the Supreme Court said, echoing the McGee ruling, judges have to interpret the rights guaranteed by the Constitution with prudence, justice and charity, but also in the light of the prevailing values. That is how a majority of the judges ruled that if there is a strong probability that the life (as opposed to the health) of the mother is in danger (even if the danger is self-inflicted), and if this risk can be avoided by a termination of pregnancy, then such an operation is permissible, under the terms of the Constitution ('with due regard to the equal right to life of the mother'). Judge McCarthy accepted that self-destruction was a real threat to the life of the young girl, which only a termination would relieve, and in that he was followed by three of the judges. The fifth maintained that the girl should be protected against self-destruction, which would preserve the life of the unborn child at the same time. In fact the most extraordinary aspect of the verdict was that the judges recognised suicide as such a real and substantial threat to the life of the mother that an abortion was deemed appropriate. Interestingly, they referred to a life in danger, whereas the psychologist who testified on the suicidal state of Ms X said that there was no doubt in his mind that 'the damage of this pregnancy to her mental health is going to be devastating'. Such a differentiation would prove crucial a few months later when the government tried to exclude health, mental or otherwise, from its proposed constitutional amendment. The majority judges omitted ruling on any time limits for legal abortions, but they only had to examine the facts of the present case. The judiciary is not meant to solve the legislators' headaches; on the contrary it could be accused of forcing things. It was now up to the legislators to define the exact parameters in which a woman could procure a termination of pregnancy (a phrase rarely employed in Ireland but employed a few times by the judges). Judge McCarthy was particularly scathing in its attack of the legislators' apathy:

I think it reasonable, however, to hold that the People when enacting the Amendment were entitled to believe that legislation would be introduced so as to regulate the manner in which the right to life of the unborn and the right to life of the mother could be reconciled. In the context of the eight years that have passed since the Amendment was adopted and the two years since Grogan's case [a SPUC v. the students case] the failure by the legislature to enact the appropriate legislation is no longer just unfortunate; it is inexcusable. What are pregnant women to do? What are the parents of a pregnant girl under-age to do? What are the medical profession to do? They have no guidelines save what may be gleamed from the judgements in this case. What additional considerations are there? Is the victim of rape, statutory or otherwise, or the victim of incest, finding herself pregnant, to be assessed in a manner different from others? The Amendment, born of public disquiet, historically divisive of our people, guaranteeing in its laws to respect and by its laws to defend the right to life of the unborn, remains bare of legislative direction.

The other aspect of the judgement is more in keeping with that of the High Court, but it is not binding, being as it were an aside. Three out of five judges, maintained that the state is entitled to prevent women going abroad for an abortion, because 'if there were a stark conflict between the right of the mother of an unborn child to travel and the right to life of the unborn child, the right to life would necessarily have to take precedence over the right to travel.' But Judge McCarthy, for his part, felt that if the mother has the right to travel, this right cannot be restrained whatever the purpose of the journey, especially if it is to avail of a legal service in another country. He added:

I cannot disregard the fact that, whatever the exact numbers are, there is no doubt that in the eight years since the enactment of the Amendment, many thousands of Irish women have chosen to travel to England to have abortions; it is ironic that out of those many thousands, in one case of a girl of fourteen, victim of sexual abuse and statutory rape, in the care of loving parents who chose with her to embark on further trauma, having sought help from priest, doctor and gardai, and with an outstanding sense of responsibility to the law of the land, should have the full panoply of the law brought to bear on them in their anguish.

Irish law had come to the same point as British law in 1939 with the Bourne case. But what was the Irish state going to do to give effect to this judgment? Amend the 1861 law in order to specify the circumstances in which a legal abortion could be performed? Organise a new referendum to repeal or amend Article 40.3.3? In any case, it had become urgently necessary to guarantee freedom of movement to Irish women, since the Supreme Court had not confirmed the supremacy of such a right, and this came as a major shock throughout the country especially at this point of European integration. The case of pregnancies as the result of rape or incest had not been tackled at all, even though the X case helped bring into light the vast issue of sexual abuse and mobilise public opinion and the authorities.

The Lavinia Kerwick case and the Kilkenny case were part of the same process – legislating through accident. Lavinia Kerwick, 19 years old, raped by a friend, expressed her anger to the media when the rapist was given a suspended sentence, which prompted the Minister for Justice to introduce the Criminal Justice (Public Order) Act, 1993, to allow an appeal against lenient sentences. As the journalist Nuala O'Faolain remarked: 'I understand progress coming about as a result of public pressure. But it's an uneasy thing when it seems to depend on completely unforeseeable events.'[7] As for the young woman at the centre of the 'Kilkenny case', she was the victim of sexual abuse and other acts of violence by her father over a period of 16 years, without any outside interference.[8] When the horror of her plight hit the headlines, it was another cathartic event, born of a groundswell of sympathy.

Another of the surprising effects of the X case was to hear parliamentarians express the inexpressible: if abortion was now legal in certain circumstances, it should be available in Ireland itself. Mary Harney, future leader of the Progressive Democrats and Secretary of State for the Environment, declared during a TV programme: 'If it is morally right in London, I can't see why it's morally wrong in Dublin.' Campaigners commented that if she had said such a thing in 1983, she would have lost her seat in no time! Other politicians followed her. This was seconded by an opinion poll published on 2 March, which showed that only 30 per cent of people thought the 8th amendment should remain as it was – an interesting result when one thinks of the 66.9 per cent who wanted its insertion in the first place – 48 per cent thought it should be modified, 18 per cent removed and only 4 per cent had no opinion. About the prospect of a new referendum, 52 per cent were in favour, 44 per cent were not.[9] These figures, compared to those of 23 February, (i.e. the 64 per cent who did not agree with the High Court judgment and the 66 per cent who wanted a change to Article 40.3.3 to allow for abortion in certain circumstances) confirm that the X case did overturn people's opinions and principles: Abortion would never again be a black-and-white issue. How were the legislators going to respond to that?

ABORTION: A EUROPEAN SERVICE

Even though the Taoiseach declared immediately after the ruling that he did not want to preside over a police state, and the right to travel would have to be restored, any solution to this, or to the 'substantive issue' of abortion as it became known, would have to be postponed because of the impending ratification of the Maastricht Treaty. The latter was an added dimension to the abortion quagmire. The right to life of the unborn child, as inscribed in the Irish Constitution, has nothing to do with Community law. But it received a European dimension when the Irish government sought to obtain a formal recognition from the EC that the Irish abortion ban would never be interfered with. This was reported in *The Irish Times* on 21 November 1991, but nobody paid it any attention. 1991 was the year when the ECJ defined abortion as a commercial service (one that the British clinics could promote in Ireland); and it was also the year the European Commission issued a report suggesting the EC adhere to the European Convention of Human Rights, which would mean that the decisions of the ECHR would take precedence over Irish law. 1991 was the year the Maastricht Treaty, successor to the Treaty of Rome and making way for a greater European integration, was drafted and a couple of the anti-abortion veterans had the idea of inserting a protocol that would protect Ireland against any future European decisions, deemed far too liberal in the socio-moral area. In the first place, to define abortion as a service was sheer nonsense and had to be nipped in the bud. Since the Treaty ensured a certain amount of delegation of sovereignty on the part of the 12 member-states, a protocol put a limitation on this delegation. Protocol 17 stated that nothing at European level would 'affect the application in Ireland of Article 40.3.3 of the Constitution of Ireland'.[10] Gerry Collins, Minister for Foreign Affairs and Ireland's main Treaty negotiator, called it 'an insurance policy' against the legalisation of abortion, and William Binchy 'an essential adjunct to the Maastricht Treaty'. It is not clear if Senator Hanafin, who first voiced this idea, had to put much pressure on the government, or if the latter was all for it and even had the idea itself, as Gerry Collins seemed to imply later. The question was certainly never debated in

Parliament, only at Cabinet level, and the wording drafted by some high-ranking civil servants, including the Attorney-General himself. Dermot Keogh suggests that the first version of the draft circulated made reference to the ban on divorce which should also be protected against European interference: 'this was not a doodle on a piece of paper. The draft in question received widespread circulation to the relevant government departments. But that piece of irresponsibility was resisted vigorously by a number of honourable people.'[11]

Such procedures, the insertion of a protocol and the 1983 amendment, are the expression of a collective paranoia whose main symptom is the fear that Europe will impose its moral choices – its immorality – on the Irish people, so far immune, it was believed, to evil practices. It also accounts for the somewhat naive attempt at copperfastening laws in stone, shielded from judges and elected representatives. Surprisingly, when one thinks about it, the European partners did not ask for any clarification on the implications of the protocol and approved it in December 1991. The Maastricht Treaty was signed on 7 February 1992, a week before the X case hit the headlines. At the time, it had not been suggested that it could limit the right to free circulation of Irish women. But the Supreme Court ruling in the X case gave it this power. Ironically, the protocol had been inserted to prevent the ratification of the Treaty from becoming entangled with the abortion question, by those who wanted to make sure that European legislation would never force abortion onto Ireland; in fact the two questions were going to become entangled, by those who wanted the rights to free circulation and recourse to European law to be clearly guaranteed. Would the Attorney-General still be entitled to stop a woman going abroad for an abortion? Could she be brought back before it took place? Could she be prosecuted on her return? The whole thing was mind-boggling, even to legal minds. Moreover, Article 40.3.3 now recognised a category of women entitled to an abortion in Ireland, so what did the protocol guarantee? That the EU recognised the right to an abortion in Ireland when the life of the mother was at risk?

To get out of this legal nonsense, which one gets into when one tries to guarantee something that has now taken on a new interpretation, removing the protocol would have contented everybody: those who feared that Irish women would lose with Maastricht part of their Community rights; and those who feared that Maastricht would copperfasten the interpretation given to Article 40.3.3 by the Supreme Court (abortion legal in certain circumstances). But this option was never really entertained. In order to guarantee the right to travel, it was necessary either to add a clause to Article 40.3.3 by referendum, or to negotiate an addendum to the protocol. The substantive issue of abortion as put forward by the Supreme Court was not an issue at all for the time being.

The government was anxious to have the Maastricht Treaty ratified by the people, undisturbed by moral considerations (Ireland was one of only two member-states requiring the treaty to be ratified by referendum). The chances of that were getting slim when Senator Hanafin and William Binchy presided over the launch of a new campaign, the Pro-Life Campaign (PLC) calling for a referendum to restore Article 40.3.3 to its initial meaning; and veterans of AAC launched the Repeal the 8th Amendment Campaign (REAC). It has to be said that the idea of a new pro-life referendum was never entertained at government level: there was no question of submitting to a lobby by far too powerful a coalition, whose campaigns had been too divisive (the government had its eyes on markets more than on moral principles, and it did not like the way it was portrayed at international level in the wake of the X case). Albert Reynolds was the new Taoiseach, having replaced Charles Haughey on 11 February, the day before the X case shook the nation. The government tried to get its European partners to accept the idea of an addendum. Adding an addendum to a protocol in a European treaty to guarantee an amendment to the Irish Constitution was getting a bit too complex even to legal experts! To cap it all, when counsel for the state admitted at the ECHR in the *SPUC* v. *ODC and WWC* case that the right to information existed in certain circumstances as defined in the X case, it became necessary to insert that right too in an addendum. In any case, the request for an addendum was rejected, as it was feared that other member-states would also want to modify the Treaty. Instead it was suggested that the twelve sign a Solemn Declaration, like the 32 others already appended to the Treaty, which are not binding but acknowledge that a problem has been identified. The Declaration stated that the signatories meant that 'the protocol shall not limit freedom either to travel between member states or, ... to obtain or make available in Ireland, information relating to services lawfully available in member states.' They declared that

> in the event of a future constitutional amendment in Ireland [about abortion] ... and which does not conflict with the intention of the High Contracting Parties hereinbefore expressed, they will, ... be favourably disposed to amending the said protocol so as to extend

its application to such constitutional amendment if Ireland so requests.

Why was it up to the Europeans to guarantee such rights which should be the concern of the national government? If Ireland was so adamant, as one of the 12 signatories of this declaration, about the right to travel, and this should be true retrospectively, what of the injunction against X? How could the 11 partners agree to consider recognising a future amendment without having the slightest idea of its content? This was too close to Des Hanafin's suggestion, disclosed on 22 March, that an addendum should state that any future constitutional amendment in connection with Article 40.3.3 would be covered by the Maastricht Treaty. Again, it seemed that a suggestion from the pro-life lobby was easily incorporated in an official document without prior Parliament consultation. Despite the Taoiseach's generous words, that he did not want to preside over a police state, the fact remains that he and Fianna Fáil were horrified that to date a psychologist's decision would suffice for an abortion to be carried out, up to the ninth month of pregnancy if need be. Were they tempted to go back to the earlier situation and quash the Supreme Court ruling? As a press editorial put it, as far as abortion was concerned, the government were 'in a state of total chassis'![12] Having the Treaty ratified while guaranteeing the right to travel and the right to information – rights that would have to be guaranteed at national level – seemed an intractable problem. Women's groups and opposition parties were hoping that a referendum on these rights would be organised before the European one, but it was announced that the Maastricht referendum would take place on 18 June, and the questions relative to abortion would be dealt with in the autumn. This was not a very convincing way of dissociating abortion from the European question. The coalition partners, the PDs, disagreed with this approach, but short of bringing down the government (and it would be politically damaging to do such a thing over the question of abortion!), they had to bow to Albert Reynolds' style of government, a kind of 'take it or leave it' approach directed to his partners in government, as well as to PLC. REAC and PLC found themselves on the same side, – calling people to vote No to Maastricht.

For REAC, it was unacceptable that Protocol 17 remain unamended, guaranteeing the application of a very ambiguous Article 40.3.3 which could make 'second-class citizens' out of Irish women. PLC were worried that any change to Article 40.3.3 (going back to an absolute ban on abortion) would not be covered by the Maastricht

Treaty once it was signed. Trying to dissociate abortion from the question of European Union, the government seemed to be doing exactly the opposite, without mentioning the political crisis Fianna Fáil's attitude had brought about. Relations with the PDs were now so strained, one wondered if the coalition would survive the November referendum or referendums on abortion! All consensus was dead, and the debate was threatening to be just as polarised and divisive as in 1983.

The Taoiseach was determined to prove he was the man of the hour, armed for the first political test of his mandate. Though opposed to abortion, the case of Ms X had moved him, and he kept saying that a pro-life referendum would be the last solution considered. Obviously, he wanted to distance himself from his predecessor, by not giving in to PLC's demands and by stressing who was in charge of the country's business. Two influential pro-PLC heads metaphorically rolled as a result: that of a High Court judge, Rory O'Hanlon, who was removed from his position as President of the Law Reform Commission for publishing an article in which he called for a new pro-life referendum, thus crossing the dividing line between the judicial and the political processes. His dismissal was a clear expression of the determination of the government to remain in control of the abortion agenda, even if it was seen as dithering and hedging. Then Senator Des Hanafin was expelled from the Fianna Fáil parliamentary party for voting against the bill putting in place the Maastricht referendum, which was contrary to party discipline. Thus Albert Reynolds dealt with those who tried to propel him into an abortion referendum!

In the later stages of the campaign though, which was getting more emotional by the day, his stance became somewhat confusing – a mixture of threats and cajoling aimed at reassuring just about everyone. There was strong pressure from within his party to see the Supreme Court judgment overturned, echoed by a declaration of the Catholic hierarchy on 14 April which 'noted with alarm that the right to life of the unborn does not appear to be on the Government's agenda at the present time' and that 'because the God-given right to life is the foundation of all other rights, the vindication of this right cannot be evaded.' In any case, on 18 June 1992, the Irish overwhelmingly voted Yes to Maastricht and European integration, and Ireland became the first member-state to ratify the treaty: 69.1 per cent voted Yes and 30.9 per cent, No with a turnout of 57 per cent. The (curious) fact that the highest Yes votes to Maastricht came from constituencies where the Yes to the pro-life amendment had been highest in 1983 gives reason to believe that the issues raised by this referendum were clearly economic, since these are rural constituencies which benefit a lot from the Common Agricultural Policy. Even the Catholic hierarchy understood that it would have been counter-productive to preach for a No vote, all the more so as PLC was already out there with this message. Their last declaration before the vote, after a long silence, was rather qualified, since they left every citizen free to vote for what s/he thought would best protect unborn human life, and demanded a new pro-life referendum.

There were two reasons for their sobriety: first, opinion polls predicted a comfortable Yes, and the authority of the Church would have been unnecessarily harmed if it turned farmers, industrialists, businesspeople and the like against them by calling for a No vote. Also, there was the Bishop Casey affair. The Bishop of Galway resigned on 7 May 'for personal reasons', and behind the formula a 17-year-old son was hiding, born to and brought up by Annie Murphy, a distant cousin of the bishop. To cap a passably sordid affair, the Irish learnt a few days later that he had used some diocesan funds to send to her. Because this scandal came out in the midst of the referendum campaign, in an emotional context owing to the renewed abortion controversy, it had a greater impact than it would have had. Irish society again had to face up to the fact that it was not so decent, perfect or pure as it liked to think it was. There would be in the following months more grim discoveries and allegations shattering the myth into even smaller fragments: the priest found dead in a gay club, with two colleagues on the spot administering the last rites; Fr Michael Cleary and his two children from his long-standing housekeeper; umpteen sexual abuse cases (clerical and otherwise), with the Brendan Smyth case having the infamous extra notoriety of bringing about the fall of the government in November 1994. On the whole, most people kept their sympathy for the Galway bishop who had always been popular if slightly eccentric, despite his preaching against family planning, sterilisation, abortion and divorce, while himself committing evil acts! In fact, many people voiced their wish to see diocesan priests marry if enforced celibacy led to that. Naturally the hierarchy could not show itself to be too absolutist in the current debate on Europe *cum* abortion, or the faithful would not listen with too much respect and would take Dr Casey's private behaviour into consideration when deciding about the morality of having recourse to contraception, abortion or divorce. So PLC lost a great part of the moral authority it was expecting from the Catholic Church.

It is abundantly clear that abortion was dissociated from Maastricht, and women did not want their No vote to be confused with that of the fundamentalist Catholics, and gambled on a Yes vote. Senator Des

Hanafin, legal adviser William Binchy, John O'Reilly, the *éminence grise* of PLC, had lost their first referendum, thus confirming they represented the 'moral minority' and not the moral majority as in 1983. There was now in Ireland an ultra-moral minority, an ultra-liberal minority and a bloc of reasonably liberal people in the middle.

In response to the Fianna Fáil backbenchers who said they felt the pressure of their constituents for a new pro-life referendum, let us look at some of the opinion polls. In May 1992, one revealed that 80 per cent of those questioned were in favour of legalising abortion in certain circumstances. Only 19 per cent felt there was no circumstances in which abortion should be allowed. Those 19 per cent represented the point of view defended by PLC, no one else supported it.[13] If one goes back to the previous polls, that of 23 February for example, it seems logical that if 64 per cent were shocked by the Costello judgment against young X, the 66 per cent in favour of a revision to the 8th amendment were of a liberal stance. On 2 March, the injunction had been lifted, but it was not yet known how the judges had reached their decision; 52 per cent wanted a new referendum, and at that time, to wish for a new referendum was to take a rather liberal position since it was not known what the Supreme Court had based their decision on. (A new referendum would have aimed at preventing such injunctions from ever happening again.) But once Article 40.3.3 itself is known to have been the basis for the Supreme Court ruling, acknowledging the threat of suicide as a legitimate ground for abortion, it becomes more difficult to determine if the 82 per cent who wanted a referendum on 11 June wanted it to recognise the judgment but guarantee certain rights, or to repeal Article 40.3.3, or on the contrary to restore its original meaning.[14] However, 83 per cent on that day thought that abortion should be made legal in certain circumstances. It is clear that the strong majority who voted for the insertion of an amendment copperfastening the ban on abortion had all but evaporated in nine years, in the wake of the X case. Was the new liberal majority going to materialise at the referendum promised by the government on abortion and related issues? Now that the Maastricht Treaty was ratified, and the future of Ireland within Europe assured, the government had to grasp the nettle. PLC was defeated, but it still benefited from a solid infrastructure and important financial resources. And it could rely once more on the support of the Catholic Church, which did not have to show consideration to the economic interests of the country. A commission, presided over by the Minister for Justice, Padraig Flynn, was asked to make recommendations on the way to deal with the issue. The same minister was also working on the White

Paper on marital breakdown, which had been postponed to avoid fighting on more than one 'religion-fraught front' at a time.[15]

ABORTION: A MORAL AND RESPONSIBLE OPTION

As far as politicians were concerned, a referendum on the right to freedom of travel and information did not raise major problems, but opinions diverged as to the way to deal with the substantive issue of abortion. Pressure groups on both sides of the legislation/referendum divide were trying to help the government come to the only possible solution, as they saw it. For example, the Second Commission for the Status of Women recommended that

> the Government should either delete the abortion clause in the Constitution or amend it to 'guarantee the right to information and travel without interfering with the rights of a pregnant woman where there is a real and substantial risk to her life' [and also that] legislation be enacted which ensures that pregnant women have the right to prompt and appropriate medical intervention, including palliative treatment, in the case of life-threatening conditions.

Informed sources said at the time that the attitude of the women's pressure groups would have a major influence on the Cabinet as it reached its decision, because there had been surprise at the virulent opposition of women in general to the Protocol. On the other side, apart from PLC, re-formed from PLAC, there were Family Solidarity and Life Interest, its official youth branch of around 1,000 members. Three hundred general practitioners had formed Doctors for Life in the wake of the X judgment, for whom there was no disease that an abortion could cure; they advised PLC, and their spokesperson was Dr Berry Kiely, a member of Opus Dei.

A new group on the scene was Youth Defence, also formed in protest at the X judgment, with over 3,000 members aged around 20. Affiliated to the National Right to Life Federation, the group would soon get a lot of (bad) publicity for the radical tactics it used, such as picketing the homes of politicians deemed to be soft on abortion or parading grim photos of aborted foetuses. All these groups had in common that they wanted a referendum to re-establish the original meaning of Article 40.3.3. There was no such thing as freedom of information if it was instrumental in the killing of a child. They were more divided on the issue of travel.

The Catholic Church made its mind known on various occasions. For example, Dr Desmond Connell preached about 'the absolute and irreparable evil of abortion.... That our Constitution may once more be enabled to express the will of the majority of our people to reject abortion.'[16] In contrast, the Protestant churches were satisfied with the Supreme Court ruling. For example, Anglican Bishop John Neill wondered 'whether a potential life conceived as the outcome of rape can be simply regarded as a divine gift of life'. In general the Protestant churches favoured a new law rather than a new constitutional amendment, which was deemed to be too blunt an instrument to take on board all the complexities of the issue. Even though the Taoiseach announced he had no intention to meet any of the pressure groups or churches, it was thought consensus would be reached when he met the leaders of the other parties.

The decision eventually taken was reached quasi- unilaterally. There would be three referendums on abortion. So, ironically, despite the dire condemnation of Judge McCarthy of the government's irresponsibility, the latter decided seven months later to put the question in the hands of the Irish people again instead of grasping the legislative nettle itself. In substance, Irish people would be asked to vote on three questions, dealing respectively with the right to travel from Ireland to another state (for an abortion), the right to obtain information relative to services (such as abortion) legally available in another state, and the substantive issue of abortion. The 12th amendment of the Constitution dealing with it would read: 'It shall be unlawful to terminate the life of an unborn unless such termination is necessary to save the life, as distinct from the health, of the mother where there is an illness or disorder of the mother giving rise to a real and substantial risk to her life, not being a risk of self-destruction.'

Interestingly, the words 'abortion' or 'termination of pregnancy' do not appear in any of the proposed amendments. Abortion opponents had said that, although they would not prevent women from going to Britain for an abortion, they would not accept the use of the word itself in the Constitution, and one notices that the government felt as prudish. Apart from the hierarchy and the anti-choice groups, most were dismayed at the prospect of deciding on such a complex isssue on the basis of a convoluted sentence. The thrust of the referendum was to facilitate the abortion route to Britain, while life-shortening and quality-of-life-destroying conditions would not be grounds for an abortion in Ireland. The particularity of the 12th amendment was that it overturned the ruling in the X case by excluding the threat of suicide as an acceptable ground for abortion, and it could diminish the right to life of the mother by trying to distinguish it from a risk to her health. The Taoiseach let it be known he was willing to discuss this second objection, but not the former. The 12th amendment implied that where a pregnant woman was suffering from a medical condition such that her life would be endangered, the pregnancy could lawfully be terminated in Ireland to save her life. The memorandum explaining the Cabinet's decision added: 'Some doctors are of the view that it is possible to treat these conditions without resorting to direct abortion. However, it seems difficult to advance a categorical statement that circumstances could never arise which would require a direct abortion to save the mother's life.'[17] This was a distinct change from the rhetoric of 1983. Unfortunately, this was soon to be contradicted by several politicians, most notably the Minister for Health, Dr John O'Connell. However, the use of terms such as 'it shall be unlawful to terminate the life of an unborn unless...' implies that abortion in certain circumstances would be allowed, and the very use of 'terminate' or 'termination' expresses an active and direct concept rather than an unintentional effect.

One could be forgiven for thinking the government was trying to win support from all sides – from the pro-lifers by assuring them that only indirect abortions would be allowed; and the others, by granting a right to abortion when the life of the mother was at risk, knowing that doctors would interpret this as they saw fit. Current medical practice already included aggressive treatment which might result in the death of the foetus for such conditions as ectopic pregnancy, cancer of various organs, pre-eclampsia, cardiac disease, etc. Would this practice change, or would it not? Was the government Machiavellian, or was the amendment badly drafted – if it did not mean what people thought it meant?

Fianna Fáil was now attacked by all the other political parties for being reactionary and anti-woman, and by the pro-lifers for condoning a category of legal abortions at all. This being said, the pro-lifers, despite their reservations, did not have much room to manoeuvre since the X case decision would have force of law if the 12th amendment was rejected; only the liberals could oppose the amendment knowing they would benefit from its defeat. Confusion increased when it was learnt that the Attorney-General had advised the government 'that the purpose of the distinction between the life and the health of the mother was to prohibit any abortion the purpose of which was to avoid a "life-shortening", as opposed to life-threatening, situation.' Ronan Fanning said aloud what a lot of people were thinking: 'What kind of a government can say, in effect, to the women of Ireland that they'll do something to prevent pregnancy taking their lives, but that if pregnancy damages their health and so shortens their lives or if unwanted pregnancy drives them in desperation to think of taking their own lives, they'll just have to grin and bear it?'[18] Women's voices, without mentioning their distress, were at no time taken into consideration, since, as a journalist put it: 'The law, as I understand it, will be inspired by bishops, interpreted by lawyers, enforced by doctors and imposed on women.'[19] There was, pervading the whole debate, a fundamental distrust of women's free will, of their capacity to reach a very private decision, of their moral conscience. Mervyn Taylor remarked: 'The debate has come full circle. It started because a small, intolerant and professionally organised pressure group decided that they did not trust the legislators. Then they decided they didn't trust the courts. Now they have decided they don't trust women.'[20] Even though the government refused to meet the demands of PLC on the insertion of a total ban on abortion in the Constitution, it would not agree to remove from its wording the distinction between the life and health of the mother, saying this would lead to widespread abortion. At the Fianna Fáil parliamentary meeting, only Brian Lenihan and Dr Jim McDaid disagreed with the distinction. The former said:

> I have great doubts about the inclusion in the amendment of the five words 'as distinct from the health' because it sets up a contrary distinction between health and life which is confusing to lawyers and doctors and unworthy as far as women are concerned.... What is the difference between life and health? Life is health and health is life. Where does the risk to health end and the risk to life begin?[21]

Fine Gael agreed with the idea of a referendum, but wanted time to clarify the situation and discuss it in Parliament, and wanted legislation to be published before the referendum. The distinction between life and health was 'unnecessary', but the exclusion of suicide threats was met with approval by most Fine Gael TDs.

Labour analysed the wording and concluded 'the bottom line effect of the amendment (whatever Government Ministers may argue) is this: If this amendment is accepted, the Constitution will provide for the carrying out of legal abortions in certain circumstances. The *principle* of legal abortion is therefore being proposed for insertion into the fundamental law of the land.' Still, they called it a 'dangerous amendment' which they could not support: some disorders (like ectopic pregnancy) could necessitate an abortion, but psychological disorders, even if they had life-threatening physical manifestations, were out.

This was offensive to women and dangerous to boot, as it might be difficult in some cases to distinguish between a life-threatening as opposed to a life-shortening or health-threatening situation! The blanket ban on suicide as a ground for termination was also unsafe. Neither was it a good idea for doctors to become moral arbiters, with no guarantee that they would not be prosecuted for procuring an unlawful miscarriage if someone disagreed with their decision, or sued for negligence if their refusal to arrange an abortion resulted in the death of their patient. The potential for litigation was great.

Democratic Left launched its policy document on abortion, sexuality and women's health on 13 October. This detailed the circumstances in which an abortion should be allowed, since, as its leader, Proinsias de Rossa, put it:

> We are, I think, the only party which has got a clearly-stated view that there is a need for pregnancy termination in Ireland and that we can no longer allow another state, Britain, to deal with the social problems that arise in Ireland.... We also need to establish the principles on which a democratic republic should operate. A republic is not about imposing the moral and ethical views of the majority on every situation. It is also about protecting the rights of the minority. It is not right to seek to insert into our Constitution the ethical view of any one group of people, whether they are a majority or not.

Democratic Left was the only party to recognise that abortion was an option chosen by a number of women (we note that DL statements always refer to women, not mothers, which is probably symptomatic) and to deny that the Irish people were implacably opposed to abortion. The PDs had to go along with Fianna Fáil, however reluctantly, since they did not want to precipitate a general election based on abortion, which is not really a party issue. Since it received no 'better' proposition, the government decided to go ahead with the three amendments as drafted. A bill giving effect in full to the Supreme Court judgment would be published before the referendum, in the hope of splitting the anti-abortion campaign and showing how reasonable the government's own amendment was. The choice would thus be between legal abortion in certain circumstances, suicide excluded, or legal abortion in certain circumstances, suicide included.

The official campaign had not yet started, but people were already at their tolerance threshold and were turned off the whole issue. Opinion polls showed that as far as freedom to travel and to information was concerned, intentions were clear. But it was difficult to identify the 'liberal vote' in the answers to questions on the abortion amendment asked in an IMS/*The Irish Independent* poll published on 22 October. Concerning the distinction between life and health, 39 per cent thought it was appropriate and necessary, 39 per cent wanted it to be removed from the amendment, and 22 per cent were undecided. Concerning the risk of suicide as a ground for abortion, 38 per cent agreed it should be excluded, but 44 per cent thought it was valid, and 18 per cent were undecided. There thus seemed to be a substantial percentage dissatisfied with the amendment for excluding suicide and health risks. However, the following result is all the more surprising. To the question. 'Every year, Irishwomen travel abroad for abortions. Some people feel that such women should be free to choose to have an abortion in Ireland. What is your opinion?' 50 per cent maintained that these women should not have their abortion in Ireland (54 per cent of women, 46 per cent of men). This seems to contradict the almost similar result that 48 per cent were going to vote in favour of the amendment, which sets out that abortion will be legal in Ireland in certain circumstances. And where were the 39 per cent opposed to the distinction between life and health? The result also contradicts earlier polls taken in the wake of the X case when large majorities were in favour of legalising abortion. There was clearly a mental block in people's minds when faced with a proposition that was more concrete than the others: the acceptance of abortions on Irish soil.

One thing remained clear: if the three amendments were adopted, someone in the same position as young X would not be allowed an abortion in Ireland; and she might not be allowed to travel to Britain, since the link between the right to life of the unborn and the right to travel was not necessarily in favour of the pregnant woman.[22] The 12th amendment created new uncertainties whereas the Supreme Court had at last brought some elements of certainty to the 1983 amendment. It was becoming clear that the abortion amendment was doomed to failure, since it did not satisfy anybody, being either too liberal or too draconian. It was promoted as a reasonable solution whereas it was as legally and medically woolly as the 1983 one. The government, in its desire to avoid drafting, debating or voting on the first Irish law on abortion, had chosen to place the problem in the people's hands, and blew hot and cold to achieve its ends. The chances that the right to information would be approved in the forthcoming referendum rose when the ECHR in Strasbourg, in the case opposing SPUC to the women's health centres ODC and WWC, ruled that the ban on information imposed by the Irish state was in breach of Article 10

of the European Convention on Human Rights. It was found that
the ban was disproportionate to the aim of protecting the right to
life of the unborn, and was not working if its aim was to reduce
the number of abortions, as the number of women travelling to Britain
had actually increased since 1987. The link between the provision of
information and the destruction of unborn life was not as clear-cut
as contended. Moreover the ban was damaging to the health of Irish
women who had their abortions later in the pregnancy due to the lack of
information and did not receive post-abortion check-ups. ODC and
WWC still had to wait for a new law, whatever the result of the referendum, before they could resume their counselling services. Nonetheless the European ruling 'has narrowed the parameters within which the
self-appointed arbitrators of right or wrong must operate when having
recourse to the law, and it has added new and enlightened jurisprudence
for the guidance of our courts and legal system.'[23]

The referendum campaign received its biggest blow when the govern-
ment fell on 5 November. Three PDs Ministers resigned, and Fianna
Fáil lost a vote of no confidence. The governmental crisis had begun on
27 October during a hearing of the so-called Beef Tribunal, of Albert
Reynolds and his Minister for Industry and Commerce, Des O'Malley.
Also, the long-awaited contribution to the debate, that of the Irish
Bishops Conference, came on that same day: Thursday, 5 November.
The bishops deplored the fact that the voters were faced with a dilemma
as the amendments all encroached on the right to life of the unborn, and
they restated their opinion that 'the law has a clear influence on most
moral perceptions, and a change in the Constitution could lead to a
weakening of moral attitudes. These are the considerations which people must weigh up in coming to a conscientious decision as to how they
should vote on these two proposed amendments.' But Archbishop
Desmond Connell declared in his diocese he could not support any of
the referendums, in which he was followed by a handful of bishops.

By then, the abortion referendums had become embroiled in a general election, all taking place on the same day, now 25 November. The
election of the 27th Dáil defused the referendum campaign, as it turned
on the questions of economic, monetary and social problems. Politicians
of all parties admitted that abortion was not an issue on the doorstep
during their canvassing, which suited them as they were after seats and
all had a mutual interest in keeping abortion from sowing discord, as it
nearly did. Confusion still abounded though, as the penultimate opinion
poll before the poll showed. Jack Jones has demonstrated that people's
attitudes towards the availability of abortion in Ireland did not match

their voting intentions when he cross-analysed them. The analysis revealed that apart from the fact that 22 per cent were still undecided, 10 per cent intended to vote Yes (for restricted abortion) whereas they were in favour of abortion on demand; 11 per cent were going to vote Yes, but thought that the risk of suicide should be a ground for abortion; 6 per cent thought that abortion should only be available when the mother's life was at risk, but they were going to vote No, which was in total contradiction with their viewpoint; 5 per cent intended to vote Yes to an amendment that sets out abortion in certain limited circumstances, but their personal view was that it should not be allowed in *any* circumstances; and 11 per cent intended to vote No and felt that abortion should not be allowed in any circumstances. In all, this meant that 32 per cent were confused about what was at stake but were unaware of it; 11 per cent were consistent, provided they campaigned later for a more restrictive position than the one set out by the Supreme Court decision which would have force of law if the amendment was defeated as they wanted; and 24 per cent who did not know how they were going to vote yet had definite opinions on abortion, which is an admittance that they did not understand what they were being asked to vote on. Only 33 per cent intended to vote consistently with their own convictions, all the others were confused to varying degrees, and this was 'an unacceptable reflection on the politicians who have referred the issue to the people. There has been no formal or practical attempt to clarify what the amendment means, and it is clear that a majority do not understand what is being presented to them.'[24] Such confusion, such irresponsibility caused the editorial of *The Irish Times* to headline: 'Women abandoned'.

The last opinion poll before the referendum, taken on 15 November, showed that a growing number of people, faced with a confusing choice, preferred to hand back the problem to the legislators by defeating the amendment: 33 per cent were in favour of inserting the abortion amendment into the Constitution, 42 per cent were against, and there were still 25 per cent undecided, a very high percentage just ten days before the poll. Jack Jones concluded his analysis by saying the amendment was likely to be defeated – which it was. Even though 62.4 per cent voted in favour of the right to travel, (the 13th amendment to the constitution) and 59.9 per cent in favour of the right to information (the 14th amendment), 65.4 per cent refused the insertion of the abortion amendment. This result proved that Fianna Fáil could not rely on the unconditional support of the Catholic Church on matters of socio-sexual morality, and vice versa. Senator Des Hanafin concluded that this No majority meant that the Irish people were saying No to even limited abortion, and were calling for another pro-life referendum. In fact liberals also said No because it opened the way to future legislation. It is interesting to compare this result with that of the general election that took place on the same day.

As we saw in Chapter 2, Fianna Fáil had not had such a bad result since 1927 (incidentally, Hanafin would lose his Seanad seat shortly afterwards), Labour had never done so well, and 12 per cent of all TDs were now women, the highest percentage in the history of the state.[25] This exemplifies a will for change, at many different levels. As Brian Girvin points out, no constituency had a majority Yes to the abortion referendum, whereas three had a majority No to all three: Cork North West, Donegal North East and Donegal South, which always return a conservative vote. On the other hand, if one looks at the constituencies where the No vote was above average (65.4 per cent), one finds that in five the No vote was or 70 per cent and more: Cork North West and Donegal North East, two rural areas whose conservatism was well known; but in Dublin South, Dublin South West and Dun Laoghaire the No vote was also over 70 per cent, and their Yes vote in the other two referendums was above the national average; these are urban areas, with a liberal vote as previous votes proved.[26] The political analyst Richard Sinnott and economist Brendan J. Whelan, in their analysis of the results, conclude that neither the conservatives nor the liberals could claim victory.[27] It is also true that confusion had remained high until the end, a fact substantiated by the number of spoiled papers. Whatever the case, without rejecting the arguments about the general confusion and an unattributable victory, it seems more pertinent to say, with regard to the result of the 1983 referendum, that there were now two opposing forces, which could even be geographically located, as we have mentioned: the old moral majority and the new liberal majority, each representing about 30 per cent of the electorate.

> These results reveal the wide divergence of opinion on abortion in Ireland. Almost one third (31.0 per cent) of those voting appear to have adopted an ultra-conservative stance (No to all three referendums). A similar proportion (28.7 per cent) appear to have taken the liberal position of YYN [Yes, Yes, No to the three questions asked]. About 27 per cent are estimated to have adopted the 'pragmatic' position.[28]

The pragmatics are those who voted Yes to all three questions and are 'categorised as either conservative or liberal pragmatists in that it was possible to vote Yes on the substantive issue on the basis that, in the circumstances of Irish politics, it was the most that could be realistically achieved either for the conservative position or for the liberal position.'[29] The liberal minority that had emerged did not see abortion as a black-and-white issue, unqualifyingly condemned; but, by rejecting the amendment on abortion itself, they showed that the right to life of the unborn could not possibly and in any way encroach on the right to live of women. The 'catalytic' events of 1992 (the X case and the resignation of Bishop Casey in particular) had forced people to reassess their values, and the editorial of *The Irish Times* on 31 December 1992 summarised the watershed:

> Eight years off the century and off the millennium, 1992 may come to be chronicled as the year of painful growing up for Ireland.... The votes for tolerance and freedom in the referendums of November 25th will stand as the most significant and far-reaching events of 1992, marking as they did, a far-reaching and permanent change of attitude.

The initiative was back in the legislators' hands, and it was legitimate to wonder, in the light of the way the referendum campaign had been handled, how long it would take the Irish government to present and adopt the first Irish law on abortion. A long time, no doubt, since, on this issue, as in the case of contraception, divorce or homosexuality, all marked by the Catholic ideology, laws were got round, flouted and unenforced, and for years fell well short of the reality. The momentum was going to be lost, and the next two years were characterised by a policy of prevarication on the part of the new government, and a new strategy on the part of PLC, the latter certainly affecting the former.

The gestation period of this new government was the longest in the history of the state, and the resulting coalition (Fianna Fáil–Labour) the most surprising. Their government programme, published on 8 January 1993, said of abortion that it would be necessary to introduce legislation to regulate the existing position, as well as to cover the right to information. This was quite vague. The Minister for Health was in charge of the dossier, but the threat of legislating in the sense of the Supreme Court decision, suicide included, would not be carried out. This delay would enable other forces to manifest themselves. For example, the ethics committee of the Irish Medical Council strongly divided opinion, medical and otherwise, when it let it be known in April, that there was 'no situation' where an abortion was a necessary part of medical treatment and any doctor performing one acted unethically unless s/he could prove otherwise. However the new medical guideline it issued only stated: 'While the necessity for abortion to preserve the life or health of the sick mother remains to be proved, it is unethical always to withhold treatment beneficial to a pregnant woman by reason of her pregnancy.' In effect, they put a total ban on abortion in Ireland, whatever a future law would say, as no doctor would ever contemplate procuring an abortion lest s/he be struck off the medical register for professional misconduct. In April, the Irish Medical Organisation, which represents around 3,500 medical practitioners, passed a motion rejecting abortion and endorsing the right to life of the unborn. A few days later, a nursing trade union blocked the publication of a new code of professional conduct from An Bord Altranais, the statutory body governing the nursing profession, as it could prevent a nurse from assisting in a legal termination as defined by the Supreme Court, and more consultation was needed. These intra-professional discussions were on the whole as vehement and as absolutist as ever, but it was all too evident that an orchestrated anti-abortion campaign was in play. The legislators let it be known they would not be discussing the Abortion Information Bill before the autumn of that year, and the substantive issue before the following autumn at the earliest.

Senior government sources admitted that the involvement of the state in the dissemination of abortion information was problematic. Clinics, magazines and doctors would be the obvious dispensers of such information, but the Health Boards could not be involved as long as the abortion legislation itself was not in place. As for that legislation, a memorandum to the Cabinet sub-committee in charge of this stated that it was 'extraordinarily difficult' to come up with proposals which would not lead to abortion on demand. In any case, it was learnt in June that the government would do nothing until after the divorce referendum (then scheduled for the summer of 1994). No further effort was made before the end of that year to clarify the confusion and uncertainty. Fine Gael TD Charles Flanagan summarised the situation:

> The present confusion represents a huge mess as the Supreme Court [in the X case] is in clear conflict with the guidelines of the Medical Council while for example in Galway, an abortion referral service is active. People still do not know whether the communication of information is legal or not. The Government has ducked this matter in the vain hope that it will simply go away.[30]

This Fianna Fáil–Labour coalition was buying time on the issues of divorce and abortion, but it is fair to bear in mind that in that year it legalised the sale of condoms from vending-machines and the practice of homosexuality, as is recounted in other chapters. Having said that, it is undeniable that the government was in no hurry to legislate on abortion. The status quo seemed, to the two government parties, preferable to the discussion of a bill relative to an issue that would once more sow discord at all levels. One notes that the opposition parties were not putting any pressure on the government to deal with the substantive issue. Publication of the information bill was announced and postponed, until after the European elections of 9 June 1994. The government wanted to avoid an acrimonious debate over social legislation before European election day, particularly on the issue of abortion referral. Nonetheless it was disclosed that, under the bill, women would have access to addresses and telephone numbers of agencies providing abortion services abroad, but also pregnancy counselling agencies in Ireland might be allowed to make appointments for women before they set out on their journey. This incensed PLC, which referred to a pledge made in 1992 by the previous administration according to which non-directive counselling would be permitted but abortion referral would remain unlawful. How could you give information on abortion without advocating a termination? How could controls be framed on abortion information in one-to-one situations, such as between doctor and patient? It seemed safer to buy time than to tackle such thorny questions.

The predictable effect of the government's waiting game was the fact that the anti-abortion activists had all the time in the world to mobilise: PLC had now an office and full-time staff, meetings were regularly organised at constituency level, TDs and European candidates were lobbied during the Euro-election. Moreover PLC had two new targets to which it was looking for support: medical organisations (the IMC and the IMO, for example), and local authorities. At local government level, up to 79 per cent of local authorities, including county councils, borough corporations, urban district councils and town commissioners, had passed resolutions calling for a new referendum. PLC had concentrated on local representatives because it had realised that the parties as such were not very receptive. Labour was in power and Albert Reynolds at the head of the government had stood up to their demands. As we saw earlier, the Department of Health did not feel bound by the pledges of the outgoing administration. There was more understanding from the IMC and from doctors and nurses' associations, and leading anti-abortion activists, such as Professor Patricia Casey and Dr Dara Scally, found their way on to the executive committees of these organisations.

Quite rightly, PLC had identified the IMC as a key player in the future of any abortion legislation. Abortion would never be introduced in Ireland as long as the IMC stuck to its ethical guidelines, by which only professionally suicidal doctors would not abide. PLC also believed that as long as the IMC said there was no evidence that an abortion was ever necessary to save a woman's life, Fianna Fáil backbenchers would favour a referendum over legislation. In fact, an opinion poll found that 71 per cent of people now favoured the introduction of legislation on the substantive issue of abortion – 30 per cent when there was a real and substantial threat to the life and health of the mother, and 41 per cent in all circumstances including a risk of suicide. Only 24 per cent were opposed to any legalisation on abortion. Concerning access to information, 71 per cent felt the government should introduce legislation to ensure that women had access to information, whereas 23 per cent were opposed.[31] With only 5–6 per cent undecided, and such a high percentage of people in favour of these laws, this poll shows that, despite the difficulties the government was having in legislating, the electorate had not changed its position on the provision of abortion and abortion information.

Was there confusion about the terminology? Some people did not call a procedure aimed at saving the life of the mother but killing the foetus in the process, an abortion, so perhaps they had answered Yes to the MRBI question for this medical practice to continue. PLC and Doctors for Life protested that the question was misleading, since it would be unconstitutional to allow abortion if only the health of the mother was in danger (just as it would be unconstitutional to legislate on excluding suicide!). The question asked by MRBI, to which 71 per cent answered Yes, was: 'Should or should not the Government legislate, as promised, to allow for abortion in limited circumstances, where there is a real and substantial threat to the life and health of the mother?' If the question included health, it was probably because some of those who rejected the 12th amendment did so because they could not accept the distinction drawn between life and health, as it amounts to the same thing. PLC had commissioned an IMS poll in June which had shown that 60 per cent of respondents favoured the holding of a 'constitutional referendum which would offer a choice between abortion being permitted in certain circumstances or abortion being ruled out in all circumstances.'[32] So the organisation was alarmed at the way in which the government was ignoring the views of the people. However, the situation was not sorted out one way or another in 1994 either.

The European election came and went, the information bill was ready and the issue had been kept out of the campaign, as it was said that the bill would be published before the summer recess. The government was hoping for a short debate to dispose of it quickly, as with the decriminalisation of homosexuality. A bill on abortion itself was on the back-burner, since the government was pledged to tackle the divorce referendum within a year, so it would be best left to the next administation. It was postponed twice until mid-October when it was announced that the Information on Termination of Pregnancy Bill, as it was now to be called, would be debated before Christmas. It was thought best to let two by-elections in Cork take place (on 10 November) first. PLC announced it would vigorously oppose the bill, and asked TDs and senators to reject it as it did not prohibit doctors and agencies from making appointments for women seeking abortions abroad (or pass on a letter to the English doctor if the woman had a medical condition). Information could not mean referral, which in effect was assistance to murder. A number of Fianna Fáil backbenchers made plain their opposition to any legislation that would allow for abortion referral, and probably prevented it from being published. The content of the bill had only been leaked, it had not reached Cabinet, and TDs had not been briefed. The question was going to be adjourned and the protagonists change a little, since Albert Reynolds resigned on 17 November as Taoiseach and leader of Fianna Fáil, in the wake of a clerical sexual abuse scandal, which brought to a head a long-standing power struggle with his deputy, Dick Spring. Putting forward his strong family values, Reynolds proceeded to reveal he had let Labour know that Fianna Fáil would not be able to deliver on abortion legislation arising out of the X case. Labour denied it and said *they* had come to the view it would not be possible for this government to deal with the substantive issue. But if a government in which Labour (strong on the liberal agenda) had been a partner had not found the courage and the leadership, despite the backing of public opinion, to introduce these laws, what could be expected of the next one? In the end, Parliament was not dissolved, and Dick Spring chose his new partners: Fine Gael and Democratic Left, another unexpected combination![33] The new Minister for Health, Michael Noonan, of Fine Gael, known for his anti-abortion stance, declared there was 'no commitment to abortion in the new Programme for Government' but legislation on abortion information would be introduced as soon as possible.

Whereas the information bill was not on the government's legislative list for the following six months, the Minister for Health chose to publish it, on the same day as the Framework Document on Northern Ireland, on 23 February 1995, as the divorce referendum had been postponed yet again because of a legal challenge. The Regulation of Information (Services outside the State for Terminations of Pregnancies) Bill, 1995 was 'part of the Government's approach to minimising the circumstances in which women seek to have abortions'.

It legalised the distribution of information on abortion, including the names and addresses of clinics, at the end of non-directive counselling sessions, but barred doctors from making appointments for women or sending letters of referral to the clinics. The bill was a distinct watering down of the bill drafted by Brendan Howlin, which had been widely reported without being published. The latter did not rule out doctors and agencies referring women for abortions abroad – 'referral' was simply not mentioned. This was acknowledging what the IFPA (linked by a commercial agreement to the BPAS) and many doctors were actually doing.

Within hours of its publication, Noonan's bill had met with sharp criticism from both sides of the abortion debate. The IFPA signalled it would discriminate against women less equipped to make appointments and arrangements on their own, whereas PLC criticised the bill for allowing doctors to promote and facilitate abortions. Where was the logic in forbidding doctors from providing women with a referral letter but allowing them to pass on a copy of their medical records? What else would there have been in the referral letter? Would the ban on doctors or agencies making appointments for their patients encourage the latter to come to them in a crisis pregnancy? Was handing a list of names and addresses of clinics simple information, or assistance in killing a child? Where did information stop and referral begin? Noonan's predecessor seemed to have decided there was no meaningful difference between the two (a view shared both by PLC and Doctors for Freedom of Information), whereas Noonan could see a distinction, but he had found the line between what was 'politically deliverable' and what was not. By taking everybody by surprise, barely into in his third month in office, he was hoping to minimise dissent and shorten the potentially divisive debate.

Politicians knew by now they had no hope of reconciling both sides of the abortion gulf, and this led to the view that the subject should be avoided or dispatched. Noonan had the backing of Fine Gael deputies. Labour and Democratic Left had decided to silence their demands for a less restrictive legislation, the PDs criticised the bill for interfering with the doctor–patient relationship, but did not threaten to vote against it. Fianna Fáil said nothing at first, but SPUC, Family Solidarity and PLC all issued strongly worded statements condemning the bill and began urging members of the Oireachtas to oppose it. They were given impetus by Judge O'Hanlon who felt he had a duty to comment on the bill:

> How can it be reconciled with Catholic teaching to propose a bill or to enact a law specifying the conditions in which it is to be legal to give information to facilitate others in the perpetration of an 'abominable crime'? ... How can we possibly say that we are protecting the life of the unborn child if we do anything to facilitate those who seek to take it away?[34]

This 'coincided' with the Fianna Fáil parliamentary party meeting where a majority of speakers, left with no guidance from their leader, emphatically opposed the legislation. But the opposition in principle of that party was not tenable, because everybody remembered it was a Fianna Fáil-led government that had proposed an information referendum so as not to be in breach of the European Convention. And in coalition with Labour it had even finalised an information bill that was more radical than the present one.

The new party leader, Bertie Ahern, was facing his first leadership crisis and not managing it very well, until the spokesperson on Health, Maire Geoghegan-Quinn, drafted a series of amendments in order to open the way for compromise without losing face and without opposing the principle of the bill. After all, as Michael Noonan said: 'the freedom to give and obtain names and addresses derives from the 1992 amendment: It is a Constitutional right since 1992, and is not a statutory right to be conferred by the Oireachtas. The bill simply sets out the conditions which govern the exercise of that freedom.'[35] Once strong opposition to the bill was in evidence within Fianna Fáil, PLC announced it was switching its lobbying to Fine Gael, to those deputies known to feel uneasy about the legislation and who are 'going to be tagged as the people who introduced an abortion culture to Ireland if it is passed.' Archbishop Desmond Connell warned in a statement:

> The first [guidance he felt he had to give] relates to legislators. They have a serious obligation in relation to this bill, which not merely accepts that abortion is permissible, but will facilitate its procurement. In forming their conscience they must give full weight to these crucially important considerations. ... The second relates to those

who, if the bill becomes law, cooperate in its operation insofar as it transgresses the moral law. Such active cooperation is as gravely wrong as abortion itself – no matter where the abortion takes place.[36]

The fact remains, the will of the people notwithstanding, that *any* political party that had put forward such legislation even a decade earlier would have been committing electoral suicide. But it was all the more extraordinary that it befell Fine Gael to do so. Many things had changed in Irish society, not least a more sceptical attitude to authority, particularly that of the Catholic Church. There was a time when an alliance of the hierarchy and Fianna Fáil would have been enough to scupper any reforming legislation. Those were the days. Nonetheless, a few hours before the vote in the Dáil, and at the end of their spring meeting at Maynooth, the Catholic hierarchy issued a strongly worded statement in which legislators and doctors were left in no doubt about their responsibility in the killing of children: 'Anybody who acts in a way calculated to facilitate abortion, anybody who helps a mother to identify or to contact those who will destroy the life of her child, is participating in the violation of that child's most basic right.' But despite the uncompromising tone of the bishops, the Dáil saw the bill through. Fianna Fáil opposed it, as announced, but at the second stage only, and the government had a comfortable majority in this division of 85 votes to 67. Noonan delivered a speech in the Dáil reminiscent of Des O'Malley's speech during the debate on contraception in 1985:

> I call on all deputies... to reject the pressure put on them by various interlocking organisations, both overt and covert, which constitute the Pro-Life Movement. I call on all deputies to reject the intrusion in our proceedings by a High Court judge who, in a piece of ludicrous hyperbole, sought to involve us in the guilt of the new holocaust. I call on all deputies tonight to reject those who would reach back into the mists of history and try to pressure us with the ghostly weapons of bell, book and candle....I call on Fianna Fáil Deputies to stand for the primacy of Dáil Éireann. I call on Deputies on all sides to ensure that...this Dáil, with Seanad Éireann, in accordance with the provision of the Constitution make the laws by which the people live their lives. That is the principle and I want the Bill to be passed by acclamation.[37]

A majority of TDs stood by the people who had already had their say on the issue. Interestingly – and we have had the opportunity before to point out such contextual incidents – the debate took place in a week when a new-born baby was found dead in a bucket and there was the alleged case of an 11–year-old Cork girl made pregnant by a 51–year-old neighbour. What is more the 14-year sentence given to the man jailed in the X case was reduced to 4 years (with up to a 25 per cent remission) causing a major uproar. This was reality, not semantics. Even this present bill (and the idea of it might sound very radical, in an Irish context) was, in the words of Alan Shatter, 'an English solution to an Irish problem. It...seeks to maintain a constitutional veil of sanctity and piety over this island which obscures our vision of the many thousands of Irish women who go to England seeking help.'[38] Once the bill passed in the Dáil, PLC lobbied senators, pointing out that most of them are elected by members of local authorities, a majority of which had adopted resolutions calling for a pro-life referendum. Notwithstanding, the bill comfortably passed the second stage in the Seanad by 29 votes to 17 on 13 March, and the committee and all remaining stages on 14 March, after a debate lasting some five hours. The bill was not amended (Noonan had introduced at report stage in the Dáil an opt-out clause for conscientious doctors) and there was no vote.

The government victory marked another defeat for the Catholic hierarchy, and this was the third time that a Minister 'chose to take note of clerical opinion before embarking on an independent course of action' on a matter of public morality.[39] The third that is, after Barry Desmond and Maire Geoghegan-Quinn had respectively made contraception more available and decriminalised homosexuality. This was a landmark for the legislature and would be hailed as a triumph for democracy by some and reviled for introducing an abortion culture into Ireland by others. It remained to be seen if the bill was constitutional.

The President, before signing it into law, could, if she had any doubts, have it tested, and indeed she referred the bill to the Supreme Court on 18 March, because it was vital that the arguments about its constitutionality be decided once and for all. If declared constitutional, no further legal challenges could be mounted against it and this would bring an end to all arguments. Unusually, the bill was challenged in court from two opposing points of view. The Chief Justice (who, incidentally, was the judge who imposed the injunction against the Dublin clinics) appointed two teams of lawyers to argue against the state on the constitutionality of the bill; one would fight for the interests of the unborn, for the first time in an Irish court, arguing that the provision of names and addresses of abortion clinics abroad, which amounted for some to referral, conflicted with the equal right to life Article 40.3.3 gives the mother and the unborn; the other would represent the interests of the mother, whether a woman in the position of X would be entitled to be referred for an abortion, and not just in Britain, under the 1992 X judgment, and whether the bill interfered with the right of all mothers to their life and health; the state's position being that the bill represented a minimalist position to regulate the provision of abortion information for which people voted in the 1992 referendum. Only two of the five judges who ruled on the X case, Seamus Egan and Hugh O'Flaherty, were still members of the Supreme Court.

The court could only deliver one judgment, and the outside world would never know about any dissension. The arguments on the unborn's side, if accepted, would have drastic implications based as they were on the natural law. One remembers that under natural law, the right to life (of the born and unborn) precedes the Constitution and no positive law or referendum can alter this. In this perspective, even the ruling in the X case did not stand, even though it did not address natural law. But the natural law thesis was an argument that 'the constitutional furniture itself needed to be rearranged' (in the words of the Attorney-General, Dermot Gleeson) and there was no place for a 'shadow Constitution' based on elusive natural law edicts. To the relief of many, in particular in government, the judges accepted that stance, as well as the fact that people had now got over the reasoning whereby giving names of abortion clinics was unconstitutional because it conflicted with the obligation to vindicate the right to life of the unborn. The Supreme Court endorsed The Regulation of Information (Services outside the State for Terminations of Pregnancies) Bill, as 'a fair and reasonable balancing of conflicting rights' and their judgment went even further than it had to. It explicitly reaffirmed the X case ruling; it broadened the Dáil interpretation of what doctors can do for women once an appointment has been made by the latter, i.e. normal communication between the Irish doctor or agency and their British colleague about a patient's condition; and, more generally, it 'cut away the umbilical cord of Catholic control inherent in the concept of natural law.'[40] Obviously the judges had a vested interest in refuting the argument, even if it was put forward by one of their colleagues, Judge O'Hanlon, that the natural law was the foundation on which the Constitution was built and was superior to the text! They asserted forcefully that the Courts, as they were and are bound to, recognised the Constitution as the fundamental law of the State to which the organs of the State were subject and at no stage recognised the provisions of the natural law as superior to the Constitution. The people were entitled to amend the Constitution ... and the Constitution as so amended by the Fourteenth Amendment is the fundamental law of the State representing as it does the will of the people.[41]

This judgment prompted an editorial in *The Irish Times* of 13 May to summarise a widely shared belief: 'it is a sane and compassionate judgement that edges this State a little further along the road to rationality when legislating on moral issues.' This recalled the situation in 1973 when the Supreme Court held that the ban on contraceptives was unconstitutional, another landmark in the separation between state and Church. However, the Pro-Life's comment in the face of legal defeat holds true too: 'The Supreme Court has given its blessing to a blatant contradiction in the law, namely, that while the unborn child is to be protected against abortion the destruction of its life may be facilitated as long as that destruction takes place outside the jurisdiction.'[42] Either that, or people's pragmatism triumphed over rights and principles. In any case, the Supreme Court judgment gave a boost to the government's confidence in tackling the forthcoming divorce referendum, but it was quite clear that nobody in government was prepared to face up to the question of abortion *in* Ireland. Noonan had already made clear that the substantive issue of abortion was long-fingered, in as distant as possible a future: A constitutional review was due to begin shortly, and would cover all aspects of the Constitution, other than Articles 2, 3 and 41 which were the subject of separate consultation. Let that Committee deal with it first! Even though the first attempt to legislate in relation to abortion had been so swiftly carried through, it would be another matter to try to legislate for the category of women entitled to an abortion in the state. It was quite convenient that abortions could be performed abroad, as that meant there were no backstreet abortions and no urgent need to acknowledge the problem. Noonan had pledged that some research would be done to reduce the number of Irish abortions in Britain, and it was hoped that the women involved would speak out. But when the Irish College of General Practitioners acknowledged that it would now be in a position to list the various costs involved in the procurement of an abortion abroad, this 'caused even the most liberal deputies to suck in breath.

This brought home to many of us here the awful reality of a crisis pregnancy situation.'[43]

Thanks to the X case, abortion was no longer condemned out of hand, and the question of the appropriateness of a pro-life article in the Constitution had been posed, which by extension led to that of the feasibility that the law should impose a particular morality. It had not been pointed out that the best way of preventing women from choosing abortion might be to prevent them from being raped, from being trapped in impossible relationships, from being marginalised if they give birth to the child, or from feeling incapable, for financial or any other reasons of bring up the child, or even from being badly informed or plain careless. Morality is also subject to social problems and to the attitude of society to them. As Louis McRedmond pointed out: 'Indeed if, as has been claimed, proportionately more Irish pregnancies end in abortion [courtesy of English clinics] than Dutch pregnancies, it has to be seriously asked whether law is at all as central to moral behaviour as we are led to believe.'[44] The annual figures relative to exported abortions had not caused a stand to be taken, whereby the sacred character of all human life was not well served by the total and stringent ban on abortion. Would not it be as moral to provide for legal abortions in well-defined circumstances? As Seán MacRéamoinn, writing in the Dominican journal *Doctrine and Life*, asked: 'Would a limited provision for "lawful" abortion as a necessary evil in certain well defined circumstances be morally preferable? I am convinced that the question should at least be asked and seriously discussed.'[45] The principle of necessary evil has as its biggest merit that it is rooted in reality.

It is most probably on the question of abortion that legislators have shown the least leadership and the most hedging, but it is also the socio-moral issue about which Irish people have developed most, have painfully questioned one of their most absolute moral principles, and it is the issue that has caused Irish society to mature most deeply and most painfully. Let us quote again the *Irish Times* editorial of 3 June, written after the original (14 year) sentence on Mr Z, the rapist of Ms X:

But in the particular circumstances of the X case a great many people woke up to the possible victimisation of their own daughters, sisters, nieces or friends. And the terrible truth dawned that if a law is enacted, purporting to reduce a profoundly complex moral issue to a simple statutory definition, sooner or later that law will be enforced.... It has been a maturing experience for this society. Perhaps more than any other event in modern times it has alerted middle-ground thinking to the dangers of allowing moral crusaders of any kind to set the legislative agenda according to their own sectional convictions. It is no truism to say that in the aftermath of this case Irish society cannot ever be the same again.

Paradoxically the Irish have been informed *ad nauseam* about the legal and medical intricacies of abortion in an effort by some to keep the procedure totally banned. Those who chose the option against all odds and those who showed compassion towards them certainly grasped the nettle long before the legislators did. The latter did eventually acknowledge abortion as an option chosen by responsible women, when they adopted a somewhat peripheral law, the Abortion Information Act, which declares in section 2.a: 'This Act applies to information that is likely to be required by a woman for the purpose of availing herself of services provided outside the State for the termination of pregnancies.' The title of the Act also uses the clinical and neutral phrase 'termination of pregnancies', putting an end to euphemisms, which is a loaded gesture in itself. Let us hope another Ms X will not have to come to the fore for the state to go one step further.[46] Instead they should take heed of what the Report of the Constitution Review Group, published on 3 July 1996, had to say:

> The review group is scathing about the confusion which has arisen out of the successive abortion amendments but does not recommend a new referendum. Instead, it proposes legislation to define the term 'unborn', protect appropriate medical intervention and set a time limit on lawful termination of pregnancy. It also recommends written certification by medical specialists of 'real and substantial risk to the life of the mother'.

Was homosexuality going to get the same long-drawn and fudging treatment, since it was, like abortion, a question which did not mobilise the public (like contraception and divorce did), and did not even inspire compassion as a woman in distress could? Would homosexual militants draw a few lessons from the other sexual socio-moral campaigns, in order to ensure the decriminalisation of their sexuality? The following chapter will tell.

7 Homosexuality: From a Crime against Nature...

A very interesting moment, in the context of a study of moral values and attitudes, occurred in January 1990, when the Catholic Archbishop of Dublin said that homosexuality was an objective disorder, which caused a ripple in public opinion. He was understood to be saying that homosexuals were sick people, suffering from an obscure disorder, and this was perceived as perhaps going a bit too far. For the people did not realise that the word 'disorder' refers not only to a disease, but also to the opposite of order. It appeared that Dr Desmond Connell was using the word 'disorder' in its scolastic meaning, as used by Thomas Aquinas and defined in our Introduction. This moment of mutual incomprehension revealed that the Irish hierarchy did not speak the same language as their flock. The fundamental source of traditional Catholic morality had become incomprehensible.[1]

The preceding chapters have shown that the Irish state, the people as well as the politicians, no longer subscribe to an order based on obligatory norms; or, to put it differently, to the need for the state to criminalise and penalise practices that are not a danger to public order. The equation according to which moral law equals penal law is no more, and, in the case of homosexuality, it has been invalidated unequivocally. It will be particularly interesting to see how the state was going to recognise homosexuals' rights, as it was not going to be forced by sheer force of numbers, as it had with the growing number of people in unhappy marriages or the large number of people practising artificial contraception. Irish homosexuals had a serious handicap in that they could never draw on strong popular demand as far as the decriminalisation of their sexual orientation was concerned.

The WHO revised its international classification of diseases (ICD) as recently as 1990, a revision that came into force as late as January 1993: ICD-10 stated explicitly that in relation to psychological and behavioural disorders associated with sex development and orientation, 'sex orientation by itself is not to be regarded as a disorder'. Indeed, in ICD-9, the formulation was such that it carried a risk of misinterpretation (homosexuality as a mental disorder). Homosexuality has always been a major threat to the socio-moral order as it fundamentally goes against a certain idea of human relationships, marriage and procreation. Sexuality must be procreative if the survival and the development of the family unit are to be assured, on which hinges social order. The homosexual act is non-procreative *par excellence* and as such has always been condemned unambiguously. It is a fact that of all the sexual deviances, homosexuality has been the one subjected to the most sustained social pressure. As Jeffrey Weeks, an authority on the regulation of sexuality in the UK, noted:

> The regulation of extra-marital sex has been a major concern for the forces of moral order throughout the history of the West, whether through the canonical controls of the church over adultery and sodomy in the medieval period, or the state's ordering of prostitution and homosexuality in the modern. Of all the 'variations' of sexual behaviour, homosexuality has had the most vivid social pressure... It is as many sexologists from Havelock Ellis to Alfred Kinsey have noted, the form closest to the heterosexual norm in our culture, and partly because of that it has often been the target of sustained social oppression.[2]

A CRIMINALISED SIN

Governments and the media have not always referred to homosexuality as a 'sexual orientation'. Indeed, during the first two-thirds of the nineteenth century, it was referred to as a 'crime against nature', one too horrible to be named (interestingly, this expression included birth control and bestiality). In the 1960s, it was considered by the medical community to be a mental disorder. The word itself, homosexuality, coined in 1869, became common usage in the English language in the 1880s, which corresponds to the very conceptualisation of this sexual variation. However, the formal regulation of homosexuality has confined itself, in the West, to male homosexual activities rather than female ones.

The laws banning homosexuality were inherited by the Irish state from the reign of Queen Victoria. They were passed in 1861 and 1885 by the British Parliament, whose concern was to regulate sexuality. The great campaigns of 'social purity' of the late nineteenth century aimed at protecting marriage and sexuality within marriage, particularly against homosexuality and prostitution – two great social evils in the legislators' minds. Sections 61 and 62 (under the heading 'Offences against Nature') of the Offences Against the Person Act only referred to sodomy, which in those days was a sin against nature, an abominable vice, whose very mention evoked horror and was 'a disgrace to human nature', in the words of Sir William Blackstone. Any act of sodomy was thus condemned, whatever the sex or the nature of the partners. Homosexuality did not seem to be considered as the attribute of one type of person, but as being potentially in all creatures. This law imposed a custodial sentence instead of the death penalty, the previous punishment for sodomy.

The use of the term 'homosexual' instead of 'sodomite' signalled a new awareness similar to that of the appropriation of the word 'gay' in the sense of 'homosexual' in the 1970s. Between 1861 and 1885, the archives of the British Home Office bear witness to the efforts made to dissociate bestiality from homosexual activity, being more and more defined as an individual trait.[3] In 1885, the Labouchere amendment, added to the Criminal Law Amendment Act (section 11), made punishable by a maximum of two years of forced labour any act of physical intimacy between two men, defined as an act of gross indecency. The concept of *gross indecency* is very vague, and as it is not defined precisely in law, jurisprudence has to do so, and it appears that no contact between the two men is necessary. For example, masturbation in the presence of another man constitutes an act of gross indecency.[4] This amendment was added late at night to a law with which it had no relation, in its first part, whose title was 'Protection of Women and Girls'. According to F.B. Smith, this extravagant amendment, later nicknamed the 'blackmailer's charter', was tabled by Henry Labouchere in an attempt to prevent the adoption of the whole law. He would have wanted to embarrass both ministers and the social purity campaigners of the time, whom he found hateful. The theory is plausible as there is no evidence that he was particularly hostile to male homosexuality. However, there were very few members present in Parliament that night and it was adopted without debate.[5] This amendment effectively criminalised any form of homosexual activity, in private as well as in public. Of course, the law was not always applied if the police or the jurors decided that public decency had not been offended; but when it was, as in the case of Oscar Wilde in 1895, its effects were harsh. At around the same time medical experts began to medicalise homosexuality: from a sin, it became a mental disorder, giving rise to the notion that a homosexual was a certain type of person. This theorisation of homosexuality applied to men and women alike, but the penal code continued to ignore women. In 1921, the British Parliament rejected a bill on lesbianism, modelled on the Labouchere amendment. The argument was that the measure would make women aware that such acts exist when the vast majority were innocent of such horrible thoughts. In effect, lesbianism was censured by silence rather than by an explicit condemnation.

As recently as 1957, the British government established a commission to examine homosexual offences and prostitution together, so close was the association in the legislators' minds. The Wolfenden Committee on Homosexual Offences and Prostitution, while deploring 'the general loosening of former moral standards', questioned in its report whether the law was the best way to repress sexual deviance such as homosexuality, which while shocking some individuals was no more a threat to the family than adultery or divorce, which were legal. Nonetheless, it is only in 1967 that the Sexual Offences Act legalised consensual private homosexual activity between adults over 21 (the Armed Forces and the Navy being exempted of the legislation). But gross indecency became punishable by up to five years imprisonment instead of two if one of the partners was under 21. In effect, the rate of recorded cases of indecency between men doubled between 1967 and 1976, that of prosecutions trebled and that of condemnations quadrupled.[6] This is the result of a law that defines more precisely which offences are still punishable by law, particularly in the area of public decency, and this has made pressing charges easier. The British climate is not altogether pro-gay. Consider the adoption of the infamous Clause 28 of the Local Government Act of 1988, which stipulates that a local authority is forbidden to 'promote the teaching in any maintained school of the acceptability of homosexuality as a pretended family relationship'.

AN OBJECTIVE DISORDER

The gay liberation movement dates back to the 1960s and was modelled on the blacks' and women's liberation movements: The Stonewall riots (New York, June 1969) had prompted the formation of the Gay Liberation Front in the United States, soon to be emulated elsewhere. The developments of the gay movement, including the Irish one, have been well discussed elsewhere so suffice it to draw a link between the creation of homosexual groups in various countries and calls for the liberalisation of anti-homosexual legislations on one side, and the fact that the Catholic Church reiterated its condemnation of homosexual activity on the other. In 1976 notably, it said that according to the objective moral order, homosexual relations are acts which lack an essential and indispensable finality. In sacred scripture, they are condemned as a serious depravity and even presented as the sad consequence of rejecting God... [this judgment] does attest to the fact that homosexual acts are intrinsically disordered and can be in no case approved of.[7]

In 1986, as the AIDS epidemic was beginning to rage, the Congregation for the Doctrine of the Faith issued the following statement, despite the fact that the Catholic Church had come to draw a distinction between homosexual activity and homosexual orientation (without having a benign attitude towards the latter!): 'Although the particular inclination of the homosexual person is not a sin, it is a more or less strong tendency ordered toward an intrinsic moral evil; and thus the inclination itself must be seen as an objective disorder.'[8] The allusion to AIDS as the gay plague was made in the following terms: 'Even when the practice of homosexuality may seriously threaten the lives and well-being of a large number of people, its advocates remain undeterred and refuse to consider the magnitude of the risks involved. The Church can never be so callous.' And a negative approach to the question of civil rights led to the following condoning of anti-gay violence: 'when civil legislation is introduced to protect behavior to which no one has any conceivable right, neither the Church nor society at large should be surprised when other distorted notions and practices gain ground, and irrational and violent reaction increase.'

In 1992, as the new *Catechism of the Catholic Church* still stood by such phrases as 'intrinsically disordered' and 'contrary to the natural law', a set of guidelines written by the Sacred Congregation for the Doctrine of the Faith for the benefit of the American Catholic Bishops provoked the indignation of the gay movement internationally. They stated that, being 'an objective disorder', homosexuality was not the source of any civil rights. The passing of anti-discriminatory legislation was thus not justified and would in effect end up promoting homosexuality. Since there was no right to homosexuality, certain forms of discrimination were actually sometimes justified. The Vatican seemed to imply that not only was homosexuality a disease, but it was also contagious; moreover, homosexuals had no self-control and had to be guarded against themselves:

Homosexuals in that they are human beings, have the same rights as everyone else... but these rights can be legitimately curbed in response to objective disordered public behaviour. That [curbing] at times is not only legitimate but obligatory. ... There are circumstances in which it is not unjustly discriminatory to take account of sexual tendency: for example in the assignation of children for adoption, in the hiring of teachers or sport coaches and in conscripting people into military service.[9]

Pope John Paul II mentioned homosexuality again in February 1994 in his 'Letter to Families', published to coincide with the UN International Year of the Family. He reaffirmed the teaching of the Catholic Church on divorce, contraception and abortion and its commitment to protect motherhood and fatherhood from 'erroneous values and tendencies which are widespread today'. He further said:

> Marriage forms the basis of the institution of the family and is constituted by the covenant whereby a man and a woman establish between themselves a partnership for their whole life. ... Only such a union can be recognised and ratified as a marriage by society. Other interpersonal unions which do not fill the above conditions cannot be recognised, despite certain growing trends which represent a serious threat to the future of the family and society itself.

This letter was published on 22 February, a few weeks after the adoption in the European Parliament of a recommendation aimed at giving homosexual couples the same rights as heterosexual couples – in particular the right to marry and to adopt children. Following this vote, the Pope had declared: 'With this resolution, the European Parliament is asking that a moral disorder be legitimised. ... A relationship between two men and two women cannot make up a real family and, more to the point, you cannot grant to such a union the right to adopt children.'[10] For the Pope, such a resolution confirmed that moral erosion progressed inexorably and that our societies really are sick. For the European Parliament, it was a matter of regularising a *de facto* situation since homosexuals live together and even get married in some EU countries, just as they have recourse to artificial insemination in the case of lesbians, or to the legal adoption of children. It was also a matter of harmonising more or less restrictive and discriminatory legislations, and to be 'tuned in' to reality.[11] The resolution was adopted by 159 votes to 98. Only seven Irish MEPs took part in this vote (out of 15) and two voted in favour of the resolution. By that time homosexuality had been legal for seven months in Ireland.

This begs the question: where did Ireland stand between the Catholic affirmation of the objective order and the European affirmation of the 'growing pluralization of lifestyles'?[12] But first, where had it stood on the question of homosexuality since the early days of the Irish state?

A NOT SO INERT LAW

The 1861 and 1885 British laws were automatically taken over by the Irish Free state, like all British common and statute law, and kept on since nothing invalidated them in the 1937 Irish Constitution. The issue was never debated in the Irish Parliament. However, the report of the Carrigan Committee, on the 1885 law in its entirety, recommended a reinforcement of some aspects of it, in particular in relation to gross indecency, i.e. homosexual activity, which, according to the members of the Committee was 'a form of depravity that is spreading with malign vigour'. The police testified thus before the Committee: 'Offences under this section should be made felonies. During the years 1928/29 we have had the following prosecutions for this offence. We believe, however, this is only a small percentage of the actual cases: ...Total for Saorstát [Free State]: 86 prosecutions; 78 convictions.'[13] It is fair to say that the Department of Justice was not altogether convinced by some of the findings of the Committee as it questioned its impartiality. The future 1935 law, drafted in the aftermath of the report, paid little heed to its conclusions, except in relation to contraceptives. Nothing more severe than what was in force was envisaged in relation to homosexuals. From then on, silence fell on this issue as on other issues of sexual ethics. The spirit of the English puritan laws was in tune with the new Catholic-inspired Irish laws, and neither were questioned until the beginning of the 1970s.

Silence in the media and in the political arena does not mean that the law was not enforced and did not sanction homosexuals. It has often been said that it was not applied, as if it was just a declaration of principle. The following facts give this argument the lie. The annual reports on prisons of the Department of Justice show that, between 1940 and 1978, an average of six men per year were gaoled for 'indecency with males', and an average of seven for 'gross indecency'. For the years 1979–87, one can refer to the figures provided by the government during the David Norris case in the European Court of Justice. They only deal with the number of prosecutions for homosexual offences in Ireland, but they do not indicate if those were consensual, committed in private or in public, nor the penalty meted out: 13 in 1979, 33 in 1980, 41 in 1981, 22 in 1982, 19 in 1983, 52 in

1984, 33 in 1985, and 25 in 1986.[14] David Norris, who will be introduced later, made his analysis in 1976 from the most recent figures he could get at that time from the police reports, the Garda Reports on Crime. As more recent figures were difficult to come by, he concentrated on 1973 and 1974, to bring to public attention not only the existence of the homosexual laws, but also the extent of their not always consistent application: 'With regard to the alleged redundancy of the law, while it is certainly correct that the proportion of prosecutions to the number of offences is infinitesimal, that fact simply indicates the existence of fundamentally bad law, which is in general inoperable, and where random attempts at enforcement are made, arbitrary and unjust in the extreme.'[15]

What was particularly shocking to David Norris was the fact that out of 23 men sentenced in 1973, and 20 in 1974, respectively 18 (78 per cent) and 17 (85 per cent) were over 21 (i.e. the age of homosexual majority in Britain, the highest in Europe). Over the period 1962–72, he registered 455 convictions, including 342 involving men aged over 21. These 342 men would not have been prosecuted if Ireland had a legislation even as restrictive as Britain's.[16]

After highlighting that anti-homosexual laws were indeed invoked, David Norris proceeded to spearhead a reform movement. A lecturer in English literature at Trinity College Dublin and a renowned Joycean, as well as a Protestant, David Norris founded the Irish Gay Rights Movement in 1974, of which he was the Chairman, a move that preceded the creation of the Committee for Homosexual Law Reform, also chaired by him.[17] David Norris will remain the figurehead of the Irish homosexual movement, which explains that he is often considered unfairly as a single-issue man. He came out in 1970 at a civil rights meeting in Dublin during which the participants praised the Republic for the liberties it afforded its citizens; to which David Norris responded: 'Of course Protestants aren't repressed – there are too few of them numerically; they are too powerful financially, and politically they are too pliable. ... But I belong to another country, the larger country of homosexuality – a minority that outnumbers all the Protestant Churches in Ireland combined, and has less rights than any other here.'[18]

He turned his frustration into indignation, did not follow his psychiatrist's advice to move abroad, and espoused the homosexual cause and thus become 'gay'. He started by drafting a bill with his friend Kader Asmal, a renowned lawyer and leader of the anti-apartheid movement in Ireland, later Minister for Forestry in the new South

Africa. The idea was to persuade a deputy to present it in Parliament on their behalf. But they could not agree on certain sections of the draft, notably the question of the age of consent and the exemption of the Armed Forces (to which Norris was totally opposed), which caused them to abandon the idea.[19] This prompted him to change tactics: It was the government's job to change the law, not his. Therefore he asked Noël Browne to intervene on his behalf, initially in the Seanad on 10 April 1975 during the debate on the Law Reform Commission Bill (which established the so-named Commission). The senator called for a debate on homosexuality, abortion and divorce (that on contraception was in progress) with a view to a radical questioning of current civil legislation in the following terms:

> There are other attitudes in our laws which are just as intransigent and inhuman, and just as unthinking. One of them is in relation to the homosexuality question. I wonder if the Attorney General will ask that consideration be given to this. Homosexuality is simply a kind of sexuality completely normal for the homosexual. ... Unfortunately it is not looked on in that way and it is still a crime in our society. ... it is absurd, like suicide or illegitimacy or any of these problems which we choose to pretend do not exist here, to pretend that there is no such thing as a homosexual problem in Ireland. Of course there is. There is no sense whatever in ignoring the fact that it is the cause of an enormous amount of great distress for many people. ... Therefore I would ask the Attorney General that we do something about at least having a debate on this subject and let people decide for and against as they did in relation to contraception. ... Important yardsticks that will have to be invoked by the Law Reform Commission will be in the areas of homosexuality, therapeutic abortion and, of course, divorce. ... One of the greatest impediments against the unity of our people is the idea that the civil law is the moral law. We must decide as parliamentarians what we consider to be desirable civil laws for the ordering of our society.[20]

Browne made a similar move in the Dáil, once elected deputy. On behalf of Norris, he asked when the government intended to review the legislation on homosexuality. This was 1977, and he was laughed off. The Minister for Justice, Gerry Collins, said evasively that the government was thinking about it.

Another priority of David Norris's was to neutralise the existing legislation. We have seen that it was applied, more or less. The argument, if one was against change, was, why change laws that are not applied anyway, but reaffirm ideals to which a society aspires? Whereas those who advocated their repeal said: Let's get a rid of legislation that is not applied and offends some people while discrediting the law in general. It was applied, but prosecuted cases were not necessarily recorded, hence the difficulty in getting an accurate picture about who was prosecuted, and for what. David Norris, with the help of a lawyer, started to appear at trials to give character evidence and defend the men prosecuted for consensual homosexual activities. As these were judged at the District Court, there are no published reports, and they were often the occasion of 'summary trials' (where it is not necessary to produce evidence). According to Norris, there were many such cases during the 1970s:

> They were consistently before the courts, There would be dozens every year. The reason why there were so many was because young gardai on the way up with a view to promotion would be looking for a string of convictions to make them look good. Because of the public climate at the time, people were very ashamed of being discovered in these situations, and they would automatically plead guilty. They would be usually let off with a slap on the wrist, a suspended sentence, a fine or they would be directed to attend a psychiatrist. They would be rarely sentenced to jail.[21]

In the late 1970s, this stream of convictions stopped, and one may wonder whether it was because these men had been so well defended that the police lost all interest:

> Prosecutions were in double figures. Then they go down and down. Because Garret and myself started to appear in court. I would be wearing a three-piece suit, a Trinity tie, a briefcase, look terribly respectable, and give character evidence. The gardai were used to people coming in a state of collapse saying I'm guilty, I'm terribly sorry, please don't.. When we started defending, and we had a string of successes, they realised it was not worth their while. And it went down to zero, they stopped prosecuting.[22]

Is it possible that there was also a change in public opinion accompanied by a change in the directives given to the police? Had the Director of Public Prosecutions decided that there should be no more prosecutions for consensual homosexual activities? The laws were still invoked until the middle of the 1980s, particularly in cases of civil marriage nullity! One couple, for example, was trying to have their marriage annulled on the grounds of the husband's homosexuality.

The judge had the proceedings stopped to warn two witnesses that it would be his duty to send the transcript of their testimonials to the DPP, who could very well decide to prosecute them. This case was unearthed, as well as another one (*C.* v *F.*, February 1988) by Mary Robinson while she was defending David Norris, to prove that the laws criminalising homosexuality were not altogether a dead letter and could be activated at any time.[23] In another case, of marital rape this time, the judge did not accept the argument that the wife liked rough sex and sent the husband to jail for sodomy, since regardless of consent, an act of buggery even between husband and wife was a criminal matter. As David Norris commented: 'This was a spectacularly unsavoury case but it does highlight the fact that one can never presume the total inertia of the law.'[24] This brings us to the Norris case itself.

8 Homosexuality:... To a Right to (Homo)sexual Privacy

By the mid-1970s, David Norris and the Irish Gay Rights Movement had acquired considerable experience of the courts, and, finding the criminal label increasingly offensive, they decided to sue the state for keeping on the statute book legal provisions that they felt were unconstitutional as they breached the civil rights of a category of its citizens. A powerful case was mounted with an impressive array of expert witnesses. It eventually resulted in the 1988 judgment of a European court.

THE NORRIS CASE: WITHOUT NORMS OR SANCTIONS

In November 1977, David Norris's case came to the High Court, where he challenged the constitutionality of sections 61 and 62 of the 1861 law and section 11 of the 1885 law. They had instilled in him the fear of blackmail, had prevented him from having open relationships and had caused him so much stress and anxiety that he had a nervous breakdown and had seen a psychiatrist for several months.[1] He invoked Article 40.1 of the Constitution to argue that the two laws discriminated against homosexuals who were thus not equal citizens before the law. He also invoked the right to privacy, as defined in the McGee case. On 10 October 1980, Judge McWilliam found against Norris. The law might be unsatisfactory, but it was not unconstitutional. He confirmed that since the Christian churches teach that the primary function of sexual organs is the reproduction of the species, human sexuality should be confined to marriage. All sexuality outside marriage and between people of the same sex was wrong. Moreover marriage was recognised and protected by the Constitution. It followed that in order to protect social order and public morality, the state was entitled to criminalise homosexual acts:

> Although I accept that the traditional attitudes of the Churches and of the general body of citizens towards homosexuality are being

challenged and may be successfully challenged in the future, it is reasonably clear that current Christian morality in this country does not approve of buggery or of any sexual activity between persons of the same sex.... Individual cases of hardship cannot invalidate statutes which can reasonably be considered by the legislature to be desirable for the attainment of the true social order and the preservation of the public order and morality mentioned in the Constitution.[2]

Two incidents happened in 1982, corroborating as it were Norris's grievances. First there was Charles Self's brutal murder, at his home, on 20 January. Gay groups, including the National Gay Federation and the Irish Gay Rights Movement, called for collaboration with the police in charge of the investigation. But it turned out that this goodwill was exploited to harass a large number of homosexuals. Investigators, under the pretext of additional questions in relation to the murder, would turn up at the home or the workplace of homosexuals who had not necessarily 'come out'. During the investigation, some 1,500 homosexuals were interrogated, photographed and put on file, as if some of the questions asked had the objective of compiling a base of information on the Dublin gay community. A new group was then established, the Gay Defence Committee, to defend homosexuals against the attacks of the police, the courts and the media.[3] The other incident happened in August 1982. A young man was beaten to death by a gang in Fairview Park, Dublin. The park was well known as a meeting-place for homosexuals and these youths had intimidated them all summer, as they had intimidated any passer-by, whatever his/ her sexual orientation. Some 20 complaints had been lodged with the police, but it became clear with this attack that nothing had been done to contain the delinquents. In fact, they were not even charged with murder, but with homicide, and received a suspended prison sentence. A protest march was followed by a gathering of some 800 people, homosexuals, trade unionists, various groups, notably feminist or affiliated to AAC (the Anti-Amendment Campaign), as it took place during the abortion referendum campaign. Homosexuals were befriending AAC and learning the campaign and lobbying tactics that were going to be indispensable to oppose what was still the moral majority of the 1980s.

This same moral majority was heard again in the Supreme Court when the judges gave their verdict in the Norris case on 22 April 1983. By 3 to 2, they confirmed the High Court judgment. At the heart of

David Norris's claim was the affirmation that the state has no role to play in the domain of sexual morality, and in particular has no right to legislate in relation to the private sexual conduct of consenting adults. But this is not something that Judge O'Higgins accepted: 'The legislature would be perfectly entitled to have regard to the difference between the sexes and to treat sexual conduct or gross indecency between males as requiring prohibition because of the social problem which it creates, while at the same time looking at sexual conduct between females as being not only different but as posing no such social problem.' He also said that encouraging homosexual activity was not in accordance with the respect due to marriage that the Constitution vowed to protect: 'I regard the State as having an interest in the general moral well-being of the community and as being entitled, where it is practicable to do so, to discourage conduct which is morally wrong and harmful to a way of life and to values which the State wishes to protect.' In a nutshell, since the Irish state is by nature Christian, and since the practice of homosexuality is morally wrong and harms both public health and the institution of marriage, a law criminalising it cannot offend against the Constitution.

However, two judges, McCarthy and Henchy, gave dissenting judgments (when they examine the constitutionality of a law, the five Supreme Court judges can disagree in minority judgments, as far as laws pre-dating the 1937 Constitution are concerned), based on the right to privacy and on the fact that the European Court of Human Rights had already given a ruling on the same sections of the same laws. As far as the right to privacy is concerned, Judge Henchy remarked it is a right that can take several forms and includes, since 1973, the right for married couples to use contraceptives, something that is still condemned by the Catholic Church as morally wrong. It is thus impossible to deny a right to private homosexual activity on the strength of this argument alone. In the McGee judgment, the judges had accepted the idea that human sexuality can be non-procreative and can express tenderness, commitment and self-expression. The judges in the Norris case did not apply this approach to consensual gay sex.

Judge Henchy added: 'One way or the other, the impugned provisions seem doomed to extinction.... The true and justifiable gravamen of the complaint against the sections under review is that they are in constitutional error for overreach and overbreadth. They lack necessary discrimination and precision as to when and how they are to apply.' According to him, the government would have to determine the conditions in which certain homosexual acts would be decriminalised and to define such terms as 'in private', 'adult' and 'consenting'. The other acts would remain illegal in order to protect the common good (for the protection of minors, handicapped people, marriage and public health). But this distinction between the two categories of homosexual acts were ignored by the majority of the Supreme Court judges who spoke in the same absolutist voice as the Catholic Church, despite the comment made by Judge Walsh in the McGee case according to which the courts should not become the arbiters of the merits of the various religious codes. This was especially pertinent in David Norris's case, as he is not a Catholic, but a member of the Church of Ireland (which was in favour of a change in the law). The Norris judgment came as a surprise as it went against the grain of previous judgments which tried to distinguish between law and private morality. A commentator said:

> The Chief Justice's declaration that he regarded the State as 'being entitled, where it is practicable to do so, to discourage conduct which is morally wrong and harmful to a way of life and values which the State wishes to protect', appeared to reverse the whole tendency in recent years to take the law out of the field of private morality. One leading barrister described his ruling as 'like something out of the 1950s'. ... In general it seemed the court was moving [until this judgment] towards a more open, liberal type of society in which greater stress was placed on the rights and privacy of the individual and that it was taking account of changing social attitudes, instances in relation to contraception and the role of women.[4]

Still, the judgment had its place in the backlash of the beginning of the 1980s, in the context of the abortion referendum campaign, for example. But one cannot help noticing a fundamental difference between the majority judgment and that of Judge Niall McCarthy, for example. In the former, the natural rights protected by the Constitution come from the Christian nature of the Irish state. But McCarthy would uphold that

> the unenumerated rights derive from the human personality and that the actions of the State in respect of such rights must be informed by the proud objective of the people as declared in the preamble 'seeking to promote the common good, with due observance of prudence, justice and charity, so that the dignity and freedom of the individual may be assured, true social order attained, the

unity of our country restored, and concord established with other nations.' The dignity and freedom of the individual occupy a prominent place in these objectives but as forming part of the promotion of the common good.

Subjective rights are thus seen as the basis of social order, and indeed promote the common good instead of corrupting it. This is the opposite of the Catholic ideology, and it is interesting to note, with the benefit of hindsight, that the spirit of this minority judgment would one day be the core of the judgment in the X case, in the mouth of that same judge.

For the time being, some in the legal profession were worried by the fact that the Supreme Court had not taken into account the decision the European Court of Human Rights had made in a very similar case, as it concerned the very same legislation. We have already mentioned the ECHR in a previous chapter; it does not create new rights, but acknowledges the right to be human, which is permanent and anterior to all political acts. This interpretation of natural rights is more in the spirit of Judge McCarthy than of Judge O'Higgins. The case that the Irish Supreme Court could have taken into consideration was *Dudgeon* v *United Kingdom*. Jeffrey Dudgeon, a citizen of Northern Ireland, challenged the homosexual laws currently in force in Northern Ireland (i.e. the same as in England before 1967, and as in the Republic at the time) under article 8 of the European Convention. A majority (15 to 4) of the European judges found that these laws did interfere with his rights as a homosexual, and one of the minority judges was the Irish representative, Judge Brian Walsh. The Irish Gay Rights Movement had helped the Northern Ireland Gay Rights Association to finance the cost of taking this case to Europe. The British government changed the law in Northern Ireland following this judgment and passed the Homosexual Offences (Northern Ireland) Order in October 1982, which repealed the relevant sections of the 1861 and 1885 laws and extended to the Province the 1967 English law. This was in defiance of the campaign organised at the end of the 1970s by Ian Paisley and the Democratic Unionist Party, the Save Ulster from Sodomy Campaign. That being said, Jeffrey Dudgeon was quoted in *The Irish Times* in December 1992 as saying that it is a change in the law that has brought about a change in attitudes in Northern Ireland. One could have hoped that the Republic would follow suit without the need for yet another trial about the same laws in the same European Court. But it did not, and David Norris felt compelled to take his own case to

Europe. It was only five years after his petition, in October 1988, that the court eventually decided the case in his favour. The majority judgment found that an individual's sexual life is part of his private life, under Article 8 of the Convention on Human Rights which says that 'everyone has the right to respect for his private life and family life, his home and his correspondence'. Ireland was thus in breach of the Convention since it did not recognise a right to homosexual privacy.

NOTHING LESS THAN EQUALITY

Now that the necessity for change had been imposed by Europe, the Irish Parliament had to give it effect. In the interval, David Norris himself had entered Parliament on 14 April 1987 and was now in the Seanad. He had received one of the highest votes. It was his sixth attempt, and he had just about managed to convince his electorate (the Trinity graduates) that he was not a single-issue candidate, but would fight for civil liberties in general (Georgian Dublin and the rights of East Timorese in particular). He was one of the three candidates elected by the Trinity graduates, together with Mary Robinson and Shane Ross. He pointed out that the Irish were not such conservatives since he was the first openly gay candidate elected to a Parliament!

I was the first person in the world elected to a national Parliament having always campaigned as an openly gay candidate, but I didn't make a meal out of that, because I was afraid they'd turn me into a freak. It made it difficult for me to get elected: it took me 10 years and six elections to get in. And about £60,000. But it was worth it. I do think, – I'm not saying anything about any talents of my own – but I think that the physical presence in the House of somebody who contributed effectively on other issues is very important because it demythologises homosexuality. Up to then there had never been a human face on gay people, and they just assumed they were child molesters, monsters roving about in the dark, giving Smartie sweets to kids, ready to prance on them ... It defused that one, a little bit, made it easier for people to deal with the fact there was a public face.[5]

To our surprise that, while in office, he had not tried to introduce a Private member's bill, as Mary Robinson had done in the 1970s, he replied that, once elected, it was out of the question that he would introduce a bill bearing his name or to which he would be closely associated. The bill would be amended so much that he would not recognise it and would be unable to give his support to clauses he would disagree with: 'I would hate to have a Bill with which I was predominantly associated used to sentence young men to prison. I said to myself: it is the Government's responsibility to produce legislation, let ME amend it.'[6] In fact the Law Reform Commission met in 1989 to study under what conditions the legislation on homosexuality could be changed. Its final report said in effect that consensual homosexual activities had to be legalised but also that the homosexual majority (or age of consent) should not be any different from the heterosexual majority. The Supreme Court had never said that it was unconstitutional to decriminalise consensual homosexuality, whatever the individual judges might think privately. It had only said that the Victorian laws were not unconstitutional. On the other hand, there was no question of decriminalising all homosexual acts, in the same way as not all heterosexual acts are legal. Minors had to be protected against both kinds of abuse, the phrase 'child sexual abuse' applying to both categories.[7]

Despite the Commission's recommendations, the government was still going to delay as long as possible the moment when it had to decide to what extent the law should enshrine the moral values of a majority, even if to breach them 'does not harm others' (the John Stuart Mill principle). However it was not the first time that Ireland had to change its legislation under pressure from the European Community. On two previous occasions, under pressure from the ECHR, two cases (also defended by Mary Robinson), *Airey* v. *Ireland* and *Johnston* v. *Ireland*, had forced the government to change its legislation. The first case led to the introduction of a system of free legal aid, and the second one paved the way for the Status of Children Act, which did away with the concept of illegitimacy. Despite these precedents, the government was in no hurry to legalise consensual homosexual acts.

This fact did not unduly irritate the gay movement which had decided on a strategy accommodating this wait-and-see policy. Indeed, their chief aim was not to get a law, any law, there and then; the reform, in a way, had already taken place, with the judgment of the ECHR. Instead, they wanted to run a campaign aimed at making the idea that any new law should be based on total equality between homosexuals and heterosexuals accepted: 'As we already had a *de facto* law reform, our initial strategy was not to call for an early law reform but to build up a consensus that an equality-based law reform was the only option.'[8] New groups, including Gay and Lesbian Equality Network (GLEN), specifically set up to campaign for equality-based legislation, and Gay Health Action, had already taken an active part in the seminar organised by the Law Reform Commission, meant as a brainstorming session, before drafting its report. Some of these groups were particularly active in the area of health, all initiative having been left to them when Ireland woke to the AIDS crisis around 1985, and the Department of Health as in so many other countries was taken unawares. They put in place the first information, prevention and support services. This being said, Gay Health Action experienced a lot of difficulty in obtaining funds from the Department of Health, apart from the cost of printing 15,000 leaflets on AIDS, for 'further funding was vetoed by the Department of Health because their legal advice was that information relating to gay sexual practices would be contrary to the criminal law.'[9] But it remains that the management of the AIDS crisis put gay and lesbian activists in contact with government agencies in a way that would have been improbable in other circumstances, and this had the effect of enhancing their visibility and legitimacy.[10]

In 1988, the Irish Council for Civil Liberties invited gays and lesbians to take part in a study with a view to publishing a report that would also be an action plan. *Equality Now for Lesbians and Gay Men,* published in 1990, was sent to every TD and senator to open and document a debate. It also fuelled submissions to the Law Reform Commission, political parties and other organisations. The fundamentalist group, Family Solidarity, replied with the publication of its own report, *The Homosexual Challenge: Analysis and Response*, which, without mentioning lesbians, referred to the gay community as 'engendering a pool of infection and disease'. The gay movement, according to Kieran Rose, lost a lot of time and energy countering the arguments of such groups: 'While the Church and lay right groups were not able to halt all change, they were able to delay law reform, AIDS initiatives, progress for young people and direct public finding for our community services. Their resistance consumed much of the scarce resources of the gay movement.'[11] GLEN got the opportunity to give another human face to homosexuality, several faces actually, by taking part in *The Late Late Show*, a TV programme presented by Gay Byrne, which had been touching on taboo subjects since the 1960s. The gays and lesbians invited, facing representatives of the right-wing lay Catholic organisations, could reassure viewers, who were, according to Kieran Rose, 'tolerant but unsure', and contribute to changing society's perception of homosexuals.[12]

The Law Reform Commission report is an important landmark in the process of imposing equality, since it marked the moment when the gay movement's argument was accepted at official level. They won a similar victory with the adoption of the Prohibition of Incitement to Racial, Religious or National Hatred Bill in 1988. This bill was discussed over a period of several months in the Seanad, where it was initiated, then in the Dáil, and again in the Seanad, once it had been substantially amended by the deputies. This bill aimed at regularising the situation in Ireland so that it could ratify the UN Convention on civil and political rights, in particular the section on the interdiction of incitement to national, racial or religious hatred. Senator David Norris was obviously the most eloquent and best informed parliamentarian, as well as the most apt at introducing an amendment to include sexual orientation as a possible reason for hatred (incitement to hatred against travellers was also strongly mentioned). As one of his colleagues put it,

> in both the Dáil and the Seanad we already have representatives of minority groupings within this State and it is logical therefore to accept that over a period we will have members of the travelling community who will be able to stand on the floor of the Dáil or the Seanad and espouse their own grouping as eloquently as Senator Norris does in the case of the gay community.[13]

He had won his case in the ECHR at that stage and hoped the government would grasp this as a golden opportunity to prove its goodwill as far as human rights were concerned. But the Minister for Justice, Gerry Collins, refused to consider for one moment the inclusion of such an amendment, since they were only trying to ratify an existing document, which did not mention hatred of homosexuals or travellers. A majority of senators were convinced by this line of argument and the amendment was rejected by 18 votes to 13. However, the vote in the Seanad had given rise to such discussions that the new Minister for Justice, Ray Burke, put forward an amendment to the original bill which the TDs approved. This is how the 1989 law, now called Prohibition of Incitement to Hatred Act, includes homosexuals and travellers even in its full title, which is: An Act to prohibit Incitement to Hatred on account of Race, Religion, Nationality or Sexual Orientation. This was history in the making: Irish parliamentarians for the first time had approved a measure in favour of homosexuals. This, of course, increased 'the "anomaly" of having a criminal offence for an activity which is being protected from hate campaigns'.[14] The very same Minister, Ray Burke, would admit some time later that 'if we did not already have legislation which penalises homosexual acts in private between consenting male adults, I do not think that today any reasonable person could seriously argue for such legislation. I do not, for example, hear of any demand to penalise homosexual activity between females.' He gave an assurance that new legislation would be brought forward and he would 'introduce it in the House during the course of next year'.[15] It was David Norris again who asked for such a debate in Parliament, and if his request was granted this time, it was maybe due to the fact that Mary Robinson had just been elected President of Ireland, and this event accounted for such goodwill. Who had not read or heard of her interview with the Irish rock magazine *Hot Press* in which she had said:

> Well, just as in other areas like wanting to remove the ban on divorce or delete sections 2 and 3, as Mary Robinson I am proud of my record and of the stands I have taken. Because they have been stands that I had to pay a price for, they've given me a reputation for integrity. Therefore I can say with integrity that as President I would be guardian of the Constitution as it is. However, I have always felt strongly that homosexuality should be decriminalised. I say it now and will say it, if appropriate, in a personal capacity, later. While I would be guardian of the Constitution as the people decide it, I could express personal reservations.[16]

But nothing further happened. The government was probably faced with the systematic opposition of some of the backbenchers, which was stronger than the unflagging lobbying of GLEN. The latter obtained from the Progressive Democrats the inclusion of this project of legislative reform in the legislative programme that this party and Fianna Fáil had reshuffled in October 1991. In 1992, David Norris threatened to take his case to Europe again, and within a few days, the Irish Ambassador to the Council of Europe, Liam Rigney, announced it was the government's intention to reform the law on homosexuality 'before the end of the year'. A few months later though, the Taoiseach said the government's current agenda was very full, and such law reform was 'at the bottom of the list of priorities'. This fuelled David Norris's frustration and anger. He 'was able to make a big meal out of that. I wrote to all the representatives of the Council of Europe ... You are supposed to be underwriting my human rights. I won a victory in your Court. And here is the Prime Minister of my country saying human rights are at the bottom of his list of priorities. What are you going to do about it?'[17] The government was now getting embarrassed, it was also embroiled in the abortion and protocol to the Maastricht Treaty controversy. Homosexuality was nearly involved too in the vote on European Union, as yet another example of European interference in Ireland's ethical principles. The spokesman for Family Solidarity warned that the legalisation of homosexual acts would have ramifications for education, child care, marriage, family and other areas of Irish life. Since opinion polls indicated that government legislation would be unacceptable to two-thirds of the people, he felt 'it would be an act of gross irresponsibility for the Government to do this, particularly during an AIDS crisis, encouraging as it does the main sexual act by which the HIV virus is transmitted.' He wondered whether this was 'another example of Europe imposing its ethical values upon Ireland, an area in which we are assured by Government that Europe has no interest'.[18]

Between May and November 1992, David Norris proceeded to disrupt the Seanad debates by tabling amendments to the order of the day at nearly every sitting of the chamber, so that his anger would be recorded in the minutes, and would also delay the discussion of what was effectively on the agenda. Supported by Brendan Ryan and John A. Murphy, he also tabled a motion criticising the government for not complying with the ECHR judgment.[19] GLEN, on the other hand, was trying to convince the Council for Human Rights within the Council of Europe to exclude Ireland from the Council until it complied with the ruling. All the political parties, except Fianna Fáil, came together against the Taoiseach to force him to include a bill on homosexuality in the current parliamentary session. There were of course other priorities, such as unemployment, but it was unlikely that changing the law on homosexuality would take up much of the chamber's time, as cross-party consensus could be expected. The Taoiseach, Albert Reynolds, said in October 1992 that such a bill would be put to the Dáil 'in due course'. Soon after he had relegated the homosexual question at the bottom of his list of priorities, to borrow his infamous phrase, President Mary Robinson invited to her residence 16 gays and 16 lesbians for tea. They represented various gay and lesbian organisations from Northern Ireland and the Republic. Jeffrey Dudgeon and David Norris, as the two persons who had contributed most to the legal recognition of homosexuality as a sexual orientation among others, were there too. Very few guests, though, felt brave enough to pose for the official photo, lest they would be recognised back home. Not for the first time the President made a symbolic gesture that would be understood as such (especially when one remembers her past outspokenness). As activist Chris Robson put it, 'the reception symbolised a national reconciliation with our community.'[20]

The Fianna Fáil–PD coalition government fell in November 1992 and elections took place on the 25th (the same day as the three abortion referendums). A Fianna Fáil–Labour government was returned and a new programme eventually published on 8 January 1993, in which David Norris was surprised not to find any explicit mention of homosexuality. In fact, there was a passing reference to forthcoming legislation to abide by the Convention on Human Rights. Another passage indicated that the government would put forward a bill to forbid all forms of discrimination on the grounds of sex, marital or parental status, sexual orientation, religion or age (the Equal Status Bill). It appears that the Campaign for Equality, the Irish Council for Civil Liberties and GLEN had made detailed submissions to the negotiators for the new government, and these reappeared in its programme.[21] This coalition would go down in history as the one that was most committed to a policy of socio-moral law reform, also called 'the liberal agenda'. Incidentally, David Norris came first in the Seanad elections that followed, with 1,149 votes more than in the previous election, i.e. 3,569 first preference votes. This would tend to confirm that his high profile in the media, which was more and more associated with homosexuals' rights, not to mention his performance in Parliament, had worked in his favour. The new Minister for Justice, Máire Geoghegan-Quinn, declared from the outset that the bill decriminalising homosexual acts would take priority, despite the fact that 87 bills in all were being drafted, and she added she was delighted to have been given the task (all the more surprising in view of the social conservatism of her party, Fianna Fáil). She can also be commended for acting as a legislator, and not 'as somebody who holds a particular view on behalf of the moral majority'.[22] She was referring there to the fact that her constituents of Galway West represented a conservative constituency.

The possible options in relation to such legislation were then presented in a memorandum from the Department of Justice for the benefit of the government. This was not a particularly radical document, which said, for example, that the government did not have any choice but to legislate, nor did it infer that the state might not have to legislate in the area of private morality. It seemed important to find a compromise between gay rights activists and the defenders of traditional family values. However, the memorandum was written in nineteenth-century language using words such as 'buggery' and acts of 'gross indecency', which betrayed the drafters' prejudice, and put gay and lesbian groups on the defensive. It was as if the intention was to make minor changes to the law so that it would comply with the Convention, rather than operate a long-overdue overhaul of the legislation, which would be a statement that a homosexual orientation was acceptable as any other. As for the age of homosexual majority, there were three possibilities: 17 (the heterosexual majority), 18 (the civil majority) or 21 (as in Great Britain). The memorandum did not seem to be in favour of a common age of consent, as this would be perceived as saying homosexuality was an acceptable lifestyle. On the whole, gay and lesbian groups were disappointed with the content of the memorandum, particularly where it envisaged copying the 1967 British law, itself inspired by the philosophy of the 1950s.

It transpired later that Labour ministers, who made up nearly half of the Cabinet, were in favour of repealing the existing legislation and introducing a common age of consent.[23] It was clear that the new legislation would legalise any sexual act between men, provided three conditions were met: the act must be consensual, it must take place in private and the two men must be over the age specified in the law. At that point, the Minister for Defence, David Andrews, announced that the Armed Forces would not be exempt from any new law. There were a few isolated deputies who voiced their opposition to any decriminalisation of sodomy and gross indecency, in order to protect public health and morality. But at that stage the die was cast, the government was determined to ensure the adoption of the bill by imposing a disciplined vote. The intense lobbying of GLEN, their interview with the Minister for Justice, their briefing letter sent to all parliamentarians were all going to bear fruit. Indeed, according to the gay protagonists, it took a meeting between Máire Geoghehan-Quinn and a young gay man's mother to convince the former of the necessity of decriminalising homosexuality in a clean-cut way. When she met Phil Moore, one of the founder members and ex-president of the Women's Political Association, adviser to Gemma Hussey while Minister for Education, and mother to a young homosexual, she was moved by what one mother had to say to another. Ms Moore showed her the dangers of a discriminatory law.

> As the mother of a gay person, I knew all about the misery and the pain. . . . I talked to Máire Geogheghan-Quinn like a mother to

another mother, I said to her: anything other than equality would be ludicrous ... Can you make 17 year olds criminals? And also, how do you prevent them from having unsafe sex? You know, we've been very good at finding Irish solutions to Irish problems, and we were so surprised when this time we got it right first time![24]

For his part, David Norris sent a letter to all deputies and senators which seems to have convinced even the most sceptical, since he received a large number of supportive replies, with the exception of one, he says. His letter, dated 30 April 1993, ended thus:

> We have a clear choice. We can do something bad and socially destructive based upon the British model or we can show our maturity as a nation and our sensitivity to the needs of a marginalised group by introducing what is in the best sense an Irish solution to a widespread human problem. This will in no way diminish the rights of the majority. In arguing for Catholic emancipation, Daniel O'Connell indicated that human liberty and dignity did not represent a finite resource but that, on the contrary, by granting liberty, dignity and equality to marginalised groups such as Roman Catholics were at the time, the dignity and humanity of all citizens was enhanced. This is also the case with the present legislation. I hope that you will feel able in conscience to support and argue for measures that will enable me and many thousands of other Irish people to feel for the first time full citizens of their country.[25]

Deaf to this kind of arguments, the Irish Catholic hierarchy published a statement the day before the opening of the debate on the bill in Parliament, which reiterated that 'sexual acts, freely chosen, with a person of the same sex, are morally wrong. They contradict the true meaning of human sexuality.... No change in State law can change the moral law. New civil laws cannot make what is wrong right.' They added: 'The Church does not expect that acts which are sinful should, by that very fact, be made criminal offences.... It is a matter of experience that legislative change is never neutral in its effects on society. In this case, the repeal of the law can be seen as giving a signal that homosexual behaviour is no longer regarded as morally unacceptable.'[26] The opponents to any change in the law, such as Family Solidarity, argued that homosexuality was not illegal, only sodomy (with a man as well as with a woman) was. This sounded like another argument heard some 20 years earlier. Contraception was not illegal, only the importation and the sale of contraceptives were!

Also, according to Family Solidarity, the propagation of AIDS was fastest amongst the homosexual community, so the government's responsibility should be to protect public health. Moreover, if only 1.1 per cent of men were homosexual, and if about 60 per cent of the population were against the decriminalisation of homosexual acts, the state had a right to refuse to change the law. (This was an allusion to new findings, according to which only 1.1 per cent (and not 10 per cent) of the population were homosexual.[27]) Family Solidarity were also worried by what they saw as the gay lobby's efforts at having more and more rights being guaranteed to gay people, such as equal rights to homosexual couples, the right to adopt children, the presentation of homosexuality in schools as a normal variation like being left-handed, the assurance of not being denied jobs even in 'sensitive' areas. Changing the law under the homosexual lobby's pressure was like saying, to young people particularly, that homosexuals were now considered normal, healthy and perfectly acceptable. Family Solidarity were active in the letter pages of newspapers, just as they had sent copies of their booklet *The Homosexual Challenge...* to all parliamentarians.

The debate on the percentage of homosexuals in the population was relaunched in Britain with the publication of *Sexual Behaviour in Britain* in January 1994. This seemed to confirm earlier American and French studies, arguing for 1.1 per cent of homosexuals in the population. Whether 1 in 10 or 1 in 100 people were criminalised for their sexual orientation was not much more than a cynical numbers game, in David Norris's mind, and should not delay the recognition of their rights. Indeed, the Irish Parliament was not going to play along these lines, as the British one did a few months later, when MPs brandished statistics when it came to liberalising the 1967 law. Anticipating slightly, let us mention that the British Parliament, on 21 February 1994, lowered the age of homosexual consent from 21 to 18 years (by 427 votes to 162); but lowering the age of consent to 16 years, which would have thus been the same for homosexuals as well as heterosexuals, had previously been rejected by 307 to 280 votes. Britain has still not solved the problem to the satisfaction of the partisans of total equality. This new law, enforceable as from the 1994 summer, was not applicable to Northern Ireland, and British gay groups were considering bringing a new case to the ECHR in Strasbourg. This was before a Labour government, elected in May 1997, promised a common age of consent.

In Ireland, the Criminal Law (Sexual Offences) Bill, was published on 16 June 1993. The sections concerning homosexuality were much more liberal than in the April memorandum. The Minister for Justice, having met various gay groups, had decided to base the bill on the recommendations of the Law Reform Commission report, so the legal age of consent would be 17 for homosexuals and heterosexuals, at the risk of alienating some Fianna Fáil backbenchers. To give an element of comparison, the countries which have a lower common age of consent are: Belgium (16), Poland (16), France (15), Spain (15) and Italy (14). It was obvious that the new law was not just a response to the Strasbourg judgment, but a truly Irish law embracing all citizens in their diversity. It is striking though that the word 'homosexual' does not appear once in the bill. In fact, the Criminal Law (Sexual Offences) Bill, like previous laws of the same kind, is not devoted entirely to homosexuality, and the government was accused of throwing homosexuality and prostitution together as a smokescreen. The bill was as liberal towards homosexuality as it was repressive towards prostitution, as if trying to silence the moralisers. *The Irish Times'* editorial on 24 June 1993 remarked: 'It is almost as if someone (incredibly) decided to compensate for taking a step forward in one area of socio-sexual legislation by taking a stride backwards in another.' David Norris himself declared he could not support such a bill, because, among other reasons, 'I do not find it flattering to be continually lumped in with prostitutes, drug abusers and child molesters.' The Minister for Justice in her introduction speech underlined that whether homosexuality was morally or socially acceptable was not at issue, but 'it is rather a matter of closely looking at values and asking ourselves whether it is necessary, or whether it is right, that they be propped up, for the comfort of the majority, by applying discriminatory and unnecessary laws to a minority – any minority.'[28] The present law repealed sections 61 and 62 of the 1861 law and section 11 of the 1885 law: sodomy has become legal between consenting adults aged 17 and over; gross indecency is not an offence under the same condition. But the concept itself has been retained to protect young boys aged 15–17 against homosexual acts (boys and girls under 15 are protected against any form of sexual assault, consensual or not). In effect, the law does not contain anything that might cause trouble to homosexuals which would not cause similar ones to heterosexuals. The government had a 41 seat majority in Parliament which guaranteed the adoption of the bill. There had only been two dissenting voices within the Fianna Fáil parliamentary group at one of its meetings to discuss the bill. The Fine Gael parliamentary group for its part wanted to table a motion for the homosexual majority to be set at 18, and one of its most virulent deputies, Brendan McGahon, would have liked to vote according to his conscience, since for him such a law was 'a wanker's charter'. As the debate opened in the Dáil, a group of people knelt in front of Parliament building, praying and bearing signs saying things like 'Ban the TD who "aids" VD' or 'Remember what happened to Sodom and Gomorrah'!

Another extraordinary thing about the adoption of this law, apart from the generosity it expresses, was the fact it was passed without a vote. As ten deputies must request a vote if there is going to be one, and only one did, it did not take place. The bill was discussed for five hours over two days, and declared passed. Most of the time was devoted to the discussion of the clauses dealing with prostitution. Several Fine Gael deputies tabled amendments to these to make sure that some of their colleagues did not have time to table their own amendments relative to the age of homosexual majority. This behaviour, called filibustering, consists in speaking as long as possible so that there is no time left for a discussion to take place. Gay rights groups, among them David Norris, applauded from the visitors' gallery when the law was declared passed by the Dáil, and bottles of champagne were opened on the steps of the Parliament building. The debate in the Seanad was shorter than expected. David Norris retraced the history of homosexuality and its criminalisation, as well as of his own liberalisation campaign which he was able to take to its rightful conclusion thanks to the fantastic expert work his lawyer and friend, now President of Ireland, had put into it: 'There is a particular appropriateness, and I hope pleasure, for the President in signing into law a Bill whose passage she was herself obliquely instrumental in securing.'[29] He also thanked the Minister for Justice for her bravery, and paid homage to all the gay groups who had fought for their civil rights but also against the AIDS crisis. It should be noted in passing that it would seem there is a relatively low rate of homosexual transmission of AIDS in Ireland, which can be accounted for by the legal ban on sex between men, but also by the early action taken by the Irish gay community. In Ireland, 18 per cent of AIDS cases are regarded as resulting from sexual intercourse between men, whereas the proportion in Britain is 64 per cent.

The legalisation of homosexual acts was hailed as one of the historic events of the decade, a satisfying conclusion to nearly two decades of commitment and involvement in the gay rights movement on the part of David Norris. As Brian Murray put it,

> he provided the environment by which the Government could change. And I've no doubt that his presence in the Senate has

resulted not only in raising the issue of homosexuality but has meant that sexual orientation is one of the things which is included in legislation as a protection of minority groups.[30]

It is also fair to say that this campaign for equal civil rights is one of the most successful such campaigns ever waged in Ireland (Chris Robson, co-chair of GLEN is tempted to say *'the* most successful').[31] Doggedness and a great sense of strategy ensured that the gay activists led Ireland to a crucial stage in its social and political history, not just for the gay community but for all minorities.

GAY VISIONS IN THE HETEROSEXUAL COMMUNITY

The ease with which this law was adopted raises the following question: Would homosexuality have been legalised if the question had been put to the people in a national referendum? Was the government, for once, ahead of public opinion? According to Micheal Mac Gréil's study, published in 1977, *Prejudice and Tolerance in Ireland*, the 2,777 Dubliners who were asked their opinion were quite divided: 39.9 per cent agreed with the statement: 'Homosexual acts between consenting adults should be a crime'; 45.2 per cent diagreed, and 14.9 per cent were undecided. Even if the 39.9 per cent in favour of the current legislation were a minority, it was a sizeable minority. But considering that this behaviour was indeed a crime, and the discriminatory climate of the time (the study was conducted in 1972–3), the fact that 45.2 per cent did not agree was a tangible sign of tolerance.[32]

An opinion poll conducted in 1993 by students in journalism using the Landsdowne Market Research methodology and asking 1,100 people from Greater Dublin, aged 16–55, from all socio-economic categories, found that 69 per cent of them were aware that private homosexual acts were a criminal offence; 78 per cent thought the law should be changed; 68 per cent believed that the homosexual age of consent should be the same as the heterosexual one (17); 51 per cent believed gay and lesbian couples should be allowed to marry, but 50 per cent thought they should not have the right to adopt children, whereas 33 per cent were in favour of adoption rights.[33] We can compare these results with those obtained by Landsdowne Market Research for *The Irish Press* and *The Sunday Press* in 1991 and 1993 respectively. In the first poll, 42 per cent disapproved of the legalisation of homosexuality and 39 per cent approved; in the second one, 50 per cent disapproved and 34 per cent approved. The June 1993 poll was carried out among a representative sample of 1,261 people, aged 18 or over, at 70 locations throughout the Republic, and the question asked was: 'The Government is planning to legalise homosexual acts between people *aged 17 and over*. Do you personally approve or disapprove of legalising homosexual acts?' We emphasise the age, to suggest that opposition to the legalisation of homosexuality might have had as much to do with the age as with the proposal itself. Also, the fact that the question 'Do you personally approve or disapprove...' was far less neutral than 'Do you think...', thus eliciting for more negative answers. As David Norris remarked:

> The vast majority of Irish people don't want to be interfering in other people's sexual lives. You get a very different response depending how the question is put... If you said 'do you think some man of 50 should be allowed to... your son of 18', they'd say Noo! Stoop! If you say 'do you think two young lads of 20–21 should be sentenced to jail for 10 years for having sex privately, for making love'... you get a different answer. It depends on the question you ask. Unfortunately the right-wing are very good at manipulating views, by pressing all the emotional stops, and you'll have all this stuff about disease, about Aids, about lengthy descriptions of anal intercourse...[34]

The poll also shows there are considerable differences between Dubliners and people from rural areas, and between young people and not so young. For example, 52 per cent of the under-25s approved the government's proposal to change the law, but only 12 per cent of the over 65s. Fianna Fáil and Fine Gael voters were more strongly opposed than Labour or PD ones, who were not enthusiastic either. The farming community and working-class voters were mainly opposed, with the middle classes being the only group approving. At the same time, IMS carried out a poll for Family Solidarity which found that 43 per cent of the sample were against a change in the law, 37 per cent were in favour and 20 per cent had no opinion. These results compare with those obtained by Lansdowne.[35] The liberal agenda did not seem to be endorsed by the people at large, even if David Norris could quote a radio poll in which out of 11,000 people, 66 per cent believed the law should be changed:

> I direct the Minister to, for example, I suppose a sort of *vox populi*, the Gay Byrne radio show, on which during a debate recently, there

was what they call a tele-poll. I am not suggesting that it is necessarily completely accurate. Everybody dismisses polls when they
do not suit them and accept them warmly when they do, but
in that poll of 11,000 people – it could not possibly have been
rigged – 66 per cent thought the law should be changed. Maybe
it is a little bit more, maybe it should be a little bit less, but it is a
very interesting indicator of the kind of support that could be
anticipated.[36]

It is hard to believe that public opinion could have changed so radically
within two and a half years. It is safer to say that a majority of Irish
people had always expressed great reserve concerning the decriminalisation of homosexuality, but also a great indifference, symptomatic of
a fair degree of tolerance. This question has only preoccupied a tiny
minority of the population, and the intervention of Europe was certainly instrumental in bringing about a change of heart on the part of
Parliament. If a referendum had been necessary to change the legislation, nothing proves that a majority of people would have voted in
favour of change, all the more so as referendums on moral questions
tend to attract answers that are more conservative than do opinion
polls or parliamentary elections.

The results of a recent study on the tolerance levels of Europeans
regarding certain deviances are fascinating if somewhat puzzling: the
Irish would appear to be the most tolerant Europeans, with the same
score as the Dutch, and far ahead of the British.[37] This result is
confirmed by another international sociological survey, ISSP (International Social Survey Programme), done in 1988, according to which the
Irish and the Dutch again had the least objections to homosexual
marriages. The question asked was: 'Do you agree or disagree that
homosexual couples should have the right to marry one another?' Only
25 per cent of the Dutch and 26.3 per cent of the Irish 'strongly
disagreed'.[38] These results are quite extraordinary, even if a higher
than average number of Irish people did not respond to this question
(71 out of 1,005); and even if 33.5 per cent 'disagreed' with the
proposition: indeed, 24.4 per cent 'agreed' with it and 2.2 per cent
'strongly agreed'. Who would have thought that 26.6 per cent of a
representative sample would agree at all with an unambiguous proposition about homosexual marriages? This is all the more unexpected
in light of the fact that Ireland has the lowest permissivity rate in
Europe: 2.49 against the European average of 3.81. And the 1994
ISSP survey had a question on same-sex relations this time, to which

57.3 per cent of the sample responded that such relations were always wrong.[39] Would this prove that the Irish are more absolutist when it comes to abstract questions, and more tolerant faced with individual cases wanting to do the right thing (marry)?

On the politicians' side, Fianna Fáil and Fine Gael were traditionally reluctant even to discuss the issue, whereas Labour and the smaller parties pressed for change. Having said that, even at a time when a Fine Gael–Labour coalition was prepared, in the 1980s, to tackle contraception and divorce, the then Taoiseach, Garret FitzGerald turned down the request of a group of homosexuals to lay a wreath in the Garden of Remembrance in Dublin, to honour all those who had been tortured or killed, over the centuries, for their sexual orientation. *The Irish Times* political correspondent reminisced on 23 June 1993: 'A spokesman said the proposed ceremony was not in keeping with the purpose of the garden.' So the wind was definitely blowing in a different direction for a Fianna Fáil-led government to pass such a liberal law, while being fully aware of not having a majority of the electorate behind it.

To return to the question, Was the government ahead of public opinion? It must be stressed that the new law was widely welcomed, notably on the streets of Dublin, where gays paraded chanting the now famous 'We're here, we're queer, we're legal!' Nobody present contradicted activist Kieran Rose when he said to the crowd:

Today we can be here, proud to be Irish citizens and proud to be lesbian and gays. We really believe that Irish people are progressive, that Irish people do support the lesbian and gay community, do support human rights and equality and have no time at all for bigotry.

When one thinks of the reception given to the Irish Lesbian and Gay Organisation in New York at the St Patrick's Day Parade that very same year (they were spat at, insulted and the target of beer cans), the attitude of the Irish is positively tolerant. To stick to the St Patrick's Day context, whereas American gay organisations cannot even take part in the New York parade, Cork was the first Irish city to include them in its parade and give them first prize for the best new float, thus vouching for 'the growing confidence of Irish society to accommodate difference.'[40]

Indeed, Ireland could now boast a most liberal and encompassing legislation on homosexuality. It could even be one of the few countries protecting its homosexuals against discrimination and harassment.

Ironically enough, some of these laws had been adopted while homosexuality was still a criminal offence. The whole range of laws and
measures aimed at equality between homosexuals and heterosexuals at
all levels of their social life includes, apart from the 1993 law: The
Video Recordings Act, 1988, which introduced a system of licences for
videos – incitement to hatred of persons because of their sexual
orientation was inserted as a reason to ban a video; The Prohibition
of Incitement to Hatred Act, adopted in 1989, which we referred to
earlier; the Health (Family Planning) (Amendment) Act, also passed
in 1993, allowing the sale of condoms in vending machines; the decriminalisation of suicide (homosexuals seem to make up a high percentage of people trying to commit suicide); the Unfair Dismissals Act of
1977, amended in 1993, and an anti-discriminatory protocol applicable
to the civil service since 1988. This civil service policy on AIDS in the
workplace, as it was called, was introduced in 1988 by Ray McSharry,
Minister for Finance, and was recently extended to local administra-
tions and semi-public bodies. Any discrimination on the basis of sexual
orientation, sero-positivity or full-blown AIDS (as long as the person is
able to work) would not be tolerated in the workplace.[41] The Irish
Congress of Trade Unions had also backed the 'struggle for equal
treatment' ever since David Norris, through his union, the Irish Federation of University Teachers, managed to put forward a resolution on
the matter to the ICTU's annual conference in the late 1970s. In June
1987, the ICTU published a radical policy document, *Lesbian and Gay
Rights in the Workplace: Guidelines for negotiators,* sent to every union
in Ireland, against discrimination towards homosexual workers.
According to Kieran Rose, 'it was the first detailed pro-gay policy
from a powerful national organisation and it resulted in significant
practical and ideological progress.'[42]

As for the Unfair Dismissals Act, 1977 which was amended on 1
October 1993, following the decriminalisation of homosexuality, it now
includes sexual orientation among the grounds for dismissals deemed
to be unfair. Let us note that the bill was actually published on 17
March, before the legalisation of homosexuality, by another woman,
Mary O'Rourke, Secretary of State for Employment. This exemplifies
GLEN's tactics which was rooted in the reality of the homosexuals'
socialisation, in particular in the workplace:

In fact at times, GLEN was putting more painstaking effort into
getting those two words 'sexual orientation' into that Act than it was
into law reform. In many ways it was a classic piece of lobbying

targeted at a major but achievable goal and identifying the precise amendment to be used, that is adding 'sexual orientation' to Section 6(2) (e) of the 1977 Act.[43]

A change in the nineteenth-century laws was necessary to remove the stigma caused by the criminalisation of homosexuality, mainly expressed in fear and guilt; to launch a campaign against discrimination in employment and housing; to enable the state to acknowledge the tremendous work done by the various gay organisations in fighting the AIDS crisis and promoting safe sex, and to offer them its financial support. Symbolically speaking, changing the law on homosexuality will have been, according to the director of Aidswise, 'the equivalent of women getting the vote, of the abolition of slavery'. For example, it saw to the implementation of the Gay Man's Health Project which was financed by the Minister for Health and based in the Royal City of Dublin Hospital. The legalisation of homosexual acts allowed a growing number of gay men, HIV-positive or suffering from AIDS, to get medical attention. This came at the end of a long period of very distant involvement on the part of the state. Ger Philpott, director of Aidswise, was very critical of the AIDS policy of the various governments:

> It wasn't until 1993 that an Irish Minister for Health had the balls to launch the first media campaign unequivocally urging people to practice safer sex and wear a condom. Brendan Howlin was responsible for this. He got a lot of praise for the campaign. It was seen to be significant. Indeed it was, but only in terms of what hadn't happened before.[44]

No attempt will be made here to measure the discrimination affecting lesbians and gays in their daily life. No such study had been done before the 1993 law, until the publication of *Poverty: Lesbians and gay men – The economic and social effects of discrimination on marginalised groups.*[45] However the McAnellan case hit the headlines and reminded us that this discrimination is invisible, as its victims are not in a position to come forward and tell their story openly. This case also proved that even though the law had changed, there were a few gaps. Donna McAnellan is the first Irish lesbian who dared come out and take to court a homophobic employer, and proudly make the headlines afterwards. She had been employed for six months as a swimming supervisor and aerobics instructor at a recently opened exclusive leisure centre in Cork. She was dismissed at no notice, in April 1993, because she had allegedly been seen kissing a woman in the changing rooms.

Three lawyers who had heard of the story on the grapevine approached her and offered to defend her, free of charge, in the Labour Court. Their argument was that, on the basis of the Employment Equality Act 1977, which forbids discrimination in employment, sexual orientation is also covered and that the young woman had been unfairly dismissed. Donna McAnellan's lawyers were hoping that the 1977 law would interpret the word 'sex' to include sexual orientation, just as it now implicitly covers sexual harassment (since the 1985 decision of the Labour Court, EEO 2/85). The employer, who did not have to produce any witness, argued that the presence of a lesbian in a leisure centre could ruin the reputation of the establishment. The court, in EEO 12/93, acknowledged that Donna McAnellan had been unjustly and arbitrarily treated, but at the same time they could not support her claim that she had been unfairly dismissed, as the law implicated did not cover sexual orientation, only sex and marital status. As a man would have been dismissed for a similar behaviour, there was no discrimination under the terms of that law.

The Unfair Dismissals Act, previously mentioned, could not be invoked as Donna McAnellan had only been employed by Brookfield for six months and not 12 as it stipulates. There was only one avenue open to the young woman, and it was the media which, in this era when the 'politically correct' reigns supreme, and homosexuality had become PC, welcomed such an opportunity. As *The Irish Times* put it on 8 February 1994:

> The '90s will be the gay decade. It's cool to be queer. It's fashionable to be gay. Kieran Rose of GLEN described the massive leaping out of closets as 'an explosion of lesbian and gay activity' which was in marked contrast to the 'very fragile' atmosphere of the mid '80s.

Overnight she became the spokesperson for Cork lesbians, a position that she ended up enjoying:

> Someone had to do it. Why not me? There are so many taking abuse and saying nothing. Someone had to stand up for our rights. I feel brilliant now that I have done it.... Through [education], through talking, through the media, people will begin to understand that we are the same human beings as them, that we have the right to choose our own sexuality...[46]

Like David Norris, Donna McAnellan wanted to give lesbianism a face, but she needed her friends' go-ahead, since by having her face plastered all over the papers, she compromised all those whose parents knew her: 'If I'm outed, they're outed, and I outed a lot of people!'[47] But the moral climate was actually such that she got the congratulations, not the leisure centre for taking its clients' best interests at heart, a little as if her action was a welcome challenge to law and authority. The Minister for Equality and Law Reform, Mervyn Taylor, pledged that, following this case, the Employment Equality Act, 1977 would be amended earlier than planned (1995), to take sexual orientation into account, since it was an obvious omission highlighted by the case. Was it really an omission? Could one really hope that the government would, in the same breath, legalise homosexuality, forbid incitement to hatred and outlaw unfair dismissals based on sexual orientation, and also forbid discrimination in employment? The moralisers would have been up in arms. The government seems to have adopted a very soft approach to the question of homosexuals' rights, very pragmatic, by which one does not appear to do much more than comply with what Europe or the UN, or WHO require, instead of tackling the issue head-on. Another reason is that amending the Employment Equality Act would require a complete restructuring, which would go hand in hand with the adoption of the Equal Status Bill. The Employment Equality Agency's brief, in particular, would be enlarged to turn it into the Equality Commission, in order to see to the enforcement of all the laws relative to the citizens' equality at all levels – this was of such magnitude it had been postponed.

More or less at the same time, the young author Emma Donoghue was herself in the news. She was featured in every book programme and book page, as well as on *The Late Late Show*. The occasion was the publication of her first novel, *Stir-Fry*. Set in Trinity College Dublin, it was about a student who awakens to her lesbianism. Representing a group that has always been considered with some circumspection, to say the least, she made quite a strong and positive impression. She still remains one of the very few public lesbians (three? four?), which is in itself extraordinary, as it would not have been allowed to happen with such indulgence only a few years earlier. Indeed, when David Norris appeared on a TV programme on RTE in 1975, some spectators complained and there was a report issued by the Complaints Advisory Committee (and published in the RTE programme guide on 30 January 1976), from which Mary Robinson, defending him, quoted:

As, at the present time, homosexual practices, even between consenting adults, are a criminal offence in Ireland, it is improper for RTE to present anything which could be reasonably regarded as encouragement or advocacy of such homosexual acts. This does not mean that a reasonable and comprehensive discussion as to whether the law should be changed is not a suitable subject for a programme.... By many, homosexuality is regarded as stemming only from moral obliquity and perversity but for others it is recognised as having physiological and psychological roots. It is probably correct to say that the majority of the Irish people retain the narrower view but even of those who accept a wider causality most regard the urge to homosexuality as a misfortune for those so affected. Any programme which could reasonably be regarded as facilitating or encouraging homosexual practices neglects the requirements of section 4 of the Code of current public affairs broadcasting practice.[48]

In 1993, passers-by shook Donna McAnellan's hand for taking on a homophobic employer. Also, when a Junior Labour Minister was questioned by the police in a notorious male prostitution area of Dublin and the media made a meal of it, the people and his colleagues did not ask for his head and he did not offer his resignation. Unlike in Britain, the professional competence of the Minister was not allowed to interfere with his private life, whether he be homosexual or bisexual (since he is married and has a family). The government was trapped in a way. Having just legalised homosexuality, could it demand the resignation of one of its most able members? Should it banish one for indulging in an illegal activity (prostitution) without the two issues being mixed together? It was decided to let the people decide at the next general election. (He retained his seat in the election of June 1997!) Parallel to the Emmet Stagg affair, the *Black Diaries* of Sir Roger Casement, the Irish hero sentenced to death by the British in 1916, were posthumously published without causing a stir. In 1916, the smear campaign engaged by the British had indeed cut short any movement asking for clemency, and he was hanged for treason and, indirectly, for his homosexuality. Eighty years later, the Irish accept that one of their heroes was homosexual: he is still a hero.

Homosexuality is, like contraception, the socio-moral issue at the core of the Catholic ideology, which has been comprehensively dealt with. A right to homosexuality has been recognised unequivocally and expressly guaranteed. The homosexuality issue, raised at about the same time as the other socio-moral ones, benefited from the torments suffered by them, be it contraception, abortion or divorce, which came first on the legislative agenda. For example gay men were a 'driving-force' in the anti-amendment campaign of 1983 in Cork, and, as Kieran Rose, co-chair of GLEN, remembers: 'While the campaign continued over more than a year and monopolised our attention, it also provided us with considerable skills, experience and confidence. The intensive local campaign resulted in the Cork City constituencies being unique in the country in having an anti-amendment vote higher than a pro-divorce vote of 1986.'[49]

The campaign also benefited from the strategical genius of one of its most tenacious and most informed spokespersons, and from a clever and unrelenting pressure group. The fact that the homosexual community is represented in Parliament by such an intellectually sound and research-conscientious man as David Norris has also contributed to the success of their long-drawn-out campaign. He had set an objective for himself, which was to include the rights of homosexuals, in the rights of the person and there would not be any giving in until the government acted in this direction:

> I got amendments into two items of legislation [Prohibition of Incitement to Hatred Bill and Video Bill] to include sexual orientation, and that was a breakthrough; that means it now goes in almost automatically, that's what I wanted to do – that the draughtsman automatically puts it in. That's crucial, you see, because that will now gow into the Anti-Discrimination Bill when it comes up, and that's where it's going to really hit.[50]

Irish lesbians commanded less of our attention since no laws and no papal pronouncements have attacked them, but it has to be said they have been involved in all liberation movements in Ireland, as the articles about them published in *Lesbian and Gay Visions of Ireland* testify. It is noticeable that whereas gay men have concentrated their efforts on law reform, and by extension, lobbying, lesbians have in the main joined efforts with other women's groups. Their representation within the Council for the Status of Women (now called NCWI) is notably strong. There are four lesbian groups affiliated to the CSW/NCWI, out of 120; they are Lesbian Equality Network, Cork Lesbian Line Collective, Dublin Lesbian Line Collective and Lesbians Organising Together (LOT). Their political activism is second to none, as the number of resolutions they put forward for the 1995 AGM of the federation proves: six out of 26, or 25 per cent. Indeed, these groups were behind the CSW motions urging the government to introduce new anti-discrimination legislation, in 1987, 1988 and 1989.[51] To prove the point further, let us note that one of these groups, LOT, obtained a £50,000 grant from the Department of Social Welfare in September 1995.

It thus seems fair to say that the Ireland of the mid-1990s, however imbued with Catholic teaching and respectful of the traditional family, can be more tolerant and more open and can show more solidarity with its gays and lesbians than France or Great Britain, to mention only her closest neighbours (and homosexuality was finally decriminalised in Ireland 11 years after France passed similar legislation, 26 years after Britain). One can imagine that the process exemplified by the legalisation of homosexuality but started a little earlier (as the adjoining legislation shows) will go further. Homosexuals have gained their civil rights and can be more open about issues affecting them; employees who feel they have been wronged by a homophobic employer have recourse to new legislation; the state can openly finance and support programmes targeted at the homosexual community about AIDS prevention and information. The bill relative to all discrimination in employment, training, education, housing and services, the Equal Status Bill, was promised by the new Government which came into office in December 1994. Already put forward by Dick Spring, while in opposition, in 1990, it was eagerly awaited by the gay community. It would give a concrete expression to a campaign which had been based on the idea of equality for all, be they women, gay men, travellers, disabled and other categories of vulnerable people, and on the necessity for global legislation that does not single out homosexuals. (Unfortunately some sections were found unconstitutional in May 1997 and would have to be redrafted.)

It should also be noted that the concept of what constitutes the family widens by the day in Ireland, and now includes single-parent families, second unions and... homosexual couples. The process by which the state officially gives its blessings, as it were, to these new family forms is well under way. Another example is the fact that barring orders are available against other persons than the lawful spouse of the opposite sex. Any violent member of the family can be thus injuncted, whether a common law spouse, whatever the sex. The Family Law (Protection of Persons) Bill, 1994, later renamed Domestic Violence Bill, 1995, prompted Kieran Rose to say that 'this amounted to the first recognition of lesbian and gay partnerships in Irish law.' And because it includes people in domestic relationships other than marriage, 'it is a much better way to go about it than to introduce a law just for lesbian and gay partnerships.'[52] If cohabitation is officially recognised one day in Ireland, and not only when it comes to violence and abuse, will it not be logical to do so without mention of the sex of the partners? As Irish homosexuals have gained their civil rights, the determined (if belated) way the state granted them lets us anticipate that it will carry on ensuring the common good through the respect of fundamental rights for everybody, as diverse as they may be.

The 1996 census for the first time asked people if they were 'living together as a couple' (and found 31,000 cohabiting family units)!

Conclusion

Having analysed in these pages the treatment meted out over 73 years to the four courses of conduct most censured by the Catholic Church and by the Irish state, one is tempted to conclude that a new order is indeed in place in the Republic of Ireland, characterised by the fact that as far as the sexual morals of consenting adults are concerned, there are no norms or sanctions any longer. Norms are not exemplified by the indissoluble, procreative, monogamous family, and those who choose to live according to different models do not risk penal sanctions. But is Ireland the victim of more promiscuity, deviance and perversions as a result? This is highly arguable, as old stories of abuse surface and suggest that the old order was to some extent fabricated, and it would appear more pertinent to focus on the fact that what is different today is that the reality of the 'non-conformers'' experience is officially acknowledged, and they are not criminals any more. Individual moral choice prevails now over adherence to obligatory norms.

These rights now recognised by the state are not really new rights, or products of modern times. But they are the extension of natural rights, superior and anterior to positive law as promulgated by the British Parliament or the Irish Free State. They have been revealed by the courts, both Irish and European. But the Irish courts interpret laws according to current notions of the common good and morality, so their judgments take into account the socio-moral climate they perceive out there: it is thus necessary for them to have perceived such a trend towards the de-catholicisation of morality among citizens. It was remarkable nonetheless that the Attorney-General, in his defence of the abortion information bill, should refute the interpretation of the natural law as the yardstick by which laws and rights are vindicated, particularly as it was in his office that law, politics, morality and religion had dramatically converged with the X case. And indeed the Supreme Court believed that Parliament had reached a 'fair and reasonable balancing' of the right to life of the unborn, the right to live of the mother and the right to have access to information on abortion abroad.

This is one of the most recent and striking examples of a non-Catholic reading of the Constitution. It would be a shortcut to conclude to the 'Protestantisation' of Ireland, primarily because the

Protestant churches do not like to be labelled 'permissive' just because they do not adhere to an absolute dogma. Also there is nothing to show that Ireland is in the process of losing its Catholic identity, if you exclude dwindling mass attendance. On the other hand, it is clear that the way Protestants consider situations as they present themselves before deciding the morality of such and such a course of action has been well integrated by the Irish courts (the X case being an illuminating example), as well as by the citizens and the legislators. Irish Catholics have reclaimed the right to think for themselves as far as sexual morality is concerned, thus overriding disciplinary norms and rejecting the Church's moral authority.

If the true value of a society, as is said, can be measured by how well it deals with its minorities, Ireland has found a balance between the traditional notion of an Irish identity imbued with Catholicism and that of a pluralist and therefore liberal democracy, which does not undermine the social order. In this process, the 'moral majority' (the militants in the pro-life and anti-divorce campaigns, the ultra-Catholic lay groups, the conservative vote) has become a minority like the others, – the homosexuals, the women who choose to terminate their pregnancy, the couples with marital difficulties, the couples co-habiting, the single-child families, the single-parent families. They bear witness to the 'widening of the ethical dissensus', in the phrase of Lipovetsky, which could very well be the supreme expression of democracy, a more convincing one than majority rule.[1]

Mary Robinson believed in 1985 that

> women should not look to Parliament as a primary source of innovation and change. At best Parliament would react to pressure from outside groups, to the consequence of successful court actions and to complying with our obligations in the EEC and under the European Human Rights Convention. This limited and mainly reactive role for Parliament poses serious problems for our democracy. Basically Ireland needs a better structured and more effective parliamentary response to the rapid pace of economic and social change taking place in society as a whole.[2]

We would argue that this reactive role is not the sole prerogative of the Irish Parliament, and that the people have not always been an agent of change in the sense of liberalism! Moreover, the Irish parliamentary system, however imperfect, has given us parliamentarians of a remarkable calibre, such as Mary Robinson, Garret FitzGerald, Noël Browne,

David Norris and others, who have been so instrumental in framing the new political culture and a more inclusive society.

Other telling signs, peripheral to the issues analysed in the preceding pages, of the dramatic changes in Irish political and judicial culture would comprise, *inter alia*, the appointment to the Supreme Court in March 1997 of the first member of the Jewish faith, Henry Barron, in replacement of Neil Blaney (at one time legal adviser to the anti-abortion campaign); the Employment Equality Bill and the Equal Status Bill, 1997, which will both provide protection for those who suffer discrimination and unequal treatment inside and outside the context of employment. These pieces of legislation were heralded as promising a great impact on Irish society for the greater equality, mutual respect and tolerance they sought to foster. Also, the Supreme Court judgment in the 'right to die case', which ruled that the right to live must also imply a right to die a natural death (as distinct from euthanasia). The recommendation of the Review Group on the Constitution that abortion must be legislated for in the sense of the Supreme Court judgment, rather than constitutionally prohibited. The legislation allowing three voluntary Dublin hospitals, including a Protestant one, to form the new Tallaght hospital, and to retain their respective ethos. Strikingly too, the Irish came to grips with genetics, ready to reconcile it with their ethics, when a state genetic counselling service was set up, in July 1994, offering at last a pre-natal diagnosis of genetic defects (amniocentesis, a service asked for by 76 per cent of 3,000 women surveyed the same year by the ESRI, despite the unconditional opposition of fundamentalist Catholics), while three centres for assisted conception (IVF for example) are running in the state.

The result of the 1995 referendum on divorce is the most momentous illustration of the advent of this new order, and it takes its rightful place in the present argument, completing as it does the range of subjective rights which are now acknowledged and guaranteed by the state and which comprise: the right to separate from one's spouse followed by the right to remarry; the right to marital privacy concerning birth control; the right of women with crisis pregnancies to travel from one European state to another for a medical service; the right to obtain all the necessary information to avail of such a service; the right to homosexual privacy. The right to an abortion on Irish soil in certain limited circumstances is acknowledged by the Supreme Court, without being enabled by the state legislation. But just as one marriage in eight ends in separation and the state had eventually to acknowledge that plain fact, the fact that one pregnancy in 10 ends in abortion will have to be faced. The state cannot legislate on this matter by referendums for ever, which contradict each other and evade the real issue.

But if the 'moral majority', to borrow the American phrase, is now as large as the 'liberal minority', in that they literally share public opinion at 50–50, this tells nothing about the future. When it comes to individual rights vigilance is *de rigueur*; particularly when one makes too regular a use of referendums, a double-edged tool of public consultation. Having said that, it will be interesting to watch how Ireland, in the long term, combines modernity and tradition, at a time when a number of its neighbours are calling for a return to traditional values and to the 'old moral order'.

Notes

INTRODUCTION; WHOSE MORALITY? WHAT SEXUALITY?

1. *Catechism of the Catholic Church*, Dublin: Veritas, 1994, p. 427.
2. See *Bunreacht na hEireann, Constitution of Ireland*, Dublin: Government Publications Office, 1937.
3. Kevin McNamara, 'Church and State', *Doctrine and Life*, 1978, p. 140.
4. Gilles Lipovetsky, *Le crépuscule du devoir: L'éthique indolore des nouveaux temps démocratiques*, Paris: Gallimard, 1992, p. 176. Quotes from Lipovetsky are translated by CH withe the kind permission of the author.
5. Ibid., p. 25.
6. See Christopher T. Whelan (ed.), *Values and Social Change in Ireland*, Dublin: Gill & Macmillan, 1994, pp. 18–21.
7. Quoted in Michael O'Sullivan, *Mary Robinson: The Life and Times of an Irish Liberal*, Dublin: Blackwater Press, 1993, p. 174.
8. 'Copperfasten' is a word that the Irish media and commentators have used profusely to describe the embedding in concrete as it were (in the Constitution) of the abortion amendment. They applied it also to the ban on divorce.

1 DIVORCE: FROM AN INDISSOLUBLE BOND...

1. See William Duncan, 'Desertion and Cruelty in Irish Matrimonial Law', *The Irish Jurist*, vol. 7, 1972, p. 214. And David Fitzpatrick, 'Divorce and Separation in Modern Irish History', *Past and Present*, no. 114, February 1987, p.174.
2. *Seanad Debates*, 22 May 1986, col. 1544.
3. Peter Finlay, 'Divorce in the Irish Free State', *Studies*, September 1924, pp. 353–62.
4. D.H. Akenson and J.F. Fallin, 'The Irish Civil War and the Drafting of the Free State Constitution', *Eire/Ireland*, vol. 5, no. 1, Spring 1970, p. 15.
5. Draft C was reproduced for the first time by Brian Farrell, 'The Drafting of the Irish Free State Constitution: III', *The Irish Jurist*, vol. 6, 1971, pp. 124–35.
6. See Eamon Duggan, *Dáil Debates*, 25 September 1922, col. 695. David Fizpatrick, 'Divorce and Separation in Modern Irish History', *Past & Present*, no. 114, February 1987, p. 188.
7. *Dáil Debates*, 11 February 1925, cols. 155–82.
8. *Seanad Debates*, 11 June 1925, col. 455.

246   *The Politics of Sexual Morality in Ireland*

9. Dermot Keogh, 'Catholicism and the Formation of the Modern Irish Society', in *Irishness in a changing society*, The Princess Grace Irish Library, Totowa: Barnes & Noble Books, p. 161.
10. *Seanad Debates*, 11 June 1925, cols. 436–7.
11. David Fitzpatrick, 'Divorce and Separation in Modern Irish History' p. 193.
12. Dermot Keogh, *The Vatican, the Bishops and Irish Politics, 1919–1939*, Cambridge: Cambridge University Press, 1986, p. 73.
13. Quoted in Michael Laffan, *The Partition of Ireland, 1911–1925*, Dundalle: Dundalgau, 1983, p. 119.
14. Dermot Keogh, 'Catholicism and the Formation of the Modern Irish Society', p. 153.
15. See John H. Whyte, *Church and State in Modern Ireland, 1923–1979*, 2nd edition, Dublin: Gill & Macmillan, pp. 49–50.
16. Quoted in *Catholic Bulletin*, vol. 25, April 1935, p. 273.
17. Brian Farrell, 'The Drafting of the Irish Free State Constitution', vol. 6, pp. 111 and 112.
18. Dermot Keogh, 'Catholicism and the Formation of the Modern Irish Society', p. 157.
19. Dermot Keogh, 'The Role of the Catholic Church in the Republic of Ireland, 1922–1995', in *Building Trust in Ireland – Studies Commissioned by the Forum for Peace and Reconciliation*, Belfast: The Blackstaff Press, 1996, p. 126.
20. Quoted in Dermot Keogh, 'The Irish Constitutional Revolution: An Analysis of the Making of the Constitution', *The Constitution of Ireland, 1937–1987, Administration*, vol. 35, no. 4, 1987, p. 84.
21. Quoted in ibid., p. 62.
22. Garret FitzGerald, *Seanad Debates*, 9 October 1981, cols. 179–80.
23. Dermot Keogh, 'The Irish Constitutional Revolution', p. 60.
24. See Yvonne Scannell, 'The Constitution and the Role of Women', in Brian Farrell (ed.), *De Valera's Constitution and Ours*, Dublin: Gill & Macmillan, 1988, p. 123.
25. *Dáil Debates*, 4 June 1937, cols. 1884–6.
26. The results of the three polls are quoted respectively from *This Week*, 25 June 1971, p. 15; Market Research Bureau of Ireland, 'Religious Practice and Attitudes towards Divorce and Contraception among Irish Adults', *Social Studies*, June 1974, vol. 3, no. 3, p. 283; *Magill*, December 1977, p. 27.
27. David Fitzpatrick, 'Divorce and Separation in Modern Irish History', p. 174.
28. For a presentation spanning several centuries, see Art Cosgrove (ed.), *Marriage in Ireland*, Dublin: College Press, 1985.
29. For the legal conditions required for denominations other than Catholic, from Presbyterians to Muslims, see Mags O'Brien, 'The Churches – The legal requirements for marriage in Ireland and the differing attitudes of various churches to divorce and re-marriage', in Mags O'Brien (ed.), *Divorce – Facing the issues of Marital Breakdown*, Dublin: Basement Press, 1995, pp. 115–16.
30. Brendan M. Walsh, 'Marriage in Ireland in the XXth Century', in *Marriage in Ireland*, p. 133.

31. David Fitzpatrick, 'Divorce and Separation in Modern Irish History', pp. 195–6.
32. *Seanad Debates*, 22 May 1986, col. 1551.
33. Garret FitzGerald, *All in a Life*, Dublin: Gill & Macmillan, 1991, p. 629.
34. Full statistics on annulments and other forms of separation are compiled in C. Hug, *L'ordre moral en République d'Irlande, 1922–1994*, doctoral thesis, Caen University, 1996, pp. 65, 73, 77.
35. *Seanad Debates*, 22 May 1986, col. 1551.
36. *Seanad Debates*, 23 May 1986, col. 1754–5.
37. *Seanad Debates*, 22 May 1986, col. 1550.
38. Figures quoted by Katherine Bulbulia, *Seanad Debates*, 22 May 1986, cols. 1588–9. See figures quoted by the Minister for Equality and Law Reform during the presentation of the Domestic Violence Bill, 1995. *Dáil Debates*, 4 July 1995, col. 1099.
39. Quoted in *The Irish Times*, 11 August 1995.
40. See Tony Fahey and Maureen Lyons, *Marriage Breakdown and Family Law in Ireland*, Dublin: ESRI Report, October 1995.
41. *The Right to Remarry – A Government Information Paper on the Divorce Referendum*, Dublin: Stationery Office, Pn. 1932, September 1995, p. 8.
42. Alan Shatter, *Family Law in the Republic of Ireland*, Dublin: Wolfhound Press, 1986 (3rd edition), p. 229.
43. Brendan M. Walsh, 'Marriage in Ireland in the XXth Century', p. 146.
44. John O'Connor (ed.), *Social Reform of marriage in Ireland*, Dublin: DAG, 1983, p. 1.
45. *Dáil Debates*, 26 February 1986, col. 450 (for an explanation of the phrase 'an Irish solution to an Irish problem', see Chapter 4). For a history of this legislation, see Peter Ward, *Divorce in Ireland: Who Should Bear the Cost?*, Cork: Cork University Press, 1993, pp. 16–18.
46. William Duncan, 'Desertion and Cruelty in Irish Matrimonial Law', *The Irish Jurist*, 1972, vol. 7, p. 220.
47. *Marital Breakdown – A Review and Proposed Changes*, White Paper, Dublin: Stationery Office, 1992, p. 19.
48. Michael O'Sullivan, *Mary Robinson . . .* , p. 119.
49. *Johnston v. Ireland*, 18/18/86, series A, vol. 112.
50. *Marital Breakdown – A Review and proposed Changes*, p. 68.
51. Michael O'Sullivan, *Mary Robinson . . .* , pp. 170–1.
52. *The Irish Times*, 9 November 1995.
53. *Seanad Debates*, 2 October 1985, col. 276.
54. Jim Walsh, Dept of Geography, St Patrick's College, Maynooth, extract of a paper published in *The Irish Times*, 27 March 1993.
55. Brendan M. Walsh, 'How divorce affects society', *The Irish Times*, 19 June 1986.
56. *Seanad Debates*, 2 October 1985, cols. 286–7.
57. Quoted in Michael O'Sullivan, *Mary Robinson*, p. 92.
58. *Seanad Debates*, 17 October 1980, col. 433.
59. *Dáil Debates*, 29 October 1980, cols. 1086 and 1089.
60. Secretary of State for Justice, Sean Doherty, *Dáil Debates*, 29 October 1980, cols. 1109–10.
61. John H. Whyte, *Church and State*, p. 418.

62. Garret FitzGerald, 'Seeking a national purpose', *Studies*, vol. 53, Winter 1964, pp. 337–51, and *Towards a New Ireland*, London: Knight, 1972.
63. Garret FitzGerald, *Towards a New Ireland*, p. 150.
64. Basil Chubb, *The Politics of the Irish Constitution*, Dublin: Institute of Public Administration, 1991, p. 87.
65. Quoted in *The Irish Times*, 29 September 1981.
66. Quoted in Raymond Smith, *Garret: The Enigma*, Dublin: Aherlow, 1985, p. 24.
67. *Dáil Debates*, 3 June 1980, cols. 1470–4.
68. *Dáil Debates*, 15 February 1983, cols. 201–5, and 15 May 1984, cols. 1009–13. Thanks to Proinsias de Rossa, while leader of Democratic Left and Minister for Social Welfare, for pointing out to us these motions for leave to introduce a Bill.
69. Text of the bill put on the record by Mary Robinson, *Seanad Debates*, 22 May 1986, col. 1543.
70. *Dáil Debates*, 26 February 1986, cols. 456–7.
71. *Dáil Debates*, 26 February 1986, col. 474.
72. Quoted in John Cooney, *The Crozier and the Dáil*, Cork: Mercier Press, 1986, p. 115.
73. Cahal Daly, *New Ireland Forum*, session of 09/02/84, no. 12, Dublin: Stationery Office, 1984, p. 2.
74. Evelyn Mahon, 'Women's Rights and Catholicism in Ireland', *New Left Review*, no. 166, November/December 1987, p. 68.
75. *Seanad Debates*, 24 May 1986.
76. Dr Cassidy, spokesman for the hierarchy, quoted in *The Irish Times*, 25 April 1986.
77. *Marriage, the Family and Divorce: A Statement by Irish Bishops*, Dublin: Veritas Publications, 1986.
78. *The Pope in Ireland: Addresses and Homilies*, Dublin: Veritas Publications, 1979, p. 79.
79. Historian and Senator John A. Murphy, quoted in *The Irish Times*, 10 June 1986.
80. Evelyn Mahon, quoted in *The Irish Times*, 22 November 1995.
81. See, for example, Cahal Daly at the New Ireland Forum, *New Ireland Forum*, p. 3.
82. Quoted in *Magill*, June 1986, p.17.
83. See 'Alibrandi: My Irish battles', an interview with John Cooney, *The Irish Press*, 10–13 October 1994.
84. Michele Dillon, *Debating Divorce – Moral Conflict in Ireland*, Lexington (KY): University Press of Kentucky, 1993, p. 141.
85. Kevin Boyle, 'Can the Republic be Trusted with its Minority?', *The Irish Times*, 24 June 1986.
86. Quoted in *The Irish Times*, 20 May 1986.
87. *Dáil Debates*, 14 May 1986, col. 843.
88. See *Financial Consequences of Marital Breakdown*, Dublin: Combat Poverty Agency, 1990.
89. John Cooney, *The Crozier and the Dáil*, p. 102.
90. *Dáil Debates*, 14 May 1986, cols 823–6.

91. Paddy O'Carroll, 'Sociology and the Politics of Fear – The Divorce Referendum of 1986', *Sociological Association of Ireland Bulletin*, no. 47, October 1986, p. 2. Thanks to P. O'Carroll for giving me a copy of his paper.
92. Brian Girvin, 'The Divorce Referendum in the Republic: June 1986', *Irish Political Studies*, vol. 2, 1987, p.96.
93. Richard Sinnott, Director, Centre for European Economic and Public Affairs, UCD, quoted in *The Irish Times*, 30 November 1994.
94. Quoted and developed in Michele Dillon, *Debating Divorce*, pp. 41–2.
95. See Jack Jones, Director, Market Research Bureau of Ireland (MRBI), in a paper which he very kindly sent us, delivered at an ESOMAR conference in Strasbourg in November 1986, 'The Irish Constitutional Referendum on Divorce – June 1986: The Role and Impact of Opinion Polls'.
96. Michael Gallagher, 'Divorce Poll a Re-run of 1983 Referendum', *The Irish Times*, 3 July 1986.
97. Quoted in *The Irish Times*, 28 June 1986.
98. See Brian Girvin's interpretation, *The Divorce Referendum in the Republic: June 1986*, Irish Political Studies, vol. 2, 1987, p. 98.

2   DIVORCE: ... TO THE RIGHT TO A SECOND CHANCE

1. *Report on Divorce a mensa et thoro and Related Matters*, LRC 8/83, Dublin: Law Reform Commission, 1983, p. 67.
2. The Irish Family League quoted in *The Irish Times*, 24 November 1988.
3. Alan Shatter, 'Ruling Finally Means the End of Century-old Marriage Laws', *The Irish Times*, 15 July 1995.
4. *The Sunday Tribune*, 6 March 1994.
5. Quoted in *The Irish Times*, 21 November 1990.
6. Dermot Keogh, *Twentieth-century Ireland: Nation and State*, Dublin: Gill & Macmillan, 1994, p. 379.
7. Renagh Holohan, 'Divorce in the Dáil', *The Irish Times*, 18 January 1992.
8. *The Sunday Tribune*, 27 September 1992.
9. *The Irish Times*, 5 October 1992.
10. *Report to the Government of the Second Commission on the Status of Women*, PL. 9557, Dublin: Stationery Office, 1993, pp. 39–43.
11. Re Matrimonial Home Bill 1993. See analysis in David Gwynn-Morgan, 'Bill is not part of the divorce agenda and could be dropped', *The Irish Times*, 25 January 1994; in Peter Ward, 'The Supreme Court finds Matrimonial Home Bill 1993 Unconstitutional', *Irish Law Times*, March 1994, pp. 62–4.
12. Unpublished judgment, High Court (*Murphy J*), 28 July 1994. See for an analysis Peter Ward, 'Relief for Thousands of Separated Couples', *The Irish Independent*, 29 July 1994, and 'Constitutional challenge to Judicial Separation Act 1989 rejected', *Irish Law Times*, September 1994, pp. 219–21. Or Alan Shatter, 'Time to Publish Divorce Proposal', *The Irish Times*, 29 July 1994.

13. Peter Ward, 'Relief for Thousands of Separated Couples'.
14. Peter Ward, *Divorce in Ireland*, p. 29.
15. *National Report of Ireland, United Nations Fourth World Conference on Women*, Dublin: Stationery Office, Pn. 2011, October 1994, pp. 2 and 100–1.
16. *A Government of Renewal – A Policy Agreement between Fine Gael, The Labour Party, Democratic Left, The Irish Times*, 15 December 1994.
17. See Chrystel Hug, 'Sans norme ni sanction: l'homosexualité dans un Etat post-moraliste', *Etudes Irlandaises*, Spring 1995, no. XX-1, pp. 205–16.
18. *The Sunday Tribune*, 14 May 1995.
19. *The Irish Times*, 27 May and 2 August 1995. See Jack Jones, 'Lessons of Last Divorce Campaign Should not be Ignored', *The Irish Times*, 2 August 1995.
20. 'Drapier – An Insider's Guide to Politics' [an unnamed TD's column], *The Irish Times*, 23 September 1995.
21. Vincent Browne, 'Coalition is Running a Strong Campaign – to Lose', *The Irish Times*, 20 September 1995.
22. Dr Gerard Casey, of the Christian Solidarity Party, 'Paradox Detected at Heart of the Pro-divorce Argument', *The Irish Times*, 25 September 1995.
23. William Binchy, 'Referendum will Decide Shape of Society for Generations', *The Irish Times*, 23 November 1995.
24. Ibid.
25. *The Irish Times* editorial, 1 September 1995.
26. *McKenna* v. *An Taoiseach and Others*, 1995, unreported. See *The Irish Times*, 18 November 1995.
27. Dr Sheila Greene, 'A Campaign not Fought on Equal Terms', *The Irish Times*, 23 November 1995.
28. *The Irish Times*, 4 October 1995.
29. *The Irish Times*, 5 October and 8 November 1995.
30. Michael Noonan, during the TV programme *Questions and Answers*, 25 September 1995.
31. Editorial 'Divorce and remarriage', *The Irish Times*, 25 September 1995.
32. *The Irish Times*, 17 November 1995.
33. *Statement on the referendum by the Irish Bishops' Conference*, Catholic Press and Information Office, 26 October 1995.
34. *The Irish Times*, 13 November 1995.
35. *The Irish Times*, 5 October 1995.
36. Phrase used by Denis Coghlan, *The Irish Times*, 8 November 1995.
37. *The Irish Times*, 8 November 1995.
38. Mary Robinson, in an interview on NBC Super Channel, quoted in *The Irish Times*, 30 October 1995.
39. Jack Jones, Chairman MRBI Ltd, 'Divorce battle has yet to be won or lost as waverers wait for guidance', *The Irish Times*, 8 November 1995.
40. Jack Jones, 'Young and Rural Voters Show Swing towards a No Vote', *The Irish Times*, 21 November 1995.

41. Joseph O'Malley, 'Narrow Win Exposes Wide, Worrying Gulf', *The Sunday Independent*, 26 November 1995.
42. Divorce became legal in Ireland on 24 February 1997 and up to the end of that year, 356 divorces were granted (out of 1,360 applications), hardly a rush to the divorce courts. See Carol Coulter, 'Money Matters Create Problems *en route* to Harmonious Divorce', *The Irish Times*, 21 February 1998.
43. Phrase used by Fintan O'Toole, 'Two Cheers for the Referendum', *The Irish Times*, 25 November 1995.
44. Joe Joyce, 'Vote Marks Coming of Age for Liberal Agenda', *The Sunday Tribune*, 26 November 1995.

3 CONTRACEPTION: FROM THE PROTECTION OF PUBLIC MORALITY...

1. See Uta Ranke-Heinemann, *Eunuchs for the Kingdom of Heaven – Women, Sexuality and the Catholic Church*, London: Penguin Books, 1991.
2. John T. Noonan, *Contraception – A History of its Treatment by the Catholic Theologians and Canonists*, Cambridge: Harvard University Press, 1986, p. 427.
3. Bryan M. McMahon, 'The Law Relating to Contraception in Ireland', in Desmond Clarke (ed.), *Morality and the Law*, Dublin & Cork: The Mercier Press, 1982, p. 22.
4. Michael Nolan, 'The Influence of Catholic Nationalism on the Legislature of the Irish Free State', *The Irish Jurist*, vol. 10, 1975, p. 131.
5. Margaret O'Callaghan, 'Religion and Identity: The Church and Irish Independence', *The Crane Bag – The Forum Issue*, vol. 7, no. 2, 1983, p. 70.
6. Ibid., p. 70.
7. *Irish Catholic Directory*, 1923, p. 612.
8. Pastoral letter of the Irish bishops quoted in John H. Whyte, *Church & State*, p. 27.
9. Sandra Larmour, *The State and Sexuality, Ireland 1929–1937*, unpublished MA dissertation in Women's Studies, University College, Cark, 1992, p. 4.
10. The Bishop of Ossory to the Minister for Justice in 1929, quoted in Dermot Keogh, *The Vatican, the Bishops and Irish Politics*, p. 161.
11. John H. Whyte, *Church & State*, p. 36.
12. Deputy J.J. Byrne, *Dáil Debates*, 19 October 1928, cols. 686–9.
13. See Jeffrey Weeks, *Sex, Politics and Society: The Regulation of Sexuality since 1800*, 2nd edition, London: Longman, 1989, p. 194.
14. Tony Fahey, 'Catholicism and industrial society in Ireland', in J.H. Goldthorpe and C.T. Whelan (eds), *The Development of Industrial Society in Ireland*, Oxford: Oxford University Press, 1992, p. 253.
15. *The Report of the Committee on Evil Literature*. Dublin: Stationery Office, 1926, pp. 15–16.

16. *Dáil Debates*, 18 October 1928, cols. 607–8.
17. See Dermot Keogh, *The Vatican, the Bishops and Irish Politics*, p. 161.
18. Sandra Larmour, *The State and Sexuality*, pp. 11–12.
19. *The Report on the Criminal Law Amendment Acts (1880–1885) and Juvenile Prostitution* (presided by William Carrigan), August 1931, National Archives, S 5998, p. 8.
20. A point raised by Sandra Larmour in her ongoing doctoral research, UCC.
21. 'Department of Justice Memorandum on Said Report', National Archives, S 5998.
22. *The Report...*, p. 41.
23. 'Department of Justice Memorandum', 10 November 1933, NA, S6489A. See Dermot Keogh, *The Vatican, the Bishops*, p. 206. Again Sandra Larmour's doctoral research might provide some clues.
24. See *Dáil Debates*, 1 August 1934, cols. 2018–19. See also *Seanad Debates*, 6 February 1935, col. 1255.
25. Sandra Larmour, *The State and Sexuality*, p. 16.
26. Quoted in ibid, p. 16.
27. See letters page, *The Irish Times*, 25 June–19 July 1934.
28. *Church of Ireland Gazette*, 7 March 1924.
29. J.H. Whyte, *Church and State*, p. 58.
30. Sandra Larmour, *The State and Sexuality*, p. 20.
31. Ibid., p. 21.
32. Michael Hornsby-Smith, 'Society and Religious Transformation in Ireland: A Case of Secularisation?', in J.H. Goldthorpe and C.T. Whelan (eds), *The Development of Industrial Society in Ireland*, Oxford: Oxford University Press, 1992, p. 275.
33. Bishop of Ferns' letter reproduced in J.H. Whyte, *Church and State*, p. 424–5.
34. Ruth Barrington, *Health, Medicine and Politics in Ireland, 1900–1970*, Dublin: Institute of Public Administration, 1987, p. 149. Such a provision was included in the Health Act 1947, in the sense that the state pledged to take control of the advertisement and sale of toilet preparations. It has not been repealed! But no order was ever made to ban tampons, which was a typical way of pleasing the men of the Church while not risking a public uproar. Thanks to Dr Barrington for helping me clarify the matter.
35. J.H. Whyte, *Church and State*, p. 230.
36. Declaration of the Catholic Truth Society of Ireland, 16 February 1969, reproduced in John Horgan (ed.), *Humanae Vitae and the Bishops*, Shannon: Irish University Press, 1972, p. 154.
37. Collective declaration of the Hierarchy, reproduced in ibid., p. 138.
38. Article quoted by Joseph Dunn, *No Lions in the Hierarchy*, Blackrock: The Columba Press, 1994, p. 140.
39. This and following quotations in Mary Maher, 'A Short History of the Pill in Ireland', *The Irish Times*, 14 March 1968.
40. Michael Solomons, *Pro-life? The Irish Question*, Dublin: Lilliput Press, 1992, p. 27.

41. Robert Rose, *An Outline of Fertility Control, Focusing on the Element of Abortion, in the Republic of Ireland to 1976*, unpublished PhD thesis in Sociology, University of Stockholm, 1976, p. 32.
42. Ailbhe Smyth (ed.), *Irish Women's Studies Reader*, Dublin: Attic Press, 1993, pp. 252–3. About the beginnings of the movement in Ireland, see also June Levine, *Sisters – The Personal Story of an Irish Feminist*, Dublin: Ward River Press, 1982.
43. For more details on this group and its evolution, see Ruth Riddick, *The Right to Choose – Questions of feminist morality*, Dublin: Attic Press, pp. 5–6.
44. *Report to the Minister for Finance of the [first] Commission on the Status of Women*, Prl. 2760, Dublin: Stationery Office, 1972, p. 225.
45. *The Irish Times*, 24 May 1971.
46. Michael Solomons, *Pro-life?*, p. 33.
47. Ibid.
48. Dr David Nowlan, *The Irish Times*, 19 April 1973.
49. Ibid.
50. Michael Solomons, *Pro-life?*, p. 35.
51. Dr. Keith Wilson-Davis, 'The Contraceptive Situation in the Irish Republic', *Journal of Biosocial Science*, vol. 4, no.4, 1974, pp. 487–8.
52. Liam Ryan, 'Church and Politics – The last 25 years', *The Furrow*, vol. 30, no. 1, January 1979, pp. 3–18.
53. Fr Denis O'Callaghan, lecturer in moral theology at St Patrick's College, quoted in *The Irish Times*, 16 March 1971.
54. Declaration to the Society of Catholic Young Men, 30 May 1976.
55. Interview for RTE Television on 30 May 1976.
56. *The Irish Times*, 15 March 1971.
57. Dr David Nowlan, 'Ireland's Year of Change', *People*, vol. 1, no. 3, April 1974, pp. 3–7. See the account of the frame-up hatched by John O'Reilly to have the family planning clinic closed in Emily O'Reilly, *Masterminds of the Right*, Dublin: Attic Press, 1992, pp. 31–3.
58. Polls: 'Contraception: What doctors think', in *Irish Medical Times*, 9 April 1971, p. 1. 'Opinion Poll on Contraception and Divorce', in *This week*, 25 June 1971, pp. 13–15.
59. John Horgan, *Seanad Debates*, 12 May 1971, col. 173.
60. *Seanad Debates*, 7 July 1971, col. 967.
61. *Dáil Debates*, 9 February 1972, col. 1448.
62. Gerard Hogan, 'Law and Religion: Church–State Relations in Ireland from Independence to the Present Day', *American Journal of Comparative Law*, vol. 35, 1987, p. 69.
63. J.H. Whyte, *Church and State*, p. 408.
64. *McGee* v. *Attorney General* (1974) IR, 284.
65. *Griswold* v. *Connecticut* (1965) 381 US 479. *Eisenstadt* v. *Baird* (1972) 405 US 438. See Maurice Dooley, 'Contraception and the Irish Constitution', *Social Studies*, vol. 3, June 1974, no. 3, p. 286.
66. See Mary T.W. Robinson, 'Reform of the Law Relative to Family Planning in Ireland', in *Dublin University Law Journal, 1976–1980*, vol. 1, no. 2, 1976, pp. 12–14.
67. *Seanad Debates*, 20 February 1973, col. 208.

68. Ibid., col. 212.
69. Ibid., col. 205.
70. Quoted in Emily O'Reilly, *Masterminds of the Right*, p. 35.
71. John A. Murphy, 'The Church, Morality and the Law', in Desmond Clarke (ed.), *Morality and the Law*, Cork: The Mercier Press, p. 109.
72. *Seanad Debates*, 27 March 1974, col. 661.
73. *Dáil Debates*, 4 July 1974, cols. 289–90.
74. Keith Wilson-Davis, 'Irish Attitudes to Family Planning', *Social Studies*, June 1974, vol. 3, no. 3, pp. 261–75.
75. Irish Marketing Surveys Ltd/*Hibernia*, 12 April 1974, p. 5.
76. Irish Marketing Surveys Ltd/*Hibernia*, 3 October 1975, p. 4.
77. Market Research Bureau of Ireland, 'Religious Practice and Attitudes towards Divorce and Contraception among Irish Adults', *Social Studies*, June 1974, vol. 3, no. 3, p. 282.
78. Dr Keith Wilson-Davis, 'Some Results of an Irish Family Planning Survey', *Journal of Biosocial Science*, no. 7, 1975, p. 443.
79. Eimer Philbin Bowman, *The Sexual Behaviour and Contraceptive Practice of a Sample of Single Irish Women*, unpublished M.A. in Psychology, Trinity College Dublin, 1976.
80. Ibid., p. 28.
81. *Fortnight*, 4 June 1976, p. 5.
82. *Dáil Debates*, 4, 11, 16 July 1974, for example.
83. *Dáil Debates*, ibid., cols. 1077–8. More interventions are detailed in C. Hug, *L'ordre moral en République d'Irlande*, pp. 268–71.
84. *Seanad Debates*, 16 December 1976, col. 1072.
85. Robert Rose, *An Outline of Fertility Control*, p. 80. Or Mary T.W. Robinson, 'Reform of the Law Relating to Family Planning', p. 13.

4   CONTRACEPTION:... TO A RESPONSIBLE SEXUALITY FOR ALL

1.   See the detailed analysis of the tactics of the militants against contraception in Emily O'Reilly, *Masterminds of the Right*, pp. 39–45.
2.   'The Life and Death of the Contraception Campaign', *The Irish Feminist Review, 1984*, Dublin: Women's Community Press and Individual Writers, 1984, p. 35.
3.   *The Irish Times*, 5 April 1978.
4.   *Dáil Debates*, 28 February 1979, col. 324.
5.   Dáil *Debates*, 28 February 1979, col. 335.
6.   See C. Hug, *L'ordre moral*, pp. 283–94.
7.   *Dáil Debates*, 28 February 1979, col. 373.
8.   *Dáil Debates*, 5 April 1979, cols 1294–5.
9.   *Dáil Debates*, 29 March 1979, col. 805.
10. *Dáil Debates*, 29 March 1979, col. 807.
11. Quoted by Dave Alvey, 'The Irish Family Planning Association on Haughey's 1979 Act', in *Church and State – A Forum of Irish Secularist Opinion*, n. 17, 1985, p. 17.

12. Ibid., p. 18.
13. *The Sunday Tribune*, 29 August 1982.
14. Ursula Barry, 'Movement, Change and Reaction: The Struggle over Reproductive Rights in Ireland', in Ailbhe Smyth (ed.), *The Abortion Papers*, p. 113.
15. *Dáil Debates*, 14 February 1985, col. 2582.
16. *The Irish Times*, 16 April 1984.
17. Presentation of his bill by Barry Desmond, *Dáil Debates*, 14 February 1985, col. 2583.
18. Anecdote related by Michael Solomons, *Pro-Life?*, p. 44.
19. All these figures are quoted by Barry Desmond, *Dáil Debates*, 21 February 1985, col. 503.
20. Results given by Barry Desmond, *Dáil Debates*, 14 February 1985, cols 2590–1.
21. *The Irish Times*, 14 December 1984.
22. *Dáil Debates*, 20 February 1985, cols 269–70.
23. *Dáil Debates*, 19 February 1985, col. 186.
24. Sean Treacy, Labour, 'dissident' on the issue, *Dáil Debates*, 14 February 1985, col. 2700.
25. John Kelly, Fine Gael, *Dáil Debates*, 9 February 1985, col. 161.
26. Quoted in *The Irish Times*, 9 February 1985.
27. J.H. Whyte, 'Recent Developments in Church–State Relations', *Seirbhis Phoibli (Journal of the Department of the Public Services)*, vol. 6, no. 3, Autumn 1985, p. 9.
28. Ibid.
29. *The Irish Times*, 15 February 1985.
30. *Dáil Debates*, 20 February 1985, cols 283–5.
31. *Dáil Debates*, 20 February 1985, col. 275.
32. John H. Whyte, 'Recent Developments in Church–State Relations', p. 4.
33. *The Irish Times*, 28 February 1991.
34. These words, by Oliver Leahy, of Welfare Hygiene Ltd, importers of the Durex brand, with the percentages can be found in 'The Sale of Condoms', *Magill*, November 1988, p. 4.
35. *The Irish Times*, 7 March 1991.
36. Andy Pollack, 'Dr Daly Mobilises Bishops to Stop the Liberal Advance', *The Irish Times*, 16 March 1991.
37. *The Irish Times*, 12 March 1991.
38. *The Irish Times*, 13 March 1991.
39. *The Irish Times*, 12 March 1991.
40. *The Irish Times*, 2 March 1991. See Micheál Mac Gréil, 'Religious practice and attitudes in Ireland. Report of a survey of religious attitudes and practice and related issues in the Republic of Ireland, 1988–89', Maynooth: Survey and Research Unit, Dpt of Social Studies, 1991.
41. *The Irish Times*, 16 December 1996. Weekly mass-going figures dipped even further to 60 per cent in an MRBI/RTE Prime Time survey published in *The Irish Times* on 4 February 1998.
42. Conversations with CH, 2 October 1995 and 13 March 1997.
43. *Dáil Debates*, 9 July 1992, col. 1266.
44. *Seanad Debates*, 15 July 1992, col. 2210.

45. *Dáil Debates*, 8 July 1992, col. 812.
46. *Dáil Debates*, 9 July 1992, col. 1268.
47. *Dáil Debates*, 9 July 1992, cols 1079–80.
48. *Seanad Debates*, 15 July 1992, cols 2225–6.
49. *The Durex Report: Ireland (a summary of research into the usage of condoms & attitudes towards them)*, Dublin: Durex, 1993, pp. 2 and 4.
50. *Dáil Debates*, 3 June 1993, col. 1789.
51. *Dáil Debates*, 3 June 1993, col. 1769.
52. *Dáil Debates*, 3 June 1993, col. 1741.
53. David Nowlan, 'Ireland's Year of Change', in *People*, no. 3, 1974, p. 5.
54. *The Irish Times*, 20 August 1982.
55. 22 February 1940, AAS 32 (1940), p. 73.
56. See W.B. Smith, 'Catholic Hospitals and Sterilisation', *Linacre Quarterly*, vol. 4, May 1977, p. 110. Quoted in Maria O'Sullivan, *Sterilisation: A Feminist Issue in Ireland*, unpublished MA dissertation in Women's Studies, University College Cork, 1993, p. 43.
57. Emily O'Reilly, *Masterminds of the Right*, p. 44.
58. 'Ethical Code for Hospitals', published in Maurice Reidy (ed.), *Ethical Issues in Reproductive Medicine*, Dublin: Gill & Macmillan, 1982, pp. 158–61.
59. Dr Andrew Rynne, quoted in *The Irish Times*, 20 August 1982.
60. *Love is for Life*, Dublin: Veritas Publications, 1985, p. 31.
61. Rev. Kenneth Kearon, Church of Ireland, in Djinn Gallagher, 'Going for the Snip: Vasectomy', *The Tribune Magazine*' (*The Sunday Tribune* supplement), 3 September 1995, p. 9.
62. Michael Solomons, *Pro-Life?* p. 37. See also Katie Donovan, 'Cut and Thrust', *Image* (Irish women's magazine), November 1991, p. 60.
63. Dr John O'Keeffe, 'Vasectomies Performed in Ireland', *Forum* (the journal of the Irish College of General Practitioners), June 1993, pp. 68–70.
64. Djinn Gallagher, 'Going for the Snip', p. 9.
65. ibid., p. 10.
66. Arminta Wallace, 'In Search of Sterilisation', *The Irish Times*, 7 February 1986. There was however a waiting list of two years.
67. Michael Solomons, *Pro-Life?*, p. 39.
68. We thank Dr Gerry Waters for giving us access to his press file relative to the opening of the clinic, as well as to his correspondence with the *Irish Medical Times*. See in particular *Irish Press*, 25 July and 28 September 1984, *Evening Herald*, 29 September 1984, *Sunday World*, 30 September 1984.
69. *Sunday World*, 30 September 1984.
70. *The Irish Independent*, 4 April 1986.
71. Arminta Wallace, 'In Search of Sterilisation'.
72. *The Irish Times*, 19 May 1993.
73. *Report of the Second Commission on the Status of Women*, p. 345.
74. Dr Oliver Lynn, 'Availability of Female Sterilisation in Ireland in the 1990's', in *Newsletter*, of the Irish Association of Family Planning Doctors (IAFPD), May 1993, pp. 2–3.
75. Maria O'Sullivan, *Sterilisation – A Feminist Issue in Ireland*, p. 54.
76. Conversation with CH, 22 September 1995.

77. *Ethical Policy and Traditions of the Coombe Lying-in Hospital, Dublin,* February 1992, pp. 5–6.
78. Maria O'Sullivan, *Sterilisation – A Feminist Issue in Ireland*, p. 25.
79. Arminta Wallace, 'In Search of Sterilisation', The list of hospitals performing tubal ligations was published in Dpt of Health, *Family Planning Policy – Guidelines for Health Boards*, March 1995, pp. 10–11. In March 1997, it was left to the doctors to queer the Department of Health's pitch: the North Western Health Board felt it had to close a vasectomy clinic in Letterkenny, Co. Donegal, after it was picketed by three doctors on pro-life and religious grounds. The Minister for Health described the action as 'a blast from the past' and pledged that a vasectomy service would be available somewhere else in Co. Donegal. The clinic eventually re-opened.
80. Dept of Health, *Family Planning Policy*, p. 14.
81. *The Irish Times*, 24 March 1995.
82. *The Irish Times*, 3 February 1995.
83. Thanks to Dr Gerry Waters for the professional attention he gave to our material and the details he contributed.
84. Having said that, the publication of a report commissioned in 1995 by the Government and carried out by a research team at Trinity College Sociology Department, *Women and Crisis Pregnancy*, showed that immature attitudes and embarrassment still abound when it comes to sexual encounters. Tony O'Brien, chief executive of the IFPA commented that this report, published in March 1998, 'completely debunked' the myth that family planning in Ireland had been 'sorted out' (*The Irish Times*, 13 March 1998).

5   ABORTION: FROM THE RIGHT TO LIFE...

1. See James Gustafson, 'A Protestant Ethical Approach', in John Noonan (ed.), *The Morality of Abortion: Legal and Historical Perspectives*, Cambridge: Harvard University Press, 1970, pp. 116–22.
2. See *Seanad Debates*, 21 February 1974, col. 356.
3. Pauline Jackson, 'Outside the Jurisdiction – Irish Women Seeking Abortion', in Chris Curtin et al. (eds), *Gender in Irish Society*, Galway: Galway University Press, 1987, p. 205.
4. NIALRA, *Abortion in Northern Ireland: The Report of an International Tribunal*, Belfast: NIALRA/Beyond the Pale Publications, 1989, p. 1.
5. In 1992 and 1993, the polls were taken for the Birth Control Trust by Ulster Marketing Services, and the results were published in the *Belfast News Letter*, 25 May 1993. The results of the third poll were also published in *The Irish Times*, in Suzanne Breen, 'Uncertainty of North's Abortion Laws "could violate Human Rights"', 14 November 1994.
6. *Report on the Position of Women in the European Community*, European Parliamentary debate, Luxembourg, June 1981, pp. 267–8.
7. Ailbhe Smyth/Irish Council for Irish Civil Liberties, *Women's Rights in Ireland – A Practical Guide*, Dublin: Ward River Press, 1983, p. 60.

8. Church of England Board for Social Responsibility, *Abortion: An Ethical Discussion*, London: CIO Publishing, 1965, pp. 61–2.
9. *G.* v. *An Bord Uchatala* (113 ILTR 25) and *McGee* v. *AG*, [1974] IR 284.
10. Maurice Dooley, 'Contraception and the Irish Constitution', *Social Studies*, vol. 3, no. 3, June 1974, p. 289.
11. William Binchy, 'Marital Privacy and Family Law: A Reply to Mr O'Reilly', *Studies*, Winter 1977, pp. 330–5.
12. See Emily O'Reilly, *Masterminds of the Right*, who retraces in detail these developments, pp. 53–5.
13. See Ruth Riddick, *The Right to Choose*, op. cit., p. 5.
14. Extract of an article published in *Magill*, July 1982, reproduced in ibid., p. 6.
15. Tom Hesketh, *The Second Partitioning of Ireland? The Abortion Referendum of 1983*, Dublin: Brandsma Books, 1990, provides a very detailed analysis, from the inside as it were and from a researcher's point of view, inclusive of internal divisions, of PLAC, and of the referendum campaign in general.
16. Emily O'Reilly, *Masterminds of the Right*, p. 74.
17. *Kilkenny Standard*, 15 May 1982. The *Workers'Life* magazine in its issue of May 1982 praised Mary Robinson for being 'one of the first and most articulate opponents of the referendum idea.' Quoted in Tom Hesketh, *The Second Partitioning*, p. 130.
18. Dean Griffin, Church of Ireland, *The Cork Examiner*, 13 May 1982. This being said, a number of Protestant men of the Church supported PLAC. See Tom Hesketh, *The Second Partitioning*, p. 79, and *The Irish Times*, 'Protestant Support for Constitutional Amendment', 28 October 1982.
19. Vicky Randall, 'The Politics of Abortion: Ireland in Comparative Perspective', *The Canadian Journal of Irish Studies, Women and Irish Politics*, July 1992, vol.18, no.1, p.126.
20. See Mary Gordon, 'Fighting for Control – The Ongoing Struggle for Reproductive Rights', *The Irish Feminist Review*, Dublin: Women's Community Press, 1984, pp. 13–22, for the genesis and the tactics of the campaign.
21. Irish Marketing Surveys/*The Irish Independent*, 17 September 1982.
22. *Seanad Debates*, 4 May 1983, cols. 565–6.
23. *The Irish Press*, 19 October 1982.
24. Results published in *The Irish Times,* 21 July1977, analysed in William Binchy, 'Marital Privacy and Family Law: A Reply to Mr O'Reilly', p. 333.
25. *The Irish Press*, 4 November 1982.
26. Tom Hesketh, *The Second Partitioning...?*, pp. 163 and 168.
27. Ibid., p. 171.
28. Garret FitzGerald, *All in a Life*, Dublin: Gill & Macmillan, 1991, p. 416.
29. Ibid., p. 417.
30. *The lrish Independent*, 9 November 1982.
31. Garret FitzGerald, *All in a Life*, p. 441.
32. *Seanad Debates*, 4 May 1983, col. 543.
33. Ibid., cols. 544–5.

Notes   259

34. Ibid., col. 560.
35. See Brian Girvin, 'Social Change and Moral Politics: The Irish Consti-
     tutional Referendum 1983', *Political Studies*, vol. 34, 1986, p. 75.
36. Ibid., p. 68.
37. *The Irish Times*, 2 September 1983.
38. St Joseph (Mayfield, Cork) priests' statement published in *The Irish
     Times*, 23 August 1983.
39. Brian Girvin, 'Social Change and Moral Politics', p. 77.
40. Ibid., pp. 76–7.
41. Brendan Walsh, 'The Influence of Turnout on the Results of the
     Referendum to amend the Constitution, to include a Clause on the
     Rights of the Unborn', *The Economic and Social Review*, vol. 15, no. 3,
     April 1984.
42. Declaration of Mary Lucey one year after the adoption of Article 40.3.3.
     Quoted in Ruth Riddick, *The Right to Choose*, p. 7.
43. *A.G. (SPUC (Ireland) Ltd)* v. *Open Door Counselling Ltd* [1988] IR 593.
44. *SPUC (Ireland) Ltd* v. *Grogan & Others* at the High Court and Case 159/
     90 (1991) ECR 4685 (ECJ). One can read William Robinson,
     'European Dimensions of the Abortion Debate', *Abortion, Law and
     Conscience, Doctrine and Life Special*, May–June 1992, vol. 42, no. 5,
     pp. 273–81.
45. For example Anne O'Connor, 'Women in Irish Folklore: The Testimony
     Regarding Illegitimacy, Abortion and Infanticide', in M. MacCurtain
     and M. O'Dowd (eds), *Women in Early Modern Ireland 1500–1800*,
     Edinburgh: Edinburgh University Press, 1991, pp. 304–14.
46. Pauline Jackson, 'Outside the Jurisdiction…', p. 212.
47. Robert Rose, *An Outline of the Fertility Control*, p. 104.
48. Pauline Jackson, 'The Deadly Solution to an Irish Problem: Backstreet
     Abortion', Dublin: the Women's Right to Choose Campaign, 20 July
     1983, p. 2.
49. P. Jackson refers to a last investigation in 1968, which did not go to court.
     Ibid., p. 6.
50. A comparative analysis of results can be found in Pauline Jackson, 'Out-
     side the Jurisdiction', pp. 214–15. See also the government commis-
     sioned report, *Women and Crisis Pregnancy*, Trinity College Dublin, 1988.
51. D. Walsh, 'Medical and Social Characteristics of Irish Residents whose
     Pregnancies were terminated under the 1967 Abortion Act in 1971/72',
     Journal of the Irish Medical Association, vol.68, no.6, pp. 143–9.
52. Seán Mac Réamoinn, 'Laylines', *Abortion, Law and Conscience, Doctrine
     and Life Special*, vol. 42, May–June 1992, no. 5, p. 319.
53. *The Irish Times*, 28 February 1997.
54. Robert Rose, *An Outline of Fertility Control*, pp. 178–83.
55. Paddy Leahy, 'Abortion: The Plain Truth', *Hot Press*, vol. 16, no. 17, 7
     October 1992, pp. 6–7.
56. Apart from the Ann Lovett case, and that of the 'Kerry babies', men-
     tioned earlier, see 'Foetus discovered in Cork', *The Irish Times*, 22 June
     1993; *The Irish Times*, 6 December 1993, 3 December 1994, 10 February
     1994 These last three babies particularly troubled the authorities. It is
     difficult to make sense of such incidences at a time when 20 per cent of

all births are outside of marriage, a phenomenon that does not carry the same stigma as it used to. One can also read *The Irish Times*, 11 November 1994 and 10 March 1995 for another two discovered dead bodies, and 14 June 1995 about a newborn buried a live but discovered in time and saved.

57. Cork Abortion Information Campaign, *Censored: Ireland's abortion reality (including a guide to abortion services for Irish women)*, Cork: CAIC, 1992, p. 15.

58. *The Sunday Tribune*, 1 March 1992.

59. 'The Silent Export', produced by Leanne Pooley, Mosaic Pictures/ BBC, broadcast on 24 April 1994 on BBC 1, widely watched in Ireland. '50,000 Secret Journeys', a documentary produced by Picture House Co. for RTE, the Irish broadcasting company, shown on 20 October 1994.

60. Dr Paddy Leahy, 'Abortion: The Plain Truth', p. 6.

61. Testimony presented to NIALRA, *Abortion in Northern Ireland: The Report of an International Tribunal*, pp. 36–7. See also the television documentary, 'The Silent Export', in which the testimony of the four women confirms this is the usual scenario.

62. See IWASG, 'Across the Water' in Ailbhe (ed.), *The Abortion Papers, Ireland*, Dublin: Attic Press, 1992, pp. 47–56.

6   ABORTION: ... TO THE RIGHT TO LIVE

1. William Binchy, 'Ethical Issues in Reproductive Medicine – A Legal Perspective', in Maurice Reidy (ed.), *Ethical Issues in Reproductive Medicine*, Dublin: Gill & Macmillan, 1982, p. 105.

2. Integral text of the X judgments in Sunniva McDonagh (ed.), *The Attorney-General versus X and others: Judgments of the High Court and Supreme Court, with submissions made by Counsel to Supreme Court*, Dublin: Incorporated Council of Law Reporting in Ireland, May 1992.

3. Cartoon by Martyn Turner, *The Irish Times*, 19 February 1992. It would be reproduced in numerous newspapers the world over.

4. Speech of Mary Robinson given to Waterford women's groups, quoted in *The Irish Times*, 20 February 1992.

5. IMS/*The Sunday Independent*, 23 February 1992.

6. Christopher T. Whelan and Tony Fahey, 'Marriage and the Family', in C. T. Whelan (ed.), *Values and Social Change in Ireland*, pp. 70–3.

7. Nuala O'Faolain, 'Why Did it Take so Long for the Perception of Women to Change?', *The Irish Times*, 3 August 1992.

8. See, for example, Mary Holland, 'Bewilderment over Society's Failure to Provide Protection', *The Irish Times*, 11 March 1993. Also Madeleine Leonard, 'Rape: Myths and Reality', in Ailbhe Smyth (ed.), *Irish Women's Studies Reader*, Dublin: Attic Press, 1993, pp. 107–21.

9. MRBI/*The Irish Times*, 2 March 1992.

10. This dimension of the abortion debate is developed in C. Hug, *L'ordre moral en République d'Irlande*, Chapter III.

11. Dermot Keogh, 'The Coalition of Conspiracy and Reaction', *The Cork Examiner*, 18 June 1992.
12. *The Sunday Tribune*, 'Abortion: a state of total chassis', 19 April 1992. Paraphrasing a famous line in Sean O'Casey's *Juno and the Peacock*.
13. MRBI/*The Irish Times*, 11 May 1992.
14. MRBI/*The Irish Times*, 11 June 1992.
15. Denis Coghlan, *The Irish Times*, 15 August 1992.
16. *The Irish Times*, 7 September 1992.
17. *The Irish Times*, 9 October 1992.
18. *The Sunday Independent*, 11 October 1992.
19. Dick Walsh, *The Irish Times*, 10 October 1992.
20. *The Irish Times*, 22 October 1992.
21. Brian Lenihan, *Dáil Debates*, 21 October 1992, col. 208.
22. See Adrian Hardiman, 'The Lesson of 1983: Constitutional Words are no Mere Gesture', *The Irish Times*, 24 October 1992.
23. Editorial, *The Irish Times*, 30 October 1992.
24. Jack Jones, 'Referendum Issues Confuse Voters', *The Irish Times*, 13 November 1992.
25. Labour is the party that presented and supported Mary Robinson during the presidential election of November 1990 (with the Workers' Party).
26. All these results in *Irish Political Studies*, no. 8, 1993, pp. 183–5.
27. Richard Sinnott and Brendan J. Whelan, 'Neither the Conservatives nor the Liberals can Claim victory', *The Irish Times*, 7 December 1992.
28. Richard Sinnott, Brendan M. Walsh and Brendan J. Whelan, 'Conservatives, Liberals and Pragmatists: Disaggregating the Results of the Irish Abortion Referendums of 1992', *The Economic and Social Review*, vol. 26, no. 2, January 1995, p.212.
29. Ibid., p.209.
30. Quoted in *The Cork Examiner*, 7 October 1993.
31. MRBI/*The Irish Times*, 8 October 1993.
32. *The Cork Examiner*, 25 June 1993.
33. See John Garry, 'The Demise of the Fianna Fáil/Labour "Partnership" Government and the Rise of the "Rainbow" Coalition', *Irish Political Studies*, vol.10, 1995, pp. 192–9.
34. *The Irish Times*, 1 March 1995.
35. *Dáil Debates*, 2 March 1995, col.27.
36. *The Irish Times*, 4 March 1995.
37. *Dáil Debates*, 8 March 1995, cols. 741–2.
38. *Dáil Debates*, 8 March 1995, col. 486.
39. Dick Walsh, 'Deep in the Moral Maze, Someone is Digging', *The Irish Times*, 11 March 1995.
40. Denis Coghlan, 'Supreme Court Closes a Door into the Past', *The Irish Times*, 13 May 1995.
41. Re The Regulation of Information (Services outside the State for Termination of Pregnancies) Bill, 1995.
42. Quoted in *The Irish Times*, 13 May 1995.
43. Drapier, 'Terminating the Abortion Issue', *The Irish Times*, 20 May 1995. See Irish College of General Practitioners, *Training Programme and*

Information for General Practitioners, in Response to the Termination of Pregnancy Information Act, 1995, Dublin: ICGP, 1995.

44. Louis McRedmond, 'Vatican II Perspectives', *Abortion, Law and Conscience, Doctrine and Life Special*, vol.42, no. 5, May–June 1992, p. 301.
45. Seán MacRéamoinn, 'Laylines', in ibid., p. 324.
46. A re-run of the X case occurred in November 1997 when a 13-year-old girl from the travelling community became pregnant after an alleged rape. Taken into care by the Eastern Health Board, her interests were defended in the District Court (under the Child Care Act 1991) and then in the High Court, where both Judges allowed the state agency to take her to England to terminate a pregnancy that was making her suicidal. Such a procedure was, in the circumstances, seen as 'medical treatment', and was paid for by the Board. This judgment was within the parameters of the X case but is itself extraordinary in light of the fact that the state was involved in such a direct way in the welfare of the girl. However, one can only dread the day another such case blows up in our faces which is not as hard, in the sense the girl won't be as suicidal, or won't have been raped enough, or won't be young enough. Worryingly, Judge Geoghegan interpreted the 13th amendment to mean it 'does not now confer a right to an abortion outside of Ireland. It merely prevents injunctions against travelling for that purpose.' Judge-made law, court case after court case, interpretation after interpretation, can get messy. In this instance the Supreme Court was not called upon to offer its views on these conflicting rights. An MRBI/*The Irish Times* poll, published on 11 December 1997, found that 62 per cent of those questioned thought the High Court Judge had taken the right decision, 77 per cent believed abortion should be permitted in Ireland in certain circumstances, and 55 per cent that the medical profession should provide abortion facilities. These results are difficult to read since, after all this, only 23 per cent believed that the Oireachtas should legislate in line with the X and C judgments, whereas 49 per cent believed it should legislate for abortion only if the bill had been approved first in a national referendum (the device used for the Divorce Act). This was indeed the approach the government now favoured, but such a bill was still well down the road. But at least there would be no going back on the X case judgment.

7 HOMOSEXUALITY: FROM A CRIME AGAINST NATURE...

1. See Fintan O'Toole, 'A Morality Debate Going Nowhere', article reproduced in *Black Hole, Green Card – The disappearance of Ireland*, Dublin: New Island Books, 1994, pp. 145–9.
2. Jeffrey Weeks, *Sex, Politics and Society*, p. 98.
3. Ibid., p. 102.
4. See P. Charleton, *Offences against the Person*, Dublin: The Round Hall Press, 1992, p. 298.
5. F.B. Smith, 'Labouchère's Amendment to the Criminal Law Amendment Bill', *Historical Studies*, vol. 17, no. 67, 1976, pp. 165–75.

6. Roy Walmsley and Karen White, *Sexual Offences, Consent and Sentencing*, Home Office Research Study no. 54, London: HMSO, 1979.
7. Sacred Congregation for the Doctrine of the Faith, 'Declaration on Certain Questions Concerning Sexual Ethics', *The Furrow*, February 1976, p. 119.
8. 'On the pastoral care of homosexual persons', Congregation for the Doctrine of the Faith, Vatican Polyglot Press, 1986, no.3, para. 2.
9. Congregation for the Doctrine of the Faith, 'Observations regarding Legislative proposals Concerned with Discrimination towards homosexual Persons', in *Origins*, vol. 22, no.10, 6 August 1992, pp. 174 ff.
10. Ibid.
11. Claudia Roth (rapporteur), *Report of the Committee on Civil Liberties and Internal Affairs on equal rights for homosexuals and lesbians in the EC*, European Parliament, Session Documents, A3–0028/94, 26 January 1994.
12. Ibid., p. 5.
13. *Garda Commissioner's Evidence to the Carrigan Committee*, National Archives, H247/41A, pp. 8–9.
14. Figures provided in appendix by the Irish government to the European Court of Justice, in *Norris Case*, Cour/Misc (88) 100.
15. David Norris, 'Homosexual law reform in Ireland: A progress report', *Dublin University Law Journal*, 1976–80, vol.1, no.2, p. 27.
16. More figures are given in Chrystel Hug, *L'ordre moral en République d'Irlande*, pp. 579–81.
17. Kieran Rose traces the history of the Irish gay movement and places it in its national and international context: *Diverse Communities – The Evolution of Lesbian and Gay Politics in Ireland*, Cork: Cork University Press (Undercurrents), 1994.
18. Quoted in *The Irish Times*, 3 June 1978. At that time, homosexuality was also illegal in Northern Ireland.
19. The text of the Sexual Offences Bill, 1975 is in David Norris, 'Homosexual law reform in Ireland: A progress report', pp. 34–6.
20. *Seanad Debates*, 10 April 1975, cols 240–3.
21. David Norris to CH, 15 March 1994.
22. Ibid.
23. See Mary Robinson in Norris Case, Cour/Misc (88) 100, p. 16.
24. David Norris, *Seanad Debates*, 29 June 1993, p. 276.

8   HOMOSEXUALITY:...TO A RIGHT TO (HOMO)SEXUAL PRIVACY

1. *Norris v. Attorney-General* [1984] IR 36.
2. Ibid., pp.46–7.
3. Dublin Lesbian and Gay Collective, *Out for Ourselves*, Dublin: DLGC, pp.192–3.
4. Michael Farrell, 'A Catholic Court for a Catholic People', *The Sunday Tribune*, 1 May 1983.

264   *The Politics of Sexual Morality in Ireland*

5. David Norris to CH, 15 March 1994.
6. Ibid.
7. Law Reform Commission, *A Law Reform Commission Report on Child Sexual Abuse*, LRC 32–1990, pp.45–9.
8. Kieran Rose, *Diverse Communities*, p. 41.
9. Ibid., p. 22.
10. William O'Connor, 'Prelude to a vision – the impact of Aids on the political legitimacy and political mobilization of gay men in Ireland', in O'Carroll Ide and Collins Eoin (eds), *Lesbian and Gay Visions of Ireland*, London: Cassell, 1995, pp.187–8.
11. Kieran Rose, *Diverse Communities*, p. 30.
12. Ibid., p. 30.
13. Katherine Bulbulia, *Seanad Debates*, 30 November 1988, cols 996–7.
14. *The Irish Times*, 16 November 1989.
15. *Dáil Debates*, 12 December 1990, cols. 70 and 72.
16. *Hot Press*, vol.14, no. 20, 4 October 1990, p. 17.
17. David Norris to CH, 15 March 1994.
18. *The Irish Times*, 16 May 1992.
19. See *Seanad Debates*, 21 May 1992, cols. 1364; 22 May 1992, cols. 1588–9; 8 October 1992, cols. 12–13; 21 October 1992, col. 324.
20. Chris Robson, 'Anatomy of a Campaign', in Ide O'Carroll and Eoin Collins (eds), *Lesbian and Gay Visions of Ireland*, p. 54.
21. Ibid., p. 54.
22. Máire Geoghegan-Quinn, *Dáil Debates*, 23 June 1993, col. 2044.
23. Chris Robson, 'Anatomy of a Campaign', p. 56.
24. Phil Moore to CH, 22 March 1994.
25. My thanks to David Norris for giving me access to this letter.
26. *The Irish Times*, 23 June 1993.
27. According to the results of the Battelle Human Affairs Research Centre, Seattle.
28. *Dáil Debates*, 23 June 1993, col. 1972.
29. *Seanad Debates*, 29 June 1993, cols. 270–84.
30. In Victoria Freedman, *The Cities of David – The Life of David Norris*, Dublin: Basement Press, 1995, p. 177.
31. Chris Robson, 'Anatomy of a campaign', p. 58.
32. Micheal Mac Gréil, *Prejudice and Tolerance in Ireland – Based on a Survey of Intergroup Attitudes of Dublin Adults and Other Sources*, Dublin: College of Industrial Relations, 1977, pp. 414–15.
33. *The Irish Times*, 5 May 1993.
34. David Norris to CH, 15 March 1994.
35. *The Irish Times*, 21 June 1993.
36. *Seanad Debates*, 12 December 1990, cols. 77–8.
37. Andrew Greely analyses some results of this European Values Systems Survey, 1990 in 'Are the Irish really losing the faith?', *Doctrine and Life*, March 1994, pp. 132–42. See also Conor Ward and Andrew Greely, 'Development and tolerance: The Case of Ireland', *Eire-Ireland*, vol. 25, no.4, Winter 1990, pp. 7–17.
38. Andrew Greely, 'Are the Irish really losing the faith?', p. 141. And Conor Ward to CH, 27 May 1994.

39. Thanks to Tony Fahey of the Economic and Social Research Institute for the complete ISSP figures and for discussing them with us.
40. Kieran Rose, *Diverse Communities*, p. 33.
41. Thanks to IMPACT, the public sector union, for letting us have access to this circular, 'Civil Policy on AIDS'.
42. Kieran Rose, *Diverse Communities*, p. 25.
43. ibid., p. 51.
44. Ger Philpot, *Deep End*, Dublin: Poolbeg Press, 1995, p. 229.
45. GLEN/Nexus Research Co-operative, Dublin: Combat Poverty Agency, 1995.
46. *The Cork Examiner*, 23 February 1994.
47. Donna McAnellan to CH, 30 March 1994.
48. Quoted in *Norris Case*, Cour/Misc (88) 100, p. 7.
49. Kieran Rose, *Diverse Communities*, p. 18.
50. David Norris to CH, 15 March 1994. Later called The Equal Status Bill.
51. Ger Moane, 'Living Visions', in *Lesbian and Gay Visions of Ireland*, pp. 92–3.
52. 'New Law to Protect Gays', *Gay Community News* (Ireland's Lesbian and Gay newspaper), August 1995.

CONCLUSION

1. Gilles Lipovetsky, *Le crépuscule du devoir*, p. 176.
2. Mary Robinson's address at the Patrick McGill Summer School, quoted in *The Irish Times*, 26 August 1985.

Bibliography

PRIMARY SOURCES

Extensive use of parliamentary debates: *Dáil Debates* and *Seanad Debates* (see notes in text)

Bunreacht na hEireann, Constitution of Ireland, Dublin: Government Publications Office, 1937.

Census 1986. Summary Population Report, Dublin: Stationery Office, 1987.

Census 1991. Summary Population Report, Dublin: Stationery Office, 1993.

Constitution of the Free State of Ireland, Dublin: Government Publications Office, 1922.

Developing a Policy for Women's Health – A Discussion Document, Pn. 1701, Dublin: Stationery Office, June 1995.

Family Planning Policy – Guidelines for Health Boards, document from the Dpt of Health for the regional Health Boards, March 1995.

First Progress Report of the Monitoring Committee on the Implementation of the Recommendations of the Second Commission on the Status of Women, Pn.0798, Dublin: Stationery Office, May 1994.

International Conference on Population and Development 1994 (Cairo), National Report on Population: Ireland, ICPD.dh4 (unpublished)

Law Reform Commission Report on Divorce a mensa et thoro and related Matters, 8/83, Dublin: LRC, 1983.

Law Reform Commission Report on Nullity, 9/84, Dublin: LRC, 1984.

Law Reform Commission Report on child sexual abuse (sections 4.24–4.32 on homosexuality), Dublin: LRC, 1990.

Marital Breakdown – A Review and Proposed Changes, White Paper of the Government, PL. 9104, Dublin: Stationery Office, 1992.

National Archives, Dublin, *Dpt of the Taoiseach* S 3301, S 4127, S 9005. Jus 95/7.

New Ireland Forum, public session 9/2/84, no. 12, Dublin: Stationery Office, 1984.

Report of the Committee on Evil Literature, Dublin: Stationery Office, 1926.

Report of the Committee on the Criminal Law Amendment Acts (1880–1885) and Juvenile Prostitution (1931) S 5998, *Department of the Taoiseach, National Archives*, Dublin.

Report of the Joint Committee on Standing Orders (private business) on the Position of Saorstat Eireann of Bills relating to Matrimonial Matters, 11 July 1924, S 4127, *Department of the Taoiseach, National Archives*, Dublin.

Report of the All-party Committee on the Constitution, Dublin: Stationery Office, Pr. 9817, 1967.

Report to the Minister for Finance of the Commission on the Status of Women, Prl.2760, Dublin: Stationery Office, December 1972.

Report to the Government of the Second Commission on the Status of Women, Pl.9557, Dublin: Stationery Office, January 1993.

Report of the Joint Committee on Marital Breakdown, Pl.3074, Dublin: Stationery Office, 1985.

Report of the Committee on Civil Liberties and internal Affairs on equal rights for homosexuals and lesbians in the EC, European Parliament, session documents, A3–0028/94, 26 January 1994.

The Right to Remarry – A Government Information Paper on the Divorce Referendum, Pn.1932, Dublin: Stationery Office, September 1995.

United Nations Fourth World Conference on Women – National Report of Ireland, Pn.2011, Dublin: Stationery Office, October 1994.

SECONDARY SOURCES

Adams, Michael, *Censorship: The Irish Experience*, University of Alabama Press, 1968.

Administration, special issue: *The Constitution of Ireland, 1937–1987*, vol. 35, no. 4, 1987.

Akenson, D.H. and Fallin, J.F., 'The Irish Civil War and the Drafting of the Free State Constitution', *Eire/Ireland*, vol. 5 (nos 1, 2 & 4), Spring, Summer & Winter 1970, pp. 10–26, 42–93, 28–70.

Ardagh, John, *Ireland and the Irish*, Harmondsworth: Hamish Hamilton/Penguin, 1994.

Barrington, Ruth, *Health, Medicine and Politics in Ireland, 1900–1970*, Dublin: Institute of Public Administration, 1987.

Barry, Ursula, 'Movement, Change and Reaction – The Struggle over Reproductive Rights in Ireland', pp. 107–18, in Smyth, Ailbhe (ed.), *The Abortion Papers*, Dublin: Attic Press, 1992,

Beale, Jenny, *Women in Ireland: Voices of Change*, Dublin: Gill & Macmillan, 1986.

Binchy, William, 'Pluralism, Liberty and the Right to Life', pp. 132–48, in Whelan, Anthony (ed.), *Law and Liberty in Ireland*, Dublin: Oak Tree Press/Trinity College Dublin Law School, 1993.

Blanshard, Paul, *The Irish and Catholic Power (an American Interpretation)*, London: Derek Verschoyle Ltd, 1954.

Brennan, Paul, 'Enjeux sociaux et relations Eglise–Etat en Irlande', *Cahiers du Centre d'Etudes Irlandaises*, no. 11, Rennes: Presses Universitaires de Rennes II, 1987, pp. 113–21.

Browne, Noël, *Against the Tide*, Dublin: Gill and Macmillan, 1986.

Chubb, Basil, *The Politics of the Irish Constitution*, Dublin: Institute of Public Administration, 1991.

Clancy, Patrick et al. (eds), *Ireland: A Sociological Profile*, Dublin: Institute of Public Administration, 1986.

Clarke Desmond (ed.), *Morality and the Law*, Cork: The Mercier Press, 1982.

Clarke Desmond, *Church and State*, Cork: Cork University Press, 1984.

Clifford, Angela, *The Catholic Church and Abortion*, Belfast: Athol Books, 1987.

Clifford, Angela, *The Constitutional History of Eire*, Belfast: Athol Books, 1987.

Coleman, D.A., 'The Demographic Transition in Ireland in International Context', pp. 53–77, in Goldthorpe J.H. and Whelan, C.T. (eds), *The Devel-*

opment of Industrial Society in Ireland, Oxford: Oxford University Press, 1992.

Cooney, John, *The Crozier and the Dáil*, Cork: Mercier, 1986.

Cosgrove, Art (ed.), *Marriage in Ireland*, Dublin: College Press, 1985.

Dillon, Michele, *Debating Divorce: Moral Conflict in Ireland*, Lexington, KY: The University Press of Kentucky, 1993.

Dooley, Dolores, 'Expanding an Island Ethic', pp. 47–65, in Lee, Joseph (ed.), *Ireland: towards a sense of place*, Cork: Cork University Press, 1985.

Dooley, Maurice, 'Contraception and the Irish Constitution', *Social Studies*, vol. 3, no. 3, June 1974, pp. 286–315.

Dublin Lesbian and Gay Men's Collectives, *Out for Ourselves: The Lives of Irish Lesbians and Gay Men*, Dublin: DLGMC, 1986.

Duncan, William, *The Case for Divorce in the Irish Republic*, Dublin: Irish Council for Civil Liberties (ICCL), 1982.

Duncan, William, 'Abortion, Divorce and the Debate about Liberty', pp. 120–31, in Whelan, Anthony (ed.), *Law and Liberty in Ireland*, Dublin: Oak Tree Press/Trinity College Dublin Law School, 1993.

Fahey, Tony, 'Catholicism and Industrial Society in Ireland', pp. 241–263, in Goldthorpe, J.H. and Whelan, C.T. (eds), *The Development of Industrial Society in Ireland*, Oxford: Oxford University Press, 1992.

Farrell, Brian, 'The Drafting of the Irish Free State Constitution', *The Irish Jurist*, vol. 5, 1970 (I: pp. 115–31, II: 343–56) and vol. 6, 1971 (III: pp. 111–35, IV: 345–58).

Farrell, Brian (ed.), *De Valera's Constitution and Ours*, Dublin: Gill & Macmillan, 1988.

Finlay, Fergus, *Mary Robinson: A President with a Purpose*, Dublin: O'Brien Press, 1990.

Finlay, Peter, 'Divorce in the Irish Free State', *Studies*, September 1924, pp. 353–62.

FitzGerald, Garret, 'Seeking a National Purpose', *Studies*, vol. 53, Winter 1964, pp. 337–51.

FitzGerald, Garret, *All in a Life*, Dublin: Gill & Macmillan, 1991.

FitzGerald, Garret, *Towards a New Ireland*, London: Knight, 1972.

Fitzpatrick, David, 'Divorce and Separation in Modern Irish History', *Past & Present*, no. 114, February 1987, pp. 173–96.

Flannery, Austin (ed.), *Abortion and Law*, Doctrine and Life Special, 1983.

Fletcher, Ruth, 'Silences – Irish Women and Abortion', *Feminist Review* (no. 50: *The Irish Issue: The British Question*), London: Routledge, 1995, pp. 44–66.

Fogarty, M., Ryan, L. and Lee, J., *Irish Values and Attitudes: The Irish Report of the European Value System Study*, Dublin: 1984.

Francome, Colin, *If You ever go across the Sea to England*, Middlesex Polytechnic: Health Research Centre, 1991.

Freedman, Victoria, *The Cities of David – The Life of David Norris*, Dublin: Basement Press, 1995, p.177.

Fulton, John, *The Tragedy of Belief: Division, Politics and Religion in Ireland*, Oxford: Oxford University Press, 1991.

Garvin, Tom, 'The Politics of Denial and of Cultural Defence: The Referenda of 1983 and 1986 in Context', *The Irish Review*, Cork: Cork University Press, no. 3, 1988, pp. 1–7.

Garvin, Tom, 'Democracy in Ireland: Collective Somnambulance and Public Policy', *Administration*, 1991, vol.39, no. 1, pp. 42–54.

Gearty, Conor, 'Constitutional Law – Homosexuals and the Criminal Law – The Right to Privacy', *Dublin University Law Journal*, vol.5, 1983, pp. 264–73.

Genovesi, Vincent, *In Pursuit of Love: Catholic Morality and Human Sexuality*, Dublin: Gill & Macmillan, 1987.

Girvin, Brian, 'Social Change and Moral Politics: The Irish Constitutional Referendum 1983', *Political Studies*, vol. 34, 1986, pp. 61–81.

Girvin, Brian, 'The Divorce Referendum in the Republic: June 1986', *Irish Political Studies*, no. 2, 1987, pp. 93–8.

Girvin, Brian, 'Social Change and Political Culture in the Republic of Ireland', *Parliamentary Affairs*, OUP, July 1993, vol. 46, no. 3, pp. 380–98.

Girvin, Brian, 'The Referendums on Abortion 1992', *Irish Political Studies*, no. 8, 1993, pp. 118–24.

Girvin, Brian, 'Moral Politics and the Irish Abortion Referendums, 1992', *Parliamentary Affairs*, OUP, April 1994, vol.47, no. 2, pp. 203–21.

Girvin, Brian, 'Church, State and the Irish Constitution: The Secularisation of Irish Politics?', *Parliamentary Affairs*, OUP, October 1996, vol.49, no. 4, pp. 599–615.

Gordon, Mary, 'Fighting for Control – The Ongoing Struggle for Reproductive Rights', *The Irish Feminist Review*, Dublin: Women's Community Press, 1984, pp. 9–27.

Greely, Andrew, 'Are the Irish really Losing the Faith?', *Doctrine and Life*, vol. 44, no. 3, March 1994, pp. 132–42.

Hamilton, Mark, *The Case against Divorce*, Dublin: Lir Press, 1994.

Hannon, Patrick, *Church, State, Morality and Law*, Dublin: Gill & Macmillan, 1992.

Hannon, Patrick, 'Church–State Relations: Post-1992', *The Furrow*, November 1993, pp. 587–95.

Hesketh, Tom and O'Leary, Cornelius, 'The Irish Abortion and Divorce Referendum Campaigns', *Irish Political Studies*, vol. 3, 1988, pp. 43–62.

Hesketh, Tom, *The Second Partitioning of Ireland? The Abortion Referendum of 1983*, Dublin: Brandsma Books, 1990.

Hogan, Gerard, 'Law and Religion: Church–State Relations in Ireland from Independence to the Present Day', *American Journal of Comparative Law*, vol. 35, 1987, pp. 47–96.

Hogan, Gerard, 'Law, Liberty and the Abortion Controversy', pp. 113–19, in Whelan, Anthony (ed.), *Law and Liberty in Ireland*, Dublin: Oak Tree Press/ in association with Trinity College Dublin Law School, 1993.

Horgan, Goretti, *Why Irish Women must have the Right to Choose*, Dublin: Bookmarks Ireland, 1990.

Horgan, John, *Humanae Vitae and the Bishops,* Shannon: Irish University Press, 1972.

Horgan, John, *Mary Robinson – An Independent Voice*, Dublin: The O'Brien Press, 1997.

Hornsby-Smith, Michael, 'Social and Religious Transformation in Ireland: A Case of Secularisation?', pp. 265–90, in Goldthorpe, J.H. and Whelan, C.T. (eds), *The Development of Industrial Society in Ireland*, Oxford: Oxford University Press, 1992.

Hussey, Gemma, *At the Cutting Edge – Cabinet Diaries 1982–87*, Dublin: Gill & Macmillan, 1990.

Hussey, Gemma, *Ireland Today: Anatomy of a Changing State*, Dublin: Townhouse-Viking, 1993.

Inglis, Tom, *Moral Monopoly: The Catholic Church in Modern Irish Society*, Dublin: Gill & Macmillan, 1987.

Irish Council for Civil Liberties, *Equality Now for Lesbians and Gay Men*, Dublin: ICLL, 1990.

Jackson, Pauline, 'The Deadly Solution to an Irish Problem – Backstreet Abortion', Dublin: the Women's Right to Choose Campaign, 20 July 1983.

Jackson, Pauline, 'Women's Movement and Abortion: the Criminalization of Irish Women', pp. 48–63, in Dahlerup, Drude (ed.), *The New Women's Movement: Feminism and Political Power in Europe and the USA*, London: Sage, 1986.

Jackson, Pauline, 'Outside the Jurisdiction – Irishwomen seeking Abortion', pp. 203–23, in Curtin, Chris et al. (eds), *Gender in Irish Society*, Galway: Galway University Press, 1987.

Jackson, Pauline, 'Abortion Trials and Tribulations', *The Canadian Journal of Irish Studies*, vol. 18, no. 1, University of Saskatchewan, July 1992, pp. 112–20.

Kennelly, Brendan and Ward Eilis, 'The Abortion Referendums', pp. 115–34, in Gallagher, Michael and Laver, Michael (eds), *How Ireland voted, 1992*, Limerick & Dublin: PSAI/Folens, 1993.

Kenny, Mary, *Goodbye to Catholic Ireland*, London: Sinclair-Stevenson, 1997.

Keogh, Dermot, *The Vatican, the Bishops and Irish Politics, 1919–1939*, Cambridge: Cambridge University Press, 1986.

Keogh, Dermot, 'The Irish Constitutional Revolution: An Analysis of the Making of the Constitution', *The Constitution of Ireland, 1937–1987*, *Administration*, vol. 35, no. 4, 1987.

Keogh, Dermot, 'Catholicism and the Formation of the Modern Irish Society', pp. 152–77, in The Princess Grace Irish Library (Monaco), *Irishness in a Changing Society*, Totowa, NJ: Barnes & Noble Books, 1989.

Keogh, Dermot, 'The Coalition of Conspiracy and Reaction', *The Cork Examiner*, 18 June 1992.

Keogh, Dermot, *Twentieth Century Ireland: Nation and State*, Dublin: Gill & Macmillan, 1994.

Keogh, Dermot, *Ireland and the Vatican: The Politics and Diplomacy of Church–State Relations, 1922–1960*, Cork: Cork University Press, 1995.

Keogh, Dermot, 'The Role of the Catholic Church in the Republic of Ireland, 1922–1995', in *Building Trust in Ireland – Studies commissioned by the Forum for Peace and Reconciliation*, Belfast: The Blackstaff Press, 1996, pp. 85–213.

Kingston, James and Whelan, Anthony, 'The Protection of the Unborn in Three Legal Orders', *Irish Law Times*, April 1992 (pp. 93–7), May 1992 (pp. 104–08), July 1992 (pp. 166–70), December 1992 (pp. 279–83).

Kirby, Peadar, *Is Irish Catholicism Dying? (Liberating an Emprisoned Church)*, Cork: The Mercier Press, 1984.

Kirby, Peadar, 'Valuing Social Change in Ireland', *Doctrine and Life*, September 1994, vol. 44, pp. 418–25.

Larmour, Sandra, *The State and Sexuality in Ireland, 1929–1937*, unpublished MA dissertation in Women's Studies, University College Cork, 1992.

Lee, Joe J., *Ireland 1912–1985: Politics and Society*, Cambridge: Cambridge University Press, 1989.

Levine, June, *Sisters: The Personal Story of an Irish Feminist*, Dublin: Ward River Press, 1982.

Luddy, Maria and Murphy, Cliona (eds), *Women Surviving: Studies in Irish Women's History in the 19th and 20th Centuries*, Dublin: Poolbeg, 1989.

McCafferty, Nell, *Selected Writings, Volume 1: The Best of Nell*, Dublin: Attic Press, 1984.

McCafferty, Nell, *Selected Writings, Volume 2: Goodnight Sisters...*, Dublin: Attic Press, 1987.

MacCurtain, Margaret and O'Corrain, Donncha (eds), *Women in Irish History: The Historical Dimension*, Dublin: Arlen House, The Women's Press, 1978.

McDonagh, Enda, 'Church & State in the Constitution of Ireland', *Irish Theological Quarterly*, vol. 28, 1961, pp. 131–44.

McDonagh, Enda, 'Church and State in Ireland: A Theological Analysis', *The Crane Bag Book of Irish Studies (1977–1981)*, Dublin: Blackwater Press, pp. 806–12.

McDonagh, Enda, 'The Winter Name of the Church', *The Furrow*, January 1995, pp. 3–12.

McDonagh, Sunniva (ed.), *The Attorney General v. X and others: Judgements of the High Court and Supreme Court with Submissions made by Counsel to the Supreme Court*, Dublin: Incorporated Council of Law Reporting for Ireland, 1992.

Mac Greil, Micheal, 'Church Attendance and Religious Practice of Dublin Adults', *Social Studies*, vol 3, n.2, 1974, p.163–211.

Mac Greil, Micheal, *Prejudice and Tolerance in Ireland*, Dublin: College of Industrial Relations, 1977.

Mac Greil, Micheal, 'Christian Family and Social Change', *Studies*, vol.7,no. 2, Spring 1983, pp. 116–26.

Mac Greil, Micheal, 'Religious practice and attitudes in Ireland. Report of a survey of religious attitudes and practice and related issues in the Republic of Ireland, 1988–89', Maynooth: Survey and Research Unit, Dpt of Social Studies, 1991.

Mac Greil, Micheal, *Prejudice in Ireland revisited: based on a national survey of intergroup attitudes in the Republic of Ireland* Dublin: Survey and Research Unit, St Patrice's College Maynooth, 1996.

McKee, Eamonn, 'Church–State Relations and the Development of Irish Health Policy: The Mother-and-Child Scheme, 1944–53', *Irish Historical Studies*, XXV, no. 98, November 1986, pp. 159–94.

MacReamoinn, Seán (ed.), *Authority in the Church*, Dublin: The Columba Press, 1995.

Mahon, Evelyn, 'Women's Rights and Catholicism in Ireland', *New Left Review*, no. 166, Nov-Dec. 1987, pp. 53–77.

Market Research Bureau of Ireland, 'Religious Practice and Attitudes toward Divorce and Contraception among Irish Adults', *Social Studies*, vol. 3, no. 3, June 1974, pp. 276–85.

Murphy, John A., 'Identity Change in the Republic of Ireland', *Etudes Irlandaises*, no. 1, 1976, pp. 143–57.

Murphy, John A., 'Religious Majorities and Minorities, North and South, Then and Now', *The Crane Bag Book of Irish Studies (1977–1981)*, Dublin: Blackwater Press, pp. 794–9.

Murphy, John A., 'The Church, Morality and the Law', pp. 103–14, in Clarke, Desmond (ed.), *Morality and the Law*, Cork: The Mercier Press, 1982.

Murphy, John A., 'Religion and Irish Identity', pp. 132–51, in The Princess Grace Irish Library (Monaco), *Irishness in a Changing Society*, Totowa, NJ: Barnes & Noble Books, 1989.

Murphy, Tim, 'Democracy, Natural Law and the Irish Constitution', *Irish Law Times*, April 1993, pp. 81–3.

Nic Ghiolla Phadraig, Máire, 'Religious Practice and Secularisation', pp. 137–54, in Clancy, Patrick et al. (eds), *Ireland: A Sociological Profile*, Dublin: Institute of Public Administration, 1986.

Nic Ghiolla Phadraig, Máire, 'Trends in Religious Practice in Ireland', *Doctrine and Life*, vol. 42, January 1992, pp. 3–11.

Nolan, Michael, 'The Influence of Catholic Nationalism on the Legislature of the Irish Free State', *The Irish Jurist*, vol. 10, 1975, University College Dublin, pp. 128–69.

Noonan, John T., *The Morality of Abortion: Legal and Historical Perspectives*, Cambridge, MA: Harvard University Press, 1970.

Noonan, John T., *Contraception – A History of its Treatment by the Catholic Theologians and Canonists*, Cambridge, MA: Harvard University Press, 1986.

Norris, David, 'Homosexuality and Law: The Irish Situation', *Dublin University Law Journal, 1976–1980*, vol. 1, no. 1, pp. 18–19.

Norris, David, 'Homosexual Law Reform in Ireland: A Progress Report', *Dublin University Law Journal, 1976–1980*, vol. 1, no. 2, pp. 27–36.

Norris, David, 'Homosexual People and the Christian Churches in Ireland: A Minority and its Oppressors', *The Crane Bag Book of Irish Studies (1977–1981)*, Dublin: Blackwater Press, pp. 770–6.

Northern Ireland Abortion Law Reform Association, *Abortion in Northern Ireland: The Report of an International Tribunal*, Belfast: NIALRA/Beyond the Pale Publications, 1989.

Nowlan, David, 'Ireland's Year of Change', *People*, no. 3, 1974, pp. 3–7.

Nugent, Robert, 'Homosexual Rights and the Catholic Community', *Doctrine and Life*, vol. 44, no. 3, March 1994, pp. 165–73.

O'Brien,, Mags (ed.), *Divorce? Facing the Issues of Marital Breakdown*, Dublin: Basement Press, 1995.

O'Callaghan, Margaret, 'Religion and Identity – The Church and Irish Independence', *The Crane Bag: The Forum Issue*, vol.7, no. 2, 1983, pp. 65–76.

O'Carroll Ide and Collins Eoin (eds), *Lesbian and Gay Visions of Ireland*, London: Cassell, 1995.

O'Carroll, J.-P., 'Sociology and the Politics of Fear – The Divorce Referendum of 1986', *Sociological Association of Ireland Bulletin*, no.47, October 1986, pp. 2–3.

O'Carroll, J.-P., 'Bishops, Knights – and Pawns? Traditional Thought and the Irish Abortion Referendum Debate of 1983', *Irish Political Studies*, vol. 6, 1991, pp. 53–71.

O Conaill, Séan, 'Scandals in the Church', *Studies*, Spring 1995, vol.84, no. 333, pp. 21–7.

O'Connor, Anne, 'Women in Irish Folklore: The Testimony regarding Illegitimacy, Abortion and Infanticide, pp. 304–14, in MacCurtain, Margaret and O'Dowd, Mary (eds), *Women in Early Modern Ireland 1500–1800*, Edinburgh: Edinburgh University Press, 1991.

O'Dowd, Liam, 'Church, State and Women: The Aftermath of Partition', pp. 3–36, in Curtain Chris et al. (eds), *Gender in Irish Society*, Galway: Galway University Press, 1987.

O'Hanlon, Roderick, 'Natural Rights and the Irish Constitution', *Irish Law Times*, January 1993, pp. 8–11.

O'Hanlon, Roderick, 'The Judiciary and Moral Law' (a reply to Tim Murphy), *Irish Law Times*, June 1993, pp. 129–32.

O'Kelly, Emer, *The Permissive Society in Ireland?*, Cork: The Mercier Press, 1974.

O'Leary, Cornelius and Hesketh, Tom, 'The Irish Abortion and Divorce Referendum Campaigns', *Irish Political Studies*, no. 3, 1988, pp. 43–62.

O'Leary, Cornelius, 'The Irish Referendum on Divorce (1986)', *Electoral Studies*, vol. 6, 1986, pp. 69–74.

O'Leary, Paul, 'Is the Church Leaking at the Edges?', *Doctrine and Life*, vol. 43, February 1993, pp. 100–7.

O'Mahony, T.P., *The Politics of Dishonour: Ireland 1916–1977*, Dublin: Talbot Press, 1977.

O'Malley, Tom, 'Norris v Ireland – An Opportunity for Law Reform', *Irish Law Times*, December 1988, pp. 279–84.

O'Reilly, Emily, *Masterminds of the Right*, Dublin: Attic Press, 1992.

O'Sullivan, Eoin, 'The 1990 Presidential Election in the Republic of Ireland', *Irish Political Studies*, no. 6, 1991, pp. 85–98.

O'Sullivan, Maria, *Sterilisation: A Feminist Issue in Ireland*, unpublished MA dissertation in Women's Studies, University College Cork, 1993.

O'Sullivan, Michael, *Mary Robinson: The Life and Times of an Irish Liberal*, Dublin: Blackwater Press, 1993.

O'Toole, Fintan, *A Mass for Jesse James – A Journey through 1980's Ireland*, Dublin: Raven Arts Press, 1990.

O'Toole, Fintan, *Black Hole, Green Card – The Disappearance of Ireland*, Dublin: New Island Books, 1994.

Philbin-Bowman, Eimer, *The Sexual Behaviour and Contraceptive Practice of a Sample of Single Irish Women*, unpublished MA dissertation in Psychology, Trinity College Dublin, 1976.

Philpott, Ger, *Deep End*, Dublin: Poolbeg Press, 1995.

Power, Patrick, *Sex and Marriage in Ancient Ireland*, Dublin & Cork: Mercier Press, 1976.

Pringle, Dennis, 'Changing Ireland – The 1990 Presidential Election', *Irish Geography*, vol. 23, no. 2, 1990, pp. 136–41.

Randall, Vicky, 'The Politics of Abortion in Ireland', pp. 67–85, in Lovenduski, Joni et al. (eds), *The New Politics of Abortion (Europe)*, London: Sage, 1986.

Randall, Vicky and Smyth, Ailbhe, 'Bishops and Bailiwicks: Obstacles to Women's Participation in Ireland', *The Economic and Social Review*, vol. 18, no. 3, April 1987, pp. 196–214.

Randall, Vicky, 'The Politics of Abortion: Ireland in Comparative Perspective', *The Canadian Journal of Irish Studies*, vol. 18, no. 1, University of Saskatchewan, December 1991, pp. 121–8.

Ranke-Heinemann, Uta, *Eunuchs for the Kingdom of Heaven – Women, Sexuality and the Catholic Church*, translated from German by Peter Heinegg, London: Penguin Books, 1991.

Reidy, Maurice, 'Moral Theology and Family Planning', *The Furrow*, vol. 32, no. 6, June 1981, pp. 343–61.

Reidy, Maurice (ed.), *Ethical Issues in Reproductive Medicine*, Dublin: Gill & Macmillan, 1982.

Reidy, Maurice, 'Civil Divorce: Clarifying the Issues', *Doctrine and Life*, vol. 36, May–June 1986, pp. 228–36.

Reidy, Maurice, 'Abortion: The Moral Argument', *The Furrow*, vol.43, no. 9, September 1992, pp. 472–80.

Riddick, Ruth, *The Right to Choose: Questions of Feminist Morality*, Dublin: Attic Press, 1990.

Riddick Ruth / Irish Family Planning Association Pregnancy Counselling Service, *Profile Report: The First 100 Clients, October 1992–December 1992*, Dublin: IFPA, 1993.

Robinson, Mary, 'Reform of the Law Relating to Family Planning in Ireland', *Dublin University Law Journal, 1976–1980*, vol. 1, no. 2, 1976, pp. 12–14.

Robinson, Mary, 'Women and the New Irish State', pp. 58–70, in MacCurtain, Margaret and O'Corrain, Donncha (eds), *Women in Irish History: The Historical Dimension,* Dublin: Arlen House, The Women's Press, 1978.

Robinson, Mary, 'The Courts, the Constitution and the Family' (on the divorce referendum), *The Irish Times*, 2 and 3 June 1986.

Robinson, Mary, 'The Constitution Means what the Courts Say it Means' (50th anniversary of the Constitution), *The Irish Times,* 29 December 1987.

Rose, Kieran, *Diverse Communities – The Evolution of Lesbian and Gay Politics in Ireland*, Cork: Cork University Press (Undercurrents), 1994.

Rose, Robert, *An Outline of Fertility Control, Focusing on the Element of Abortion, in the Republic of Ireland to 1976*, unpublished PhD dissertation in Sociology, Stockholm: 1976.

Ryan, Liam, 'Church and Politics – The Last 25 Years', *The Furrow*, vol. 30, January 1979, p. 3–18.

Ryan, Liam, 'Faith under Survey', *The Furrow*, vol. 34, January 1983, pp. 3–15.

Ryan, Liam, 'The Changing Irish Family', *The Furrow*, vol. 45, April 1994, pp. 212–20.

Ryan-Sheridan Susan, *Women and the New Reproductive Technologies in Ireland*, Cork: Cork University Press (Undercurrents), 1994.

Rynne, Andrew, *Abortion: The Irish Question,* Dublin: Ward River Press, 1982.

Saunders, Kate and Stanford, Peter, *Catholics and Sex,* London: Heinemann, 1992.

Siggins, Lorna, *The Woman who Took Power in the Park – Mary Robinson, President of Ireland, 1990–1997*, Edinburgh & London: Mainstream Publishing, 1997.

Sinnott, R., Walsh, B.M., and Whelan, B.J., 'Conservatives, Liberals and Pragmatists: Disaggregating the Results of the Irish Abortion Referendums of 1992', *The Economic and Social Review,* January 1995, vol. 26, no. 2, pp. 207–19.

Smith, F.B., 'Labouchère's Amendment to the Criminal Law Amendment Bill', *Historical Studies*, vol. 17, no. 67, 1976, pp. 165–75.

Smith, R., *Garret: The Enigma*, Dublin: Aherlow, 1985.

Smyth, Ailbhe, *Women's Rights in Ireland, a Practical Guide*, Dublin: Ward River Press, 1983.

Smyth, Ailbhe, 'Femme: pouvoir en puissance dans l'Irlande contemporaine', *Cahiers du Centre d'Etudes Irlandaises*, no. 11, Rennes: Presses Universitaires de Rennes II, 1987, p. 41–71.

Smyth, Ailbhe, ' "A Great Day for the Women of Ireland": The Meaning of Mary Robinson's Presidency for Irish Women', *The Canadian Journal of Irish Studies*, vol.18, no. 1, December 1991, pp. 61–75.

Smyth, Ailbhe (ed.), *The Abortion Papers, Ireland*, Dublin: Attic Press, 1992.

Smyth, Ailbhe (ed.), *Irish Women's Studies Reader*, Dublin: Attic Press, 1993.

Smyth Ailbhe, 'States of Changes – Reflections on Ireland in Several Uncertain Parts', *Feminist Review* (no. 50: *The Irish Issue: The British Question*), London: Routledge, 1995, pp. 24–43.

Solomons, Michael, *Pro-life? The Irish Question*, Dublin: Lilliput Press, 1992.

Staines, Michael, 'The Concept of the "Family" under the Irish Constitution', *The Irish Jurist*, vol.XI, 1976, pp. 223–42.

Treacy, Bernard (ed.), *Abortion, Law and Conscience, Doctrine and Life Special*, vol. 42, no. 5, May–June 1992.

Treacy, Bernard and Whyte Gerry (eds), *Religion, Morality and Public Policy, Doctrine and Life Special*, vol.45, no. 1, January 1995.

Valiulis, Maryann Gialanella, 'Neither Feminist nor Flapper: The Ecclesiastical Construction of the Ideal Irish Woman', *Newcomb College Center for Research on Women Working Papers*, Tulane University (New Orleans), vol.14, no. 2, Spring 1994, pp. 9–11.

Walsh, Brendan, *Ireland's Changing Demographic Structure*, Dublin: Gill & Macmillan, 1989.

Walsh D. et al., *Termination of Pregnancy – England – 1984 – Women from the Republic of Ireland*, Dublin: The Medico-Social Research Board, 1985.

Ward, Conor and Greely, Andrew, 'Development and Tolerance: The Case of Ireland', *Eire-Ireland*, vol.25, no. 4, Winter 1990, pp. 7–17.

Ward, Peter, *Financial Consequences of Marital Breakdown*, Dublin: Combat Poverty Agency, 1990.

Ward, Peter, *Divorce in Ireland: Who Should Bear the Cost?*, Cork: Cork University Press (Undercurrents), 1993.

Ward Peter, 'The Path to Divorce?', *Irish Law Times*, February 1994, pp. 29–31.

Ward Peter, 'The Family Law Bill 1994 – An Overview', *Irish Law Times*, April 1994, pp. 76–9.

Weeks, Jeffrey, *Sex, Politics and Society: The Regulation of Sexuality since 1800*, 2nd edition, London: Longman, 1989.

Whelan, Anthony (ed.), *Law and Liberty in Ireland*, Dublin: Oak Tree Press/ Trinity College Dublin Law School, 1993.

Whelan, Christopher T. (ed.), *Values and Social Change in Ireland*, Dublin: Gill & Macmillan, 1994.

Whyte, John H., *Church and State in modern Ireland, 1923–1979*, 2nd edition, Dublin: Gill & Macmillan, 1980.

Whyte John H., 'Recent Developments in Church–State Relations', *Seirbhis Phoibli* (*Journal of the Department of the Public Services*), vol. 6, no. 3, Autumn 1985, pp. 4–10.

Williams, Bruce, 'Homosexuality: The New Vatican Statement', *Theological Studies*, no. 48, 1987, pp. 259–77.

Wilson-Davis, Keith, 'Irish Attitudes to Family Planning', *Social Studies*, vol. 3, no. 3, June 1974, p. 261–275.

Wilson-Davis, Keith, 'Some Results of an Irish Family Planning Survey', *Journal of Biosocial Science*, 1974, no. 7, pp. 435–44.

Wilson-Davis, Keith, 'The Contraceptive Situation in the Irish Republic', *Journal of Biosocial Science*, 1974, no. 4, pp. 483–92.

Index

Divorce, contraception, abortion and homosexuality will be mainly discussed in the chapters devoted to them (see Contents). Commentators quoted in the text are not listed here, but in the Bibliography.

278   *The Politics of Sexual Morality in Ireland*